The Cinema of Yorgos Lanthimos

The Cinema of Yorgos Lanthimos

Films, Form, Philosophy

Edited by

Eddie Falvey

BLOOMSBURY ACADEMIC
NEW YORK • LONDON • OXFORD • NEW DELHI • SYDNEY

BLOOMSBURY ACADEMIC
Bloomsbury Publishing Inc
1385 Broadway, New York, NY 10018, USA
50 Bedford Square, London, WC1B 3DP, UK
29 Earlsfort Terrace, Dublin 2, Ireland

BLOOMSBURY, BLOOMSBURY ACADEMIC and the Diana logo are trademarks of
Bloomsbury Publishing Plc

First published in the United States of America 2022

Volume Editor's Part of the Work © Eddie Falvey, 2022
Each chapter © of Contributors

For legal purposes the Acknowledgments on p. ix constitute an extension
of this copyright page.

Cover design: Eleanor Rose
Cover image: *The Lobster*, 2015, Dir. Yorgos Lanthimos, starring Colin Farrell and Rachel
Weisz © Canal+ / CNC / Cine+ / Collection Christophel / ArenaPAL www.arenapal.com

All rights reserved. No part of this publication may be reproduced or transmitted
in any form or by any means, electronic or mechanical, including photocopying,
recording, or any information storage or retrieval system, without prior permission in
writing from the publishers.

Bloomsbury Publishing Inc does not have any control over, or responsibility for, any
third-party websites referred to or in this book. All internet addresses given in this
book were correct at the time of going to press. The author and publisher regret any
inconvenience caused if addresses have changed or sites have ceased to exist,
but can accept no responsibility for any such changes.

Library of Congress Cataloging-in-Publication Data
Names: Falvey, Eddie, editor.
Title: The cinema of Yorgos Lanthimos : films, form, philosophy / edited by Eddie Falvey.
Description: New York : Bloomsbury Academic, 2021. |
Includes bibliographical references and index. | Summary: "The first book
dedicated to the cinema of Yorgos Lanthimos, offering a range of
critical approaches to his work"–Provided by publisher.
Identifiers: LCCN 2021060140 (print) | LCCN 2021060141 (ebook) |
ISBN 9781501375491 (hardback) | ISBN 9781501375507 (paperback) |
ISBN 9781501375484 (epub) | ISBN 9781501375477 (pdf) |
ISBN 9781501375460 Subjects: LCSH: Lanthimos, Yorgos, 1973–Criticism
and interpretation. | Motion picture producers and directors–Greece. |
Motion pictures–Greece–History.
Classification: LCC PN1998.3.L3838 C56 2021 (print) | LCC PN1998.3.L3838 (ebook) |
DDC 791.4302/33092–dc23/eng/20220314
LC record available at https://lccn.loc.gov/2021060140
LC ebook record available at https://lccn.loc.gov/2021060141

ISBN: HB: 978-1-5013-7549-1
ePDF: 978-1-5013-7547-7
eBook: 978-1-5013-7548-4

Typeset by Newgen KnowledgeWorks Pvt. Ltd., Chennai, India

To find out more about our authors and books visit www.bloomsbury.com
and sign up for our newsletters.

CONTENTS

List of Illustrations viii
Acknowledgments ix
A Note on Titles x

1 (A Late) Introduction: Framing Yorgos Lanthimos's Weird Worlds 1
   Eddie Falvey

Part I Origins and Identity

2 Greek Screen Cultures and the Scopic Regimes of the Long 1990s: Exploring Yorgos Lanthimos's Early Works 19
   Afroditi Nikolaidou

3 The Anti-Foundationalist Cinema of Yorgos Lanthimos: The Case of *Kinetta* 35
   Vrasidas Karalis

Part II Experiencing Lanthimos

4 On Confinement, Sameness, and Grieving: Yorgos Lanthimos's *Alps* 55
   Asbjørn Grønstad

5 Bodies Out of Place: Ontological *Adriftness* in *The Lobster* 67
   Ina Karkani

6   Notes Toward a Cinema of Apathy in the Films of Yorgos Lanthimos 81
    Eddie Falvey

Part III Form and Authorship

7   Kafkaesque Themes in *The Lobster* 103
    Angelos Koutsourakis

8   Animal Instincts: Fear, Power, and Obedience in the Films of Yorgos Lanthimos and Stanley Kubrick 117
    Michael Lipiner and Nathan Abrams

9   Consider the Absurd: Uneasy Proximity in *Dogtooth*, *The Lobster*, and *The Killing of a Sacred Deer* 133
    Nepomuk Zettl

10 Dog, Lobster, Deer, Rabbit: Yorgos Lanthimos's Animal Metaphors 149
    Savina Petkova

Part IV Genre and Variation

11 Art-House Thriller: Auteur Meets Genre in *The Killing of a Sacred Deer* 165
    Geoff King

12 Myth and Mythopoeia in the Films of Yorgos Lanthimos 183
    James J. Clauss

13 Rethinking the Heritage Film: Gothic Critique in *The Favourite* 199
    Alex Lykidis

Part V Gender, Sex, and Sexuality

14 Young Women's Deadly Rebellions in the Early Films of Yorgos Lanthimos 221
    Tonia Kazakopoulou

15 The "Weird" Sex Scenes of Yorgos Lanthimos 239
Alice Haylett Bryan

16 The Queer Posthumanism of *The Lobster* 259
Marios Psaras

Yorgos Lanthimos's Primary Feature Filmography 277
Notes on Contributors 281
Index 285

ILLUSTRATIONS

Figure 5.1   A woman shoots an unsuspecting donkey during the opening scene of *The Lobster* 69
Figure 5.2   Asymmetrical relations in *The Lobster*: David, his dog, and his wife off-screen 70
Figure 5.3   Becoming animal in *The Lobster* 74
Figure 9.1a and b   Close-up of heart surgery opens *The Killing of a Sacred Deer* 135
Figure 9.2a and b   Absurd *mise-en-scène* in the hospital spaces of *The Killing of a Sacred Deer* 139
Figure 9.3a and b   Communication and sacrifice in *The Lobster* 143
Figure 15.1   Incestuous sex in *Dogtooth* 245
Figure 15.2   Genuine affection in *The Lobster* 248
Figure 15.3   Marital sex in *The Killing of a Sacred Deer* 250
Figure 15.4   Abigail's wedding night in *The Favourite* 253

ACKNOWLEDGMENTS

I would like to start by acknowledging the support shown by Katie Gallof and others at Bloomsbury Academic who were enthusiastic about this book from the off. Next, I would like to thank each of my contributors for their work, and for showing professionalism and resilience during a time of global uncertainty and, for many of us, panic. I would also like to thank the peer reviewers who helped shape the book and its chapters. A thousand thanks also to Calum Baker who meticulously cross-checked every word of the manuscript before publication, though of course I accept full responsibility for anything that was missed. I would like to thank my family for their ongoing love and support and, last but not least, Fiona, who despite liking lighter films never faltered in being there as I buried myself in this project. Thank you all.

—Eddie Falvey

A NOTE ON TITLES

The titles of Lanthimos's main feature films will be presented as follows:

Kinetta (2005)
Dogtooth (2009)
Alps (2011)
The Lobster (2015)
The Killing of a Sacred Deer (2017)
The Favourite (2018)

As this is a work in the English language on a director who has worked in multiple languages, it is important to offer clarification on titles and how they will be presented across the chapters that comprise this volume. Incorporating Lanthimos's later films—*The Lobster*, *The Killing of a Sacred Deer*, and *The Favourite*—is straightforward enough as they are firstly presented in English (though note the British English spelling in the case of the last). Lanthimos's earlier films, however, require more clarification due, first, to their Greekness and, second, to tensions that arise in translation. *Kinetta* has been released in all territories under that name and therefore presents no obstacle. *Alps* (*Alpeis*) provides a direct translation. *Dogtooth* (*Kynodontas*) is perhaps the most interesting title to note. *Kynodontas* more or less translates to "canine," a more commonly adopted English designation for the fang-like teeth of mammalian anatomy than "dogtooth." In many territories, the film has been released as *Canine* and derivatives of it. Distinctions between *Canine* and *Dogtooth* in the English translation are small but meaningful, for not only does the latter present an additional element of uncanniness for being a less common term, it also more concretely invokes the theme of animality that prefaces the film's representation of violence against the imprisoned children. For the titles of films not directed by Lanthimos, in all instances the most commonly adopted English title has been chosen, with the original title included in parentheses in the first instance of citation (all original titles are typed in the Latin alphabet). Finally, I made the decision early on in my own writing to present *The Killing of a Sacred Deer*'s title in full. Despite appearing clumsy when repeated across short distances due to its length, when simplified to either *Killing* or *Sacred Deer*, the emphasis shifts focus from a holistic ritualized process to either a single act or victim. I will not speak to the reasons why other writers also chose to write this particular title in full, but it is curious that, like me, they all did.

—Eddie Falvey

1

(A Late) Introduction: Framing Yorgos Lanthimos's Weird Worlds

Eddie Falvey

And what weird worlds they are!
 While it is pleasing from an editor's perspective that this book represents the first of its kind, it is nevertheless surprising that it has taken so long for a dedicated, book-length companion to Yorgos Lanthimos's oeuvre to emerge, especially given his centrality to the discussion of a series of isolated, adjacent, and overlapping contexts relating to twenty-first-century film cultures. Indeed, Lanthimos's concise but acclaimed body of work is frequently invoked as being indicative of some of the prevailing landscapes and modes of the contemporary art film. With qualification, Lanthimos has operated close to the center of what has been referred to as the Greek New Wave—or Weird Wave—that typifies new forms of experimentation to emerge out of Greek cinema in the late twentieth and early twenty-first centuries. The Greekness of Lanthimos's cinema is equally interesting for being both self-evident and increasingly troubled by aspects of his international, or transnational, coproductions. Having started out on a markedly Greek, transmedial art scene as a prominent, if artfully inclined, director of commercials and music videos, Lanthimos's early work was culturally and geographically rooted in its Greekness, with his second feature *Dogtooth* remaining, for many, the archetypal text of the Weird Wave. *The Lobster*, however, Lanthimos's debut English-language feature,

was inversely characterized by an unrootedness, from the internationality of its financing to the placelessness of its setting, while more recent features *The Killing of a Sacred Deer* and *The Favourite* make permeable the boundaries between the mythic, historical, and modern to express the timelessness of humanity's more corrupt designs.

Taken together, Lanthimos's films reflect, in little and large ways, authorial continuity between them, marked by their repeated contravention of aesthetic, thematic, and generic boundaries. With reference to the auteur—a contentious but influential framework for exploring the film director's privileged status within the context of a film's production—Lanthimos's name brings a certain weight of expectation for the uniqueness of his style and the heft of his theses on structural violence and oppression, arguably the most sustained thematic preoccupation of his current corpus. In spite of a critical tendency to structure readings around directors, Lanthimos's role within a network of collaborators on both sides of the camera illuminates the important labor done by others, from his work with producers that include Athina Rachel Tsangari and Ed Guiney—thus marking a transnational Greek–Irish exchange occurring in Lanthimos's mid to late productions—to regular cowriter Efthymis Filippou, and recurring on-screen stars ranging from Greek compatriots Angeliki Papoulia and Ariane Labed to Hollywood-adjacent international film stars Colin Farrell and Rachel Weisz.

If Lanthimos's films are in many ways typical of the art-house mode, then they are nevertheless marked by a series of distinctions, not least for his tendency to traverse boundaries in terms of production strategies, as well as the textual, or aesthetic, variation offered by his key works. I have chosen to present this introduction parenthetically as a late one to acknowledge Lanthimos's already established position within contemporary film scholarship, a position that many of the chapters in this book seek to expand upon. Indeed, various analyses already exist that situate Lanthimos within certain waves and cycles. Of these, the aforementioned Weird Wave framework, following Steve Rose's coinage of the term,[1] has gained the most traction in both popular and scholarly discourse on Lanthimos and his contemporaries, but like other broad categorizations it fails to account for the full range of histories and textual elements it has been designed to encompass. Moreover, it goes without saying that weirdness alone does not account for all aspects of his form. For Alex Lykidis, who continues his work on Lanthimos in this volume, the style of the films associated with the Weird Wave invokes the complex sociopolitical milieu of the nation at a time of widespread cultural crisis: "The social effects of the financial crisis are addressed in these films through a narrative emphasis on isolated or alienated characters, dysfunctional family relationships, desperate or anti-social behavior and breakdowns in communication. Aesthetically, these dynamics are conveyed through unexpressive acting, stilted dialogue, performative gestures, an absence of continuity editing, absurdist deviations from narrative logic, excessive referentiality and claustrophobic *mise-en-scène*."[2] There is nothing to contest in this or other descriptions of the style of these films, which speaks not only to Lanthimos but also to a range of other contemporary Greek filmmakers including Tsangari, Yannis Economides, and Panos Koutras. Rather, problems start to arise when the implication is that the adoption of similar formal devices expresses a singular function between practitioners (akin to the French *Cahiers du cinema* filmmakers of the 1950s or the Denmark-based Dogme 95 movement), which is contested by scholars and filmmakers alike as not necessarily being the case.

Ever the disrupter, Lanthimos has even sought to overturn assumptions on this matter and contest the "ethnicity" of his films, as he does in regard to *The Lobster*:

> It's fascinating to see how people view work that springs from another culture. And then transporting it into another culture. I'm obviously Greek, but I made this film in English, and—well, I don't know what the film's ethnicity is—it was shot in Ireland. The cast is from all around the world, which was intentional because the whole story just felt right being something contemporary and close to the societies that we live in, that I live in.[3]

Therefore, the Greekness of Lanthimos's cinema is at once a given and an obstacle for positioning his later works, which oscillate from the local to the global and from the contemporary to the historical. Moreover, while the Weird Wave is specifically Greek in rhetoric, under scrutiny it discloses a more transnational enterprise with historical roots in various forms of postmodernism. As unique as they are in many ways, Lanthimos's films arguably sit within a much larger web of influences than neat categorizations account for.

One such context, intertwined as it is with the art film, is the extreme film. But while textual and philosophical parallels to European extremists including Catherine Breillat, Claire Denis, Michael Haneke, and Gaspar Noé convey transnational (and transgeneric) inheritance for the intellectually minded extremist forms and affects with which Lanthimos works—*Dogtooth* and *The Lobster* arguably being as extreme as they are weird—his films also have roots in more straightforward genre traditions. That *The Killing of a Sacred Deer* is in many ways a straightforward revenge thriller and *The Favourite* is a variation on the period drama are evidence that Lanthimos's films trouble distinctions between forms. While the former pairs a familiar Greek myth (Euripides's *Iphigenia in Aulis* [*c*. 408–406 BCE]) with a Pasolinian nihilism that is redolent of *Salò, or the 120 Days of Sodom* (1975)—arguably the archetypal extreme film—the latter playfully inverts the generic tropes of the heritage film by dehistoricizing its subject, producing a hyperreflexive sex comedy in period dress that comments on the perniciousness and absurdity of power. In aid of describing Lanthimos's various sources of influence, it should be noted—as some of the writers contained herein do—that these films bear more than a little in common with the works of Stanley Kubrick, another prominent filmmaker known to traverse and, in doing so, trouble generic and art house–mainstream distinctions.

If individual chapters included here seek to engage with some of the key aspects of Lanthimos's films, their form, and philosophical proclivities, then the book as a whole comes together to provide a Lanthimosian panorama that offers multifaceted critical pathways into one of the more unique voices of contemporary film. Over the course of the fifteen chapters that comprise this book, a diverse cohort of Lanthimos experts cast their historical and theoretical nets wide to expand on and complicate existing ideas about the director and his work, while in some cases embarking, as Lanthimos so often does, into realms as yet unknown.

Lanthimos at Home and Abroad: From the National to the Transnational

Much of the early scholarship on Lanthimos was keen to position him as a new filmmaker with pronounced national specificity. But as much as Lanthimos's Greek identity is incontestable, his filmmaking is punctuated by the sort of postmodern hybridity that invites further scrutiny for its contravention of boundaries. As Lydia Papadimitriou, Vangelis Calotychos, and Yannis Tzioumakis write on this topic,

> for all the facile arguments that exploit the coincidence and conveniently place the astonishing success of Lanthimos's *Dogtooth* at the origins of this New Wave, there remain legitimate debates as to whether these new trends (and the crisis itself) emerged at an earlier time in the decade, not only in the work of filmmakers who have since been identified with these trends, but also in the work of other Greek directors working in film.[4]

Beyond any tension caused by a critical over-determination to position *Dogtooth* this way, its signifying potential as reflective of a certain tendency in Greek filmmaking has had substantial impact on discourses relating to it. These debates have been registered in a variety of formats, from popular film criticism to academic scholarship, and will return in citations at intervals throughout this volume. Yet, the style of Lanthimos's films appears to traverse several historical and national contexts, linking late modernists such as Kubrick, Robert Bresson, Roy Andersson and Greek compatriot Theo Angelopoulos to the present, via further nodes of influence that include British art and popular cinema, European extreme cinema and even the form-melding of the likes of Peter Greenaway and Charlie Kaufman. It should be unsurprising that a filmmaker as obsessed with boundary-crossing as Lanthimos offers evidence of this aspect in his work in both textual and extratextual ways.

* * *

Georgios (or Yorgos) Lanthimos was born in Athens in 1973 and was educated, after a short stint in business studies, at the famous Hellenic Cinema and Television School Stavrakos in Athens where he specialized in directing. His early career was marked by experimentation across formats, including television commercials, short films, theater productions and video dances. Echoing the origins of other acclaimed contemporary international directors, including Anton Corbijn, Jonathan Glazer, Michel Gondry, Spike Jonze and Mark Romanek, Lanthimos is yet another modern filmmaker who has roots in the music video industry, where he directed stylized shorts for acts such as Despina Vandi, Sakis Rouvas and Xaxakes, and, later, Leon of Athens and Radiohead, all of which are in some way redolent of his aesthetic strategies going forward. It was this context, against the backdrop of an expanded film industry that emerged in Greece between the 1990s and the mid-2000s, that formed the conditions for Lanthimos's cinematic breakthrough. Vrasidas Karalis, in his book *A History of Greek Cinema*, writes of the emergent traditions of the period:

> With all of these films it was becoming obvious that a new movement, an innovative gaze full of curiosity, ingenuity, and contradiction was gradually crystallizing and that the new directors had totally abandoned the excesses of auterish [*sic*] and commercial traditions alike, and had formed distinct styles of their own. A renaissance of independent cinema, uncontrolled by state bureaucracy, was well under way. A distinct narrative language was slowly being put together based on a new hybrid style of representation, intermingling documentary and fiction, combining elements of burlesque and pastiche, and paying homage to the great names of world cinema, while showing both continuity with and departure from the conventions and certainties of the past. Now the whole world becomes the studio, as the camera moves everywhere without stylization or illusionist techniques. The openness of space has created a roaming camera, insatiable and curious, discovering elements of a new cinematic language in the most trivial and insignificant details of everyday life.[5]

It is notable that Karalis's suggestion of formal synchronicity is not based on mutual aims per se, but rather on a common stylistic verisimilitude that is marked by independence from and innovation of preceding traditions in Greek and world cinema, of which Lanthimos's films function as an exemplar.

Lanthimos's feature film career is usually understood to begin with *Kinetta*, or even *Dogtooth* for those less familiar with his roots, but it in fact began earlier than that when he made his start codirecting *My Best Friend* (*O kalyteros mou filos*, 2001) with popular Greek filmmaker Lakis Lazopoulos. Held against Lanthimos's later work, *My Best Friend*—a comedy that follows the wanderings of a man who recently found his wife in bed with his best friend—bears little in common with the structurally integrated violence of *Kinetta*, *Dogtooth*, or indeed any of his later works. Despite casting shadow visions of Lanthimos's style in the film's strange dialogue and offbeat humor, not to mention his prevailing interest in the weirdness of sex, it is, for the most part, Lazopoulos's film—indeed, it is not currently listed on Lanthimos's official website, suggesting a desire on the director's part to distance or even divorce himself entirely from it. Rather than complicate understandings of his oeuvre—which, I would argue, it does not, given the evident if diluted stylistic correspondence with his later work—*My Best Friend* reveals much about the collaborative landscape of the early twenty-first-century production cultures in Greece where Lanthimos got his break. As Maria Chalkou writes of early twenty-first-century Greek film, hybridity and a culture of collaboration was key to its success: "Arthouse and popular films in the 2000s seem to have arisen to a great extent from the same matrix, an over-expanded commercial audio-visual industry that has experienced growth, overproduction, prosperity and creativity in several fields of audio-visual culture."[6] If *My Best Friend* reflects Chalkou's claim to some degree, then its correspondence with Lanthimos's subsequent Greek-language films compounds her notion that boundaries between popular and art-house forms of filmmaking were constantly being traversed and renegotiated in light of the Greek industry's pointedly transmedial and inherently collaborative production economy.

Lanthimos's first solo feature, *Kinetta*, was coproduced by HAOS Film—its second film after *The Slow Business of Going* (Athina Rachel Tsangari, 2000)—and marked the beginning of a productive relationship between Lanthimos and producer Tsangari, who would continue to work with him on all of his Greek-language productions going forward. Though HAOS Film, which was founded by Tsangari herself, served as the primary production base for *Kinetta*, the film's completion was made possible only by the assistance of several regional advertising companies (Modiano, Stefi, and Top Cut) that contributed additional funding, demonstrating the transmedial symbiosis that characterized Greece's visual culture industries at this time.[7] Despite featuring on the festival circuit—most notably in Berlin and Toronto, where it premiered in 2005—*Kinetta*, which arguably remains the most avant-garde of Lanthimos's early films, was ultimately met with mixed reviews. Many critics were perplexed by the opaque weirdness of it, a sentiment that was largely sustained in the film's retrospective evaluations that followed Lanthimos's ascent to a critical darling following *Dogtooth*.[8]

Despite the explosive, career-forging reception of *Dogtooth*, it was largely born out of similar circumstances to *Kinetta* before it, with the notable addition of a small bursary of state funding. Tsangari and HAOS Film returned to coproduce, once again with the support of an advertising company (Boo), as well as a new production company, Horsefly Productions, headed by another significant Greek independent producer, Yorgos Tsourgiannis. The circumstances of *Dogtooth*'s financing are illustrative once again of a symbiotic, coproducing film culture in Greece, albeit one that was short-lived due to the imminent financial crash. In her analysis of this dimension, Papadimitriou echoes Chalkou, stating that Lanthimos's first two solo features "were sponsored by advertising companies, introducing a new kind of synergy between art and commerce in Greece."[9] The first mark of *Dogtooth*'s success came with its premiere at the 2009 Cannes Film Festival, where it won the top prize in its category (*Un Certain Regard*). Perhaps the biggest sign of Lanthimos's breakout came after, with *Dogtooth*'s Oscar nomination in the category of Best Foreign Language Film. Lanthimos's selection on the occasion of just his second feature is significant for the fact that the Foreign Language Film category has favored middlebrow (and often historical) dramas over the avant-gardist pursuits of *Dogtooth*. Despite historical precedents for off-kilter winners, including the likes of *Through a Glass Darkly* (*Såsom i en spegel*, Ingmar Bergman, 1961) and *The Discreet Charm of the Bourgeoisie* (*Le Charme discret de la bourgeoisie*, Luis Buñuel, 1972), which were both directed by firmly established European auteurs, few winners or even nominees have brought the same level of outlandish style or provocation to the Oscars circuit as *Dogtooth*.

While the abundance of scholarly attention bestowed on *Dogtooth* has arguably caused some issues with its placement within film discourse, especially as a work of the Weird Wave, it is certainly one marker of its status as a contemporary classic.[10] I, like many, generally balk at the aggressive canonization that accompanies "best of" lists; however, such discursive maneuvers are in this case useful for making sense of Lanthimos's rapid ascension from the fringe to the center of the European art-house. Both at home in Greece and internationally, *Dogtooth* garnered recognition for the confidence of Lanthimos's direction, the cast's performances, and the overall thematic preoccupations with the family home and, by inference, the state. British film critic Peter Bradshaw admired the film's ability to make strange the "benchmark[s] of normality: the family, a walled city state with its own autocratic rule and untellable secrets."[11] Many words have been spilled in advance of this volume making sense of Lanthimos's films, starting with *Dogtooth*.[12] However, next to *Dogtooth*'s identity as a Greek production and the bearing that has on the announcement of national waves, it is largely Lanthimos's style and themes that have provided a basis for his discussion in popular and scholarly film writing.

Between *Kinetta*, *Dogtooth*, and then *Alps*, Lanthimos was fast developing a tendency toward high-concept, metaphoric filmmaking with a distinct—though principally ambiguous—philosophical component. If *Dogtooth* finds Lanthimos unpicking the conceptual baselines of modern identity politics and, next to it, political authority—made manifest in the metaphor of the family as state—then *Alps* moves in equally strange, though more muted, directions. Less shocking than *Dogtooth* before it, *Alps* portrays empathetic abundance to convey the personal and social dynamics of mourning. In appearance, *Alps* continues to belong to Lanthimos's early Greek productions, though in reality it demonstrates his impending departure for pastures new or, at least, funding sources new. There are, of course, external dimensions to the internationality of *Alps*. Who would have thought that, after the coast-to-coast success of *Dogtooth*, Lanthimos would experience anything close to difficulty when it came to financing his next film? Enter the Greek national debt crisis. The Greek financial crisis started in the crucible of the global crash of 2008, though it extended well into its aftermath, accelerated by infrastructural weaknesses in the national economy and the precariousness of Greece's standing within the European Union's economic zone. The trajectories and various impacts of the Greek financial crisis are complex and numerous, but the upshot regarding state film funding is that there was no longer the money for it. Indeed, whatever incentive there had been to expand the film industry internationally in the 1990s and the early 2000s was wiped out by the material consequences of the nation coming, economically speaking, to its knees.

Karalis notes that "under such a period of a presumed economic boom followed by a total collapse, Greek cinema continued its own independent and lonely path."[13] Determined as it was by contextual factors beyond its control, the historical insularity of the Greek film industry was propagated and prolonged by a period of sustained economic crisis that eventually led to Lanthimos's migration. So, while *Alps* is certainly Greek in appearance— that is, performed in the language and made by a largely domestic cast and crew—and is a Greek coproduction financially speaking, it in fact found Lanthimos acquiring additional funds from France, the United States and Canada, so marking the beginning of the director's transnational wanderings. Papadimitriou summarizes it so: "Realizing that staying in Greece would mean facing continuous financial struggles, especially as the country was getting deeper into crisis, Lanthimos left Greece for the UK. From there, he was able to tap in to significantly better funding opportunities, international casts, as well as global distribution and visibility."[14] It transpired in the end that whatever heightened visibility Lanthimos had received due to the critical success of *Dogtooth* would not be matched in responses to *Alps*, which despite a warm reception among critics came and went with little in the way of a commercial fanfare.

At a projected cost of $4 million, *The Lobster* was Lanthimos's largest production thus far. The film was coproduced by independent studios from across Europe, including Element Pictures (Ireland), Faliro House (Greece), Film4 (UK), Haut et Court (France), Lemming Film (the Netherlands), and Scarlet Films (UK), and received US distribution assistance from A24, a budding hub for art-house genre films.[15] The film followed *Dogtooth*'s success at Cannes by winning another prize for Lanthimos (the *Prix du Jury*) before securing him another Oscar nomination, this time for original screenplay. Bolstered by the commercial support of working in the English language and with international film stars Colin Farrell and Rachel Weisz, *The Lobster* went on to earn rave reviews and more than four times its budget at the international box office.

By the time *The Killing of a Sacred Deer* was in production under the auspices of A24, Element Pictures, HanWay Films (UK), the Irish Film Board, Limp (UK), and New Sparta (UK), Lanthimos had shed the last of his links to Greek production companies. Papadimitriou writes that while the "international recognition [of the Weird Wave filmmakers] has conveyed a renewed sense of possibility and confidence among art-film/festival-oriented directors and producers ... the financial conditions for film production [in Greece] worsened since the crisis."[16] Though *The Killing of a Sacred Deer* largely retained Lanthimos's favor among critics—it also won at Cannes, for its screenplay, and was met by mostly positive to very positive reviews—it made significantly less money than *The Lobster*, despite boasting Farrell once again, this time joined by Nicole Kidman in the film's other lead role. Its failure to resonate with audiences could be attributed to a number of factors both in and out of its makers' control, though it is worth noting that *The Killing of a Sacred Deer* is arguably Lanthimos's bleakest and most humorless film, not to mention potentially the most "art-house" of his English-language output.

With a budget in the region of $15 million, *The Favourite* placed Lanthimos's work into the realm of moderately priced productions, akin to the sort of art-house independent studio films that typified the opening out of the American studio system from the 1980s onward—albeit one that is styled in Lanthimos's unique formal mode.[17] *The Favourite*—which, at the time of writing, is Lanthimos's most recent feature film to have been released—was coproduced once again by a conglomerate of small production companies including returning investors Element Pictures, Film4, and Scarlet Films, as well as new United States-based collaborators Arcana and Waypoint Entertainment. Though the industrial dimensions of *The Favourite* are in some ways similar to Lanthimos's other English-language films, they also mark a significant departure for the fact that Lanthimos was hired to direct from a pre-exisiting screenplay rather than working from his own material (albeit most often coauthored) as he had done since *Kinetta*. As critics were starting to make sense of Lanthimos's working method as one of the preeminent writer–director auteurs of his generation, he did something markedly against type with *The Favourite*, accepting a script written by British historian and first-time screenwriter Deborah Davis and worked on later by Australian screenwriter Tony McNamara. Having been passed around for some years, during which time producer Ceci Dempsey had struggled to muster support, Ed Guiney of Element Pictures injected the project with fresh enthusiasm. Amid the company's rising success with a series of mid-sized British–Irish co-productions that include the *Palme d'Or* winner *The Wind That Shakes the Barley* (Ken Loach, 2006) and a run of collaborations with Lenny Abrahamson on *What Richard Did* (2012), *Frank* (2014), and *Room* (2015), Element and Guiney began working with Lanthimos starting with *The Lobster*. It was around that same time that Guiney introduced Lanthimos to the Davis's screenplay for *The Favourite*; the director was reportedly enticed by the central relationship among the three female leads.[18]

The Favourite arguably offers the most expressive showcase of Lanthimos's unique style, which elevates Davis's and McNamara's acerbic deconstruction of the political economies of the eighteenth-century court with an eccentric dynamism brought on by fish-eye lens shots, irregular framing, and various other visual flourishes. Indeed, it was Lanthimos's unique style that suggested him to Guiney for *The Favourite* in the first place. Guiney recalls:

> We knew that if Yorgos were to take on the British costume drama, he would re-shape it to create something utterly unique. That was exciting. Yorgos is someone who not only has a vision, but can marshal that vision to say something bold, distinctive and inspiring. When you find people with that kind of vision, you roll with them wherever they might take you.[19]

Regardless of the more collaborative elements, it is through the uniqueness of Lanthimos's direction that *The Favourite* may be positioned in direct continuity with his other works. Beyond experimenting with the spatiality of the *mise-en-scène*, *The Favourite* abjures the more regular dimensions of the heritage film in its irregular narrative style and generic playfulness. Indeed, the film focuses less on historical verisimilitude than it does on the central relationships between Queen Anne (Olivia Colman) and her combative court favorites (Rachel Weisz and Emma Stone),[20] whereby significant events play second fiddle to the sexual mores of the characters, which in turn become the symbolic basis for the film's political showcase. Eschewing the political into the personal, *The Favourite* provides a revisionist approach to history (and indeed the historical film) that is more intent on commenting on the pernickety and precarious nature of power than it is on providing an accurate history lesson.

By the time this book hits the shelves, Lanthimos's next film *Poor Things* will have likely been released—however, at the time of writing, one can still only speculate as to the form it will take. What we do know is that it will follow his work in a number of interesting ways. Lanthimos will be working, once again, under the auspices of Element Pictures (and therefore Guiney), alongside Film4 and Fruit Tree, a new production company run by Emma Stone and Dave McCary. Stone will also return onscreen, this time in the lead role. Tony McNamara, meanwhile, fresh from his success with *The Favourite*—not to mention Disney's *Cruella* (Craig Gillespie, 2021) and his *Favourite*-esque ahistorical TV series *The Great* (Hulu, 2020–)—is once again on screenplay duties. *Poor Things* is an adaptation of Scottish author Alasdair Gray's novel of the same name, in which a young woman who commits suicide to escape an abusive marriage is brought back to life with the brain of her unborn child. A reworked *Frankenstein* (Mary Shelley, 1818), *Poor Things* is "postmodern in its game-playing with literary conventions … within a neo-Victorian frame" that "intermingles science fiction and fantasy … and combines both with realistic settings and generally realistic, if sometimes extreme, human reactions to circumstances and situations."[21] So far, so Lanthimos.

Prefacing *Poor Things*' possible detour into horror proper, in 2019 Lanthimos produced a cryptic short film, *Nimic*, in which a seemingly serendipitous encounter on a subway sees a professional cellist (Matt Dillon) lose grip on his life as a stranger, a woman, quite suddenly enters his life to replace him. The short film demonstrates Lanthimos's box of formal tricks while utilizing horror iconography relating to the *doppelgänger* to convey the existential dread of late modernity. Finished in 2020, with the Covid-19 pandemic underway, *Nimic* acquired a surprising second level of thematic purchase upon its release. In the context of a global crisis that required distancing of oneself from another, *Nimic* hauntingly showcases how existing social orders have sacrificed individuality and facilitated detachment to the extent that we already operate as disconnected and potentially replaceable automatons. *Nimic*'s coldly intelligent yet direct take on the impersonal dynamics of the modern world echoes *The Lobster*'s thesis on dehumanizing forms of governance, marking once again thematic cohesion between Lanthimos's various "storyworlds."

Framing Lanthimos's Weird Storyworlds

As *The Favourite* illustrates, Lanthimos's style is distinct even when working alongside collaborators, so much so in fact that one could plausibly imagine a world in which the characters of his films might coexist. Without going so far as to propose a Lanthimos extended universe, there is nevertheless space to explore the interconnectedness of his works. Despite the fact that the notion of the "archi-film," following Peter Wollen,[22] is rooted in traditional (and arguably somewhat antiquated) ideas concerning the auteur, it is nevertheless an enticing framework through which to explore the explicit and implicit connections between a filmmaker's works, especially when said filmmaker employs what appears to be formal continuity. My starting point for this consideration of Lanthimos's works is Warren Buckland's semiotic analysis of the "storyworlds" of Wes Anderson, which he defines as "an abstract totality encompassing everything that fictionally exists across a director's films."[23] Following this method, Buckland writes that "a storyworld emerges from abstract codes and structures—paradigms, kinship structures, binary oppositions, mediators, systems of exchange and rules of transformation."[24]

Suffice it to say, one need not have a full grasp of Anderson's or indeed Lanthimos's films to understand that the two directors have little in common with each other. Nevertheless, the "storyworld" method brings new dimensions to readings of Lanthimos's work that explores them as parts of a wider film project. Themes that recur include the ruthlessness of parental and/or state authority, unbeatable systems, exchanges of power, animality and human–animal boundaries, legacies of loss and trauma, the absurd and its variations, false truths, the staging of violence, god-like egos and the mythopoeic, and so forth. Taken together, the studies conducted in this book arguably provide evidence of Lanthimos's "archi-film," which emerges from the ties that bind these readings together.

In Part I, "Origins and Identity," Afroditi Nikolaidou and Vrasidas Karalis position Lanthimos in relation to the Greek film cultures that precede his emergence in the mid-2000s. In the first chapter, Nikolaidou brings focus to Lanthimos's early works, up to the making and release of *Kinetta*, that saw the director experiment with various types of media. In doing so, Nikolaidou explains Lanthimos's development as symptomatic of a series of changes that were happening in the shadow of Greek *eksynchronismos*/"modernization." Karalis then looks at the complex range of influences that *Kinetta* exhibits. He explores *Kinetta* in a way that demythologizes Lanthimos's style and authorship by contextualizing it against key historical movements in Greek film that preface the Weird Wave. Karalis's chapter works to explore *Kinetta* as reflective of an emergent mode while dispelling many prominent ideas about the Weird Wave, which demonstrably has antecedents in earlier national movements.

In Part II, "Experiencing Lanthimos," the collection turns to questions of spectatorship. Asbjørn Grønstad opens the section discussing confinement in *Alps*, a film that he finds demonstrates Lanthimos's expanded thesis on the machinations of modern life and how best to negotiate it. Next, Ina Karkani explores her concept of *adriftness* in *The Lobster*, observing how the film presents bodies out of place that, as she puts it, "threaten to violate familiar ontological boundaries as we have come to know them." Finally, my own chapter explores how the apathetic, or affectless, style of Lanthimos's films constructs a spectatorial contract that engages the viewer to watch ethically, asking them to unpick the images of violence to understand their symbolic currency.

In the longest part of the book, "Form and Authorship," my contributors consider the historical, formal and theoretical contexts that frame Lanthimos's film style. The section opens with Angelos Koutsourakis's chapter on the Kafkaesque genealogy evident in *The Lobster*. Tracing Kafkaesque resonances in the style of the film, Koutsourakis observes how Lanthimos reformats those themes to provide commentary on the contemporary crisis of neoliberalism. Continuing the theme of textual inheritance, in the next chapter, Michael Lipiner and Nathan Abrams explore stylistic correspondence between Lanthimos and Stanley Kubrick. Their study finds echoes at the level of form and content in which Lanthimos's films come to mirror Kubrick's often cynical view of humanity's struggle against the absurd violence of the universe. Next, Nepomuk Zettl explores the spatial, social, and semiotic relations that characterize Lanthimos's film worlds. Zettl argues that Lanthimos's films utilize spatial proximity to recode and deconstruct recurring themes such as family and intimacy. Finally here, Savina Petkova explores how the specific ontological position of Lanthimosian animals helps to overcome anthropocentric discourse by reconfiguring relationships between humans and animals. For Petkova, Lanthimos's use of animals (and animal metaphors) entices new ways of thinking about human–animal ethics, human behavior, and the political systems that account for them.

Part IV of the book, "Genre and Variation," opens with Geoff King continuing to explore his interests in the art film by making use of *The Killing of a Sacred Deer* as a case study to observe how, and to what extent, Lanthimos's cinema occupies the relatively more commercial end of the art–mainstream film spectrum. King's study focuses on how Lanthimos utilizes and defies generic expectations at a textual level, evident in certain dimensions that include narrative, audiovisual style, characterization, and moral ambiguity. Next, classicist James J. Clauss explores the mythic resonances of Lanthimos's oeuvre. Beginning with its most obvious contender, *The Killing of a Sacred Deer*, a reworking of Euripides, Clauss comes to observe a link between the antique and modern where recurring classical elements reflect the timelessness of some of Lanthimos's central themes. In the final chapter of this section, Alex Lykidis considers how *The Favourite* revises the conventions of the British heritage film to provide a more critical perspective on history, politics and contemporary society. Lykidis notes that the innovative visual and narrative style of Lanthimos's film avoids the pictorialism, pastoralism and nostalgia that previously characterized the heritage genre, and instead presents an unflinching portrayal of undemocratic systems of power that are reflective of Lanthimos's preoccupation with authoritarianism, proceduralism and disempowerment.

In the opening chapter of Part V, "Gender, Sex, and Sexuality," Tonia Kazakopoulou provides a more critical reading of Lanthimos's work than many of the other chapters. Kazakopoulou considers the motif of young women's deadly rebellions against the restrictive, and invariably patriarchal, regimes they inhabit in Lanthimos's Greek-language films. She explores what she sees as a paradox inherent in these films, where images of resilience and rebellion are offset by systems of representation that ultimately lead women not to liberation but to death. Alice Haylett Bryan follows with a chapter on the use of sex in Lanthimos's works. Haylett Bryan adopts weirdness as a critical prism that has long trailed Lanthimos, linking it to European extremity, to explore how his presentation of sex explicates not only his positioning at the fringe of corresponding movements, but also how it explains the affective resonances that his films inspire. Finally, Marios Psaras looks at *The Lobster* through a queer, posthumanist lens. In this last chapter, Psaras considers how Lanthimos's film presents a subversive deconstruction of normative discourses on the human, highlighting the body's representational potential to convey new horizons beyond what has been adopted as an anthropocentric and heteropatriarchal realism.

The fifteen chapters that comprise this book draw on various critical frameworks in their approach to Lanthimos and his body of work. Each framework offers insight into the various historical, cultural, industrial, formal and philosophical pathways that might unlock the mysteries of his films. I do not present this book as one that is exhaustive, but rather as a point of entry for those interested in Lanthimos and his evidently weird worlds. While I sincerely hope that researchers, students, and teachers of film, and indeed anyone else who encounters it, find the book to be a worthy and versatile companion to his works, it is also my hope that the pathways it uncovers invite ongoing critical discourse that will continue beyond its pages. Indeed, while he may be one of the more distinct filmmakers of his generation, he still has much to offer—I, for one, cannot wait to see how the rest of his career progresses and whether it will underscore or complicate the ideas contained here.

Notes

1. Steve Rose, "Attenberg, Dogtooth and the Weird Wave of Greek Cinema," *The Guardian*, Aug 27, 2011, available at https://www.theguardian.com/film/2011/aug/27/attenberg-dogtooth-greece-cinema.
2. Alex Lykidis, "Crisis of Sovereignty in Recent Greek Cinema," *Journal of Greek Media and Culture*, 1, no. 1 (Apr 2015): 9–27, at p. 10.
3. Quoted in Peter Strickland, "Yorgos Lanthimos by Peter Strickland," *Bomb Magazine*, Mar 15, 2015, available at https://bombmagazine.org/articles/yorgos-lanthimos/.

4   Lydia Papadimitriou, Vangelis Calotychos, and Yannis Tzioumakis, "Revisiting Contemporary Greek Film Cultures: Weird Wave and Beyond," *Journal of Greek Media and Culture*, 2 (2016): 127–31, at pp. 128–29.

5   Vrasidas Karalis, *A History of Greek Cinema* (London and New York: Continuum, 2012), 264–65.

6   Maria Chalkou, "New Cinema of 'Emancipation': Tendencies of Independence in Greek Cinema of the 2000s," *Interactions: Studies in Communication and Culture*, 3, no. 2 (2012): 243–61, at p. 249.

7   See Lydia Papadimitriou, "Greek Cinema as European Cinema: Co-productions, Eurimages and the Europeanisation of Greek Cinema," *Studies in European Cinema*, 15 (2018): 215–34.

8   For example, writing in 2019, film critic Ben Kenigsberg of the *New York Times* concedes that "time hasn't made it more than a cryptic curiosity" ("Kinetta Review," *New York Times*, Oct 17, 2019, available at https://www.nytimes.com/2019/10/17/movies/kinetta-review.html).

9   Papadimitriou, "Greek Cinema as European Cinema," 224.

10 See *Dogtooth*'s regular inclusion in lists dedicated to the best films of the twenty-first century (e.g., Peter Bradshaw, Cath Clarke, Andrew Pulver, and Catherine Shoard, "The 100 Best Films of the 21st Century," *The Guardian*, Sept 13, 2019, available at https://www.theguardian.com/film/2019/sep/13/100-best-films-movies-of-the-21st-century).

11 Peter Bradshaw, "*Dogtooth* Review," *The Guardian*, Apr 22, 2010, available at https://www.theguardian.com/film/2010/apr/22/dogtooth-review.

12 See Rosa Barotsi, "Whose Crisis? *Dogtooth* and the Invisible Middle Class," *Journal of Greek Media and Culture*, 2, no. 2 (2016): 173–86; Mark Fisher, "*Dogtooth*: The Family Syndrome," *Film Quarterly*, 64, no. 4 (2011): 22–27; Stamos Metzidakis, "No Bones to Pick with Lanthimos's Film *Dogtooth*," *Journal of Modern Greek Studies*, 32, no. 2 (2014): 367–92.

13 Karalis, *A History of Greek Cinema*, 267.

14 Papadimitriou, "Greek Cinema as European Cinema," 224.

15 See my own work on A24 and independent North American horror: Eddie Falvey, "'Art-Horror' and 'Hardcore Art-Horror' at the Margins: Experimentation and Extremity in Contemporary Independent Horror," *Horror Studies*, 12, no. 1 (2021): 63–81.

16 Papadimitriou, "Greek Cinema as European Cinema," 224.

17 See Geoff King, *Indiewood, USA: Where Hollywood Meets Independent Cinema* (New York: Bloomsbury, 2009).

18 "*The Favourite* Production Notes," *Fox Searchlight* et al., available at http://dps03o6uurl7v.cloudfront.net/FAVOURITE_Production_Notes.pdf, 4–8.

19 Ibid., 6.

20 Tony McNamara stated that

> As an Australian and a Greek, Yorgos and I weren't attached to English history, so maybe we felt more free to be fast and loose with it … there's a

fundamental truth to the big events and the big frame of the story, but we were mostly concerned with exploring these three women. So where the established history was useful to us it stayed, and where it wasn't useful to us we let it go. It was quite fun to do. (ibid., 7)

21 John Glendening, "Education, Science and Secular Ethics in Alasdair Gray's *Poor Things*," *Mosaic: An Interdisciplinary Critical Journal*, 49, no. 2 (2016): 75–93, at p. 75.
22 Peter Wollen developed this concept when studying the films of Jean Renoir, leading to the proposition that some directors spend their lives making a single film: "Underlying the different individual tales was an archi-tale, of which they were all variants" (*Signs and Meaning in the Cinema* [London: British Film Institute, 1972], 93).
23 Warren Buckland, *Wes Anderson's Symbolic Storyworld: A Semiotic Analysis* (New York and London: Bloomsbury, 2019), 5.
24 Ibid.

PART I

Origins and Identity

2

Greek Screen Cultures and the Scopic Regimes of the Long 1990s: Exploring Yorgos Lanthimos's Early Works

Afroditi Nikolaidou

Introduction

Yorgos Lanthimos is undoubtedly one of the most intriguing filmmakers of the twenty-first century. He is commonly regarded as one of the exemplary figures of contemporary world art cinema, having paved his way within the consolidated and often bureaucratic systems that comprise the European film industry. There, Lanthimos has successfully navigated the creative possibilities and pitfalls that lie between regulation, the hierarchies of big production companies, and the work of intermediaries—sales agents, festival directors and programmers, film promoters, and marketers—that have all in their way impacted the production of art films in Greece as well as elsewhere. His films pose questions about world cinema and the auteur in the age of postnational identity, and about transnational film production processes, demonstrating mobility between the periphery and center that illustrates uneven relationships within the film industry. Moreover, most of the current scholarship on Lanthimos's oeuvre focuses on the cultural criticism inherent to it, and mostly commits to the philosophical and aesthetic decipherment of his films. His entire oeuvre, however, comprises—as well as his six feature films—a significant number of short films, music and dance videos, theater performances, television commercials, fashion films, and photographic work, which have not yet been incorporated into the academic work on Lanthimos and, thus, are yet to be discussed as a substantial part of his creative signature. Consequently, various areas of inquiry have been ignored, like those concerning the status of auteurs in the age of media convergence,[1] as well as questions relating to authorship and intermediality,[2] intertextuality,[3] and paratextuality,[4] especially if one is to consider paratexts—including promotional dance performance videos—as autonomous works of art belonging to a filmmaker's filmography. Each of these industrial and media contexts and modes of production, pertinent to Lanthimos's development as a filmmaker, shape and are shaped by artistic choices, themes, and styles that are all worthy of deeper consideration.

For that reason, I suggest that we consider Lanthimos's career in three phases. The first phase might be called Lanthimos's experimentation phase and includes everything from the second half of the 1990s to the early 2000s, encompassing Lanthimos's television commercials, music and dance videos, the short film *Uranisco Disco* (2002), and his collaboration with Lakis Lazopoulos on the film *My Best Friend* (*O kalyteros mou filos*, 2001). Elsewhere, this period has been defined by the political and social discourse of *eksynchronismos*/"modernization," by the advent of advertising and popular cinema in Greece, and also by the development of certain tendencies in the performative arts (including dance theater and devised theater). After the Athens Olympic Games in 2004, Lanthimos entered his second artistic phase as a Greek filmmaker, in which he established his unique style in *Kinetta*, *Dogtooth* and *Alps*. This period is marked by steady collaborations with a group of creative professionals, by his repudiation of dysfunctional ties with state-funding bodies, and by the international success of his films. In the third phase, Lanthimos becomes established as an international auteur as he moves into making larger, English-language coproductions, thus becoming an exemplar for transnational European art filmmaking.

In this chapter, I aim to reconsider the first period of Lanthimos's career, approaching the past in a prospective way that establishes a genealogy in his work, and that finds points of entrance for the critical discourse that has addressed his later films. I argue that although Lanthimos's visual style during this first phase appears to be different to that of his later work, intertextuality[5] and intermediality[6] become strategic objectives that address specific "scopic regimes" of the late 1990s to the early 2000s while paving the way for the performative and kinesthetic forms of his later work. My approach aims to connect contexts, paratexts, and texts: contexts, relating to the historical and cultural conditions that shape textual processes of production; paratexts, namely the catalogues and promotional materials of the archive of the VideoDance Festival and its parent organizer, the Thessaloniki International Film Festival (Athens and Thessaloniki,

2000–2007), administered by the VideoDance Festival artistic director, Christiana Galanopoulou;[7] and texts, including films, music, and dance videos, accessed from the VideoDance's archive, the Greek Film Centre, and the great living archive that is YouTube.

Considering that this corpus contains both mainstream films and popular music videos, I turn to Martin Jay's concept of "scopic regimes"[8] to understand the director as modulator and explorer of ideas relating to this period. The "scopic regime," coming from Christian Metz's psychoanalytical theory on film,[9] refers to the way a society sees and organizes its visual culture. It encapsulates both the technologies that facilitate and the conventions of representation that determine how a society imagines and engages with itself during a specific cultural moment. The moment in question spans the late 1990s to the early 2000s, which has been understood to encompass a period of *eksynchronismos*/"modernization" in which elements of postmodernity were becoming dominant in the Greek arts and media. Jay argues that there is not only a "unified scopic regime," but that it can be "discerned, if often in repressed form" within "competing ocular fields,"[10] meaning that there is a dominant form, but that subcultures with contested visual approaches propose other "scopic regimes" also. As Jay argues of "the scopic regime of modernity," it "may best be understood as a contested terrain, rather than a harmoniously integrated complex of visual theories and practices."[11] Therefore, at the end of the 1980s, Jay argues that there is not only one definitive "scopic regime," but rather also "a differentiation of visual subcultures, whose separation has allowed us to understand the multiple implications of sight in ways that are now only beginning to be appreciated."[12]

Looking at Lanthimos's early material through this prism allows one to see the contested visual forms that emerge in his work as coming from specific cultural discourses and practices with which he was involved (such as the "video dance"[13]). Furthermore, two interweaving "scopic regimes" reveal themselves via this method: one that is based on "intertextuality," including the types of generic pastiche that are considered by Fredric Jameson,[14] and another that privileges "intermediality" and "fusion"[15] between coproducing forms of media. "Intertextuality" and "pastiche" are integral parts of the discourse on postmodernism and, in that sense, express a dominant trend in Greece at the end of the twentieth century that conforms to corresponding trends in the arts and film and television cultures. On the other hand, "intermediality" is not only a practice that Lanthimos exercises in his "video dances," but also one that expresses a specific environment of experimentation operating across various forms of media in Greece during the late 1990s. Through the conceptual prism of "fusion" that does not discern between film, dance, theater and performance art, as well as other visual and sound arts, one is not only able to reconceptualize the notion of the auteur in accordance with aesthetic shifts taking place, but also to position that figure as a fluid, in-between medium "in continuous change and interchange,"[16] one which helps situate Lanthimos's earlier and later proclivities as an artist.

The Long 1990s: The Years of *Eksynchronismos*/"Modernization"

The long 1990s[17]—between 1989 and 2004—represent for the performing arts, a period of experimentation and visual research, of contested boundaries marked by "scopic regimes" that privilege dynamic visual cultures, as well as somatic and kinesthetic experiences. As I will argue, seeds for the performativity, experimentation, and fusion of pop culture with the high arts that perfuse the Greek Weird Wave[18] are to be found in this period that culminated with the Athens Olympic Games in 2004. Dimitris Papaioannou, the award-winning stage director, choreographer, visual artist, and artistic director of the ceremonies, as well as Athina Rachel Tsangari, Yorgos Lanthimos, and other contemporary artists—many of whom have been collaborators since the mid-1990s—participated in the creative process and contributed toward the visual identity of the opening and closing ceremonies.

More specifically to screen media, the late 1980s in Greece are marked by the launch of private television channels. The end of state monopolization of the television industry led to more competition and media "deregulation" and the rise of what has been called "promotional culture."[19] These changes resulted not only in the rapid expansion of the Greek advertising industry and the rearrangement and redistribution of political powers within the media sector, but also in the formal transformation of information delivery and entertainment.[20] Coinciding with this period of change, a dominant message emerged around *eksynchronismos*/"modernization," a political and social discourse associated with Europeanization and the rationalization of the state, as well as its harmonization with Western structures and wider European economic development.[21]

During this period, the practices and mechanisms of cultural representation and communication were responding to global trends in a manner that are expressive of a Greek orientation toward *eksynchronismos*/"modernization." The "practical philosophies," following Nicolas Sevastakis,[22] of this period include artistic and social representations that are disengaged from *laikotita*/"authentic popular culture," and convey symbolic content that bears the tensions between old and new codes of Greek identity. In cinema and television there are three primary manifestations of these tensions. In the first type, tradition is modernized not just in a state of "negotiation and coexistence," as in the case of popular television series,[23] but also in "nostalgia films" including *Peppermint* (Costas Kapakas, 1999) and *A Touch of Spice* (*Politiki kouzina*, Tassos Boulmetis, 2003). In the second type, old and traditional signifiers are reappropriated, rediscovered, and reunited into new forms of signification—for example, in the ironic, parodic distance that typifies Panos Koutras's first feature, *The Attack of the Giant Moussaka* (*I epithesi tou gigantiaiou mousaka*, 1999).[24] In the third type, there are new trends to borrow from European forms that demonstrate a synchronous intertextuality, as in the case of *From the Edge of the City* (*Apo tin akri tis polis*, Constantine Giannaris, 1998), which echoes the spatial and visual organization of urban-set French *banlieu* films such as *La Haine* (Mathieu Kassovitz, 1995).

Prominent Greek directors including Panos Koutras, Constantine Giannaris, Angelos Frantzis, Yannis Economides and, later, Dennis Iliadis all made their feature debuts between 1996 and 2004, and collectively represent a new generation of filmmakers adopting new technologies and styles developed in advertising to create independent productions and television coproductions.[25] Parallel to the advertising industry, another area for experimentation with new technologies is the music video format, which also flourished during that same period. MAD TV, a Greek private music television station, was established in 1996 and created space for production within a markedly postmodern format that reflected changing celebrity cultures in the Anglo-American music video industry.[26] The rise of popular stars such as Sakis Rouvas showed movement away from both folk and *entechni/*"art" music toward an "intensification of the discourses of celebrity around pop music" reflective of the cultural environments of the West.[27]

Theater, performance art and film all functioned as communicating media. During the 1990s, Michael Marmarinos, Theodoros Terzopoulos, and others acclimatized a generation of spectators and young artists to postdramatic theater art. Accordingly, dance theater companies responded to the tensions of "modernization" revolutionizing dance.[28] Playful repetition, expressionless acting styles, awkward movements, and body posture—the "performative aesthetics"[29] that Lanthimos and others of his generation embrace in their theatrical and film work—are to be found in these innovating theatrical approaches. These, in short, are the cultural, political, and mediatic contexts that predicated a young generation of filmmakers preoccupied with "the rhetorics of the end—the end of century, the end of history, the end of representation, the end of the grand narratives, the end of Greece, even the end of cinema."[30] Television commercials aside—a format that traditionally rejects auteurism, since it does not often rely on the identity and publicity of its creator—Lanthimos developed his style in two primary arenas: video dances and music videos, particularly those in collaboration with popstar Sakis Rouvas. It is in these formats that Lanthimos explores— via a variety of techniques, mechanisms, and styles—elements to be found in his later work, namely the relations of the ocular to the kinesthetic.

Music Videos and Pastiche: Lanthimos's Film Lab

During the second half of the 1990s, Lanthimos directed a number of music videos, working with a series of major pop artists, including Rouvas, Despina Vandi, and the alternative group Xaxakes. His music videos frequently explore male and female sexuality (and contain a lot of nudity) via iconoclasm, nostalgia, and pastiche, as well as various forms of media archeology. Most significantly, they represent studies in specific genres. This diverse body of work borrows from the narrative and visual devices that were at the time associated with the postmodern in film, recalling Jameson's "nostalgia"[31] in the music video for Sakis Rouvas's song "*Ipirhes panta*" (1998), as well as Giuliana Bruno's ideas relating to "post-industrial decay"[32] in "*Den ehei sidera i kardia sou*" (1998), and Jim Collins's "eclectic irony"[33] in "*Antexa*" (2000). His music videos also promote a "stylish style" through "rapid editing, bipolar extremes of lens lengths, reliance on close shots and wide-ranging camera movements,"[34] and place emphasis on generic exploration and "transtextuality."[35] In his music videos, Lanthimos introduced cinematic aesthetics that transplanted narrative and stylistic conventions from different genres and films of the 1990s into an emerging television format.

The 1997 music video for the song "*Sta xafnika*" by Xaxakes employs rapid editing, colorful roaming shots, canted framing, frequent use of a wide lens to distort its figures, and a costume style and body choreography reflective of the same excessive camp aesthetic to be seen a couple of years later in Panos Koutras's *The Attack of the Giant Moussaka*. The saturated color and the extreme camera movement, in combination with the song, recalls Wong Kar-wai's 1990s film aesthetic (see, e.g., *Chungking Express* [1994]). Working with Rouvas, "*Den ehei sidera i kardia sou*" contains nods to various American science-fiction films, while "*Ipirhes panta*" has the look of a 1950s road movie shot on Super 8 film. "*I kardia mou*" is shot as a black and white noir narrative that fetishizes, via close-ups, various parts of Rouvas's body. "*Antexa*" comprises a single take of four and a half minutes and is evocative of both Francis Ford Coppola's adaptation *Bram Stoker's Dracula* (1992) and Neil Jordan's *Interview with the Vampire* (1994). The continuous shot conveys a *mise en abyme* narrative in which another 16-mm camera simultaneously films an erotic sequence with the pop star. At the end of the music video, a clapboard reveals the director to be Buck Rogers—another genre reference, this time to American science fiction. The music video for "*Thelis i den thelis*" (Sakis Rouvas, 1998) was awarded the Best Music Video in 1998 by the Pop Corn Music Awards. The fragmented way in which Lanthimos films Rouvas transforms him into an object of sexual commodification. In these roles, Rouvas exhibits his adaptability as an actor working not only in popular cinema, but also in more niche works like Tsangari's *Chevalier* (2015). Motifs and themes in Lanthimos's later works are also present in this music video, from a reflexive framing of sex and sexuality to the presence of games that recur in *Dogtooth* and beyond.[36]

As Jameson asserts, pastiche represents an "imitation of a peculiar or unique, idiosyncratic style, the wearing of a linguistic mask, speech in a dead language."[37] Systematically employed from video to video, Lanthimos's music video pastiches are a kind of self-reflexive play that reproduces the prevailing trends of the period. Lanthimos's method of filming Rouvas, for example, often provides a pastiche of the overtly sexualized customary means of filming the bodies of female actors and pop stars. As a cultural form, pop music videos have "a heterogeneous and inconsistent cultural presence" that "mixes the mainstream with more avant-garde tendencies."[38] Although Lanthimos's music and dance videos explore a variety of cinematic techniques and genres, within the context of *eksynchronismos/* "modernization," such works express and shape the scopic regimes reflective of Greek postmodernity in which the "stylish style" of world cinema of the 1990s interplays with an erosion of boundaries between popular and high art within the prevailing "promotional culture," elements that combine to produce a culture of "endless chain[s] of mutual reference[s] and implication[s]."[39]

One may read *My Best Friend*, a romantic comedy codirected by Lakis Lazopoulos and Lanthimos, in the same way. *My Best Friend* is paradigmatic of mainstream popular Greek cinema, which combines television actors with era-specific dialogue, advertising aesthetics, product placement, and themes pointing to the tradition of the Boulevard Theatre. Lazopoulos, the film's producer, actor, and codirector, was already a major Greek television celebrity, establishing himself with the popular satirical television show *Deka mikroi Mitsoi* (1992–2003). At the time, he collaborated with many young and talented artists, among whom were Yorgos Lanthimos and the choreographer Constantinos Rigos. Though the film does not reflect the directorial style that Lanthimos will bring to his solo feature film *Kinetta*, it does connect with the stylistic and technological devices of the "promotional culture" that he employed for his commercial and music video work. Lanthimos's short film *Uranisco Disco* is another meticulous exercise in intertextual pastiche that refers to Alexandre Rockwell's *In the Soup* (1992) and points to erotic films of the 1970s, as it does to the directorial style of Paul Thomas Anderson's own intertextual homage to the era, *Boogie Nights* (1997). Moreover, in both *My Best Friend* and *Uranisco Disco* it is obvious that a synergetic production culture is being developed among young and talented professionals, including editor Yorgos Mavropsaridis, production designer Anna Georgiadou, costume and production designer Elli Papageorgakopoulou, and director of photography Thimios Bakatakis, all of whom will return as creative personnel for Lanthimos's later films. Operating within this promotional culture, Lanthimos adopts, on his own terms, what was being formalized by 1990s world cinema and MTV: "a specific set of qualities—aggressive directorship, contemporary editing and FX, sexuality, vivid colors, urgent movement, nonsensical juxtapositions, provocation, frolic, all combined for maximum impact on a small screen."[40] As much as these elements constitute the style of a Greek postmodernism more generally, as audiovisual cues expressive of a wider discourse of *eksynchronismos*/"modernization" in operation, they also represent cultural and formal building blocks—and a preparatory stage—for Lanthimos: a laboratory of colliding cultures and film techniques that set the platform for his later experimentation.

Video Dances: An Intermedia Practice

Encounters between film and dance take diverse forms. Dance constitutes a key mode of visual ethnography and features often in narrative films as well as forming the basis of specific genres. Otherwise, dance performances in theaters or other spaces may be filmed for promotional reasons or to experiment with image and body movement. At the first VideoDance Festival that took place in Athens and Thessaloniki in 2000,[41] artistic director Christiana Galanopoulou defined "video dance [a]s a meeting point between dance and the camera."[42] Galanopoulou explains the form further: "The dancer, the choreographer, the director, the visual artist, the musician can meet in a performance. What makes the difference between a dance performance and a dance film is the camera and its gaze ... This gaze must become the real medium between the dance and its viewer within the cinema."[43] Defined by an act of looking that constitutes an interactive relation between subject and spectator, Galanopoulou's outline presents the video dance as a characteristically intermedial form, where dance, music, and film fuse in such a way that they cannot exist separately. In that sense, a video dance is itself a uniquely performative act. For the event, Galanopoulou released an open call through the Greek Choreographers Association to showcase and record various encounters between dance and film. In the end, she screened seven video dances directed by Lanthimos, which attests to his engagement with experimental forms of filmmaking during the second half of the 1990s. He was one of very few notable directors to practice and create within this genre.

The screenings took place largely in industrial or obsolete spaces, creating a mystical and ritualistic experience. The VideoDance Festival provided the platform for a unique mode of cultural ambience, a space of convergence between the performing and visual arts and new forms of technology. The first two productions on this platform were Yorgos Lanthimos and Katerina Papageorgiou's *9 a.m.* (2001) and Dimitris Koutsiambasakos and Elefthria Rizou's *Frida* (2001). From 2001 until 2007, the program created a production culture that nurtured artistic and aesthetic synergies between art, film, and technology. From a media history point of view, these festivals nurtured collaborations between choreographers, performers, visual artists, and filmmakers, renewing the scopic regimes in Greek visual culture into one that was transmedial, formally expanded, and multisensory.

Of the thirteen video dances screened during the first festival, seven were directed by Lanthimos, proving that his engagement with the genre was not minor. His video dances include *Counted Time* (chor. Maro Tsouvala-Vasso Barboussi, 1995), *Private Closet* (chor. Konstantinos Rigos, 1997), *Raping Chloe* (chor. Konstantinos Rigos, 1998), *Woman in White* (chor. Konstantinos Rigos, 1999), *Icarus* (chor. Konstantinos Rigos, 1999), *Song of '99* (chor. Dimitris Papaioannou and Omada Edafous, 1999) and *The Date* (chor. Katerina Papageorgiou, 2000). It is worth additionally noting that Lanthimos was collaborating with dancers from two of the most important dance companies of the time: Oktana (led by Konstantinos Rigos) and Omada Edafous (led by Dimitris Papaioannou).

Lanthimos's videos for Oktana and Omada Edafous—in combination with the works of company SineQuaNon—provide evidence for the changing environment of dance in the mid-1990s. The three dance companies were associated with a "dance boom" and "new dance" in this era of cultural *eksynchronismos*/"modernization."[44] As Tsintziloni summarizes in her research on the aesthetic elements that these groups brought to the dance scene in Greece: "[Omada Edafous] used a choreographic language based on visual elements, while Oktana Dance theatre stressed the tactile (material) presence of bodies on stage and the psychological depth of the characters. SineQuaNon, through its movement vocabulary, energy and movement dynamics, foregrounded the kinesthetic dimension of dance."[45]

Encounters between film and dance in this period are part of an aesthetic program that performed the tensions of *eksynchronismos*/"modernization" by situating a new mode of bodily expression in a period where the corporeal (lived) political body became less involved with political action and was disappearing from the public sphere.[46] In the same manner, dance sequences in the films of the Greek Weird Wave—such as key dance sequences that feature in both *Dogtooth* and *The Lobster*—could be read as an inextricable stylistic element that comments on the (bio)political situation of post-2009 Greece. Moreover, if one considers Rigos's integration of classical forms in *Daphnis and Chloe* (2000) as part of a modernized dance style,[47] Lanthimos's adjacent uses of dance in *Dogtooth* and *The Lobster* can be seen as belonging to a fertile tradition aiming to reshape dance on film into a new form of visual and political expression.

The video dances were not merely being filmed for posterity—in some cases, they were produced as promotional material—yet all of them stand as unique works where filmed visuality transcends their liveness and ephemerality. Framing, camera movement and editing reveal the performances' cinematic quality and emphasize their intermedial nature; as Dick Higgins writes of intermediality, "fusion" and "continuity" become "the hallmark of our new mentality."[48] *Woman in White*, directed by Lanthimos and choreographed by Rigos, for example, also functions as a music video for Alexia Vassiliou, a well-known pop and jazz singer. The video is influenced by prevailing music video aesthetics of the 1990s,[49] utilizing slow motion in its study of the human body. At the same time, the scenography contains diverse equipment akin to that of a strange, antiquated laboratory: a refrigerator, an old monitor, streetlamps, and doctor's chairs present remnants of a civilization bound in plastic wrap. Reflecting the fusion Higgins discusses, Lanthimos's *Woman in White* evades strict categorization and can be discussed both as a music video and as a video dance.

The Date and *9 a.m.* stand out as examples due to the fact that the choreography appears to be specifically designed for the camera. Lanthimos collaborates with Thimios Bakatakis—his future director of photography on *Kinetta, Dogtooth, The Lobster* and *The Killing of a Sacred Deer*—for *The Date*, a video dance that tells the story of a couple through dance, lighting, and scenography, as well as camera movement and editing. The video dance opens with a woman in the middle of a room with a white table, dancing alone in an otherwise empty space. A man joins her and the couple dances their date. Lanthimos uses a variety of techniques, like oblique framing and fast editing that disorient the viewer. His style creates blurred images from the movements of the dancers, while out-of-focus shots and intensified match cuts unite the female and male body in unconventional ways. The gaze of the camera is inextricably interwoven with the movements to the extent that it is part of the choreography, which is in turn formulated by the gaze. *9 a.m.*, meanwhile, mixes analogue with digital media, combining Super 8 film with digital video. Set in part on the streets of New York City, *9 a.m.* otherwise depicts everyday practices in mundane spaces—the main dance sequence takes place in an all-white bathroom, for instance. The video dance utilizes uncanny imagery of a woman in a sleeping mask—masks and blindfolds being a visual motif for Lanthimos—or dancing in her red dress as she is trapped in the small bathroom to convey a struggle between night and day, dream and reality, a theme that is embodied in the materiality of the production that appears to capture film technology in transition. Both video dances are preoccupied with the changing materiality of the scopic regimes of late modernity while Lanthimos's gestures toward an expanded cinema are marked by a symbiosis between film and dance.

Conclusion

One of the most important formal interfaces between Lanthimos's early and later years is the establishment of metonymy as a core trope of his visual style. Metonymy, as Dimitris Papanikolaou suggests, is a nodal characteristic of the films of the Weird Wave that will follow. He writes:

> [U]nlike metaphor, in which substitution is based on analogy or similarity (something is like something else), metonymy is based on the way in which two elements are combined along a horizontal axis: One stands for (and eventually could link to) another because they are close, because they touch, because they belong in a list or an assortment or an entity, or because they are related through a line of cause and effect, container and contained, and so on.[50]

Metonymy relates not to "stable signification," but to more complex "structures of meaning."[51] It is constructed on a basis of unfamiliarity paired with proximity, contiguity, and closeness, thus differentiating it from the use of metaphors or symbols deployed by the auteurs of the New Greek Cinema of the 1970s. Metonymy equally expresses the forms of the period, both in the subtle collapsing of boundaries and in Lanthimos's intermedial legacy where forms come to "touch," if one follows Papanikolaou.

Kinetta, Lanthimos's first feature film, sets the scene for the next phase of the filmmaker's career. Production-wise, *Kinetta* was by no means an ordinary affair. An Athina Rachel Tsangari production, *Kinetta* also lists coproduction credits belonging to Modiano Inc, Top Cut, Stefi and Kino (four production companies with stakes in the advertising industry). *Kinetta*'s production model circumvents or avoids state funding bodies, even from private financiers or television companies. The time-consuming bureaucracy of such official procedures could last up to two years before a project is accepted or rejected, disrupting the creative process.[52] As Lanthimos stated in one of his interviews: "We just started making our own films—a few friends asking for favors, using friends' houses, clothing and cars. By making commercials, investing the money we were making and working with friends, we were able to eventually make our first film without much other support, which in Greece was negligible anyway. That's how we made *Kinetta*, *Dogtooth* and *Alps*."[53] Approaching Lanthimos's oeuvre in relation to the three distinct phases it encompasses allows one not only to see evidence of continuation, tensions, overlap and evolution, but also to explore Lanthimos's complex and nodal relation to the Greek (and later world) screen and art industries. Both aims pose wider questions about Greek film history and its relation to European cinema in the era of transnational and intermedial practices.

In conclusion, Lanthimos's experimentation with style via other art forms is clearly crucial to his development. In his music and dance videos, he explores themes and motifs that he will return to later; he masters cinematic devices—the long shot, slow motion, art-house aesthetics, genre conventions—that he will continue to use or reject later; in terms of production he invests in collaborations with a loyal and talented creative crew, from his production designer to editor to director of photography who will each return at intervals for his later features; he works to transcend the boundaries between low and high forms of culture, between mass media and visual and performative arts; he continues to explore different ways to film and edit the body and its movements. Many of these features return in various forms in his later work. Intertextuality becomes a core directorial strategy in this work, and intermediality will continue to shape its "performative aesthetics."[54] From early on in his career, Lanthimos moves through media forms and genres within different industry environments, on one hand exhibiting a chameleonic professional attitude and on the other hand establishing his identity as an auteur able to understand and adapt modes of audiovisuality for a new era of filmmaking.

Notes

1. See Henry Jenkins, *Convergence Culture: Where Old and New Media Collide* (New York: New York University Press, 2008).
2. See Dick Higgins with Hannah Higgins, "Intermedia," *Leonardo*, 34, no. 1 ([1965] 2001): 49–54.
3. See Gérard Genette, *Palimpsests: Literature in the Second Degree*, trans. Channa Newman and Claude Doubinsky (Lincoln, NB, and London: University of Nebraska Press, 1997). Following Julia Kristeva's use of "intertextuality," (*Desire in Language: A Semiotic Approach to Literature and Art*, 1980) Genette proposes the term "transtextuality" that comes in five types, one being "intertextuality." In this chapter, I prefer the term "intertextuality" as it conveys implicit or explicit references to specific films or styles, which is close to Genette's definition.
4. See Gérard Genette, *Paratexts: The Thresholds of Interpretation*, trans. Jane E. Lewin (Cambridge: Cambridge University Press, 1997); Jonathan Gray, *Show Sold Separately: Promos, Spoilers, and Other Media Paratexts* (New York and London: New York University Press, 2010).
5. See Genette, *Palimpsests*.
6. See Higgins, "Intermedia," 49–54.
7. I would like to thank, the VideoDance artistic director, Christiana Galanopoulou, for sharing valuable archival materials and information with me.
8. See Martin Jay, "Scopic Regimes of Modernity," in H. Foster, ed., *Vision and Visuality* (Seattle, WA: Seattle Bay Press, 1988), 3–23.
9. Christian Metz, *The Imaginary Signifier: Psychoanalysis and the Cinema* (Bloomington: Indiana University Press, 1982), 61.
10. See Jay, "Scopic Regimes," 3–4.
11. Ibid., 4.

12 Ibid.
13 I prefer the term "video dance" over "dance video" since this term is also used in Greek and better implies the transmedial aspect I am interested in.
14 See Fredric Jameson, *Postmodernism, or, the Cultural Logic of Late Capitalism* (Durham, NC: Duke University Press, 1991).
15 Higgins, "Intermedia," 49–54.
16 Ágnes Pethö, *Cinema and Intermediality: The Passion for the In-Between* (Cambridge: Cambridge Scholars Publishing, 2011), 1.
17 See Lars Bang Larsen, "The Long Nineties," *FRIEZE*, issue 144 (Jan 1, 2012), available at https://www.frieze.com/article/long-nineties; Jeremy Gilbert, "Captive Creativity: Breaking Free from the Long '90s," Conference Talk, *Capitalism, Culture and the Media*, University of Leeds (Sept 7–8, 2015), available at https://jeremygilbertwriting.files.wordpress.com/2015/09/the-end-of-the-long-90s1.pdf.
18 For an overall historiographical and critical conceptualization of the "Greek Weird Wave," see Dimitris Papanikolaou, *Greek Weird Wave: A Cinema of Biopolitics* (Edinburgh: Edinburgh University Press, 2021).
19 See Andrew Wernick, *Promotional Culture: Advertising, Ideology and Symbolic Expression* (London: SAGE Publications, 1991).
20 See Maria Komninou, *Apo tin agora sto theama* (Athens: Papazisis, 2001), 180–86; Stylianos Papathanassopoulos, *I tileorasi ton 21o eona* (Athens: Kastaniotis, 2005), 284–320; Ioanna Vovou, "*Stihia gia mia meta-istoria tis ellinikis tileorasis. To meso, I politiki, o thesmos,*" in I. Vovou, ed., *O kosmos tis tileorasis: Theoritikes proseggisis, analisi programmaton kai elliniki pragmatikotita* (Athens: Irodotos, 2010), 93–139.
21 See Nicos Mouzelis, "The Concept of Modernization: Its Relevance for Greece," *Journal of Modern Greek Studies*, 14, no. 2 (1996): 215–27; Kevin Featherstone, "'Europeanization' and the Centre Periphery: The Case of Greece in the 1990s," *South European Society and Politics*, 3, no. 1 (1998): 23–39.
22 See Nicolas Sevastakis, *I kinotopi chora: Opsis tou dimosiou chorou ke antinomies axion stin simerini Ellada* (Athens: Savvalas, 2004).
23 Vassilis Vamvakas, "Modernizing Tradition: Love, Friendship, Family and De-Urbanization in Greek TV Fiction (1993–2018)," *FilmIcon: Journal of Greek Film Studies*, 6 (2019): 17–39, at pp. 18–19.
24 See Afroditi Nikolaidou, *Poli ke Kinimatografiki Morfi: I Tenies Polis tou Ellinikou Kinimatografou 1994–2004*, PhD Thesis (Panteion University, 2012), 165.
25 See Dan Georgakas, "Greek Cinema for Beginners: A Thumbnail History," *Film Criticism*, 27, no. 2 (2002): 2–8; Nikolaidou, *Poli ke Kinimatografiki Morfi*.
26 See Will Straw, "Popular Music and Postmodernism in the 1980s," in S. Frith, A. Goodwin, and L. Grossberg, eds., *Sound and Vision: The Music Video Reader* (London and New York: Routledge, 1993), 2–17.

27 Ibid., 4.
28 See Steriani Tsintziloni, *Modernizing Contemporary Dance and Greece in the Mid-1990s: Three Case Studies from SineQuaNon, Oktana Dance Theatre and Edafos Company*, PhD Thesis (London: University of Roehampton, 2013).
29 Panayis Panayotopoulos and Vassilis Vamvakas, "*I elefsi tis meseas taxis. Ilika ke simvolika apotipomata*," in P. Panayotopoulos and V. Vamvakas, eds., *GR80s. I Ellada tou Ogdonta stin Technopoli* (Athens: Technopoli, 2017), 47–51, at p. 47.
30 See Geli Mademli, "The Importance of Being Weird: On Language Games in Contemporary Greek Films," *FilmIcon: Journal of Greek Film Studies* (2015), available at https://filmiconjournal.com/blog/post/41/the-importance-of-being-weird.
31 See Fredric Jameson, "Postmodernism and Consumer Society," in H. Foster, ed., *The Anti-Aesthetic: Essays on Postmodern Culture* (Seattle, WA: Seattle Bay Press, 1983), 111–25.
32 Giuliana Bruno, "Ramble City: Postmodernism and 'Blade Runner,'" 41 (Oct 1987): 61–74, at p. 63.
33 Jim Collins, "Genericity in the 90s: Eclectic Irony and the New Sincerity," in J. Collins, H. Radner, and A. Preacher Collins, eds., *Film Theory Goes to the Movies* (New York: Routledge, 1993), 242–63.
34 David Bordwell, *The Way Hollywood Tells It: Story and Style in Modern Movies* (Berkeley: University of California Press, 2006), 121.
35 Genette, *Palimpsests*.
36 See Mademli, "The Importance of Being Weird."
37 Jameson, *Postmodernism*, 17.
38 See K. J. Donnelly, "Experimental Music Video and Television," in L. Mulvey and J. Sexton, eds., *Experimental British Television* (Manchester: Manchester University Press, 2007), 166–79.
39 Wernick, *Promotional Culture*, 187.
40 See Rob Tannenbaum and Craig Marks, *I Want My MTV: The Uncensored Story of the Music Video Revolution* (New York and London: A Plume Book, 2012).
41 *VideoDance 2000 Catalogue*, Thessaloniki International Film Festival, 2000.
42 Christiana Galanopoulou, "VideoDance: The Camera-Spectator, the Camera-Choreographer," *VideoDance 2000 Catalogue*, 5–6.
43 Ibid.
44 Tsintziloni, *Modernizing Contemporary Dance*, 4–5.
45 Ibid., 7.
46 Ibid., 115.
47 Ibid., 190–91.
48 Higgins, "Intermedia," 50.
49 Galanopoulou, "VideoDance," 8.

50 Papanikolaou, *Greek Weird Wave*, 54–55.
51 Ibid., 20.
52 See Lydia Papadimitriou, "European Co-Productions and Greek Cinema Since the Crisis: 'Extroversion' as Survival," in L. Hammett-Jamart, P. Mitric, and E. Novrup-Redvall, eds., *European Film and Television Co-Productions: Policy and Practice* (London: Palgrave Macmillan, 2018), 207–22.
53 Quoted in "Yorgos Lanthimos: Interview by Clare Shearer," *Issue*, available at https://issuemagazine.com/yorgos-lanthimos/#/.
54 Afroditi Nikolaidou, "The Performative Aesthetics of the 'Greek New Wave,'" *FilmIcon: Journal of Greek Film Studies*, 2 (2014): 20–44.

3

The Anti-Foundationalist Cinema of Yorgos Lanthimos: The Case of *Kinetta*

Vrasidas Karalis

Greek Cinema Is Imported to Greece

In one of the best considerations of Yorgos Lanthimos's cinematic language, Maria Katsounaki, a persistent reviewer of his work, relates the following incident between the young director and Pantelis Voulgaris, the patriarch of grand narrative movies in Greece, and one of the last remaining directors of the so-called New Greek Cinema of the 1970s: "Let's have a test," says Voulgaris to Lanthimos, during shooting. "Do you see the window opposite us? What does exist behind it?" "Nothing, just empty rooms," Lanthimos replies. It is October 2009 and *Dogtooth* is being released the same week as Voulgaris's *With Heart and Soul* (*Psihi Vathia*, 2009).[1] In some ways, empty spaces set against a deeper, more encompassing field of vision defines the relationship that was being established between a new generation of filmmakers with a patricidal gaze trying to define the boundaries of their visual fields and the established gaze of the New Greek Cinema inaugurated in the 1970s. Furthermore, the juxtaposition is more than indicative of the directions that were "thinkable" and therefore realizable in early twenty-first-century Greek cinema precisely before the great financial crisis that engulfed the whole of Europe and its regional cinematic industries. We cannot understand the genesis and the development of Lanthimos's cinematic idiolect without exploring its genealogy, and without grounding it first to the particulars of the dynamics that were dominant in his native country between 1995 and 2005. This also gives the opportunity to delineate the implicit dialogic lines between him and other directors during the same time and frame certain aesthetic and formal parameters of his work.

The central point of my approach here is that Lanthimos's work belongs today to global cinema and is not confined to the cinematic tradition of his country of origin. Despite the fact that his first three feature films bear clear affinities with Greek cinema, his most recent films are truly transnational and even global, contributing to an emerging trend of simultaneous foreignization and indigenization that has taken place during the last twenty years. I leave out here the notorious and superfluous question of "Greekness" that has bedeviled Greek film studies, as the Greek elements of Lanthimos's films deny and confront all concepts of Greekness. It would be more appropriate to call Lanthimos the first *glocal* filmmaker since, together with a considerable number of directors, he follows a cultural trend which, according to Victor Roudometof, is "the refraction of globalization through the local. The result is glocality—a blend of the local and the global."[2]

Through the prism of his ambivalent *glocality*, we can clearly explore the cold frisson that Lanthimos introduced initially to Greek cinema and that later led to the internationalization of his work and his elevation to the status of a contemporary master, next to other international superstar directors such as Alejandro González Iñárritu, Steve McQueen, Alfonso Cuarón, and Bong Joon-ho. The simultaneous existence of universalizing and particularizing elements in his work, hallmarks of contemporary globalization, relocates Lanthimos's work to a different conceptual framework of interpretation if taken in its entirety. Furthermore, Lanthimos's cinematic language per se was from the beginning an amalgam of various forms, encompassing different genres, visual modes, and iconographic patterns that changed considerably since his first feature film in 2005, which is the object of analysis here.

Lanthimos's evolution as director, and we can clearly detect his distinct unfolding over the last twenty years punctuated by ruptures and reconsiderations, gives a rare opportunity to explore and investigate some of the most persistent elements of the structuration of his film. As I stated in a review of his film *The Lobster*, Lanthimos's language "transforms, or indeed re-imagines, the well-established codes of telling a story cinematically, into a new open-ended plot structure which for the time being frustrates and puzzles."[3] In an interview, he formulated his exodus from Greece to the great global scenes as follows: "If you want to make film outside the borders of your country, you must be conscious of your identity and be confident that you can make it everywhere in the world, without being afraid that you will be swallowed by any space or any place."[4]

However, before being recognized by international audiences and critics, Lanthimos had to deal with the limited and somehow restricted models of production that is evident in his native country, together with the limitations imposed by the cinematic practice as an industry. The peculiar position of cinema in Greece needs more discussion both for the realms of visuality and for the underlying structures or restructures that made them possible. Indeed, while his films are often linked to the financial crash, Lanthimos in fact emerged during years of extreme affluence leading to the Athens Olympics of 2004, when television channels proliferated and the advertising industry was thriving. Furthermore, in the beginning of the twenty-first century, and given the new funding opportunities that Greece's participation in the Eurozone created in 2002, film production in the country experienced a sudden and somehow unexpected exposure on international circuits.

The only director who had secured funds from international consortia until then was predominant Greek auteur Theo Angelopoulos, whose magisterial poetic elegy *Eternity and a Day* (*Mia aioniótita kai mia méra*, 1998) won the *Palme d'Or* prize at the Cannes Film Festival, its highest honor, with a stellar international cast led by Bruno Ganz. Angelopoulos's success also led to a keen international interest in the overall production output of the country. At the same time, his very presence was the embodiment of what had to change in Greek cinema, according to the new up-and-coming filmmakers like Panos H. Koutras, Filippos Tsitos, Athina Rachel Tsangari, and of course Lanthimos himself. In a French report by Laurent Rigoulet on the state of Greek cinema after Angelopoulos, aptly entitled "*Cinéma grec: après Angelopoulos, le vrai déluge?*" ("Greek Cinema after Angelopoulos: The Great Deluge"), Lanthimos expressed fierce criticism against Angelopoulos, the established grand master of contemplative yet political Greek cinema: "With his stature, his notoriety, he embodied everything we hated in Greek cinema. He represented the establishment, the privileges, the implicit rights, the weight of a system in which all funding without change and since the beginning of time went to the same cinematographers."[5]

Lanthimos was right to criticize the funding models of the Greek film industry, which conveyed an almost unconscious policy of promoting a style of cinema that followed in the footsteps of the so-called New Greek Cinema of the 1970s. At that time, production was divided between commercial blockbusters—namely comedies, melodramas, and dazzling biopics—and art-house movies that were still popular amongst the urban middle-class elites with abundant intellectual pretensions and fanciful delusions of revolution. The traditional narrative cinema of Voulgaris produced international blockbusters like *Brides* (*Nyfes*, 2004) and some others that followed (including *With Heart and Soul* [*Psihi Vathia*, 2009] and *Little England* [2013]), which signaled the revival of Hollywood-inspired spectacles in a regional context; with Voulgaris's films one had the perception that they were watching a Douglas Sirk, Elia Kazan, or Robert Powell production presented in glorious Technicolor or Eastmancolor, often at the expense of any substantial narrative or structural innovation. In a strange way, with Voulgaris's films, which served a nostalgia for grand visual narrativizations of recollected historical experiences, *mise-en-scène* and mood took precedence over story and expression, something that Angelopoulos tried to address in his last two, rather underrated, films, *The Weeping Meadow* (*To Livadi pou dakryzi*, 2004) and *The Dust of Time* (*I skoni tou chronou*, 2009).

At the other end of the spectrum, a new visual form started to emerge during the same period, with a series of low-budget, antinarrative, and esoteric films that along with *Dogtooth* were beginning to spark conversation under the adopted rubric, the Weird Wave. Steve Rose, who coined the term, avoids a direct definition of the term, which remains to this day somewhat vague and fluid. In a way, the article responds to its own rhetorical question: "Is it just coincidence that the world's most messed-up country is making the world's most messed-up cinema? *Attenberg* might not speak directly about Greece's financial crisis, but in its own way, it reflects on today's generation of Greeks and the legacy they've been handed."[6] The phrase makes and imposes its own assumptions about Greek cinema without a solid understanding of the cinematic forms and self-reflexive historicity of Greek filmmaking. It went unrecorded that the cinematic idiom that Lanthimos, Tsangari, Alexandros Avranas, and Ektoras Lygizos adopted originated in a mode of profound questioning that was established long before the 2009 crisis and were mostly cinematic in their nature, referring to an implosion of representation as such that became dominant around the beginning of the new millennium.

Rose's Weird Wave thesis, for example, fails to mention Yannis Economides's most subversive films (including *Matchbox* [*Spirtokouto*, 2003] and *Soul Kicking* [*I psihi sto stoma*, 2006]), yet makes reference to Koutras's film *The Attack of the Giant Moussaka* (*I epithesi tou gigantiaiou mousaka*, 1999) as a gay cult film, something that obviously had nothing to do with the Weird Wave itself, as well as his subversive but structurally familiar film *Strella* (2009), which was released close to *Dogtooth*. In an interview with Ariane Labed for Hilary Weston, Lanthimos also introduced another international, indeed transnational, Greek filmmaker, Nico Papatakis, and his radical, explosive film *The Shepherds of Calamity* (*Oi voskoi*, 1967) as one of the stylistic progenitors to his work: "It's just the most amazing—not only Greek—film. It's brilliant. It's black and white. I can't describe it. It takes place in this village and it's a bit bucolic, but so absurd and modern at the same time. You couldn't believe that this film was made in Greece back in the sixties."[7] Lanthimos's recollection of Papatakis's "absurd" film indicates that one should take seriously his attempt to delineate a genealogy from within his own tradition.

Lanthimos's first film *Kinetta* opened in the middle of the aforementioned battle of old and new visual languages as well as clashes over film funding. Rose thought of his cinema as "weird," but historically it is the product of intense collision of cultural imaginaries in Greece and, later, Europe that corresponded with how the new realities of producing films in the era of bureaucratized funding would affect cinematic representation itself. For Lanthimos, his own cinema has nothing to do with weirdness. In an interview, he stated:

> In essence we determine spectators' reactions, by the way we write our script. We build a dramaturgic system in which we make characters have a specific trajectory and behavior. With Efthymis Filippou [his screenwriter] we work together for many years. So, our idea is constructed over a long period of time, shaped and crystallized. We don't remember the origin of many things. We don't try to make something weird. Maybe something more original but not more weird.[8]

The term "weird" is useful mostly for problematizing the asymmetrical structure of cinematic representation developed by Greek filmmaking during a certain period of production, but it is not sufficient to talk about a complete self-conscious movement with its own principles, values, and ideas, as for example with the Danish Dogme 95 collective.

The number of films produced until and after the so-called crisis of 2009 is also not great enough to talk of such trends as a specific "wave" of cinematic rebellion.[9] The rebellion against the cinema of the great paternal figures had already started with Yannis Economides's *Matchbox* and *Soul Kicking*, as well as with the master of subversive cinema Nikos Nikolaidis's films *Singapore Sling: The Man Who Loved a Corpse* (*Singapore Sling: O Ánthropos pou Agápise éna Ptóma*, 1990), *See You in Hell, My Darling* (*Tha se Do stin Kolasi Agapi mou*, 1999) and his experimental film *The Zero Years* (2005), which I have argued elsewhere captures the "fossilization of a visual style which had transformed itself into a self-conscious manneristic extravaganza."[10] It is arguably Nikolaidis who started the gradual destructuration of the dominant ways of seeing in the Greek cinema as well as a denarrativization of its prevailing mythopoetic forms. Furthermore, Nikolaidis also diffused the lucid and transparent polychromatic patterns that dominated Greek cinema by privileging dark and grey monochrome *tableaux vivants* as negative takes on emblematic films such as Otto Preminger's *Laura* (1944) and Jean-Luc Godard's *Alphaville* (1965).

As evidenced by its history, Greek cinema was arguably always in search of grand narratives to convey the historical experiences of the country via film texts; however, the only contender for that title was Angelopoulos's *The Travelling Players* (*O thiasos*, 1975), which was produced in the 1970s under extreme circumstances. Angelopoulos's film encapsulated the long duration of Greek history as a series of repetitions through archetypal myths and mythopoetic structures. In many ways, with his first film, *Kinetta*, Lanthimos confronts the visual language of Angelopoulos, and other Greek filmmakers working in his mold, as he searches for a visual idiom with its own structural markers and ambitions. Theodoros Lennas wrote that in *Kinetta* we encounter,

> a policeman obsessed with cars, a woman searching desperately for pain and sadness and a strange photographer, encountering death through its reconstruction. Although the dialectical part of the film is rather atonal and "unbuttoned," many of Lanthimos's motifs make their presence felt. All these happen under the music of pop songs of the 60s and 70s and the voice of Jenny Vanou accompanying melodiously this interesting but immature cinematic "enigma."[11]

The film is consciously awkward and irregular in the offbeat visual strategies that constitute its story and style. There is a distinct and somehow persistent attempt by Lanthimos to unfocus his camera from any action that happens in front of it, or to maneuver his actors as if he were a puppeteer. The implicit story remains amorphous and plotless, and the film searches for a center through its form, in the layering of its images.

The Filmmaker as an Absurdist

Lanthimos was born in 1973 in Athens and studied filmmaking at the famous Stavrakos School in the Greek capital. He began his career in the advertising industry; before his first feature film, he directed music videos for pop singers including Sakis Rouvas and Despina Vandi, as well as some extremely successful commercials in the quirky, melancholic tradition of Roy Andersson. Some of these commercials, with their uncanny juxtaposition between tradition and modernity in Greek society (especially the ones for telecommunication companies), could reasonably function as the best introduction to Lanthimos's outlandish symbiosis of absurd satire and operatic tragedy. During the same period, Lanthimos made two other films: a short entitled *The Rape of Chloe* (*O viasmos tis hlois*, 1995) and the black comedy *My Best Friend* (*O kalyteros mou filos*, 2001) that he codirected with the grand master of contemporary Greek comedy, Lakis Lazopoulos. Another short film followed in 2002, a Tarantino-like comedy *Uranisco Disco*, which set the tone for the spasmodic and antinarrative forms that would find full expression in his first solo-directed feature film *Kinetta*.

Before the 2004 Athens Olympics, Greek cinema went through a period of intense reorganization and reorientation, as the old funding models, exclusively administered by the Greek Film Centre, were becoming scarce for young directors as the funding body sought to target big international productions in the style of Pantelis Voulgaris's *Brides* (2004), Angelopoulos's *The Weeping Meadow* (2004), and Yannis Smaragdis's *El Greco* (2007).

Meanwhile, within this period of extreme spending and reckless affluence, all based on money borrowed from the European Union, some new "gazes" started to emerge that led to the paradoxical explosion we find in *Kinetta*. Most of these films were implicitly dismantling the visual narratives that had dominated Greek cinema, especially regarding their visualization of history and politics. They were also discarding altogether the tropes and discursive practices that presented the Greek experience as a coherent, uninterrupted, and meaningful journey from antiquity to the new millennium, and in doing so dismantling any suggestion that postwar visual forms maintained contemporary relevance.

A dominant narrative of Greekness found its most spectacular and at the same time specular expression in the opening ceremony of the Athens Olympics, as the event was consciously designed to establish links between the nation's mythic past and then-present, creating continuity via a majestic genealogy of Greek visual culture. Such ideas about what constituted Greekness were being subverted elsewhere by the fragmented, fast-paced, and episodic cinema of filmmakers such as Koutras, Constantine Giannaris, and Sotiris Goritsas. By 2005, a number of interesting and provocative films including *Hostage* (*Omiros*, Constantine Giannaris, 2005), *Honey and Pig* (*Loukoumades me meli*, Olga Malea, 2005), *The Heart of the Beast* (*I kardia tou ktinous*, Renos Haralambidis, 2005), *A Dog's Dream* (*To oneiro tou skylou*, Angelos Frantzis, 2005), and *The Crossing* (*To perasma*, Dimitris Stavrakas, 2006) were foregrounding new orientations and departures in Greek cinema in the period that directly followed the spectacularization of the local visual imaginary through the opening (and closing) ceremony of the Athens Olympics.

The new frisson that was gradually taking over Greek film productions articulated a new filmic temporality that was at odds with the very structural intentionality of preceding cultural poetics, as sponsored by the Greek state through the Greek Film Centre. The hegemonic mythopoeia was also subjected to relentless scrutiny especially from the underfunded margins whose dismissive approach received less attention by the media. However, the tradition of transgressive cinema was a hidden yet present undercurrent in the filmic culture of the country. If Lanthimos stands close and is related to the cinematic absurdism of Andersson, he was also coming out of another current of film productions that appeared and disappeared with the tendency to parody the dominant forms of visual discourse. There was already a well-established tradition that began with one of the most bizarre films of Greek cinema—Andreas Thomopoulos's *Aldevaran* (1975), a film that visualized an antisociety that dreamers and visionaries were struggling to imagine after the collapse of the dictatorship in 1974. Thomopoulos abandoned the radical experimentations later, a task that was continued by Nikos Alevras's explosive *A Hail of Bullets* (*Peftoun oi sfaires san to halazi ki o travmatismenos kallitehnis anastenazei*, 1977), a film of extreme irreverence and eccentricity. Such filmmakers were collectively fighting against the tradition of realism that was becoming more and more dominant in Greek cinema, especially after 1981 when the Panhellenic Socialist Movement (PASOK) led by Andreas Papandreaou was elected to government and the funding models started to privilege socialist sagas and idealized the Greek civil war *ad nauseum*.

The main structural underpinnings of these films were the parodic elements of their stories together with small budgets and their being made at the periphery of the distribution circuit. The most interesting of these films appeared in 1983 with Nikos Zervos's *The Dracula of Exarhia (O Drakoulas ton Exarheion)*, a hilariously absurd parody of dominant visual tropes from an anarchist perspective. Such parodic absurdism was formulated as a fully-fledged minority language since the 1980s with Stavros Tornes and his political irrationalism and aesthetic radicalism, in films like *Balamos* (1982), *Karkalou* (1984), and especially *Danilo Treles: The Famed Andalusian Musician (Danilo Treles: O fimismenos Andalousianos mousikos*, 1986). Tornes became the Samuel Beckett of Greek cinema, producing independent films in a style that was "beyond the restriction of narration ... based on associations, peculiar humor, memory fragments, imaginaries and poetry."[12]

Tornes's poetic and antinarrative films created a trend of anti-illusionist and antinaturalist cinema that showed a tendency to dismantle the regularities of preceding film conventions, opting rather for a nonsequitur style where the ruptures of oneiric imagery are held together by humor, satire, and parody. With its quirky structure and irregular narrative, Haralambidis's later film *No Budget Story* (1997) can be seen as a bridge to the more radical experiments with visual temporality and structure that were to follow. Despite these quite radical films, experimentation of this kind in Greek cinema ended sometime in the late 1990s, and certainly by the time Antouanetta Angelidi released her last film *Thief or Reality* (*Kleftis i pragmatikotita*, 2001), when melodramas, comedies, and grand biopics came to dominate the national film industry.

After Tornes's death in 1988, the latency period of Greek cinematic absurdism started and ended as great historical events started transforming the country into a society built around consumer capitalism yet without the necessary economic and organizational infrastructure. Just as Greece joined the Eurozone in 2002, Tsangari's film *The Slow Business of Going* (2002) encapsulated a profound sense of growing disconnection, imagined in the film through the global adventures of a woman with a rocking chair. This was the first "weird" comedy, without plot or any distinct story, which indirectly paved the way for the kind of films that were to become increasingly visible by the end of the decade. Although the film was mostly ignored by critics, it was visually expressive of a mode less interested in narrative or plot, but in mood and imagery. Tsangari transformed the odd presence of the woman into a unique catalyst for reconsidering cinematic language, a project that she would continue with *Attenberg* (2010) and *Chevalier* (2015).

From the same period, the feature film that most preempts Lanthimos's own experiments with form and representation is arguably Economides's *Matchbox*, a film that destructured narrative, dismantled plotlines, and derationalized dialogue to produce an extraordinary atmosphere of pointless action, verbal transgression, and violent libidinal psychodynamics. Economides continued his experimentation with space, narrative, and light with his next two films, which paved the way for the strange amalgam of narrativity and absurdism that culminated with *Dogtooth*. Economides's *Soul Kicking* and *Knifer* (*Mahairovgaltis*, 2010) are probably the most important signposts in the cultural semiotics of Greek cinema for establishing a horizon of expectation for the novel atmosphere of what might be called *positive cinematic negativity* that would eventually frame the cinema of transgression and negation that emerged after 2010. Following Economides, Dennis Iliadis released his gritty and gruesome *Hardcore* (2004), which won a major prize in Germany and gave him the opportunity to start an international career with the remake of *The Last House on the Left* (2009) in the United States. As funding sources expanded and new possibilities for international productions were set in place, Iliadis serves as forerunner for the internationalization of regional Greek filmmakers, while at the same time other filmmakers continued to vie for local funding and institutional support.

In the middle of this process and at the center of its context stands *Kinetta*, which accelerated the transformation of Greek cinematic language into something fluid and indeterminate, and in doing so created a wave of revisions and revisualizations to the dominant forms of seeing in European cinema. Despite the despotic presence of directors like Angelopoulos, Nikolaidis, and Voulgaris, the visual regimes and their discursive justifications were already shaken by the impact of global auteurs including Andersson, Iñárritu, and Joon-ho, as well as Lars von Trier, Aki Kaurismäki, Wong Kar-wai, Ang Lee, and Gaspar Noé. In the case of Lanthimos, also, Andersson's *Songs from the Second Floor* (*Sånger från andra våningen*, 2000) especially, can be seen as influential for its fusion of abstraction and figuration, comedy, and tragedy in a form reminiscent of Beckett's *Waiting for Godot* (1953). Also, in a strange but distinct manner, Andersson's commercial work presents, in a condensed form, the elliptical and minimalistic quirkiness that took shape with Lanthimos in completely different ways. As Andersson stated in an interview:

> I like it both figurative *and* [italic in the original] abstract. All of these things you and I talking about now—expressionism, impressionism, simplicity—I think that, within us, we have all of these things. My

abstract side was always there. After having passed naturalism and realism, I found that side of myself. I used it to condense and purify and simplify the scenes.[13]

The fusion of ellipsis and expressionism in Lanthimos's first film can be traced back to his early experiments with the same ideas, and even to Angelopoulos's abstract and elliptical masterwork *Days of '36* (*Meres tou '36*, 1972), which features narrative discontinuity, sparse dialogue, and monochromatic immersion.

The established tradition of parodic absurdism is there in the background of Lanthimos's early films; *Kinetta* can be taken as an attempt to discard the ideological and political elements that are dominant in Angelopoulos's film, and furthermore to destructure, de-found, and reimagine its expressive potential. In *Kinetta*, as an obsessive forensic policeman (Costas Xikominos) struggles to reconstruct with a photographer (Aris Servetalis) how a crime was committed (which the film later drops abruptly, leaving everything in abeyance), Lanthimos also recalls Angelopoulos's first film, *Reconstruction* (*Anaparastasis*, 1970), which is turned upside down as the search for what really happened is transformed into an act of reconstruction, presenting various different versions of what might have happened as perceived from different points of view. Nick Riganas aptly synopsizes the complex story as follows:

> During off-season at the Greek seaside resort of Kinetta, three perfect strangers—a police officer out of uniform with a thing for German luxury cars and Russian women, an eccentric photographer, and a hotel chambermaid—join forces for a rather strange reason: to recreate homicides. Meticulously and with an almost ritualistic approach, the unlikely trio re-enact crime scenes of brutal murders, to the point where the boundaries of their own private lives slowly begin to blur. Does this alliance lead somewhere?[14]

The dead end of their alliance, the inconsequentiality of their working together, and the inability of the three strangers to overcome their alienation through shared concern, foreground minimalistic ellipsis as the central visual strategy, and ellipsis is, according to Angelopoulos, "a tremendous option for the spectator to become the filmmaker's partner in the creative process."[15] In a way, Lanthimos searches for this same partnership with his audience, though in a context different to Angelopoulos.

In his way, Lanthimos adopts a mode of pure representation, without hypertextual indexes or intertextual inferences. This style arguably reaches its peak in *Alps*, though Lanthimos gradually turns to narrative "emplotment," as found in his later films including *The Killing of a Sacred Deer* and *The Favourite*. *Kinetta* therefore offers a critical vantage point for exploring the gradual construction of Lanthimos's cinematic language over the last twenty years. In a way, it expresses more lucidly even than *Dogtooth* what Mark Fischer pointed out as "a kind of ongoing extemporized Dadaist theatre"[16] that "delighted in exaggerating the pompous absurdity of the ceremonies that authority needs in order to legitimate itself, and Lanthimos's anatomization of patriarchal power in *Dogtooth* partakes of the same spirit of coldly savage caricature."[17]

"When You Film Reality, It Is Transformed into Something Else": *Kinetta* and Its Others

When *Kinetta* was released in 2005 it caused mixed reactions.[18] Maria Katsounaki's perceptive eye understood immediately that something new and uncanny was emerging out of Lanthimos's camera: "A hand-made and unembellished movie … Its eccentricity is welcome despite the fact that it initially makes you puzzled. You don't know if you reject it or you are taken over by its unprocessed form." Katsounaki continues:

> Lanthimos has an unconventional gaze, which wavers between what is artistically extreme and narratively (still) indeterminate. As the director himself has indicated (after a ten-year career in the publicity industry) this is a not a linear story. It focuses on the characters, their relations, on moments, and on the peculiarity of their behaviour. The film is an attempt of writing, which is structured in *statu nascendi* [in a nascent state].[19]

After the success of his later films, Ben Kenigsberg observed the "cryptic seeds of Lanthimos's imagery" in *Kinetta*, pointing out that "viewing *Kinetta* with the benefit of hindsight, you can see inklings of visual and staging ideas that Lanthimos would explore more fully later on. Clearly, he had already developed his interest in tableaus of near-mute characters making spastic, dancelike movements—a motif that resurfaced in *Dogtooth* and his 2011 film *Alps*."[20] The sparse dialogue, the lack of an obvious plot, and the awkwardness of the hand-held camerawork are also mentioned, indirectly bringing attention to the construction of his cinematic language *vis-à-vis* the forms of his storytelling and *mise-en-scène*. *Kinetta* hovers in the space between a narrative in search of a story and a purely visual form exploring its limitations. A desire to philosophically question the function of cinematic images underpins his first feature, as Lanthimos exposes the artifice of representation: the *thing itself* does not really exist in his film. *Kinetta* is about absent stories and absent characters: the characters we see are simply reflections of reflections, referential markers of other characters and actions existing and taking place elsewhere. They exist as images from other films, as imprints on the wax tablet that constitutes Plato's metaphor for memory.[21] Lanthimos's visual memory is also a memory of replication and repetition: what it tries to foreground is the artifice in the mnemonic reconstruction of the past, and of experience itself.

Lanthimos's film language emerged to confront the grand narrative structures that dominated the imagination of the public and, to a certain degree, the box office for decades. Art-house films dominated the market and had established a certain expectation about the content of "quality" films. By the late 1990s, Greece had seen a rise of comedies and glossy television series that started taking over from the forms of the so-called New Greek Cinema as established in the 1970s, which culminated with Angelopoulos winning the *Palme d'Or* at Cannes for his mournful elegy *Eternity and a Day*. Paradoxically, Angelopoulos's triumph also marked an end for that type of film.

A central strategy of Lanthimos's films is to question how foundation images can make claims on truth. The antifoundationalist iconography of Lanthimos is pertinent throughout all his cinema, up to and including *The Favourite*. Starting with his work on television commercials and music videos, Lanthimos had to deal from the beginning with the hyperreal, or indeed antireal, function of images in the "society of the spectacle," as Guy Debord defined this period of late capitalism.[22] Lanthimos's films capture the illusory and alienating character of contemporary experience as mediated by technologized images and reproduced photographs. Yannis Fragoulis, in a short and perceptive review of *Kinetta*, points out that "the film work is never completed, and we understand that we deal with a movie-exemplar that shows the director's good intentions but nothing else."[23] For Fragoulis, the film medium itself is central to the message of the film: it is not merely technological apparatus for framing, but emerges as functionally expressive of the film's thesis on modern society.

The implied dialogue with other films must also be mentioned. The deconstructive function of the film's language must be considered against the archetypal film of the New Greek Cinema, Angelopoulos's *Reconstruction*. Andrew Horton wrote this about the film:

> The film thus fuses documentary, drama, tragedy, myth, and folk ballads (the lemon tree song). Yet the film is in structure and theme also, as the title suggests, a series of reconstructions. One is forensic: the district police have arrived in the village to re-create the crime as part of their investigation. Another is journalistic: the police are soon followed by the media trying to get a "hot" story for the press and for television. The film demands our close attention because the switches between the "real" events and the reconstructed ones are jumbled. We are not allowed to follow the simple chronological drive of a genre police film.[24]

Angelopoulos himself stresses the importance of duality to his narrative strategy, as well as his artful inversion of the Aristotelian concept of unified space and time:

> The plot moves constantly between these two elements in a manner that is quite different from a logical narrative. To give you an example, the film concludes with a scene that should have been at the very beginning: the murder itself. But what exactly happens there is still a mystery, because the camera remains outside, never witnessing the deed itself, just hearing the voices.[25]

The use by both directors of amateur actors and a minimalist script offers another form of dialectical symmetry: an exercise in antithesis between the two films, with one (Angelopoulos) inaugurating something while the other (Lanthimos) closes out the era by way of funereal parody. A prominent film and cultural critic, Elias Kanellis, called Lanthimos's cinema "the Angelopoulian copy for our age" expressing "the adoration of an audience deeply impressed by exoticism, even if there is no sufficient interpretation for it."[26]

Film critic John DeFore is keen to address the subtexts that dominate Lanthimos's film. He stresses that the sexual psychodynamics that permeate the film fashion a dominant male gaze that autoerotically toys with its own reflection:

> Viewers who have only recently encountered the idea of the male gaze will have a field day here; one of the more satisfying ways to view the movie is as a bitterly funny dissection of the fantasies men and women construct—fantasies that, if not kept in check by interaction with the real world, can grow so increasingly specific and ritualized that they prevent real-world satisfaction.[27]

The fantasies of all characters in the films are intricately interwoven in the fabric of the narrative; viewers cannot distinguish between what is seen and what is imagined, as the camera and the photographer in the film coexist in each other's specular gaze. This is exactly what Roger Moore misses in describing the film as follows: "the wholly Greek *Kinetta* is more overtly navel-gazing, obscure to the point of suggesting obscurant. It's a 95-minute exercise in minimalism, behavior studies and psychology … and boredom."[28] The mysterious spatial boundaries that the film constructs was referred to later in an extended review of Lanthimos's oeuvre by Eric Kohn: "The movie provides the first rough glimpse of Lanthimos's aesthetic—a disturbing self-contained world that adheres to its own logic, sounds ludicrous on paper, and somehow remains credible as it plays out onscreen."[29]

In a strange and rather adversarial way, Lanthimos's film is caught in a dialogue with what Angelopoulos refers to in his interview as the "mystery of what exactly happens." Lanthimos's cinematic language in *Kinetta* oscillates between pure representation and an antinarrative structure: in his later films, especially *The Killing of a Sacred Deer* and *The Favourite*, he returns to the former tactic, but it is in his early films that he most engages with the latter, here and to a lesser extent in *Dogtooth*. Fragoulis observes in *Kinetta*: "an unprocessed stylistic nostalgia for the seventies, absence of dialogue and spasmodic camera movement, that withdraws from any attempt for the identification with the viewer whereas at the same time places us in a subjective optical angle which penetrates voyeuristically the obsessions of his characters and abandons himself to the ecstatic worship of the non-encounter."[30]

The "non-encounter" as a key part of Lanthimos's filmic temporality raises one of the most important questions that permeates his form: on what foundation, both ontological and epistemological, are specular images grounded, and to what extent is such a foundation justified and comprehensible? The absurdism of Lanthimos's works, following Charlie Chaplin, Buster Keaton, Daniil Kharms, and Beckett, is not mere posturing or a matter of style; beyond anything else, it offers a nonfoundationalist ontology of images, consisting of the traces of other images that ultimately constitute a visual agnosticism about representation and visuality. What appears to interest Lanthimos is the essential contingency and the contestable character of film images, and what such elements can reveal about human consciousness. This also encompasses the entirety of the performances contained in his work, which confront the realist fallacy of film imagery. Colin Farrell, who worked with Lanthimos on *The Lobster* and *The Killing of a Sacred Deer*, recalls, "The best direction in 20 years of doing this job I've ever heard is [Lanthimos] screaming from a monitor to an actor 'stop trying to be so naturalistic!'" to which Lanthimos adds, "because that's the worst! You see the effort of someone trying to be like real life ... don't do that."[31]

Lanthimos's antifoundationalist project is nihilistic and political at the same time. Stanley Fish however argues that antifoundationalism "leaves the individual firmly entrenched within the conventional context and standards of enquiry/dispute of the discipline/profession/habitus within which s/he is irrevocably placed."[32] Language, imagery, and setting all firmly contextualize the project and the individual within specific cultural and social networks of meaning and communicative actions. In *The Lobster*, Lanthimos struggles to deterritorialize action and dialogue from within an established framework of anachronistic fusions. Elsewhere, *The Favourite* can also be seen as a fantastic reconstruction of other films, as a pastiche of interfilmic transcriptions confronting dominant culture and its imaginaries. With his first film, *Kinetta*, Lanthimos articulated a profoundly deconstructive, antiepistemological and deessentializing visual idiom that confronted the certainties and the norms of hegemonic visual languages. As such, the project was destined to remain incomplete and somehow fragmented. After leaving Greece, Lanthimos restored the primacy of foundational mythos with his more recent films that entertain dialogue with the works of other filmmakers such as Stanley Kubrick or David Lynch.

Ten years after his international debut at Cannes in 2009 with *Dogtooth*, Lanthimos stated that filmmakers of his generation "have a great responsibility … to remain open to everything new that cinema has to offer. To look at cinema with newness."[33] Reaching that point of "newness," however, required a long and contradictory process that went through a subversive dismantling of the grand narratives of Greek cinema. Yet, a question still remains concerning what these "new eyes" can enable one to see and how they will impact the experience of what can be seen. In his most recent films, Lanthimos seems to do away with the antifoundationalist aesthetic of his early films and opts for an opulent narrative linearity, which prompts further discussion over how this reorientation is incorporated into his visual idiom. In the end, it seems that *new eyes* are eventually destined to confront their own *newness* and articulate ever newer reconsiderations and resignifications that are encompassed in and expressive of their form.

I contend that the new eyes do not frame any Weird Wave but construct what I have referred to elsewhere as a "cinema of abeyance" that brings together "acausal episodes"[34] and startling snapshots without rational or clear causal connection with each other. Disenchantment with the world and encasement in a world without windows, to return to the interview that opened this chapter, is gradually abandoned as the visual euphoria of a new cinematic anthropology emerges. Lanthimos's engagement with seminal film texts like Angelopoulos's *Reconstruction*, or a classical myth, as in *The Killing of a Sacred Deer*, or the thick semiology of Stanley Kubrick's cinema, underscore an abeyant visuality in which his images maintain strong traces of an empathic rationality that cannot be easily traced. In a way, they foreground the postmodern fragmentation of experience by making visible "its nature as fable," as Gianni Vattimo argues.[35] However, Lanthimos the confabulator now belongs to a new conversation: perhaps with "*new* eyes" he has finally started to look back at the worlds *Kinetta* dismantled with nostalgia, curiosity, and possibly even affection.

Notes

1 Maria Katsounaki, "The Bizarre Universe of Lanthimos," *Kathimerini*, Jan 28, 2019, available at https://www.kathimerini.com.cy/gr/politismos/to-allokoto-sympan-toy-lanthimoy.

2 Victor Roudometof, "Theorising Glocalization: Three Interpretations," *European Journal of Social Theory*, 19, no. 3 (2016): 391–408, at p. 403.

3 Vrasidas Karalis, "Yorgos Lanthimos's *The Lobster* and the Cinema of Abeyance," *FilmIcon: Journal of Greek Film Studies*, Dec 18, 2015, available

at http://filmiconjournal.com/blog/post/48/the-lobster-and-the-cinema-of-abeyance.

4   Alexandros Voulgaris, "Interview with Yorgos Lanthimos," *Moter*, 2019, 34.
5   Laurent Rigoulet, "*Cinéma grec: après Angelopoulos, le vrai déluge?*" *Telerama*, May 25, 2012, available at https://www.telerama.fr/cinema/cinema-grec-apres-angelopoulos-le-vrai-deluge,80441.php.
6   Steve Rose, "*Attenberg*, *Dogtooth* and the Weird Wave in Greek Cinema," *The Guardian*, Aug 27, 2011, available at https://www.theguardian.com/film/2011/aug/27/attenberg-dogtooth-greece-cinema.
7   Hilary Weston, "Talking Greek Cinema with Yorgos Lanthimos and Ariane Labed," *Criterion*, Oct 2, 2015, available at https://www.criterion.com/current/posts/3731-talking-greek-cinema-with-yorgos-lanthimos-and-ariane-labed.
8   Katsounaki, "The Bizarre Universe of Lanthimos."
9   The magazine *Cinema* in its special issue on the topic characterized it as a "trend" and not a "wave." Orestes Andreadakis argues that these filmmakers are not united by any common set of principles, but that "they surrender to a peculiar jocular attitude and refuse any parochial grouping" ("*Mia exaisia proklisi*" ["An Exquisite Challenge"], *Sinema/Cinema*, 219 [Winter 2011]: 44).
10 Vrasidas Karalis, *A History of Greek Cinema* (New York: Continuum, 2012), 268.
11 Thodoris Lennas, "Yorgos Lanthimos, the Path of a Controversial Visionary to the Top," *Artic*, Feb 20, 2019, available at https://artic.gr/giwrgos-lanthimos-afierwma/.
12 Dimitris Babas, "The Self-Existent Cinema of Stavros Tornes," *Cinephilia*, available at http://www.cinephilia.gr/index.php/prosopa/hellas/1549-stavros-tornes.
13 Ignatiy Vishnevetsky, "Figurative and Abstract: An Interview with Roy Andersson," *Mubi*, Aug 9, 2009, available at https://mubi.com/notebook/posts/figurative-and-abstract-an-interview-with-roy-andersson.
14 Nick Riganas, "Synopsis of *Kinetta*," *IMDb*, available at https://www.imdb.com/title/tt0477991/.
15 Dan Fainaru, *Theo Angelopoulos: Interviews* (Jackson: Mississippi University Press, 2001), 12.
16 Mark Fischer, "*Dogtooth*: The Family Syndrome," *Film Quarterly*, 64, no. 4 (2011): 22–27, at p. 27.
17 Ibid., 23.
18 "Exclusive Interview with Yorgos Lanthimos, Kostas Xykominou, Evangelia Randou and Aris Servetali," *Camera Stylo Online*, Jan 24, 2012, available at https://camerastyloonline.wordpress.com/2012/01/24/kinetta-giorgou-lanthimou-24-1-2012-et1/.
19 Maria Katsounaki, "Kinetta," *Kathimerini*, Dec 11, 2005, available at http://trans.kathimerini.gr/4dcgi/_w_articles_qsite1_1_22/03/2007_185384.

20 Ben Kenigsberg, "'Kinetta' Review: Cryptic Seeds of Yorgos Lanthimos's Imagery," *New York Times*, Oct 17, 2019, available at https://www.nytimes.com/2019/10/17/movies/kinetta-review.html.
21 Plato, *Theaetetus*, trans. John McDowell (Oxford: Oxford University Press, 2014), 196a.
22 Guy Debord, *Society of the Spectacle* (London: Rebel Press, 2004).
23 Yannis Fragoulis, "*Kinetta*: Movie Without End," *Cinema Info*, 2007, available at https://web.archive.org/web/20110415083124/http://www.cinemainfo.gr/films/opinion/2007/2/kineta/index.html.
24 Andrew Horton, *The Films of Theo Angelopoulos: The Cinema of Contemplation* (Princeton, NJ: Princeton University Press, 1997), 92.
25 Fainaru, *Theo Angelopoulos: Interviews*, 3–4.
26 Elias Kanellis, "Like Angelopoulos for 2010: On *Dogtooth*," *The Book's Journal* (Athens, 2011), 75.
27 John Defore, "'Kinetta': Film Review," *Hollywood Reporter*, Oct 16, 2019, available at https://www.hollywoodreporter.com/review/kinetta-1248353.
28 Roger Moore, "Movie Review: Yorgos L. Gets His Start with the Cryptic and Obscure *Kinetta*," *Movie Nation*, Apr 1, 2020, available at https://rogersmovienation.com/2020/04/01/movie-review-yorgos-l-gets-his-start-with-the-cryptic-and-obscure-kinetta/.
29 Eric Kohn, "'The Favourite' Director Yorgos Lanthimos Reveals the Method to His Madness," *IndieWire*, Nov 21, 2018, available at https://www.indiewire.com/2018/11/yorgos-lanthimos-interview-the-favourite-greece-1202022576/.
30 Elias Fragoulis, "Kinetta," *Free Cinema*, 2007, available at https://freecinema.gr/home-cinema/kinetta/.
31 Jake Coyle, "Q&A: Kidman, Farrell on the Surrealism of 'Sacred Deer,'" *AP News*, Oct 26, 2017, available at https://apnews.com/article/10c63c7d790e42959e84b3916c369985.
32 H. Aram Veeser, *The Stanley Fish Reader* (London: Wiley-Blackwell, 1999), 213.
33 Poly Lykourgou, "Jury Press Conference: 'I Wish to See the Cinema with Different Eyes' Said Yorgos Lanthimos," *Flix*, May 14, 2019, available at https://flix.gr/news/cannes-2019-jury-press-conference.html.
34 Karalis, "Yorgos Lanthimos's *The Lobster*."
35 Gianni Vattimo, *The End of Modernity: Nihilism and Hermeneutics in Postmodern Culture*, trans. J. Snyder (Baltimore, MD: John Hopkins University Press, 1988), 30.

PART II

Experiencing Lanthimos

4

On Confinement, Sameness, and Grieving: Yorgos Lanthimos's *Alps*

Asbjørn Grønstad

If the characters in the films of Yorgos Lanthimos had been real people, they would probably have an advantage over the rest of us in the weeks following the March 2020 Covid-19 lockdown. An experience of confinement infuses films such as *Dogtooth*, *The Lobster*, and, to some extent, *The Killing of a Sacred Deer*. While the subject of physical entrapment was apparent enough from the beginning, the measures of social distancing imposed on so many of us in the wake of the pandemic serve to put this motif into even clearer relief. So much of Lanthimos's cinema seems to address rigorous systems of social governance and how to negotiate them. In fact, one could argue that the fixation on various forms of performativity, imitation, and play in his films may be understood within the context of a critique of biopolitical regimes. In the process of both conforming to and resisting the ritualized control of institutional power structures, Lanthimos's characters marshal strategies of adaptation that tend to blur the boundaries between alterity and imitation and, likewise, between authenticity and performance. Unsettling our notions of the various ways in which authority is socially constructed, Lanthimos's provocative films interrogate distinctions between the absurd and the dystopian, as well as between the familiar and the uncanny. Profoundly destabilizing the dynamic of the gestic and the pathetic, his oeuvre invites us to reconsider the relationship between theatricality and ethics.

The intricate entanglement of performativity and biopolitics aside, I want to suggest that the swiftly and extensively adopted practices of social distancing provide us with a bountiful prism through which to comprehend the nature of Lanthimos's projects. It is difficult to pinpoint exactly what the filmmaker is trying to show us, but a close scrutiny of his oeuvre, *Alps* in particular, has led me toward the following hypothesis: Lanthimos's films seem to explore the psychic architecture of confinement. This entails delving into the tensions and gaps between identity and imitation, normality and aberration, inimitability and substitution, and, last but certainly not the least, social constraints and what one might call the universe within. Pondering the implications of Covid-19 for the refiguration of domestic space, Maud Ceuterick observes that "micro-social relations" are worth studying for the way in which they "convert spaces into sites of meaning and power."[1] This exchange, whereby a certain spatial formation is imbued with significance as a result of the specific material relations that come to inhabit it, appears relevant to Lanthimos's films as well.

On the surface, his is a body of work that shares a conspicuous resemblance to a particular tradition within cinematic modernism, especially the stylized, dedramatized, and depsychologized movies of someone like Robert Bresson and, in a later generation, Michael Haneke. There is also a hint of the minimalism of the Dogme 95 movement; moreover, Lanthimos incorporates enough disturbing elements in his films for him to be seen as heir to the transgressive art cinema of the late 1990s and the early 2000s, to which both Lars von Trier and Haneke were significant contributors.[2] What is notable about Lanthimos's style, in the context of aesthetic traditions, is that his approach coalesces the two "opposite trends" that Mario Perniola considers in his influential *Art and Its Shadow* (2004).[3] One of these revolves around "appearance," as well as "separation" and "distance," whereas the other gravitates toward "reality" and modes of "participation."[4] Where the aesthetic impulse behind the former is "de-realization," that behind the latter is "perturbation."[5] Lanthimos's fictional universe is often laced with detachment, populated as it is with characters who are expressionless much of the time. For this reason, in part, it can be a cold and prohibitive world, which might explain why so many of my friends and colleagues abhor Lanthimos's films. Yet, the jarring intrusion of transgressive acts into this universe—the unsettling sex scenes in *Dogtooth*, the shooting of the donkey in *The Lobster*—can be just as shocking as, say, the orgy in von Trier's *The Idiots* (*Idioterne*, 1998) or the suicide in Haneke's *Hidden* (*Caché*, 2005). Tonally, then, these films embody an uneasy alliance of dispassionate feeling and severe affect. Drawing on the work of Hungarian philosopher Aurel Kolnai, Perniola hypothesizes that disgust might be the principal emotion accompanying the new aesthetic that he labels "psychotic realism" or alternatively "crude realism," which he associates with the work of authors such as Bret Easton Ellis and artists such as Orlan and Sterlac.[6]

What Perniola calls art's *remainder*—an "incommunicable nucleus" that for him replaces both metaphysics and institutionalism as a candidate for the essence of the artwork—is richly apparent in films like *Dogtooth*, *Alps*, and *The Lobster*, referring as it does to that which is "opposed to, and resists, homogenization, conformity, the process of mass consensus at work in contemporary society."[7]

Lanthimos's peculiarly transgressive cinema of anemic detachment and simmering affect thus comes close to capturing Perniola's concepts of disgust and the remainder. In simple terms, we could say that the very point of his cinema is to scrutinize the psychology of convention as well as what happens when social expectations and norms are upended. Not unlike the protocols of *ostranenie* that preoccupied Viktor Shklovsky and the Russian Formalists, Lanthimos's poetics foreground human behavior and actions that seem alien to any received notion of realism.[8] The absurdist, vaguely Dadaist comedy of *Dogtooth*, shot before the financial crisis but often considered the inauguration of the so-called Greek New Wave, or Weird Wave, exhibits many layers of such defamiliarization; the excessive confinement of the children, the bizarre private and "unnatural" language invented for them, the aberrant sense of sexuality, and the raw, unexpected violence.[9] Critics have also noted other idiosyncratic components in the film, such as the unusual forms of intimacy, which Mark Fisher dubs "antiseptic," the routine consumption of the family's own home movies, and the vilification of everything external to the household.[10] Likewise important to an understanding of the film's transgressiveness is the scene in which the family starts to behave like canines, another instance of Lanthimos's "performative realism" that some have seen as an act of filial "de-humanization."[11]

The unhealthiness of the patriarchal family is plainly a key theme in *Dogtooth*, and one that reappears in different guises throughout the director's filmography. Critics have correctly pointed out that the dissection of "sexual politics" in films like *Dogtooth* and *The Lobster* exploits the narratives' relative immobility in order to zero in on "the social gestures and micropolitics of everyday life."[12] The chief morality that manages this politics tends toward the untainted and the pure, something to which *Dogtooth*'s punishing elimination of almost everything that makes up a life world attests—freedom of mobility, healthy social and filial relationships, a sense of personal autonomy, genuine communication. For some critics, it is this "obsessive quest for purity" that defeats "the actual humanity" of family life.[13] In the dystopian society of *The Lobster*, the interdiction of homosexuality and masturbation expresses an ideological preference for a similar purity. Its rulers have criminalized singledom, and those without a partner of the opposite sex have to undergo an arduous process of conditioning that entails compulsory intermingling and dating. If the candidates fail, they will be converted into an animal of their own choosing.

As in *Dogtooth*, it could be argued, Lanthimos plays with the idea of the creaturely as a possible way out of the rigid conformism of biopolitically engineered systems of governance. In the intellectual tradition that stretches back to Rainer Maria Rilke's *Duino Elegies* (1922), and whose principal articulation may be found in the work of Giorgio Agamben and Eric Santner, the concept of *Das Offene* invokes an experiential realm beyond the symbolic representation and processes of mediation.[14] Thus, while the idea of being existentially demoted to an animal might seem like a bleak and grisly fate, there is also a sense in which Lanthimos imbues it with a kind of emancipatory heft.

But according to some critics, animality permeates not just Lanthimos's work but also several of the films that fall under the umbrella of the Greek New Wave. As Rosalind Galt sees it, for example, animality becomes a trope through which "subjectivity, power, and social relations" may be conveyed.[15] Noting that the acronym for the European Union countries that have struggled the most financially is the racist PIIGS (for Portugal, Italy, Ireland, Greece, and Spain), Galt suggests that the Greek New Wave has produced allegorical narratives, marked by a certain level of opacity, that connect both with the monetary crisis and the fraying of patriarchal family structures. "Animals, their lives, and their representability," she claims, "are the very medium of *The Lobster*'s critique."[16] Narratively extraneous animals like the flamingoes function as what Galt calls "disruptors," simultaneously fulfilling their roles as extradiegetic creatures and "fictional signifiers"; the name she gives to this aesthetic modality is *default cinema*, "films [that] refuse to play by the rules of neorealist poverty porn."[17] On an altogether different interpretive level, the inclusion of an assortment of animals—ponies, sheepdogs, peacocks—might be construed as a means by which to confront the filmic universe's amelioration of sameness and homogeneity with the freedom inherent in diversity and heterogeneity.

A politics of equivalence, or analogy, lies at the heart of the social order in *The Lobster*. Remaining unattached poses a threat to its very logic of operation, and only those who are in a heterosexual relationship can prove valuable to the maintenance of this order. It does not matter if one's solitary status is voluntary or unwelcome; singles are simply disposable whatever their reasons for failing to achieve coupledom. One consequence of the rigidity of such a system is that it drastically diminishes the ontological range of the human. In her reading, Galt offers the interpretation that the film shows us "a particularly wry version of the posthuman," which is what awaits "if you forfeit the right to humanity by refusing to obey."[18] This is true in the most literal, narrative sense; the fate of animality is what comes chronologically after being a person if one is unsuccessful in hooking up with a life partner of the opposite sex. But in a different sense, the metamorphosis that the singletons are forced to endure is a process not of posthumanization but of dehumanization. As an evolutionary condition, bestiality precedes the human.

More significant than the issue of posthumanism to grasping the meaning of *The Lobster*, however, are the acts of compulsory self-management taken up by David (Colin Farrell) and the others in his situation. In order to find a suitable companion, they have to adhere to a rather stringently encoded routine, a kind of perverted notion of "best practice" meant to ensure realization of their objective within the span of the forty-five days that they have available. Indispensable to this regimen is mimetic competence, as well as an aptitude for socioemotional forgery. To some extent, then, *The Lobster* anticipates the seismic conceptual shift considered by some scholars from biopolitics to what has been termed *aretaics*, that is, from "life itself" to "life as it is lived."[19] A convergence of Michel Foucault's notions of biopolitics and self-care, the concept of the aretaic entails a "somatization of identity," a new body that is not so much biological as "relational" and "context-dependent."[20] What scholars like Peter Lindner have in mind here is the increasingly pertinent role that digital technologies play in shaping the human. The rise of wearables and sensor-software gadgets occasions an ontological change whose transformation of human subjectivity and agency portends a new ethical future. The informational self is a transgressive entity in the sense that it is not anchored in a universal understanding of "life" but rather on models of "best practice." In their function as mediators between corporeal behavior, the self, and the social sphere, wearable technologies transgress both what is visible and sensible. Fundamentally, they are about datafication rather than the molecularization of biopower that has previously preoccupied scholars such as Nikolas Rose, and their mode of operation is preventive rather than curative.[21] Wearable technologies transcend the limitations of our sensorium and usher in "entirely new forms of body surveillance, control and optimization."[22]

While Lanthimos does not directly address wearables, health apps, and other digital gadgets intended to enhance psychosomatic wellness, the arduous protocols for mating in *The Lobster* call to mind the reliance on data rather than experience that characterizes the use of dating apps such as Tinder and Happn.[23] In the aretaic regime, the hunt for a partner always proceeds on the basis of compatibility rather than complementarity. "Likeness," in this particular universe, as Sarah Cooper points out, "is the only sought-after foundation for love."[24] The society that Lanthimos depicts therefore has little use for difference. In turn, the cultivation of similarity and the concomitant evasion of alterity inevitably encourage the acquisition of mimetic competence. The social exaltation of mimeticism and conformity, furthermore, is ultimately what drives the affinity for performance and reenactment in Lanthimos's cinema. A problem, of which the filmmaker may or may not be aware, that arises with the aretaic regime is that a system that unyieldingly favors performance and imitation over authenticity and alterity will remain stagnant and barren. Change and becoming are processes in which the mimetic has no place.

Lanthimos's most pungent articulation of the delirium of mimesis, I would like to argue, can be found in *Alps*, his 2011 follow-up to *Dogtooth*. Shot on a limited budget, *Alps* unveils a narrative premise so preposterous that even trying to recount it to people who do not know the film might be tinged with a certain awkwardness. Alps is the cryptic name of a small group of characters—a nurse (Angeliki Papoulia), a gymnast (Ariane Labed), her coach (Johnny Vekris), and an orderly (Aris Servetalis)—who offer a rather improbable service. Their secret agency caters to the recently bereaved by impersonating their departed loved ones. Among their clients are the parents of a 16-year-old tennis player, an older widow, and a man whose friend was in the army. The name of their organization appears to have no discernible connection to the nature of their work—which is possibly a residue from the language games in *Dogtooth*—except that its internal logic adumbrates the more conceptual dimension of the service provided. In an early scene, the paramedic informs his colleagues that he has selected the name Alps firstly because it gives nothing away and secondly because the mountain range—to his mind—conveys something to us about the business of substitution. So magnificent and grand are the Alps that they can replace any other mountain chain in the word, but no other mountain can supplant the Alps. This is a rather apt metaphor, since the film is above all else an exploration of the foundations of identity and the ethics of (ir)replaceability.

While having garnered less exposure than both earlier and later films such as *Dogtooth*, *The Lobster*, and *The Favourite*, *Alps* is certainly no less Lanthimosian. On display are stylistic trademarks like the immobile camera and the relatively long takes, the use of widescreen shots, the penchant for dorsality, compositions in which characters or objects are partially out of the frame, a disjointed narrative. Familiar themes also abound: being and pretending, normality and deviance, performance, play, imitation, mediation, behavioral absurdity, and the pressures on autonomy from austere social systems. But into this recognizable synthesis Lanthimos introduces the subject of loss (I first wanted to write "mourning," but upon further reflection I realized that the film is surprisingly reluctant to examine the condition of grieving), inspiring the viewer to ponder questions such as: what remains of the deceased after they are gone? How do you reconstruct the uniqueness of an individual? How can a sense of singularity be refashioned from habits or objects that in themselves are rather generic?

The members of Alps seem, on the whole, to approach the requirements of reenactment forensically. They are preoccupied with the smaller details that define the deceased, such as their favorite cuisine, what type of glasses they wore, their shoe size, their hairstyle, their preferred perfume, and their habits of speech (one was particularly inclined to begin sentences with the word "anyway," we learn). Someone's barber has passed away and one of his distinctive traits, we are told, was that he was always very particular about the sideburns being of exactly equal length. But the labor of imitation can also take less trivial and more animated—even disturbing—forms, as when the couple in the lamp store bicker aggressively with one another, or when, later on, he administers oral sex to her. In a later scene that vaguely recalls the atmosphere and style of Roy Andersson's films, one of the Alps recreates an adulterous setup in which the widow catches her late partner having an affair. One practically compulsive question that continually resurfaces in the group's work concerns the favorite actor of those departed. Jude Law, Morgan Freeman, and Robert Redford all get a mention, as do singers Harry Belafonte and Prince. In a film about performance and pretense, these allusions to Hollywood stars might come across as too obvious, but at the same time they help cement the idea that the film rebukes the neoliberal "commodification of everything, even mourning," as one critic puts it.[25] The ardent interest that the characters take in American popular culture suggests not only the degree to which everyday life has been commodified and colonialized by salable cultural imaginaries, but it also underscores the leveling of subjective experience that can be a corollary of the homogenizing impetus of imitation and sameness.

The thesis that identity is shaped by a mediated image appears to be internalized also by the diegetic characters; a term such as "substitution," for example, is in use by the Alps crew themselves. In the context of their work, impersonation is intended to function as an analgesic, to "ease the grief," as the nurse with the nickname Monte Rosa tells the parents of the adolescent tennis player. Choreography and acting thus become a kind of antidepressant. But an identity nourished by imitation and performed rather than spontaneously lived flags up the issue of authenticity. External attributes and patterns of behavior may be successfully emulated, but is not any given individual more than that? The logic of imitation, what I refer to above as the politics of equivalence, always risks succumbing to the powers of reduction. That the world of *Alps* is one in which experience is overwhelmingly influenced by mediated matter that tends to flatten rather than augment subjectivity is for example made clear by the use of Carl Orff's clichéd anthem O *Fortuna* in the opening scene in the gymnasium. At one point the athlete gets so discouraged by her coach's opposition to her practicing to pop music that she attempts to hang herself (at least that is an inference the film invites us to make). For many of the protagonists it is as if the more impersonal sphere of popular entertainment—of stars such as Prince and Jude Law, who in a certain sense are images more than persons—holds greater existential significance than that of their friends and colleagues.

The need for escapism (possibly due to the Greek recession and austerity measures from which Lanthimos has seemed determined to distance himself) might to some extent account for this appetite for American popular culture as a resource for the self, but that is hardly the whole story. Lanthimos's fictional environments are populated by characters who misapprehend the relation between sameness and plurality that Hannah Arendt discusses at length in *The Human Condition* (1958). In her account, sameness involves neither similarity of manners or beliefs nor a kind of identificational cloning, but refers, rather, to a common humanity shared in spite of our innumerable differences. In a passage about the public and the private realms, she writes that "[o]nly where things can be seen by many in a variety of aspects without changing their identity, so that those who are gathered around them know they see sameness in utter diversity, can worldly reality truly and reliably appear."[26] But a recurring problem for many of Lanthimos's characters is that they fail to discern this "sameness in utter diversity"; instead, they tend to see a largely unwanted diversity that gets in the way of their recognizing sameness in a truer, Arendtian sense. This is especially apparent in *The Lobster*, in which the system goes to great lengths to eliminate diversity in the name of a misguided sense of sameness that presumes, erroneously, that it must be ascribed to particular rather than universal phenomena such as forms of sexual practice or social organization. But this perverted sense of sameness can also be seen in the *Dogtooth* family's virtually surgical eradication of the outside world, as well as in *Alps*' obsession with ersatz sociality. The idea that anything can be replaced is predicated both on the conviction that differences can be ironed out and on an unrealistic confidence in the art of imitation.

The dead cannot be brought back to life, and they cannot be replaced, however great the efforts of reenactment might be. Despite the crew's best endeavors, a service such as that offered by the Alps is destined to fail because ultimately the actors' inescapable divergence from the departed will only serve to accentuate their absence. The company extended by Monte Rosa and her associates will likely only get in the way of the grieving process, for which acceptance of the loss is a condition for enduring it. While in the care of the Alps' carefully curated performances, the mourners are actually stuck in a limbo of sorts; thus, the phrase I use above, the "psychic architecture of confinement," also applies to this cognitive–emotional state. The children in *Dogtooth* and David and the others in *The Lobster* also suffer from this. In the former, the haywire referentiality of signs and meanings considerably shrinks the life world of the children, and in the latter the almost comical inflexibility of the social system likewise functions to restrict the characters' emotional selves.

Cinema has its own genre of confinement, as Thomas Connelly has shown, comprising films where much or sometimes all of the narrative action takes place in just one single space.[27] Canonical examples would be *Rope* (Alfred Hitchcock, 1948), *The Passion of Anna* (Ingmar Bergman, 1969), *Talk Radio* (Oliver Stone, 1988) and *Panic Room* (David Fincher, 2002). *Dogtooth* fits this pattern, *Alps* less so (although its narrative does return to a limited set of locales: the gym, the hospital, and the small apartment). But confinement as a psychological experience—and social distancing as an outcome of emotional glacialization—seems to be a vital part of the internal landscapes Lanthimos surveys in *Alps*. Although the director has refused to acknowledge the correlation, it is nonetheless not unlikely that the limitations and constraints caused by the recession, rising unemployment, and dire economic prospects have informed *Alps* on an allegorical level. The ramifications of a financial downturn for the individual citizen may very well be situations of confinement: being trapped in a tiny apartment because it is all one can afford, sleeping in the car or on the street, ending up in prison, or simply being unable to travel anywhere due to insolvency. Finally, the psychology of confinement may even materialize in the work of imitation and acting itself. We often hear that pretending to be someone else can be liberating, but it might also come with its own set of restrictions. The element of repetition is prominent in reenactment. What the Alps crew does is essentially to reiterate habits, attributes, and situations associated with those they impersonate. But repetition of course represents its own form of confinement. If one's whole life becomes just a series of repetitions, one can easily feel trapped. And pretending to be someone else can be not only energizing but also self-alienating; if social mores dictate that one cannot really be oneself, acting can come to mean a kind of blockage, an existential impasse that forecloses growth and opportunity.

In Leos Carax's *Holy Motors* (2012)—a work that *Alps* foreshadows in its emphasis on impersonation and death—the main character Oscar, an actor, is asked why he chose his profession. "For the beauty of the gesture" is his reply. If there is anything recuperable in Lanthimos's rather dismal spaces, where intransigent rules and perfunctory simulation threaten to consume all authenticity, it might be the incolonizability of the human body and the ways in which its gestural language tends to exceed the pre-prepared protocols of imitation. One of the most gripping scenes in *Alps* occurs toward the end when Monte Rosa visits the dance parlor and with an older woman initiates a dance that turns increasingly violent, culminating in an assault on the floor. In this scene, there is a sense that her behavior—unlike that of the scene in the lamp store, for instance—is spontaneous, wild, and unrehearsed. Perhaps fitting for a filmmaker who used to shoot dance and theater performances, Lanthimos, in this scene, shows how the deeply corporeal life of gesture, posture, and carriage can remain impervious to the stifling demands of conformity and sameness. In the end, what Lanthimos's cinema might convey is the ambiguity or two-sidedness of performance. On the one hand, its mimetic drive generates sameness and repetition; on the other, there is a utopian prospect in any act of performance that is linked to the possibilities of improvization and instant invention. The films themselves corroborate this equivocality, which manifests as the paradox that such a pessimistic engagement with the pathology of conformity and imitation can be realized in such an inimitable cinematic language.

Notes

1 Maud Ceuterick, "An Affirmative Look at a Domesticity in Crisis: Women, Humour and Domestic Labour during the COVID-19 Pandemic," *Feminist Media Studies*, 20, no. 6 (2020): 896–901, at p. 897.

2 For more on this trend, see Tanya Horeck and Tina Kendall, eds., *The New Extremism in Cinema: From France to Europe* (Edinburgh: Edinburgh University Press, 2011). See also my work, *Screening the Unwatchable: Spaces of Negation in Post-Millennial Art Cinema* (London: Palgrave Macmillan, 2012).

3 Mario Perniola, *Art and Its Shadow*, trans. Massimo Verdicchio (New York: Continuum, 2004), 3.

4 Ibid.

5 Ibid.

6 Ibid., 7, 22.

7 Ibid., 11, 66.

8 Viktor Shklovsky, "Art as Technique," in D. Lodge, ed., *Modern Criticism and Theory: A Reader* (London: Longman, [1917] 1988).

9 Dionysios Kapsaskis, "Translation as a Critical Tool in Film Analysis: Watching Yorgos Lanthimos's *Dogtooth* through a Translational Prism" (*Translation Studies*, 10, no. 3 (2017): 247–62, at p. 253. In the aftermath of the financial crisis of 2007–2008, Greece faced a more severe recession than other advanced mixed economies, with rampant debt, the implementation of grim austerity measures, and the loss of income and property.

10 Mark Fisher, "The Family Syndrome," *Film Quarterly*, 64, no. 4 (2011): 22–27, at p. 22.

11 Angelos Koutsourakis, "Cinema of the Body: The Politics of Performativity in Lars von Trier's *Dogville* and Yorgos Lanthimos' *Dogtooth*," *Cinema: Journal of Philosophy and the Moving Image*, 3 (2012): 84–108, at p. 104; Stamos Metzidakis, "No Bones to Pick with Lanthimos's Film *Dogtooth*," *Journal of Modern Greek Studies*, 32, no. 2 (2014): 367–92, at p. 384.

12 Kapsaskis, "Translation as a Critical Tool," 253; Koutsourakis, "Cinema of the Body," 104.

13 Metzidakis, "No Bones to Pick," 384.

14 See Giorgio Agamben, *The Open: Man and Animal* (Stanford, CA: Stanford University Press, 2004); Eric L. Santner, *On Creaturely Life: Rilke, Benjamin, Sebald* (Chicago: University of Chicago Press, 2006); and Rainer Maria Rilke, *Duino Elegies: A Bilingual Edition* (New York: North Point Press, 2001).

15 Rosalind Galt, "The Animal Logic of Contemporary Greek Cinema," *Framework: Journal of Cinema and Media*, 58, nos. 1–2 (2017): 7–29, at p. 7.

16 Ibid., 9.

17 Ibid., 9, 11.

18 Ibid., 21.

19 Peter Lindner, "Molecular Politics, Wearables, and the Aretaic Shift in Biopolitical Governance," *Theory, Culture and Society*, 37, no. 3 (2020): 1–26, at p. 1.
20 Ibid., 7, 9.
21 Nikolas Rose, *The Politics of Life Itself: Biomedicine, Power, and Subjectivity in the Twenty-First Century* (Princeton, NJ: Princeton University Press, 2007).
22 Lindner, "Molecular Politics," 4.
23 Reviews of the film have picked up on this correspondence. See, for instance, James Farrell, "*The Lobster*: A Bleak, Unique, Twisted Tale of Online Dating," *SiliconAngle*, Feb 16, 2016 available at https://siliconangle.com/2016/02/16/the-lobster-a-bleak-unique-twisted-tale-of-online-dating/; Annalee Newitz, "At Last, a Sci-Fi Movie that Accurately Captures the Horrors of Dating," *ArtsTechnica*, May 13, 2016, available at https://arstechnica.com/gaming/2016/05/at-last-a-sci-fi-movie-that-accurately-captures-the-horrors-of-dating/; and Liam Ball, "Swipe Left: Modern Dating in *The Lobster*," *Film Inquiry*, Jun 23, 2016, available at https://www.filminquiry.com/swipe-left-modern-dating-lobster/.
24 Sarah Cooper, "Narcissus and *The Lobster*," *Studies in European Cinema*, 13, no. 2 (2016): 163–76, at p. 163.
25 Eleni Varmazi, "The Weirdness of Contemporary Greek Cinema," *Film International*, 17, no. 1 (2019): 40–49, at p. 46.
26 Hannah Arendt, *The Human Condition*, intro. Margaret Canovan (Chicago: University of Chicago Press, [1958] 1998), 57.
27 Thomas Connelly, *Cinema of Confinement* (Evanston, IL: Northwestern University Press, 2019).

5

Bodies Out of Place: Ontological *Adriftness* in *The Lobster*

Ina Karkani

There's much more to be said about losing oneself in worldly space than can be referenced—or remediated—by recourse to the abstract objectivity of a map.[1]

VIVIAN SOBCHACK

Yorgos Lanthimos's *The Lobster* thematically and stylistically deals with bodies out of place, living under the constant threat of transmogrification. In the diegetic universe that *The Lobster* presents, animals function as indexical markers for pending existential crises that threaten to violate familiar ontological boundaries as we have come to know them. The dissolution of the human/animal binary creates an affective sensation of *adriftness* that makes up the "worldhood"[2] of the film. By withholding clear expositional markers, Lanthimos invites the viewer to feel their way around *The Lobster*'s ambiguous fictional space in which humans and animals epitomize "the extreme collapse between the figural and the real."[3] It is a conceptual disruption that breaks from common modes of representation of humans and animals. This feeling of being *adrift* does not play out in the leisurely fashion of the modernist *flâneurs* of *The Darjeeling Unlimited* (Wes Anderson, 2007) or *Midnight in Paris* (Woody Allen, 2011), an affective mode building on Walter Benjamin's city-dwelling urban character.[4] Nor do we feel *adrift* in the unpleasurable, fatiguing sense in keeping with André

Bazin's conceptualization of duration (*dureé*)[5] that is evident in the works of slow cinema auteurs such as Béla Tarr, Kelly Reichardt, Lucretia Martel, and Tsai Ming-liang, filmmakers who regularly employ animals as spatiotemporal markers to deliver the affect of "'stuckness,' non-productivity, and inability to progress within the harsh demands of an exhausting, social, material world."[6] *The Turin Horse* (Béla Tarr, 2011), for example, incorporates the laboring animal in its diegetic world to reframe the relationship between the characters and their harsh surroundings. Tarr's film employs realism and utilizes the animal to comment on social conditions pertaining to both species, creating a sense of "stuckness" that conveys the themes of the film; in this respect, distinctions between species (or lack thereof) provide a commentary on our own ontological boundaries and oppressive laws of governance.

The Lobster, on the other hand, resists the tidy frame of reference and clear ontological categorization that defines *The Turin Horse*. The fact that animals are transmogrified humans that share the frame with human characters removes all traces of what is naturally animal about them.[7] This distortion of an otherwise conceptually determined physical signifier demonstrates *The Lobster*'s design to create a viewing experience that makes the viewer feel *adrift*. *Adriftness*, as I use it here, corresponds with what Jean-François Lyotard refers to as "drifting," a style that employs spatial "connotations of non-linearity and unpredictability and potentiality … provoking shifts and movements, transformations and becomings."[8] For one example, consider filmmaker Chris Marker's timeless aesthetic that opts for a geographical rather than a chronological approach to consciousness. In *La Jetée* (1962), Marker portrays characters that go through the difficulties of living in an oppressing reality while trying to find a way to escape it. Marker's film explores this theme by constructing a time travel narrative out of black-and-white photography and cine-roman sequences that are tied together by an off-screen voice that organizes the film elements into continuity, giving them logic or order otherwise unseen.

Echoes of Marker's patchwork diegesis are immediately clear in *The Lobster*'s three-minute long opening scene that begins with the shooting of an unsuspecting donkey by an unknown middle-aged woman framed against a rainy, rural landscape (see Figure 5.1). The ambiguous sequence unfolds in a long shot that captures the action from inside the woman's parked car as intermittent windshield wipers provide mechanized sounds. The film cuts to a man sitting opposite his dog in a living room as an emotionless, off-screen voice belonging to his wife explains her decision to leave him. The man is subsequently removed from his home by two mysterious men wearing long, white aprons. These bizarre interactions culminate with the accompaniment of Beethoven's dramatic String Quartet and the monotonous voice of the female narrator who, as we later find out, is a main character named Short Sighted Woman (Rachel Weisz). Contrary to *La Jetée*'s distinct authorial voice, the narrator does not provide the viewer with an explanation of

FIGURE 5.1 *A woman shoots an unsuspecting donkey during the opening scene of* The Lobster.

the strange events, but rather with some equally strange details about the deported man, revealed to be named David (Colin Farrell).

The affective charge of the scene is bewildering, much in the same way as the *fait accompli* that opens the film; with the cold treatment of both donkey and husband, the viewer is thrown into a world that looks familiar but unfolds as an ambiguous viewing experience. At this point the viewer might suspect that in this world humans and animals share common characteristics in a way that challenges our everyday understandings of their differences. This impression is amplified in the following scene where David, at the check-in desk of an ominous hotel, introduces his dog Bob as his brother who stayed at the hotel some years ago but "did not make it." David delivers this bizarre information along with intimate details about his sexual preferences, which figure as part of the standard procedure for registering as a guest at the hotel. The strange tone of these opening scenes introduces the unusual regulations of the world of *The Lobster*. It is revealed that the hotel functions as a space for match-making where citizens without a partner are given forty-five days to find a suitable mate. Premarital sex and masturbation are strictly forbidden and, indeed, punishable. In the case that guests do not succeed in pairing up, they face transmogrification into an animal of their own choosing in a chamber called the "transformation room." The opposing yet equally totalitarian belief system within *The Lobster*'s world is represented by a faction of forest-dwelling renegades called the Loners. There, coupledom—as well as any other form of affection—is an offense that faces brutal physical punishment. In the forest, pigs, flamingos, and peacocks ambiguously populate the edges of the frame; in fact, both worlds

FIGURE 5.2 *Asymmetrical relations in* The Lobster: *David, his dog, and his wife off-screen.*

are home to a range of domestic and exotic animals of different biological classifications, which may or may not be former humans.

The Lobster presents asymmetrical character arrangements that prompt new engagement with the natural order of things on an aesthetic level (see Figure 5.2). Consider the formal elements of that earlier scene in which the spatial alignment of David and his dog/brother Bob pushes David's wife out of the frame, rendering her invisible. While alluding to contemporary ecological anxieties, these film scenes do not simply convey messages about humans, species hierarchy, and/or animal ethics.[9] Rather, Lanthimos's film shows an interest in deconstructing representational images; as such, *The Lobster* employs affective, material images that prompt the viewer to wonder about the connection between humans and nonhumans and to question their epistemological relationship to their environment. In this chapter, I want to consider how what I call affective *adriftness* shapes meaning in *The Lobster*. I want to question how Lanthimos generates affecting images that challenge our ontological understanding of the world.

The Lobster was released during a time in which European cinema was becoming increasingly preoccupied with the repercussions of new ecological and ongoing economic crises, and Lanthimos's work contributes to that tradition by articulating the social dynamics of the vertigo-inducing experience of existing in the age of ontological uncertainty. These ideas are activated in Rosalind Galt's article on *The Lobster*, which explores the links between images of animals and subject formation in Lanthimos's film. Galt explores this theme in relation to contemporary politics on migration, arguing that such films take "for granted cross-species bonds" and "imply that subjectivity is not determined or limited by species."[10] Similar interest in subject formation in Greek cinema has been expressed by Vrasidas Karalis in his discussion of *The Lobster*'s "aesthetics of abeyance," wherein animals become symbols to reflect upon the "characters who lack identity, centre and ideal self[hood]."[11] Elsewhere, Sarah Cooper's discussion of Narcissus and *The Lobster* brings Lanthimos's film in dialogue with the ethics of Emmanuel Levinas and Jacques Derrida, exploring how the animal gaze, particularly that of Bob, offers one way of thinking about radical alterity. Cooper argues that Bob, through his anthropomorphic relationship to David, becomes a medium for experiencing a radically different subject position in the film.[12] These scholarly approaches point to the centrality of the animal to readings of *The Lobster*, a film whose "creaturely"[13] elements explicate the affective value of the drift to offer new possibilities for exploring subject relations.

Compared to *The Turin Horse*, where the animal constitutes a referential site that illuminates social tensions and uncertain knowledge through affective investment, it becomes clear how *The Lobster*'s drifting style further complicates the human–animal interplay, thereby rendering the human body increasingly unstable and fragile. Lanthimos's ambiguous style disputes the authority of narration and subverts regular systems of meaning by creating film worlds that lack spatiotemporal integrity. This is evident in Lanthimos's earlier film *Dogtooth*, which tells the story of a totalitarian family regime in which the cat behind the fence is "the most dangerous animal that exists" while the new family member is "a dog that will come out of the mother's womb." *Attenberg* (2010), a coproduction with its writer-director Athina Rachel Tsangari, meanwhile transforms an industrial town into an imaginary animal habitat in which the preferred method of socialization is to watch animal documentaries and then imitate them in a shared ritual of chest-beating and shrieking. Indeed, just as *Dogtooth* and *Attenberg* "cut together images and bodies that appear and withdraw without much spatiotemporal coherence or narrative significance,"[14] so does the weird idiosyncratic style of *The Lobster* complicate compositional expectations and resolutions. *The Lobster*'s challenging ontological address of the human body places Lanthimos's cinema more explicitly in relation to a new contemporary cinema of the body that I will outline in due course. It is my position that the film's strangeness and flouting of expectations comes to impact the consciousness of the viewer; as Lanthimos's minimalist, impersonal style withholds information from the viewer, feelings and thoughts of characters become increasingly unclear, leaving the viewer in a narrative position one might describe as disadvantageous, if not vulnerable. The viewer's "witnessing bod[y]"[15] leads to a slippery subjectivity generated by Lanthimos's style that deploys an intentionally contrapuntal relationship between body, sound, and filmic space. As such, this chapter considers *The Lobster* in such terms, as a film that reflects on sociocultural uncertainties by creating a particular form of embodied viewership that conveys the experience of being dislocated, disoriented, and *adrift*.

Thomas Elsaesser's discussion of Walter Benjamin's twin concepts of *Erlebnis* and *Erfahrung* is fruitful ground on which to reflect on this type of viewing experience as it offers one explanation for the interrelationship between spectatorial agency and affect.[16] *Erlebnis* is explained as "an immediate, passive, fragmented, isolated and unintegrated inner experience," while *Erfahrung* is associated with a more complete understanding synonymous with "wisdom, of epic truth."[17] As demonstrated in the film's opening scene, a sense of *Erfahrung* is withheld as the donkey is shot and the husband divorced, leaving the viewer with an unstable ontological frame of reference due to the fragmented signifiers presented in the scene. It is in relation to such instances that Elsaesser points to the importance of the body and its affective states, as a perceptual rather than merely metonymical surface on which experiences manifest despite an uneven distribution of narrative knowledge or blocked agency.[18] In *The Lobster*'s opening scene, the spectator is set *adrift* by the lack of agency that comes from minimal narrative markers.[19] Embodied *adriftness*, then, describes the sensation of a viewer experiencing insufficient narrative information and blocked agency. Such a viewing experience recalls what has been named the "vertigo effect" after Alfred Hitchcock's *Vertigo* (1958), a sensation that employs compositional effects to reflect upon the characters' unstable mental states of mind.

The Lobster creates a similar effect, one that is amplified by the presence of animals whose fictional status as transmogrified humans surpasses their specificity as animals. I observe that this element is reflected in a cluster of thematically linked films of different genres and production backgrounds, including *On Body and Soul* (*Teströl és lélekröl*, Ildikó Enyedi, 2017), *The Shape of Water* (Guillermo del Toro, 2017), and *Border* (*Gräns*, Ali Abbasi, 2018), films that foster reformulations of spectatorial agency and reflect on the relation between the human and animals. Interests in the field of posthumanist animal studies intersect with ongoing discussions within film spectatorship theory. Laura McMahon states that films featuring animals are "shaped by their particular historical moment and by a set of contemporary cultural trends which are characterized by cultural and social transfigurations related to today's ecological and economical crisis."[20] Elsewhere, Matthew Calarco has called for "an alternative ontology of animal life, an ontology in which the human–animal distinction is called radically into question."[21]

In tandem with such ontological anxieties, postcontemporary studies have been trying to establish the need for a "forward-looking"[22] film language. Michael J. Shapiro, for example, has addressed the necessity for new corporeal language within film discourse that engages with the labor of looking.[23] The existential uncertainty that comes by way of affect has been described by Vivian Sobchack as feeling "lost" in "unfamiliar, worldly space, always mutable and potentially threatening."[24] The spatialization of emotions have been the interest of phenomenological film scholars such as Carl Plantinga and Greg M. Smith who write that films occupy a central place in the "emotional landscape of the modern world as one of the predominant spaces where societies experience feelings."[25] Giuliana Bruno has discussed the "circulation of emotions" and the construction of "geopsychic space,"[26] referring to writing and visual arts as "imaginative terrains of emotion" that carve out "psychogeographic route[s]" with a "sensorium of emotions."[27] By this Bruno attests that the visual arts embody a voyage in the form of an emotional landscape and carve out "itineraries of emotions."[28] These interests have come together in recent work by Alexa Weik von Mossner who focuses on the role played by affect and emotion in the production and reception of films that "centrally feature natural environments and nonhuman actors."[29] I will conclude this theoretical framing by returning to Lyotard's notion of the drift. Lyotard explains that what is significant in a text is "not what it means, but what it does and incites to do. What it does: the charge of affect it contains and transmits. What it incites to do: the metamorphoses of this potential energy into other things—other texts ... photographs, film sequences."[30] Lyotard's redirection of affect from one space into another offers inspiration for examining the emotional resonances of drifting, or of feeling *adrift* as a viewer of this or indeed other films.

Toward the beginning of *The Lobster*, the hotel guests are taken to the forest where they are expected to hunt the Loners. The activity is framed as a competition that grants the guests extra days at the hotel, depending on the number of Loners they manage to immobilize. As the guests are released from their transportation vehicle, the film switches to slow motion and is accompanied by the mournful song "*Apo Mesa Pethamenos*" ("Dead Inside"), performed by the Greek singer Danae. The dramatic lyrics detail the pain of unrequited love, which provides a haunting accompaniment to the visual field as the group of hunters is unleashed into the forest. The slow, haunting song embodies and emphasizes the spatiality of the sequence, or to borrow from Thomas Elsaesser and Malte Hagener, "it gives film a body."[31] As time is slowed down, the viewer's attention is drawn to the strange spectacle of the hunters' bodies as they wade through the forest stumbling and falling over. The sequence evokes the affective state of *adriftness*, of not being properly anchored in space and time, an affect echoed in the form as the action plays out in slow motion. This *adriftness* is further indicated in the slow transition from the vehicle into nature that suggests a point of entry into a drastically different environment, providing a transition from inside to outside, just as the sequence intimates another transition, ontologically speaking, from human to animal. And indeed, during the hunting scene, the guests are portrayed as predators driven by bestial instincts to survive. At one point, David lifts his gun and his target materializes as a cat—an ongoing threat against his personhood, possibly a former human who did not make it—which then jumps across the fauna.

FIGURE 5.3 *Becoming animal in* The Lobster.

The scene is photographed by Thimios Bakatakis whose preferences for soft lighting to capture earthly colors is out of balance with the images of explicit physical violence (see Figure 5.3). Elsaesser by way of Gérard Genette has conceptualized affect on spatiogeographic terms, that it "prestructure[s] horizons of expectation and call[s] forth promises of identification," as well as indicating the "semantic instability and tectonic shifts and turbulence of texts, as inside and outside are never quite stable and fixed and their boundaries become fuzzy or jagged."[32] Indeed, the viewer experiences similar instability or "turbulence" when navigating the jarring slow motion sequence that nurtures feelings of haptic *adriftness* which characterize the film. Bruno uses psychogeographic language to describe haptic affect, which constitutes "reciprocal contact between us and the environment both housing and extending communicative interface."[33] Affective tensions are further articulated between the haptic texture of the sequence and the deadpan acting style that withholds interiority and character depth. Again, the viewer's experience is guided not by the characters' subjectivity but by the sensations embodied in watching the surfaces of the film.

Thomas Morsch explains the role of actors and acting styles in relation to the process and experience of viewing films.[34] He emphasizes the experiential dimensions that are projected onto the actors' bodies that enable identification.[35] Viewers are tasked with figuring out the order of things by observing the characters' behavior as a form of language. This localization of the production of meaning to features of the body materializes in characters besides David and his dog Bob not given proper names, but who are instead referred to by their physical traits, for example

Nosebleed Woman (Jessica Barden), Limping Man (Ben Wishaw), Biscuit Woman (Ashley Jensen), Lisping Man (John C. Reilly), or, depending on the occasion, simply by their hotel room numbers. As the viewer engages with such characters, their viewing position retreats ever further from any form of subjective alignment; they are uncoupled from any agentic grasp on the characters that might offer a consoling sense of *Erfahrung*. The extent to which *The Lobster*'s characters are emotionally evacuated becomes particularly explicit in critical moments in the film. Toward the middle of the film, Biscuit Woman laments that her time at the hotel is coming to an end; in a detached tone, she goes on to reveal that she will jump out of a window of the hotel room should she not find a suitable partner soon, but realizes that, practically speaking, she faces a problem in that her room does not have any windows. She coldly if desperately makes David an offer: "Can I come to your room sometime for a chat? I can give you a blow job or you could just fuck me?"

There is a precedent for such affective techniques, for example, in Todd Haynes's environmental thriller *Safe* (1995). Roddey Reid observes how the style of the film blocks identification with the protagonist, offering "neither Hollywood conventional identification nor avant-gardist ironic critique"[36] that creates a discomforting subjective position for the viewer. Reid identifies what he describes as "blank time" as a key compositional element in *Safe* that explains the uneasy tension created by the affective *adriftness* and the uncertain knowledge of what may happen; "blank time" might also indicate a nothingness, where "the indifferent thereness of things has taken over and has nothing to say."[37] It can be argued that Reid's notion of "blank time" plays out in *The Lobster* also, where an absence of clear identification extends to other elements of the *mise-en-scène*. The guests at the hotel, for example, often appear blank, wearing identical clothes for each of the planned events. They don colorful cocktail dresses and black suits for evening wear, as well as identical green jackets to go out hunting in the forest. Meanwhile, *The Lobster*'s detached, pragmatic language points to another blankness, characterized as a lack of agency where the characters do not appear to be "acting on behalf of the self."[38] This point is further articulated by the female narrator who initially functions as an auxiliary for David's lack of charisma (she later enters the film as Short Sighted Woman), and who provides the viewer with further information about his internal condition. Consider the information the narrator provides as David's wife leaves him:

> He decided that his brown leather shoes were the best pair to wear. His back hurt a little bit, not like some other times in the past when the pain was intolerable. He was thinking his wife did not love him at all anymore. He didn't burst into tears and didn't think that the first thing most people do when they realize someone doesn't love them anymore is cry.

Deadpan moments of affective *adriftness* characterize Lanthimos's style in ways that comment on current ruptures in the collective human experience. Lanthimos's film explores the oppressiveness of global sociopolitical climates by constructing hermeneutically ambiguous ontologies that throw the body out of place, showcasing feelings of uncertainty toward a range of contemporary topics, including politics, global epidemics, hygiene discourses, and various forms of social and personal trauma. The film's ambiguity plays into various discussions surrounding contemporary body politics. Susie Orbach, for example, points to the "difficulty of living in the bodies we currently inhabit, with their many predicaments, and the promise of trouble-free, almost body-free existence as we move towards futures constituted by algorithms and synthetic biology."[39] It can be argued that in the fictional universe of *The Lobster*, Lanthimos's adoption of outwardly pragmatic but horrifying resolutions to social ills reveals various crises regarding the individual and their relation to an existing reality, a theme that manifests in the film's unclear ontological distinction between human and animal. Later in the Loner's forest, David and Short Sighted Woman attempt to secretly communicate with one another using body language for fear that their illegal attraction might be met with cruel consequences. The film switches once again to slow motion and, again, the scene is accompanied by a dramatic string arrangement, as well as the voice of the narrator (Short Sighted Woman) who attempts to orientate the viewer within the ambiguous ontological abyss of the forest. Framed before a lush, green background, the camera lingers in close-up on the hands and torsos of the "lovers" as they perform a human intimation of an animal mating ritual. The narrator explains:

> We developed a code so that we could communicate with each other even in front of the others without knowing what we were saying. When we turned our heads to the left, it means "I love you more than anything in the world" and when we turned our heads to the right, it means "watch out we are in danger" … When we raise our left arms it means "I want to dance in your arms," when we make a fist and put it behind our backs it means "let's fuck."

Their unique language of love echoes *Attenberg*'s zoomorphic approach to communication that is both fully embodied and strangely stylized. The scene manifests what Marios Psaras has described in spatial terms as an "idiosyncratic cartography of the human body's exploratory, yet often frustrating, oscillation between mobility and stasis across the monotonous and oppressive contours of social life."[40] It can be argued that in this moment *The Lobster* demonstrates *adriftness* that is embodied by both characters and the viewer, culminating in a moment of stylistic and thematic convergence with a cinematic image with the sustained texture of *Erfahrung*. In desperate need of communication, David and Short Sighted Woman reconfigure their agency by creating a new, clandestine language with concrete semiotic markers.

This connection has violent ramifications in the film's controversial closing scene. Short Sighted Woman has been punished with blindness after the romantic notes in her diary have been revealed. David and Short Sighted Woman decide to escape the Loners' regime and make their way toward the city, where they nevertheless have to abide by the rules of conformity, and David, fearing a newfound incompatibility, resorts to blinding himself with a steak knife. Echoing *Dogtooth*'s bathroom scene in which Elder Daughter attempts to break free of her oppressive family prison by mutilating herself, so too does David stand in front of mirror, prepared to let his indoctrination by the authoritarian rules of the state rob him of his sight, even after he has finally escaped them.

Rather than answer the question of what the modern person (or animal) is, *The Lobster* attempts to convey the ever more challenging condition of being human. Dislocated, disoriented, and *adrift*, Lanthimos's human is endlessly caught up in the mist of modern day uncertainties of "incalculable environmental risks, threatened identities and partial knowledges."[41] *The Lobster* resists concrete temporal or ontological development or categorization, but nevertheless provides sensorial insight into the film's historical moment. With a lack of clear referents or concrete points of entry, everything in *The Lobster* feels *adrift*. As such, Lanthimos's film, with its myriad ambiguous contextual markers, employs style to create potential for a multitude of productive readings of the film as a critical reflection on what it currently feels like to be human.

Notes

1 Vivian Sobchack, *Carnal Thoughts: Embodiment and Image Culture* (Berkeley: University of California Press, 2004), 15.

2 Translated from Martin Heidegger's concept "*Weltlichkeit*." See Martin Heidegger, *Being and Time*, trans. J. Macquarie and E. Robinson (Oxford: Wiley-Blackwell, [1927] 2005).

3 Jonathan Burt, *Animals in Film* (London: Reaktion Books, 2002), 44.

4 Anke Gleber, *The Art of Taking a Walk: Flanerie, Literature, and Film in Weimar Culture* (Princeton, NJ: Princeton University Press, 1999), 55.

5 See Karl Schoonover, "Wastrels of Time: Slow Cinema's Laboring Body, the Political Spectator, and the Queer," *Framework: The Journal of Cinema and Media*, 53, no. 1 (2012): 65–78.

6 Elena Gorfinkel, "Exhausted Drift: Austerity, Dispossession and the Politics of Slow in Kelly Reichardt's *Meek's Cutoff*," in T. de Luca and N. Barradas Jorge, eds., *Slow Cinema* (Edinburgh: Edinburgh University Press, 2016), 123–35.

7 Ibid., 111.
8 John Hodgkins, *The Drift: Affect, Adaptation and New Perspectives on Fidelity* (London and New York: Bloomsbury, 2013), 138.
9 The asymmetrical relationship between species has been discussed extensively by interdisciplinary animal and film studies and will complement the framework for this discussion.
10 Rosalind Galt, "The Animal Logic of Contemporary Greek Cinema," *Framework: The Journal of Cinema and Media*, 58, nos. 1–2 (2017): 7–29, at p. 9.
11 Vrasidas Karalis, "Yorgos Lanthimos's *The Lobster* and the Cinema of Abeyance," *FilmIcon: Journal of Greek Film Studies*, Dec 18, 2015, available at http://filmiconjournal.com/blog/post/48/the-lobster-and-the-cinema-of-abeyance.
12 Sarah Cooper, "Narcissus and *The Lobster*," *Studies in European Cinema*, 13, no. 2 (2016): 163–76.
13 I am borrowing Anat Pick's notion of living bodies here. See Anat Pick, *Creaturely Poetics: Animality and Vulnerability in Literature and Film* (New York: Columbia University Press, 2011).
14 Marios Psaras, *The Queer Greek Weird Wave: Ethics, Politics and the Crisis of Meaning* (Basingstoke: Springer Nature, 2016), 124.
15 Roddey Reid employs Carol Clover's formulation to comment on the correlation between the body onscreen and off-screen in Todd Haynes's *Safe* (1995) in which he regards the portrayal of the protagonist's slowly disintegrating character as a radical critique of 1990s health discourses. See Roddey Reid, "UnSafe at Any Distance: Todd Haynes' Visual Culture of Health and Risk," *Film Quarterly*, 51, no. 3 (1998): 32–44, at p. 38.
16 Thomas Elsaesser, "Between *Erlebnis* und *Erfahrung*: Cinema Experience with Benjamin," *Paragraph*, 32, no. 3, *Passage-Work: Walter Benjamin between the Disciplines* (2009): 292–312.
17 Ibid., 294.
18 Ibid., 302.
19 See David Bordwell, *Poetics of Cinema* (Oxford: Routledge, 2007).
20 Laura McMahon, *Animal Worlds: Film, Philosophy and Time* (Edinburgh: Edinburgh University Press, 2019), 10.
21 Matthew Calarco, *Zoographies: The Question of the Animal from Heidegger to Derrida* (New York: Columbia University Press, 2008), 141.
22 Burt, *Animals in Film*, 35.
23 Michael J. Shapiro, *Politics and Time* (Cambridge: Polity, 2016).
24 Sobchack, *Carnal Thoughts*, 15.
25 Carl Plantinga and Greg M. Smith, eds., *Passionate Views: Film, Cognition, and Emotion* (Baltimore, MD: Johns Hopkins University, 1999), 1.
26 Guiliana Bruno, *Atlas of Emotion: Journeys in Art, Architecture, and Film* (London: Verso, 2002), 9.

27 Ibid.
28 Ibid., 2.
29 Alexa Weik von Mossner, ed., *Moving Environments: Affect, Emotion, Ecology and Film* (Waterloo, ON: Wilfrid Laurier University Press, 2014), 1.
30 Jean-François Lyotard, *Driftworks*, trans. Roger McKeon (Los Angeles, CA: Semiotexte, 1984), 9–10.
31 Thomas Elsaesser and Malte Hagener, *Film Theory: An Introduction through the Senses* (New York: Routledge, 2010), 136.
32 Ibid., 42.
33 Bruno, *Atlas of Emotion*, 6.
34 Thomas Morsch, "*Der Körper des Zuschauers: Elemente einer somatischen Theorie des Kinos*" ["The Body of the Spectator: Elements of an Embodied Theory in Cinema"], *Medienwissenschaft: Rezensionen/Reviews*, 14, no. 3 (1997): 271–289, at p. 278.
35 Ibid., 274.
36 Reid, "UnSafe at Any Distance," 33.
37 Ibid., 35.
38 Elsaesser, "Between *Erlebnis* und *Erfahrung*," 302.
39 Susie Orbach, "Will This Be the Last Generation to Have Bodies that Are Familiar to Us?" *The Guardian*, Aug 23, 2019, available at https://www.theguardian.com/books/2019/aug/23/susie-orbach-that-will-bodies-be-like-in-the-future.
40 Psaras, *The Queer Greek Weird Wave*, 124.
41 Reid, "UnSafe at Any Distance," 39.

6

Notes Toward a Cinema of Apathy in the Films of Yorgos Lanthimos

Eddie Falvey

Apathy, noun.
1. Freedom from, or insensibility to, suffering; hence, freedom from, or insensibility to, passion or feeling; passionless existence.
2. Indolence of mind, indifference to what is calculated to move the feelings, or to excite interest or action.[1]

OXFORD ENGLISH DICTIONARY

Introduction: From Cruelty to Apathy

Troubling or alien actions accompanied, often, by violent repercussions sit at the heart of Yorgos Lanthimos's films. His cinema has been discussed in a range of different ways, with "weird,"[2] "absurd,"[3] and "extreme"[4] being chief among the most frequently employed terms. In my reading of it, Lanthimos's cinema is distinctly apathetic; his style employs affective distance that amplifies a sequence's horror, developing a form of address that engages the viewer to take up the role of an active spectator who thinks about the ethical dimensions of what they are seeing. Paying close attention to three films by Yorgos Lanthimos—*Dogtooth*, *The Lobster* and *The*

Killing of a Sacred Deer—this chapter will explore how Lanthimos's films construct a Cinema of Apathy in which the viewer is asked to negotiate (or renegotiate) their relationship to violence onscreen.

In this chapter I will pay considerable attention to the weird style that characterizes Lanthimos's cinema, though of course these elements, often rooted in the writing and performances, are not the only dimensions of what I refer to here as an apathetic mode. Indeed, the apathetic register of Lanthimos's cinema permeates far more than just certain features. From generic hop-scotching to the construction of the *mise-en-scène* to a range of cinematographic choices to the selection and implementation of music and so forth, various aspects converge and culminate in an atmosphere of dislocation and otherness that constitutes Lanthimos's style and the film worlds it produces. This chapter, therefore, does not aim to provide an exhaustive reading of Lanthimos's films that explores each and every pathway apathy uncovers, but rather offer a new framework for considering them that not only invites but encourages further application and scrutiny.

In most cases I would empathize with any reader compelled to roll their eyes at the proposition of yet another chapter that comes bearing the familiar "Cinema of X" template; however, in this case it is fitting, especially given the thematic and stylistic cross-pollination that occurs between Lanthimos's films.[5] Apathy, per the definition above, describes a form of dislocation that manifests as indifference to suffering. It is my position that Lanthimos's films draw on apathy specifically as a means of activating critical engagement on the part of the viewer.

The simple fact is Lanthimos's cinema is demanding; it employs extreme imagery and disorienting affects that dissociate the spectator, thus forcing them to scrutinize the text for meanings that are abstruse, uncomfortable, or withheld entirely. Films that foster a need to scrutinize necessitate ethical film-watching for the fact that they discourage passivity on the viewer's part. The ethical dimension of challenging films features in Catherine Wheatley's work on the cinema of Michael Haneke, an equally demanding filmmaker:

> the object of a morally consequent film must be to work through the specific forms of spectatorial address which are functions of the binding of narrative and space, in a manner that disturbs and ultimately cannot be contained. This is precisely what Haneke's films do, prompting us to assume a position of moral spectatorship, in which we are able to consider the content of his films and the cinematic situation (and the relationship of the two) in accordance with our existing moral principles. More than just a narrative schema, Haneke's works comprise a certain conjunction of elements, diegetic and non-diegetic, which contribute to their overall moral effects. His cinema is not didactic, but it is educational, for it asks the spectator questions

and places them in a position whereby they are able to make up their own mind about the possible answers.⁶

For Wheatley, it is precisely due to the indeterminacy of meaning that an educational dimension to Haneke's films comes through. Without losing sight of the stylistic discrepancies between these two bodies of work, one might suggest that the same is true of Lanthimos's films—indeed, Wheatley's description of Haneke could fit both directors, subject to qualification. I would posit that Haneke's films are more concretely thesis-driven than Lanthimos's—see, for example, *Hidden* (*Caché*, 2005), *The White Ribbon* (*Das weiße Band*, 2009), or *Amour* (2012), all of which appear to mount a tangible argument on each of their subjects. Lanthimos's films, on the other hand, are more willfully abstruse, with their dispassionate, apathetic style facilitating a contract to rationalize, fostering spaces of contemplation in which to engage his weird, affectless worlds.

In Lanthimos's films, intellectual engagement is cultivated in their form. By way of the apathetic mode, Lanthimos's films extinguish reasonable grounds for character identification, a formal tactic that triggers the spectator to reconsider the moral dimensions of identification itself, especially where it relates to structural violence. Lanthimos's films do not shy from the notion that the world is a cruel place made up of cruel people and utilize disorienting forms to compound their theses, with the attendant suggestion that ignorance breeds complicitness. In all his films, but especially those under consideration here, Lanthimos adopts a style that withholds or inverts logical forms of affect: emotions are unclear, desires unformulated, and so forth. The result is that the viewer is compelled to activate their own rationalizing subjectivity; in doing so, I argue, they confront their relationship to visible forms of violence and oppression in the films, and in general.

Linking spectatorial distance to ethical film-watching has theoretical antecedents in the works of Bertolt Brecht by way of Jacques Rancière. Brecht's *Verfremdungseffekt*—otherwise known as the distancing or alienation effect—describes a variation of Russian formalist Viktor Shklovsky's "estrangement theory" and is characterized by the very sort of apathetic style that I am interested in here, albeit to different ends. Brecht writes that "the alienation effect intervenes, not in the form of absence of emotion, but in the form of emotions which need not correspond to those of the character portrayed."⁷ If Brecht explains the style of Lanthimos, then Rancière expounds the effect. Leaping quickly from Brecht to Rancière, then, spectatorial emancipation comes when agency is conferred back onto the spectator. Rancière writes of "emancipation as re-appropriation of a relationship to self lost in the process of separation."⁸ Emancipation, therefore, is the result of the spectator returning agency to the self, who then acts as an intellectually able (and, crucially, active) participant in the production of meaning: "Being a spectator is not some passive condition that we should transform into activity. It is our normal situation. We also learn and teach, act and know, as spectators who all the time link what we see to what we have seen and said, done and dreamed."[9] By synthesizing these two principles from Brecht and Rancière, it becomes evident how the style of a work might foster a certain form of engagement with it. If one accepts the premise that many works of popular film consciously or otherwise rely on a separation between film watching and the activities of ethical spectatorship—how else might one accept a character such as Batman as a hero?—one can see how filmmakers have their work cut out to disrupt passivity with the aim to effect critical, and therefore ethical, forms of engagement with their work.

Passive acceptance of a film's moral formulation is the basis of what has been referred to as the Cinema of Cruelty, William Blum's term adapted from Antonin Artaud's "Theater" of the same.[10] Key to Artaud's theoretical model is the twinned premise that human beings are all capable of cruelty, and not just the worst of them, and that Cruel works present a "mirror image of what they [the audience] are."[11] Taking up Artaud's notion, Blum explored a group of films as works of Cruelty, including *The Wild Bunch* (Sam Peckinpah, 1969), whose impact, he argued, is embroiled in an aim to make viewers understand the place of violence in the world:

> To watch *The Wild Bunch* demands much more than an open, objective mind. It requires a difficult confession, and a vast amount of courage. Submitting to the experience of a work of Cruelty acknowledges, and such a work insists, that you are not your own man, that forces exist inside you beyond your control, forces that can make you tear out a man's throat or burn his children.[12]

If the Cinema of Cruelty asks a film's viewer to accept the place of violence on certain conditions—to, as Blum puts it, "interpret the intolerable in acceptable terms"[13]—then it does so by constructing an ethical realm in which those terms function as law. If the order of law in Cruel films is an eye for an eye (or worse), then the viewer is asked to adopt that law and feel satisfied when justice is met, regardless of the means of its delivery.[14] If the film asks its viewer to go further than practiced morality will regularly permit, it is doing so on rational (if internally constructed) terms that are consistent with prevailing cultural ideas about justice and its mode of delivery.

William Brown has considered how other types of expressively Cruel films work to more explicit ends, a process that for Brown specifically invites ethical engagement on the spectator's part. Brown writes that such films ask their audience to acknowledge "that we all have the capacity for monstrous behavior and that monsters are all too human, as opposed to being inhuman or supernatural. This is difficult because it asks us to view ourselves as potentially very bad, violent people."[15] For Brown, analyzing several more recent Cruel films including *The Great Ecstasy of Robert Carmichael* (Thomas Clay, 2005), revulsion is the thing that prompts ethical involvement, forcing the viewer to confront the very bad thing and ask if they would allow themselves to give in to the instincts that led the characters there. I would contend that whether a film asks its viewer to accept violence as a necessary course—in the way that a Batman film does (pick one, any will do)—or to reject it wholesale, as in the case of *The Great Ecstasy of Robert Carmichael*, most works tend to present violence in at least relatively straightforward terms as either necessary (and therefore "good") or intolerable (and therefore "bad").

Violence in Lanthimos's films is not so straightforward; in their complex formations of power and oppression, his films ask that more ethical work is done on the part of the viewer. If Lanthimos's films appear to be cruel also, then it is specifically for their ambiguity concerning violence that I differentiate the Cinema of Apathy from the Cinema of Cruelty that precedes it. In apathetic films, dissociation from actions leads to active ethical spectatorship, as illustrated in *The Killing of a Sacred Deer*, for example, where Steven and Anna circumvent a moral duty to protect their children. While both forms might appear to be violently consequent, it is precisely when narrative cruelty is made inexplicable that the apparatus of ethical spectatorship kicks in. Ethical spectatorship can take many forms; in Wheatley's aforementioned work on Haneke's films, she makes the case that "the sadism depicted in his films, and exhibited to the audience, serves a pedagogical function, for the intention of his work is to place spectators in a position whereby they can lucidly assess the content of the film."[16] I have chosen to call this mode the Cinema of Apathy to address both the style and effect of Lanthimos's films, where alien atlases of emotion establish affective ambiguity in such a way as to promote sustained critical engagement, per Rancière's concept of the "emancipated spectator."

Stanley Cavell has come close to describing something similar to the Cinema of Apathy in his analysis of a key scene in *Cries and Whispers* (*Viskningar och rop*, Ingmar Bergman, 1972) in which Karin (Ingrid Thulin) mutilates her own vagina. Cavell struggles to make sense of the intention of the scene and asks: "Are we to be disgusted by this? Is she? Is her husband meant to be?" before uncertainly concluding that the character "is perhaps doing this as a sign of remorse and surely as an expression of rage, of revenge."[17] I contend that such uncertainty marks the difference between a cruel and an apathetic sequence and places Bergman alongside Haneke and Lanthimos as a filmmaker employing violence to incite critical, and therefore ethical, film watching, or for pedagogical means following Wheatley. The Cinema of Apathy likewise registers in the style of Lanthimos's films; it is a mode that finds characters deviating from natural forms of affect to such an extent that the spectator is forced to mediate the repercussions of the characters' actions on their own terms, therefore inviting ethical engagement firstly with the films and then with the forms of violence reflected in them.

In an essay on variation, distance, and violence in *Dogtooth*, Eugenie Brinkema places great emphasis on the trigonometric symbol *sine* which features both on the film's marketing posters and again, epigraphically, at the very beginning of the film. Brinkema writes,

> [w]hat a sine wave is is a formalized map of variation; it describes oscillation and displays repetitive deviation ... Lanthimos's entire film could be redescribed as a pure form of this graph of relation and variation, the formalizing of oscillation and repetitive deviation: the putting on display of *variation* in language, *variation* in framing, and *variation* in violence.[18]

For Brinkema, the *sine* symbol provides a simple yet powerful cue for Lanthimos's tendency to utilize form in ways that complement, and even expand upon, his thematic preoccupations. Chief among Brinkema's observations is a disavowal of the critical tendency to base readings of *Dogtooth* on the act of translation. Indeed, the temptation to translate aspects of Lanthimos's films is not limited to the language of *Dogtooth*,[19] but can equally be applied to the placelessness of *The Lobster* and the allegorical dislocation of *The Killing of a Sacred Deer*. In my reading of his films, speculation over the allusive properties of Lanthimos's films—represented by the urge to find direct translations—is less important overall than understanding the ways in which they facilitate a specific form of spectatorship. That is not to say that Lanthimos's films do not work allegorically—they almost certainly do—but that their form is at least as interesting as their function. As formally disparate islands of uncanny affect, Lanthimos's films shake the spectator into asking profound questions of human nature and its ongoing tendency toward barbarism. His films use strange circumstances and random acts of violence to prompt the spectator to reflect on how the medium works on their senses and their sense of moral certainty, in turn compelling them to think critically about authority and its applications, as well as their own subjectivity and, accordingly, nature. I will consider aspects of a group of Lanthimos's films to evidence this mode of address.

Adopting Trauma in the Absence of Affect in *Dogtooth*

For all of *Dogtooth*'s disturbing, eruptive scenes of violence—narratively situated within the Father's (Christos Stergioglou) draconian practices that maintain the home/prison environment in which his adult children are being held captive—a principal way in which the film demonstrates affective discontinuity is in its treatment of the sexual activity taking place between the three siblings. The sex in *Dogtooth* exhibits a "real," unsimulated element to compound the feelings of revulsion that scenes of forced incest are clearly intended to elicit. On close inspection, while there are clear instances of unsimulated sexual touching in several sequences—including during a shared bath in which Son (Hristos Passalis) chooses which of his sisters (Elder Daughter [Angeliki Papoulia] or Younger Daughter [Mary Tsoni]) will be his sexual mate—other sequences are shrouded in just enough mystery to suggest that the sex may or may not be "real" (one might call it Schrödinger's sex act). The choosing ceremony in the bathtub is followed by an equally weird, and pointedly apathetic, sequence in which Mother (Michele Valley) garishly applies make-up to Elder Daughter in preparation for sex with her brother. The scene cuts to Son's bedroom where the siblings sit side-by-side on his single bed; apathetic as automatons, neither of their expressions convey any feelings toward what is to follow. The sex begins with Elder Daughter masturbating Son to erection before he repositions their bodies to initiate intercourse, which is initially framed at a tight low angle where the viewer's proximity to close thrusting makes the likelihood of actual penetration ever more plausible.

Until this point, apathy has been the sole mode of communication; it is only after the sex has ended that either one of them exhibits some form of an emotional response. The siblings lie side by side in a canted shot that is overwhelmed with oppressive negative space, an image that formally conveys the distorted world in which they exist. Unequipped with the necessary language to explain her feelings toward what has happened, Elder Daughter scorns Son with a violent threat that feels as if it has been taken directly from one of the video tapes she secretly acquired: "Do that again, bitch, and I'll rip your guts out. I swear on my daughter's life you and your clan won't last long in this neighborhood."

Beside augmenting the horror of the forced incest, the "realness" of the siblings' sex—either in fact or mere appearance—contrasts significantly with the artificiality of Elder Daughter's film-like response. In some ways, the "realness" of it all, formally speaking, presents a double bluff on the filmmaker's part, reinforcing the fact that notions of unsimulated contact and actual "realness" remain at odds with each other, bound up in the context of a performance that naturally departs from whatever "real" intimacy is conceptually thought to be. The real/false binary that the scene stages not only reinforces a discontinuity in the characters' emotional register—another case of the erasure of plausible affect—but simultaneously disrupts the viewer's understanding of the "real," of authenticity as it is used to describe a performance and its effect.

By this point in the film the three siblings have already exchanged sexual favors for various personal items of varying significance, though this encounter registers differently for Elder Daughter. She is clearly traumatized by the sexual intercourse with her sibling that has been imposed on her by her parents, a matter confirmed by her violent threat toward her brother, even if it comes across as uncannily theatrical and disembodied. Her coldly delivered rebuttal is strange on the ear—impassioned yet completely impersonal— made even more discordant by its staginess. Since it has been constructed out of pieces of speech heard in films, Elder Daughter's overtly stylized threat only partially belongs to her. Elder Daughter's inability to appropriately communicate her trauma illustrates how apathy and affective dislocation operate within Lanthimos's film worlds to profound effect. Her threat is demonstrative of an inhibitive lack of language wherein she is unable to transmit feelings from a void of affect that has formed in her, thrust upon her by parents who modify word meanings to prolong their children's captivity. Indeed, vehicles for escape are systematically repressed; airplanes are taught to be the size of toy models while the word telephone is explained to mean salt. In keeping with Lanthimos's tenacity to stretch metaphors to absurd and then extreme lengths—consider (as David Foster Wallace did[20]) *The Lobster*— Father's methods to establish the cognitive dissonance that maintains his children's imprisonment demonstrates, *in extremis*, the dangerous effects of ideological indoctrination. Beginning with the corruption of her vocabulary, Elder Daughter is systematically denied the tools to form autonomy over her subjectivity. The sex sequence acts as a narrative catalyst for Elder Daughter's desire to escape while compounding the film's central thesis on fascism as a corrupting influence on free will, with the implication that fascism does not always present as such to those living under it.

Elder Daughter's threat toward her brother, disembodied as it is, is in keeping with her experiences within her home environment. In the context of the home/prison complex in which she and her siblings exist, her impulse to threaten violence is consistent with her experiences at the hands of Father, who employs violence as punishment, such as in the scene in which he beats her with the video tapes she has acquired in secret. The film's message that fascism enacted under the law of the Father (or state) forces its citizens to act against their nature becomes transparent in Elder Daughter's volatile behavior and desire to escape. Without the tools to protect herself, Elder Daughter decides to leave the home/prison, but the law of the Father, which states that first she must lose her "dogtooth," still has authority over her. She enters the bathroom, where she smashes her face with a dumbbell until her "dogtooth" comes loose. When the act is finally over, Elder Daughter smiles manically into the blood-smeared bathroom mirror. Recalling Cavell's response to the self-mutilation in *Cries and Whispers*, it is not entirely clear how one is supposed to react to this violent act of self-harm, yet the affective dislocation expressed in Elder Daughter's deranged smile forces the viewer to confront the extent of her lot and contemplate the lengths to which she is willing to go to free herself from tyranny. Her apathy toward the act of self-mutilation forces the viewer to adopt trauma in the absence of affect, made all the more consequential for the extent to which Elder Daughter remains bound to Father's law, even in the act of her possible, but by no means guaranteed, escape.

Performing Apathy in *The Lobster*

While the groundwork for a budding style is notably evident in his earlier work, I contend that it is in Lanthimos's English-language debut *The Lobster* that his apathetic style most evidently infiltrates all aspects of the *mise-en-scène*. *The Lobster*'s vision of a society in retrograde operates at the edge of recognizable experience, opaquely intimating—as in *Dogtooth*—the dangers of authoritarian political schemas. The film presents a near-sighted, absurdist portrait of competing forms of fascism, with each sect having their own unique taste for heteronormative programming. The authoritarian *modus operandi* of each group manifests in systems of control over intimate relationships. Moreover, coinciding with the fascism analogy, the film's coincidence with changes in modern dating, in which apps provide algorithmic solutions for romantic and sexual encounters, offers multivalent metaphoric pathways to be traversed by readers. When linked to sex and relationships, authoritarian politics often constitute what Michel Foucault has described as a "procedure of power," which promotes regressive paradigms in order to naturalize and ensure ideological conservatism, thus protecting the power of oppressors under the guise of nostalgia for a backward status quo.[21] And if that sounds equally like the description of a Lanthimos film and of the state of a nation on the precipice of a fall back toward conservative ideology, then that should go some way toward explaining the power of his allegorical devices. Ultimately, the fascist behaviors of the opposing, if effectively mirrored, authoritarian parties that each demand compliance to their specific system of control convey, in the absence of an alternative, a failed future or state of terminus for the political systems they engender.

The world of *The Lobster*, then, represents only a partially estranged reality, one that conveys various sources of anxiety in its guarded allusions to real-world correspondents. This thematic estrangement is matched by the formal variation offered in the style of the actors' performances. Indeed, affective discontinuity pervades the film's fabric, evident not only in *The Lobster*'s dystopian atmosphere and setting—a reflection of a locked system of political dogmatism that typifies neoliberal conservatism—but also in virtually every interaction that takes place between the central characters. The apathetic mode as a style and form of address is rooted in conceptual breaks from routine affective techniques. For Murray Smith, "recognition in film is normally dependent upon exterior, perceptible traits—the body, the face, and the voice."[22] By any metric, the affectless world-building that constitutes Lanthimos's formalism offsets recognition to such an extent, per the aforementioned Brechtian notions of the *Verfremdungseffekt*, that it dislodges the viewer's perceptive faculties to create a new form of engagement, as in the case of *Dogtooth* which entices spectatorial dislocation *in extremis*. By unseating the viewer from classical spectatorial paradigms, Lanthimos's style uses apathy against them, forcing the viewer to forensically examine their role as spectators of oppression, per Rancière by way of Artaud. Michele Aaron has written on "spectatorial agency as a marker of socio-political responsibility," constructing it as an "understanding reached between the spectator and culture."[23] As aforementioned, *The Lobster*'s interpolation of wider cultural points of reference is markedly abstruse, and presents a knot of allegorical pathways that evade clear correspondents in the world. Naturally, these pathways have already enticed a number of critical readings, including several more that feature elsewhere in this book. Rather than trace the allegories, I am primarily interested in the ways in which Lanthimos's apathetic style reinforces a specific form of spectatorship.

Indeed, affective discontinuity abounds in *The Lobster*, though as a sensation it emerges in the text in a variety of different forms. Beyond the generally dissociated style of performances in the film, there are moments where Lanthimos is clearly trying to comment on apathy as a form of social engagement. Take, for instance, the sequence in which David (Colin Farrell) attempts to seduce Heartless Woman (Angeliki Papoulia). Having previously shown affection toward David, Biscuit Woman (Ashley Jensen) has since spiraled into a depression and attempts suicide by leaping from an upstairs window of the match-making hotel. As Biscuit Woman lies screaming in agony, David sees it as an opportunity to win over Heartless Woman with performed heartlessness. After modifying his expression to feign apathy, the following interaction takes place between the two of them:

DAVID: What happened?
HEARTLESS WOMAN: She jumped from the balcony of Room 180.
DAVID: I hope she dies right away. On second thought, I hope she suffers quite a bit before she dies. I just hope her pathetic screams can't be heard from my room because I'm thinking about having a lie down and I need peace and quiet. I was playing golf and I'm quite tired and the last thing I need is a woman dying slowly and loudly.
HEARTLESS WOMAN: I can't hear you with all this screaming. We'll talk some other time when it's quieter. Bye.

It is interesting that in this sequence David has incrementally (though consciously) adjusted his behavior to appeal more to Heartless Woman's eponymous trait. His display of heartlessness is awkwardly theatrical ("the last thing I need is a woman dying slowly and loudly"), though not entirely removed from his generally detached demeanor. If most—if not all—of the interactions in *The Lobster* are notably cold and stilted, this sequence reflexively brings the film's apathetic register plainly into view. *The Lobster* is a film that could be about a great many things, including how performative gestures have been adopted and co-opted as a tactic for self-preservation. While the placelessness of *The Lobster* already contributes toward an affective dislocation that facilitates epistemological lines of inquiry, the conscious adoption of apathy in an already apathetic world explicates some aspects of the film's wider social commentary. Angelos Koutsourakis, in his analysis of *Dogtooth*, for instance, writes that "the actors' bodies are not simply the carriers of dramatic *agon*, but the medium through which the filmmaker captivates the most ordinary aspects of human behaviour, so as to dissect them and analyse them."[24] This logic is similarly evident in *The Lobster*, where affective distance in the performers, who participate in the construction of an atmosphere of apathy, functions as the prism (or medium) through which to reconcile its exegesis.

There are readings to be made of Heartless Woman as a facsimile for a certain type of blankness that constitutes modern interpersonal relations, but the question remains, what exactly makes her an attractive prospect to an introvert such as David? It is not as though he is lacking safer options. Indeed, in a previous encounter, Biscuit Woman promises David a reverie of sexual favors in exchange for intimacy: "Can I come to your room sometime for a chat? I could give you a blow job or you could fuck me. I always swallow after fellatio and I have absolutely no problem with anal sex, if that's your thing." It is another instance in which the timbre of the writing is matched by the glacial emotional resonance proffered by the performers. Whether or not anal sex is for David is beside the point, yet in a universe in which intimacy is negotiated via economies of exchange—from the overbearing social dogmas that demand matched characteristics as evidence of romantic compatibility, to Biscuit Woman's offer of sex acts for companionship and, therefore, survival—it seems unusual that David chooses to hedge his bets with a match as potentially volatile as Heartless Woman. Such is the value of ruthlessness in the world of *The Lobster* and the actual world that serves as the source of its symbolic currency. David's performance explicates an understanding of the environment in which he has found himself, wherein Heartless Woman and, therefore, heartlessness itself as a state of being offers a logical means of protection and, therefore, survival in a world that is institutionally fascist and fundamentally cruel.

David's deception comes to light after he displays empathy following the death of his brother/dog Bob, who has been kicked to death in the corridor by Heartless Woman. As in *Dogtooth*, *The Lobster* demonstrates apathy as a formal system designed to provoke the viewer into interrogating devolutions in human conduct. Koutsourakis writes that "Lanthimos's emphasis on the body—reinforced by the blockage of linguistic communication—draws the audience's attention to the fact that what passes as 'real' cannot be understood outside socially constructed representational systems."[25] Both films convey the stickiness of living under dominant hegemonic logic that represses the tools—that is, language, for Koutsourakis—to take back freedom. There is a distinction to be made between not wanting to see and being unable to, though David's relationship to sources of governance remains complicated; even if he, unlike the children in *Dogtooth*, is aware of his fascist environment, he nevertheless remains at the mercy of the ideology expounded by its caretakers. After ridding himself of their direct control he finds himself bound by instinct to continue to serve the established rules of law. Outside the law of the hotel, David is quickly inculcated in a new system of control that has a zero-tolerance policy on any form of intimacy. Yet, by the end of the film, having escaped with Short Sighted Woman (Rachel Weisz), with whom he has finally found a connection, David remains beholden to the need for sameness explicated by both movements he has appeared to overcome, to the extent that he considers blinding himself to match Short Sighted (now Blind) Woman's recent maiming (her punishment for exhibiting intimacy). Of the bleakness, ambiguity, and affective potential of this ending, Sarah Cooper writes, "David chooses sameness and ultimately blindness but by shattering the mirror of the self-image and surrendering narcissism to a realm beyond sight, leaving spectators too with a position from which we cannot see."[26] David's reasoning is unclear but speaks to the depth of his indoctrination within overlapping systems of oppression; nevertheless, and due in part to his apathetic blankness in it, the scene produces strange affective resonances that conspicuously deviate from regular modes of identification that urges the viewer to do work in order to ascertain its meaning(s). Cooper explains Lanthimos's construction of spectatorship in this finale as one that is blocked to form "a position from which we cannot see." David is both free and not; even after his emancipation he remains bound to laws that continue to render him docile to discipline. In the ambivalent and affectless scene that ends *The Lobster*, Lanthimos demonstrates that apathetic invocations of violence produce a spectatorial paradigm designed to engage the viewer to labor for meaning, producing an ethically consequent system in which violence is not allowed to exist without scrutiny.

Paternal Horror in *The Killing of a Sacred Deer*

Tarja Laine, in the introduction to her 2011 book *Feeling Cinema: Emotional Dynamics in Films Studies*, writes that "we [the viewers] are *part* of cinema in its emotional eventfulness ... cinematic emotions [are] processes that are intentional in a phenomenological sense, supporting the continuous, and dynamic exchange between the film's world and the spectator's world."[27] Her interest in cinematic emotions is explored in relation to a number of works that either facilitate or offset subjective alignment. Laine concedes that cinematic emotions are potentially erratic things, that "cinema as an emotional event is conditioned not only by its aesthetic system, but also by the spectators' view of the world, their sense of self, their valuation of phenomena such as love that are important for their own well-being, and their willingness to 'accept' the film in general ... same films move different spectators in emotionally distinctive ways."[28] Put differently, Laine identifies the contract that is generated between style and affect, even if the forms of affect shift in line with a viewer's own experiences and values.

Subjective as it ultimately may be, arguably one of the most disruptive forms of emotional apathy coincides with the neglect of children, a theme that bridges Lanthimos's work from *Dogtooth* to *The Killing of a Sacred Deer*. In the latter, Steven Murphy (Colin Farrell), a distinguished but haunted surgeon, has been tasked with choosing which of his two children to forfeit for the death of Martin's (Barry Keoghan) father, for which Martin holds Steven responsible. By this time Steven's wife Anna (Nicole Kidman), having witnessed the supernatural power that Martin has over her children, Kim (Raffey Cassidy) and Bob (Sunny Suljic), is now convinced not only of the fact that Martin can make good on his threat to kill them, but that Steven is also responsible for the crime for which he stands accused. In the next room Kim and Bob are lying in twin hospital beds where they are connected to intravenous support machines, their strength dwindling under Martin's power. In the kitchen, Steven sits eating at the island while Anna looks on from her seat on the counter. As Steven eats his meal, he expresses mundane pleasures and wishes, commending the meat and expressing a desire for mashed potatoes, before Anna finally rebukes him: "Our two children are dying in the other room, but yes, I can make you mashed potatoes tomorrow." Anna's inability to stomach Steven's trivial (and, importantly, selfish) observations in the shadow of her family's impending doom is amplified by a slow zoom that comes to rest on a close-up of Kidman's unblinking expression, her face wracked with the horror of what must follow; the inevitable consequence of a power that at this point must appear to her as nothing short of providential. The challenge that Anna brings against Steven's indifference at last inspires a rare moment of emotional release in him, and he erupts with the following retort:

> So what do you suggest? Tell me. Oh wait, I know. I've got it. There's a way we can put a stop to all of this. All we need to do is find the tooth of a baby crocodile, the blood of a pigeon and the pubes of a virgin. And then we just have to burn them all before sunset. Let me see, do we have

any spare teeth lying around? Teeth, pubes? Nope, none here! Let me see, do we have any here? Pubes? Teeth? Nothing in this box either. Where are they? I'm sure they were here earlier. I put them here myself. Who's been moving things around? Fucking unbelievable! I don't suppose you have any pubes I could have, by any chance? Oh, I forgot, you don't have any left. We don't have any of the things we need.

Steven's weird list of requirements conveys not only frustration, but also an epiphany on the mythic nature of Martin's power.[29] However, Steven's outburst also reveals an apathy toward suffering that characterizes him and, indeed, many other characters that populate the weird storyworlds of Yorgos Lanthimos's films. Steven has finally realized that there is no way to beat the system: he has been presented with a puzzle he cannot solve. His outburst conveys neither guilt nor love, sentiments that one might expect to guide the actions of someone whose children have been threatened. Rather, Steven expresses affective distance, as he has throughout the film, declaring that it is the rules of a system he is helpless against that are to blame for the family's circumstances, an act of self-deception in which he finds that it is easier to invoke divine authority than to confront the reality of his (in) humanity.

In a desperate bid to regain control of his situation, Steven takes Martin as his prisoner in the basement of the family house where he beats him in the vain hope that he might relent on the torment. Knowing by faith if not by evidence that it is impossible to cheat Martin's design on her family, Anna employs a new tactic. After releasing Martin, she heads upstairs to proposition Steven. Anna kisses Steven on the hand before straddling him and removing her nightdress. She lies back, displaying her naked body perpendicularly across the bed, an erotic yet markedly cold invitation for sex, the image itself presenting a facsimile for intimacy, once removed (at least) from its original function in their lives as husband and wife. Steven is unmoved by Anna's strange advances, and promptly turns off the bedside light. Anna does not retreat, but instead moves in closer, where Kidman monotonally delivers Anna's final proposition: "I believe the most logical thing, no matter how harsh this may sound, is to kill a child. Because we can have another child. I still can and you can. And if you can't, we can try IVF, but I'm sure we can." Whether or not Anna is just using her sexuality as a ploy for her protection, or if she has a different agenda, remains unclear; what is clear, however, is that time is running out for them all and that she must make a case for her survival. The children have each already appealed to Steven for their lives, despite knowing that the price will be their sibling's death. Yet, Anna's claim is by far the most cunning: faced with the realization that Steven holds all the cards (and that she cannot trust how he will play them), Anna presents her reproductive faculties as a dowry for her life.

Though *The Killing of a Sacred Deer* cannot be straightforwardly understood as a horror film, at least not in the traditional sense,[30] Anna's solution threatens to place her on a long list of monstrous mothers on film for her contravention of one of the most customary emotional contracts, the universality of love for one's children.[31] If by this point of the film Steven's failures (both as a father and more generally as a human being) is taken as given, then Anna's inability to sacrifice her own life for the lives of her children provides a new source of horror, and one that will no doubt translate for some viewers as tantamount to infanticide, even in spite of the hellish circumstances in which the desperate mother has found herself. For Steve Jones, films that employ this theme "give voice to deep-seated fears about 'the worst that could happen'; since parenthood entails being responsible for a child's life, infanticide is the ultimate negation of the guardian role."[32] The natural horror elicited in Anna's openness to infanticide, even as it is presented here as a last resort, follows Steven's outburst to offer yet another case of affective discontinuity; all in all, Anna's argument demonstrates Lanthimos's utilization of apathetic strangeness as a stylistic strategy. By distorting or removing logical or relatable forms of affect—emotion, desire, disposition—from the characters' psychic registers, the audience is forced to fill in the (quite literal) blankness that forms in them; in doing so, I argue, his audience is forced to confront their relationship to violence and its figuration onscreen. Following Laine's view of films as emotional events that encourage viewers to accept or not accept their systems of affect, *The Killing of a Sacred Deer* goes to lengths to upset the viewer with scenes of paternal horror, coldly demonstrating that for some there is no such thing as going too far in aid of self-preservation.

Conclusion: The Form(s) of Apathy

The Killing of a Sacred Deer once again demonstrates a tendency in Lanthimos's cinema to create atmospheres of affective ambivalence. At the film's end, having killed Bob in a blindfolded shootout, Steven and his remaining family take an evening meal at a local diner. Accompanied by the dramatic build-up of "*Passio secundum Joannem*" (Johann Sebastian Bach, 1724), the shot transitions from Bob's dead body slumped on the sofa to a slow-motion long shot of Martin entering the diner. Anna's eyes flicker in Martin's direction as he passes the family's table, though Steven does not let on that he has seen Martin until he has already passed. The shot cuts to Kim watching Martin. Martin returns her gaze as she drowns her french fries in tomato ketchup (a favorite food of Martin's). The camera approaches slowly in corresponding shots marked by eye-line match cuts to establish further the perverse connection maintained between Kim and her family's foil. Clearly uncomfortable with Martin's presence, Anna initiates that they leave the diner; as they do, Anna glances at him nervously while Steven refuses to look at all, potentially conveying his shame. Kim, however, looks back and offers Martin the slightest of smiles and the film ends on a shot of Martin looking on as he slurps on the straw in his water cup.

By the end of the film Lanthimos has arguably already achieved a near-constant atmosphere of ambiguity, punctuated by formal invention in tandem with disorienting uses of baroque music. In the final scene, the filmmaker exhibits no intention to relent on his weird style. After *Dogtooth* and *The Lobster*, this sequence once again fails to offer a clear form of identification or navigation for the viewer. Where does the family go from here? What does Kim's smile mean? Is Martin human, supernatural, or a god? Returning one last time to Wheatley's work on Haneke, she writes, "[r]ather than eschew what we might call 'Hollywood technique' entirely, Haneke's films enter into dialogue with and draw upon existing narrative forms and genre conventions in order to generate a new spectatorial experience which focuses on the spectator's ethical position in relation to the film."[33] Meanwhile, Brinkema, in a piece of writing that dazzlingly brings the work of Emmanuel Levinas to the cult horror film *The Human Centipede* (Tom Six, 2009), considers the affective consequences of watching extreme acts of violence:

> In routing its violence through the representational form of the diagram, *The Human Centipede* gives form to the suffering need to escape and structural inability to escape in the more radical sense by which Levinas theorizes it—the brutality of being's rivetedness to itself. The film attests to the extremest formality of the violence of this suffering. Violence is not in the sewing and stitching of the thing; violence is in the non-modifiable givenness of the diagrammatic attestation, the notational impossibility of any pure getting out.[34]

On the surface, one might question to what extent Six's "torture porn"[35] horror film has much in common with an art-house film like *The Killing of a Sacred Deer*, but it warrants comparison for the shared establishment of a particular affective form. It is interesting how horror, or at least films that provoke the viewer with violence and disquieting forms of affect, manifests as one of the more effective vehicles for the discussion of the ethical dimensions of spectatorship. Extrapolating Wheatley's evidence of an ethical dimension to unpleasant films that seek to engage the viewer, as well as Brinkema's notion that film formalizes violence into patterns of representation, it is clear that even in Lanthimos's more generically hybridized, if no less horrifying, cinema the employment of apathetic characters mobilizes similar affective forces, informing the viewer that they have work to do, and that although they might not always understand the experiences of others (or the Other), those individuals are nevertheless subject to violent forces beyond their control. An affective gambit such as this works to destabilize any grounds for willful ignorance on the viewer's part by displacing emotional understanding (achieved by recognition) with violent affect. In essence, Lanthimos's films evade the muddy matter of cause by violently concretizing effect in a way that shocks the viewer into confronting the ethical pitfall of accepting without scrutiny the role of a bystander to oppression.

Notes

1 "Apathy," *OED* (Oxford: Oxford University Press, 2021), available at www.oed.com/view/Entry/9052.
2 See Vangelis Calotychos, Lydia Papadimitriou, and Yannis Tzioumakis, "Revisiting Contemporary Greek Film Cultures: Weird Wave and Beyond," *Journal of Greek Media and Culture*, 2, no. 2 (2016): 127–31; Eleni Varmazi, "The Weirdness of Contemporary Greek Cinema," *Film International*, 87 (2019): 40–49.
3 See Nepomuk Zettl's chapter in this book. In relation to the present topic, pay close attention to Zettl's exploration of what he refers to as "uneasy proximity" to describe the familial dynamics at work in *Dogtooth* and *The Killing of a Sacred Deer*.
4 See James Quandt, "More Moralism from that 'Wordy Fuck,'" in T. Horeck and T. Kendall, eds., *The New Extremism in Cinema: From France to Europe* (Edinburgh: Edinburgh University Press, 2011), 209–13.
5 Indeed, aesthetic unity is a theme that propels many of the chapters in this book.
6 Catherine Wheatley, *Michael Haneke's Cinema: The Ethic of the Image* (New York and Oxford: Berghahn Books, 2009), 45–46.
7 Bertolt Brecht, "Alienation Effects in Chinese Acting" in J. Willett, ed., *Brecht on Theatre: The Development of an Aesthetic* (London: Eyre Methuen, [1936] 1964), 91–99, at p. 94.
8 Jacques Rancière, *The Emancipated Spectator* (London and New York: Verso, 2009), 15.
9 Ibid., 17.
10 See Antonin Artaud, "The Theater of Cruelty (First Manifesto)," in S. Sontag, ed., *Antonin Artaud: Selected Writings* (New York: Farrar, Straus & Giroux, 1976), 242–51.
11 Antonin Artaud, "An End to Masterpieces," in S. Sontag, ed., *Antonin Artaud: Selected Writings* (New York: Farrar, Straus & Giroux, 1976), 253–59, at p. 254.
12 William Blum, "Toward a Cinema of Cruelty," *Cinema Journal*, 10, no. 2 (1971): 19–33, at p. 33.
13 Ibid.

14 Consider, e.g., the case of Batman's heroism. Or, to offer another example from straight genre cinema, consider how in the first *Taken* film (Pierre Morel, 2008) the viewer is asked to accept Bryan Mills's (Liam Neeson) methods to retrieve his kidnapped daughter (Maggie Grace) *by any means necessary*. *Taken*, a variation on the rape–revenge genre made popular in the 1970s and 1980s, presents extreme violence as both a necessary and appropriate means of enacting justice. In my reading of it, the film operates as a work of Cruelty for its presentation of justice as just, no matter the means of procuring it. It is a tendency of such films to frame *by any means necessary* as a heroic rite (and right), a trope that cruelly asks the viewer to erase whatever moral fortitude they might bring to the film.

15 William Brown, "Violence in Extreme Cinema and the Ethics of Spectatorship," *Projections*, 7, no. 1 (2015): 25–42, at p. 39.

16 Wheatley, *Michael Haneke's Cinema*, 189.

17 Stanley Cavell, "On Makavejev on Bergman," in W. Rothman, ed., *Cavell on Film* (New York: SUNY Press, 2005), 11–40, at p. 35.

18 Eugenie Brinkema, "e.g., *Dogtooth*," *World Picture*, 7, 2012, available at worldpicturejournal.com/WP_7/Brinkema.html.

19 I should like to point out by way of aside that I do not mean to suggest that there is such a thing as a correct or an incorrect reading of this, or indeed any, film; rather, my observation, following Brinkema, is that scholarship on *Dogtooth* has reached critical mass on this particular aspect. See Philip Brophy, "The Prisonhouse of Language," *Film Comment*, 46, no. 2 (2010): 16; Dionysios Kapsaskis, "Translation as a Critical Tool in Film Analysis: Watching Yorgos Lanthimos's *Dogtooth* through a Translational Prism," *Translation Studies*, 10, no. 3 (2017): 247–62.

20 See David Foster Wallace, "Consider the Lobster," in D. Foster Wallace, ed., *Consider the Lobster and Other Essays* (New York and Boston, MA: Little, Brown & Company, 2006), 235–54.

21 Michel Foucault, *The History of Sexuality 1: The Will to Knowledge* (London: Penguin Books, [1979] 1998), 47.

22 Murray Smith, *Engaging Characters* (Oxford: Oxford University Press, 1995), 114.

23 Michele Aaron, *Spectatorship: The Power of Looking On* (London: Wallflower Press, 2007), 88.

24 Angelos Koutsourakis, "Cinema of the Body: The Politics of Performativity in Lars von Trier's *Dogville* and Yorgos Lanthimos's *Dogtooth*," *Cinema: Journal of Philosophy and the Moving Image*, 3 (2012): 84–108, at p. 96.

25 Ibid., 103.

26 Sarah Cooper, "Narcissus and *The Lobster*," *Studies in European Cinema*, 13, no. 2 (2016): 163–76, at p. 173.

27 Tarja Laine, *Feeling Cinema: Emotional Dynamics in Film Studies* (New York: Bloomsbury, 2011), 1–2. Emphasis in the original.

28 Ibid., 6.

29 For a chapter-length discussion on the antique heritage of *The Killing of a Sacred Deer*, see James Clauss's chapter in this book.

30 I have explored elsewhere the generically dislocated style of recent "art-horror" films: see Eddie Falvey, "'Art-Horror' and 'Hardcore Art-Horror' at the Margins: Experimentation and Extremity in Contemporary Independent Horror," *Horror Studies*, 12, no. 1 (2021): 63–81. While *The Killing of a Sacred Deer* would need additional qualification as a horror film, I believe that it might be possible to do so under the terms that I set out in that article. As evidence of what can be gleaned by recasting a nonhorror film as horror, see Charlene Regester, "Monstrous Mother, Incestuous Father, and Terrorized Teen: Reading *Precious* as a Horror Film," *Journal of Film and Video*, 67, no. 1 (2015): 30–45.

31 Other recent films that fall into this category include *The Babadook* (Jennifer Kent, 2014) and *Hereditary* (Ari Aster, 2018). For scholarship on this topic, see Barbara Creed, *The Monstrous-Feminine: Film, Feminism, Psychoanalysis* (London and New York: Routledge, 1993).

32 Steve Jones, "Torture Born: Representing Pregnancy and Abortion in Contemporary Survival-Horror," *Sexuality and Culture*, 19 (2015): 426–43, at p. 432.

33 Wheatley, *Michael Haneke's Cinema*, 87–88.

34 Eugenie Brinkema, "Violence and the Diagram: or, *The Human Centipede*," *Qui Parle*, 24, no. 2 (2016): 75–108, at p. 90.

35 See Steve Jones, *Torture Porn: Horror Cinema after Saw* (Basingstoke: Palgrave Macmillan, 2013).

PART III

Form and Authorship

7

Kafkaesque Themes in *The Lobster*

Angelos Koutsourakis

Introduction: Kafka and Animality

In a 2018 interview with Jonathan Romney, Yorgos Lanthimos acknowledged that he used to be a dedicated reader of the work of Franz Kafka.[1] Indeed, Lanthimos's work is indebted to the Bohemian author both formally and thematically. Key Kafkaesque traits in his oeuvre include deadpan humor, a tragic–comic aesthetic, the critique of liberalism and humans' compliance with absurd and repressive authority. But it is in his first English-language film, *The Lobster*, where the Kafkaesque motifs become even more demonstrable. In this chapter, I focus on the Kafkaesque themes in *The Lobster*; I draw analogies between Kafka's interest in animality as a route of escape from human alienation and the motif of metamorphosis in the film. My key argument is that the film follows Kafka's critique of conformity in its caustic satire of the disciplinary forces behind the individual's desire for amorous relationships. I suggest that whereas in the Bohemian author's work animality is seen as a liberating path away from human alienation, the characters in *The Lobster* resist it because they remain vulnerable to the neoliberal narrative of success that values homogeneity and compliance to authority. The fear of animality can therefore be seen as a fear of change, which is indicative of the erasure of political alternatives in the neoliberal present.

Before moving to an analysis of the film, a few comments on Kafka and animality are in order. In many of the author's stories focusing on the thin boundaries between human and nonhuman animals, animality is presented as a condition that allows one to reflect on the social conditions of alienation. This is certainly evident in *The Metamorphosis* (1915), a short story about Gregor Samsa, an alienated worker, being suddenly transformed into an insect and eventually abandoned by his family. When his transformation takes place, he manages to reflect not only on his alienating labor, but also on the patriarchal set-up in his family, where he is supposed to toil to make a living for his parents and his sister. Interestingly, the former take this for granted and their relationship ends up being aloof, as described in this passage:

> They had been good times, which never occurred again, at least not in such glory, even though later Gregor made so much money that he was in a position to take on the expenditure of the whole family—and did so. They just got used to it, the family as much as Gregor; they accepted the money gratefully, he provided it gladly, but there was no longer any particular warmth about it.[2]

Gregor's transformation into an animal brings into sharp focus not only the estranging labor he has to perform, but also the labor hierarchies in his department as evidenced by the visit of the chief clerk who is distressed by the employee's unexpected absence from work. It is the metamorphosis into a nonhuman animal that enables him to contemplate the circumstances he took for granted.

In "The Burrow" (1931), human anxiety is paralleled with the extreme precautions taken by an unnamed animal, which tries to fortify itself in its labyrinthine burrow out of fear of invasion. As Siegfried Kracauer comments, there is an interesting dialectic involved in the story, where it is hard to discern whether the anxiety stems from the architectural complexity of the burrow, which aims to protect the animal, or from the fear of external assault.[3] The animal's thoughts as communicated in the story can be read as broader reflections on twentieth-century anxieties related to the diminished human agency in modernity.[4] Finally, in "The Investigations of a Dog" (1922), the anthropomorphized dog character muses on the individualism that characterizes human beings: "But one thing is too obvious to have escaped me; namely how little inclined they are, compared with us dogs, to stick together, how silently and unfamiliarly and with what a curious hostility they pass each other by, how only the basest of interests can bind them together."[5] In these and other stories with animal characters, Kafka uses animals not to distract our attention from human anxieties, but in order to highlight them.

Scholars have paid heed to the link between animality and human alienation in Kafka. In their seminal study, *Kafka: Toward a Minor Literature*, Gilles Deleuze and Félix Guattari contend that animals play a key role in Kafka's stories even in those that feature no animal characters. For these writers, animality in Kafka points to ways out of the impasses of modernity; they are careful, however, to explain that the escape should not be confused with freedom. It is rather a way of dealing with situations that could not have been imagined by humans. As they write, "We would say that for Kafka, the animal essence is the way out, the line of escape, even if it takes place in place, or in a cage. A line of escape, and not freedom."[6] In other words, the metaphor of animality allows humans to rethink and eventually resist the narrative of Enlightenment progress, which promises human liberation and freedom, but ends up producing more subtle forms of social control and oppression. But importantly—and this is very much relevant in the case of Lanthimos—Deleuze and Guattari draw parallels between animality and bachelorhood in Kafka. Both resist accepted forms of sociality and dominant patterns of social behavior and are somehow perilous because they challenge established forms of social reproduction. As they write, "With no family, no conjugality, the bachelor is all the more social, social-dangerous, social-traitor, a collective in himself."[7] In other words, both the animal and the bachelor in Kafka's world are figures that cannot be fully integrated into the productive world; their nonintegration renders them threatening. Josef K in *The Trial*, who leads a bachelor's life, is accused of something that even his persecutors fail to articulate and ends up being killed "like a dog,"[8] as he says, when facing his executioners. Gregor in *The Metamorphosis* is excluded from the family and even his compassionate sister abandons him when they realize that his parasitic status will not just affect their social standing, but also their economic well-being, since his presence upsets the household lodgers.

Oriented by Deleuze and Guattari's paralleling of the animal with bachelorhood in Kafka, Chris Danta has developed this point further, arguing that the uniqueness of animal characters in Kafka's work is that they are in between, that is, they share both human and animal characteristics. According to Danta, Kafka's stories focusing on animality such as *The Metamorphosis* and "A Report to an Academy" (1917) deploy the motif of metamorphosis so as to perpetuate the characters' bachelorhood. Bachelorhood acts as a metaphor for the exclusion of an individual from the world of the humans. Thus, both animality and bachelorhood point to the estrangement among human beings in modern societies. They are another form of parody of anthropocentrism and rationalistic narratives of human progress. As he writes, "for Kafka, to depict our proximity to other animals is at the same time to figure our alienation from each other."[9] In a way, becoming animal is a negative response to social conditions that call into question the liberal view of the individual as a free agent who has the capacity to rationally respond to the pressures of its social environment and achieve positive change.

The Lobster: Animality and Bachelorhood

Kafka's deployment of animality and bachelorhood as a commentary on human alienation speaks to broader issues related to the disbelief in liberal democracy and economic liberalism following the late nineteenth-century economic recession and the traumatic experience of the First World War. The Marxist historian Eric Hobsbawm explains that on account of these historical experiences, "liberalism was in full retreat throughout the Age of Catastrophe," a neologism he uses for the twentieth century.[10] These events shook the foundations of the liberal view of history as a route to progress and the Enlightenment conception of the state as a social organization motivated by the values of reason. Furthermore, these historical experiences demonstrated how economic/democratic liberalism could become as hegemonic as the political paradigms it opposed. For Kafka then, the blurring of the boundaries between human and nonhuman animals was not just a parody of the liberal narrative, but also a response that displayed some form of skepticism to other alternatives that took for granted ideas of human rationality. Embracing animality was a way to acknowledge human vulnerability and the inability to respond to the historical impasse. Metamorphosis into animals entails a mockery of the structures that perpetuate alienation.

Of interest in Lanthimos's *The Lobster* is how the characters are so alienated that they prefer to integrate at all costs to the very reality that oppresses them and resist their transformation to animals. Infused with references to Kafka, the film is set in an unknown place and time. It follows a recently divorced man, David (Colin Farrell), who participates in a competition in a rural hotel where people are urged to find a partner within a forty-five-day timeframe. Failure to do so will result in their being transformed into an animal of their own choosing. The hotel residents are urged to find a partner who shares similar characteristics, something that makes many of them manipulate the system; for instance, John (Ben Whishaw), a man with a limp, ends up faking nosebleed crises to gain the attractions of a young woman, who suffers from frequent nosebleeds (Jessica Barden). David himself ends up doing something analogous, pretending to lack emotions so as to pair with the Heartless Woman (Angeliki Papoulia), who is incapable of showing any empathy or feelings. To confirm that David is not faking, she kills his brother, who has been transformed into a dog for failing to find a partner; when David starts sobbing, she decides to inform the Hotel Manager (Olivia Colman) of his dishonesty. David manages to escape with the help of a maid (Ariane Labed), who helps him flee to the forest and live among the Loners, an underground group hunted by the hotel residents who embrace single life and strictly ban relationships among their members. David eventually falls for a woman who also suffers from myopia, the Short Sighted Woman (Rachel Weisz); this angers the autocratic leader of the Loners (Léa Seydoux), who punishes her with blindness for breaking the rules. Toward the end of the film, we see David pointing a knife at his eyes presumably in order to blind himself and mate with his blind partner successfully on the basis of their shared disability.

The society pictured in the film is a heavily disciplined one; in the hotel, residents are asked to follow the rules, and noncompliance is punished heavily; for instance, the penalty for masturbation is forcing one's hand in a toaster. Monitoring and surveillance to ensure compliance are the key strategies deployed by the hotel owners, who create a claustrophobic atmosphere to ensure that the rules are followed. Similarly repressive is the group of Loners that uses analogous means to force their own type of discipline and control. Those caught being in a relationship are forced to perform a "red kiss," which involves forcing them to kiss after cutting their lips, and there is also a higher punishment called the "red intercourse" based on a similar premise.

Evidently, both in the hotel and in the Loners' society homogeneity is the key criterion for integration. People in the hotel are asked to find a partner on the basis of likeness, whereas in the Loners' universe, it is expected that everyone acts as an isolated individual, responsible for digging their own grave and for avoiding romantic relationships. Both environments are premised on individualism: in the hotel, finding your other half involves pairing with a mirror image of one's self; in the woods, where the Loners reside, one is literally asked to be only for her/himself. In both cases, uniformity is expected and enforced through monitoring and surveillance.

The key parallel with Kafka in *The Lobster* is the depiction of bachelorhood as threatening and dangerous to the status quo. The bachelor is treated as a pariah by the hotel owners because she/he is synonymous with the unproductive subject, whose single status renders her/him synonymous with the nonintegrated individual. A sequence that is remarkable in this respect sees the hotel residents being cautioned about the danger of being single through a series of performances by the hotel staff. The first begins by showing a man eating alone, who suddenly chokes after swallowing his food too quickly. After repeated coughing, he ends up dying. The following performance demonstrates the benefits of being a couple, showing how the same person would have had a different fate due to the support that would be provided by a partner. This performance is accompanied by another episode showing the hotel maid stimulating David's genitalia to keep him focused on his objective to find a romantic partner. In the third performance, the hotel staff perform another small piece showing the dangers facing women walking alone at night. We see a woman being assaulted and raped by a man as she walks a street alone. This small episode is intercut with the punishing of Robert (John C. Reilly), who has been caught masturbating. In the counter-performance that follows, we see the woman accompanied by a partner and the aggressor now reluctant to attack her as he did in the previous episode.

What is striking about this sequence is how the value of being in a relationship has little to do with affectionate and romantic fulfilment but strictly with practical matters. The sequence is performed in the typically affectless Lanthimos style, something that reinforces its absurd quality. The bachelor as perceived in this dystopian society cannot fit in because she/he is not resilient enough to cope with the threats of the modern world. To be useful requires resilience, and resilience can only be achieved by being in a relationship. The ones who fail to achieve this do not deserve to be part of the human world and need to be downgraded to the world of the animals, which stands for creatures with no "rational agency." This emphasis on resilience has overtones that push further the modernist critique of liberalism as a political model predicated on the importance of insecurity as a narrative that can stimulate adaptability—even to the most absurd circumstances—instead of political engagement and change. Brad Evans and Julian Reid have made a strong case about the link between insecurity as a form of political governance in classically liberal and contemporary neoliberal societies. As they explain, the narrative of insecurity endorses an individualist worldview, according to which the subject is responsible for adapting to a constantly insecure environment. Adaptability and resilience are, therefore, values that can guarantee the maintenance of the status quo. Failure to adapt is an individual failure and not a social one. As they explain,

> the liberal discourse of resilience functions to convince peoples and individuals of the risks and dangers of the belief in the possibility of security. This is an extension of the classical trope of liberal thinking, reaching back to the origins of liberal tradition which has always taken insecurity as the condition of possibility for political rule. To be resilient, the subject must disavow any belief in the possibility to secure itself and accept instead an understanding of life as a permanent process of continual adaptation to threats and dangers which are said to be outside its control. It is all about "thriving" in times of unending chaos without losing the faculty of neoliberal reason. As such the resilient subject must permanently struggle to accommodate itself to the world. The resilient subject is not a political subject who on its own terms conceives of changing the world, its structure and conditions of possibility. The resilient subject is required to accept the dangerousness of the world it lives in as a condition for partaking of that world and accept the necessity of the injunction to change itself in correspondence with threats now presupposed as endemic and unavoidable.[11]

Evans and Reid cogently suggest that the narrative of insecurity and resilience go hand in hand and their ultimate aim is the depoliticization of the social actors and the public sphere. Put simply, insecurity and the emphasis on resilience seek to condition individuals to a world of perpetual risk. Expectations of adaptability to this uncertain environment imply that the subject is responsible for identifying individual solutions for social problems.

In the context of Lanthimos's film, we can see how the narrative of insecurity is promoted by the hotel management, so as to alert the residents to the importance of finding a partner and integrating efficiently into a world of risk. To be a risk-taker implies devising solutions within the confines of a system and it is not accidental that many of the participants in this matchmaking exercise must cheat in order to succeed, despite the hotel's strict rules. John pretends to suffer from nosebleeds so as to match with a woman who has a similar problem, and David pretends to lack emotions so as to match with the Heartless Woman and avoid the humiliating transformation into an animal. In a way, cheating convincingly is encouraged by the hotel owners. The person who can play the part credibly without being found out is rewarded. It is not accidental that when the Loners assault the hotel and the couples, they concentrate on exposing the performative and constructed nature of their relationships by exposing the fake similarities between the couples and the false love between the hotel manager and her partner (Garry Mountaine). In a scene with references to George Orwell's *1984* (1949) and Sarah Kane's *Cleansed* (1998), the Loners give him the option to be killed so as to save his wife or to be spared and to kill her. He chooses the latter option, only to realize that the gun with which he is asked to kill her is not loaded. Here the narrative of individualism is pushed to its ultimate extremes showing how the value of adaptability is synonymous with an affectless worldview in which romantic relationships are founded on expediency rather than affective connection.

Perhaps what is so unsettling about the film's characters are the lengths to which they are ready to go in order to integrate even further into this alienating reality. They are even ready to physically self-harm, like John, or as in the case of David to feign (unsuccessfully) emotional indifference at his brother's murder by the Heartless Woman, in order to ensure their continued presence in the hotel. This is another iteration of Kafkaesque themes, where we see characters ready to accept anything in order to blend in an environment despite its oppressive quality. K. in *The Castle* (1926), a story that has also been seen as a parable of Jewish assimilation, is eager to accept all forms of humiliation in order to keep on hoping to be accepted by the Castle authorities. Josef K. in *The Trial* (1925) understands the absurdity of being accused of an unspecified crime, but still holds faith in the legal system while trying to prove his innocence. Similarly, Karl Rossmann in *Amerika* (1927) is willing to accept all forms of abuse to be able to fit in the new world of American capitalism. The irony is that the more estranging conditions they encounter, the more these characters try to become a part of these environments so as to avoid the status of being pariahs. Kafka makes a parody of the liberal narrative of the autonomous individual, with the view to showing the fallacy of the liberal conception of the subject as an active agent, who acts upon the world rather than being acted upon. The liberal view of the subject according to one of its proponents, Isaiah Berlin, suggests that liberal freedom is predicated on an individual with agency, which is "self-directed and not acted upon by external nature or by other men as if I were a thing, or an animal."[12] Inherent in this approach is the view of animality as a condition that describes lack of agency. Kafka's world, however, raises the question of whether individual agency is relevant in the modern world, since subjects are expected to operate within rules and structures of regimes of control that are absurd and incomprehensible. In drawing attention to the irrationality of modern structures of governance and apparatuses of control, Kafka parodied the liberal ambition of the self-determined subject who "wishes to be his own master."[13]

Yet, as has already been stated in the previous section, it is in Kafka's animal stories that characters somehow resist alienation and embrace their animality as an alternative to the alienated world they are part of. Kafka reflected on this in his conversations with Gustav Janouch:

> Every man lives behind bars, which he carries within him. That is why people write so much about animals now. It's an expression of longing for a free natural life. But for human beings the natural life is a human life. But men don't always realize that. They refuse to realize it. Human existence is a burden to them, so they dispose of it in fantasies.[14]

Kafka later comments that in everyday life people prefer the security of social integration as opposed to reacting against their oppression. Seen this way, characters in *The Lobster* have reached an analogous stage of alienation, since they are willing to do anything it takes to resist their animality. Bachelorhood and thus animality need to be avoided at all costs even if this involves a conscious participation in a coercive performance that guarantees acceptance and inclusion. Sarah Cooper cogently argues that the film raises questions about performance/imitation as a key to social acceptance and the securing of social uniformity.[15] Extending her argument, it is legitimate to suggest that in the film's universe, accepting the rules of the game and being in a relationship on the basis of likeness does not simply involve the preservation of a monogamic tradition, but it also suggests that those involved are capable of reproducing the very reality in which they participate. Finding a partner in these terms is analogous to mimetically reproducing the status quo, whose perpetuation is predicated on coercive training procedures.

One can read the characters' willingness to accept uniformity and alienation as a commentary on the lack of political alternatives in the neoliberal present that has limited their social imaginary to such an extent that they are reluctant to consider ways out. This is effectively conveyed in a sequence where John reproaches David and Robert for being weak and unable to perform productively. Characters seem to have internalized the regulations and the narrative of individualism and performance. In another sequence, when David encounters Robert in the forest, he begs him not to shoot him, only for the latter to retort that he has two days remaining and he needs to shoot a Loner to get an extension. David, on his part, attempts to change his mind by telling him that he considers him his best friend. The performing quality of social integration turns literal here since the affectless acting on the part of the actors exposes their exchanges as shams. Later, even David's rebellion against the Loners' regulations of celibacy takes place within the prescribed parameters of matching through likeness since he is attracted to the Short Sighted Woman with whom he shares the same condition. The rules of the game are somehow accepted by all participants who are an index of a society in which alternatives have no firm foothold. To embrace "humanity" over animality in *The Lobster* stands for the social reproduction of the familiar, and the familiar in the neoliberal present is based upon models of competitive socialization, reproduction of uniformity structured around market criteria, and the disabling of political imagination through a politics of monitoring and fear.

No Alternative: Community and Compliance

In *The Lobster*, it is revealing that the lack of political imagination is evidenced by the promotion of a competitive individualism that characterizes both the world pictured in the hotel as well as the underworld of the Loners. Uniformity and repression go hand in hand in both environments, where individualism and repression are the norm. In the hotel, the value of couplehood is endorsed on the basis of individual accomplishment and social reproduction, but any meaningful social and collective bonds among the inhabitants are absent. Competition rules even between best friends as it is poignantly shown when the Nosebleed Woman tries to console her best friend (Emma O'Shea) for her impending transformation into an animal after failing to find a partner. After reading a letter in which she describes shared memories, the latter responds abruptly by slapping her and refusing the offer to spend her last day as a human together. Of note in this scene is how the letter read by the Nosebleed Woman, which is aimed at offering comfort and support, sounds antagonistic as if she is displaying an air of superiority for not sharing her fate. Her best friend's aggressive response reconfirms this hypothesis.

The antagonistic individualism that characterizes the environment of the hotel is also applicable to the world of the Loners, where one is individually responsible for not being caught by the hunters, digging his or her own grave, and obeying the rules of celibacy imposed from the top. Both settings are reminiscent of disciplinary institutions operating through fear and repression and valorizing individual responsibility at the expense of communal unity. Commentators have noted this resemblance. Aidan Power contends that "[t]aken at face value, the Loners' outlook appears to be little more than an exact reversal of state policy, their methods every bit as brutal."[16] Along these lines, Yonca Talu suggests that "though their principles are at odds with each other—one is a capitalist institution that marginalizes loneliness while the other a civic society that promotes it—their tactics are similarly despotic and both inflict atrocious punishments upon disobedient members."[17] Valerie Andrews similarly argues that the Loners "prove as flawed as the bureaucrats with their unforgiving rules."[18]

In a scene charged with absurd humor, we get to see the Loners dancing on their own while listening to music in their headphones. The absurdity of the situation is that this is a collective gathering, which is, however, predicated on atomic isolation and lack of engagement with one another. Thus, endemic in both universes is an enforced individualism and the absence of community. This is symptomatic of a neoliberal reality structured around competition and individual initiative and the model of the consumer replacing that of the active citizen. Then again, this understanding of the individual as a self-determined agent was also prevalent in classical theories of liberalism against which modern authors like Kafka, W. H. Auden, Bertolt Brecht, T. S. Eliot, and Virginia Woolf reacted. Modernists from the left and the right of the political spectrum criticized liberalism's view of human agents as independent entities. Emblematic in this respect is Auden's famous condemnation of liberalism:

> By denying the social nature of personality, and by ignoring the social power of money, it has created the most impersonal, the most mechanical and the most unequal civilisation the world has ever seen, a civilisation in which the only emotion common to all classes is a feeling of individual isolation from everyone else, a civilisation torn apart by the opposing emotions born of economic injustice, the just envy of the poor and the selfish terror of the rich.[19]

The modernist destabilization of the self-determined liberal subject implicitly suggested that true individuality cannot be accomplished outside of a community, which provides a pertinent framework for approaching the fragmentary and unstable subject of modernist literature, theater, and cinema.

In Kafka's universe, for example, the individual is abandoned to the mercy of institutions that are more interested in reproducing themselves rather than serving the collective benefit. This is why Kafka has been discussed as the author who anticipates totalitarianism; as Deleuze and Guattari suggest, he anticipates the emergence of "Fascism, Stalinism, Americanism, diabolical powers that are knocking at the door."[20] What connects these three models, fascism, Stalinism, and free-market capitalism—what the two philosophers call Americanism—is this sense of abandonment faced by the individual even in systems that are supposedly in service of the community, but aim actually at the reproduction of their own institutions; this is certainly the case in fascism and Stalinism, while in market capitalism individual competition officially replaces social solidarity. Kafka's animal stories comment on this lack of collective bonds and social solidarity: "To the inhumanness of the 'diabolical powers,' there is the answer of a becoming-animal: to become a beetle, to become a dog, to become an ape, 'head over heels and away,' rather than lowering one's head and remaining a bureaucrat, inspector, judge, or judged."[21] We saw in the first section how Deleuze and Guattari considered Kafka's bachelor threatening because she/he represents an imminent collective force that may challenge the existing state of things. In these terms, becoming animal is a means of joining a community that opposes the human inclination for competition. Illuminating from this point of view is Danta's commentary on the dog's critique of the humans in "The Investigations of a Dog" mentioned in the first section of this chapter. Danta suggests that one cannot read this passage without recognizing "a lament about the fact of human alienation—of how little, compared to dogs, humans stick together."[22]

Taking these into account, *The Lobster* has many parallels with the crisis of subjectivity in twentieth-century modernist literature, a crisis that was a reaction against the decline of communal bonds in the liberal democracies of the time. In *The Lobster*, the disintegration of the communal bonds characterizes both systems pictured in the film, which are structured around strategies of monitoring and surveillance that are deployed to guarantee compliance and conformity. The inhabitants of the hotel are not solely monitored in their everyday interactions that assess their progress in their pursuit of a partner, but also through apparatuses of control that are suggestive of depersonalized institutions. A good example is the mechanical announcer notifying David every morning of his remaining time in the premises. But in a way, each individual monitors each other and this is achieved through tactics of competitive exclusion such as the hunting of Loners that can secure them extra days in the hotel. This spirit of individualism and competition also permeates the Loners' community. When David suspects a man (Michael Smiley) of flirting with the Short Sighted Woman, he physically attacks him to confirm that he is not short-sighted, and thus a match with her. The antagonistic terms in which the society of the Loners also operates are pictured clearly in a scene showing a man participating in a military drill where he is caught by an animal trap. He is immediately encircled by the group who are reluctant to offer a helping hand. The leader of the Loners chastises him for not trying hard enough to free himself, something that provokes scornful laughter from the rest. She then emotionlessly explains to him that if he manages to free himself but thinks there is a chance of dying of blood loss, he is advised to move immediately to his grave. As such, neoliberal models of individual responsibility and self-management seem to be the norm even in this underground group, which reacts against the imposed conformity of the hotel with its own disciplinarian strategies of surveillance and control.

In this regard, it is legitimate to conceive the film's negative portrayal of the two antithetical societies, which are both founded on a nihilistic individualism, as a reflection on the present lack of credible political alternatives to the status quo following the failure of the twentieth-century emancipatory narratives. Zygmunt Bauman referencing Cornelius Castoriadis suggests that the impasse facing societies founded on the no-alternative principle is that they cease to engage in self-criticism that can enable individuals to think differently.[23] Symptomatic in this respect is the valorization of survival and endurance by both political models pictured in the film, which are values bereft of a utopian vision of progressive change. Instead, the film's characters are ready to conform and comply even when they temporarily rebel. David, for instance, subscribes to the idea of matching with somebody based on likeness even after abandoning the hotel and joining the Loners as well as after escaping from the woods, where we see him attempting to blind himself in order to be a match with his blind partner. Again, the solution proposed here is that of conformity to the very reality that produces oppression in the first place.

One needs to point out, however, that the film leaves the narrative open to different interpretations including the transformation of David to an animal, an act of escape from the alienated human community. When asked about the character's choice in the last scene, Colin Farrell responded,

> Honest to God, part of me thinks he does it. Then part of me thinks that when the camera cuts back to Rachel Weisz, I'm already in a fucking Uber, heading down the road as fast as I can. And part of me goes to the third option—that he doesn't do it but he goes back to her and tells her that he did.[24]

Farrell is correct in pointing out the film's various conclusions; at the same time, it is of interest to consider an observation by Shelby Cadwell: following the ending of the last song during the film's credits we hear the sound of some crushing waves, something that potentially implies that David has chosen animal transformation instead of pairing with somebody on the basis of likeness.²⁵ This interpretation would be a conscious reiteration of Kafka's view of animality as an escape from human alienation as voiced by the animal character narrator in "The Investigations of a Dog," who compares human individualism to the dogs' communal spirit:

> Consider us dogs, on the other hand! One can safely say that we all live together in a literal heap, all of us, different as we are from one another on account of numberless and profound modifications which have arisen in the course of time. All in one heap! We are drawn to each other and nothing can prevent us from satisfying that communal impulse; all our laws and institutions, the few that I still know and the many that I have forgotten, go back to the longing for the greater bliss we are capable of, the warm comfort of being together.²⁶

Being together in the animal world envisaged by Kafka means being part of a community as opposed to the capitalist relations experienced by humans, which are premised upon individualism and competition. David's potential metamorphosis in *The Lobster* suggests something similar, since none of the human models of governance pictured in the film are founded on the principles of collective coexistence and collaboration.

I have been arguing in this chapter that Yorgos Lanthimos's *The Lobster* reanimates Kafkaesque themes that parallel animality with bachelorhood and link it with an escape out of human alienation. While scholars have identified the film's indebtedness to Kafka, little has been written in detail on the film's reiteration of Kafkaesque themes and how they speak to a different historical reality, which also experienced a crisis of liberalism. In acknowledging the film's Kafkaesque themes, we can get a better understanding of its complex politics and aesthetics as well as of the reasons why its reanimation of a modernist aesthetic is not a nostalgic gesture, but one deployed to comment on current historical contradictions.

Notes

Research for this chapter was supported by the Arts and Humanities Research Council, Grant Ref: AH/T005750/1.

1 See Jonathan Romney, "Yorgos Lanthimos, Director of *The Lobster*, on His Wild, Star-Studded Life of Queen Anne," *The Guardian*, Dec 9, 2018, available at https://www.theguardian.com/film/2018/dec/09/yorgos-lanthimos-the-favourite-interview.

2 Franz Kafka, *The Metamorphosis and Other Stories*, trans. Joyce Crick (Oxford: Oxford University Press, 2009), 49.

3 See Siegfried Kracauer, *The Mass Ornament: Weimar Essays* (Cambridge, MA, and London: Harvard University Press, 1995), 268.

4   Interestingly, Peter Kuper's recent graphic reimagination of the story complicates the portrayal of the burrow as an animal environment filled with human gadgets such as televisions and hoarded industrially produced dry food. See Peter Kuper, *Kafkaesque: Fourteen Stories* (New York: W.W. Norton, 2018).

5   Franz Kafka, *Collected Stories*, trans. Willa and Edwin Muir (New York, London, and Toronto: Everyman's Library, 1993), 421.

6   Gilles Deleuze and Félix Guattari, *Kafka: Toward a Minor Literature*, trans. Dana Polan (Minneapolis: University of Minnesota Press, 1986), 35.

7   Ibid., 71.

8   Franz Kafka, *The Trial*, trans. Mike Mitchell (Oxford: Oxford University Press, 2009), 165.

9   Chris Danta, *Animal Fables after Darwin: Literature, Speciesism, and Metaphor* (Cambridge: Cambridge University Press, 2018), 54.

10 Eric Hobsbawm, *The Age of Extremes: The Short Twentieth Century, 1914–1991* (London: Abacus, 1994), 112.

11 Brad Evans and Julian Reid, *Resilient Life: The Art of Living Dangerously* (Cambridge: Polity, 2014), 41–42.

12 Isaiah Berlin, *Incorporating Four Essays on Liberty*, ed. Henry Hardy (Oxford: Oxford University Press, 2002), 178.

13 Ibid.

14 Gustav Janouch, *Conversations with Kafka*, trans. Goronway Rees (New York: New Directions, 2012), n.p.

15 See Sarah Cooper, "Narcissus and *The Lobster*," *Studies in European Cinema*, 13, no. 2 (2016): 166–67.

16 Aidan Power, *Contemporary European Science Fiction Cinemas* (London: Palgrave Macmillan, 2018), 145.

17 Yonca Talu, "Review: *The Lobster*," *Film Comment*, 52, no. 2 (2016): 69.

18 Valerie Andrews, "Clawing Your Way to the Bottom," *Jung Journal*, 11, no. 1 (2017): 75–80, at p. 77.

19 W. H. Auden, *The Far Interior* (London: Barnes & Noble Books, 1985), 51.

20 Deleuze and Guattari, *Kafka: Toward a Minor Literature*, 42.

21 Ibid., 13.

22 Danta, *Animal Fables after Darwin*, 153.

23 See Zygmunt Bauman, *Liquid Modernity* (Cambridge: Polity, 2000), 215.

24 Quoted in Andrews, "Clawing Your Way to the Bottom," 78.

25 See Shelby Cadwell, "*The Lobster*, by Yorgos Lanthimos," *Science Fiction Film and Television*, 11, no. 1 (2018): 136–39, at p. 138.

26 Kafka, *Collected Stories*, 421.

8

Animal Instincts: Fear, Power, and Obedience in the Films of Yorgos Lanthimos and Stanley Kubrick

Michael Lipiner and Nathan Abrams

Introduction

Although filmmaker Yorgos Lanthimos has refrained from citing Stanley Kubrick directly as a major influence, the legendary American auteur has had a profound stylistic effect on Lanthimos's English-language films. Lanthimos's *The Lobster*, *The Killing of a Sacred Deer*, and *The Favourite* bear more than a passing resemblance to the films of Kubrick. Indeed, as an auteur, Lanthimos's authorial voice is conveyed through a specific cinematic style and vision that includes distinctive off-kilter camera angles, shots, and the use of fish-eye lenses to elevate the viewer's sense of disorientation and unease.[1] Many of these techniques draw from Kubrick's oeuvre reflecting the dark themes he explores, namely "the way individuals are stripped of their identity and autonomy, and … the gradual yet lethal process by which people are psychologically manipulated and enslaved,"[2] specifically by an outsider who threatens to dissemble the family unit and enforces the ultimate sacrifice. Like Kubrick, Lanthimos's films delve into what Jennifer Barker observes as "the relation between human and animal as a mutual entanglement … with an eye toward dissolving static and binary concepts of species, gender, and the relation between them."[3] As we aim to demonstrate in this chapter, both filmmakers attempt to provide a deep psychological understanding of the family unit, human obedience, fear, power, authority, resistance, and Western civilization through notions of sex, freedom, violence, and the human versus animal binary.

Stylistic Similarities

Both filmmakers are primarily self-taught. It is well known that Kubrick was an auto-didact who learned to make movies by watching every film he could before picking up a motion-picture camera to direct three documentaries and then a feature film, *Fear and Desire* (1953). Similarly, Lanthimos has expressed dissatisfaction at the quality of the infrastructure and training in his native Greece; despite having studied at Hellenic Cinema and Television School Stavrakos in Athens, he recalls, "I learned about making films by going into advertising, making commercials. I learned about it by watching films."[4] The similarities extend to how Lanthimos echoes, in particular, such Kubrickian cinematic devices as the "wandering camera" or *camera gaze*,[5] as well as a painterly aesthetic, reverse zoom, and an unidentified narrator. Thus, the camera gaze in his films is voyeuristic and rarely at eye-level. It enters many elaborate, often largely ornamented, rooms filled with unruly characters where strange camera angles and fish-eye lens shots lend a claustrophobic feeling that the characters have no way to escape their bleak fate. The gaze is also rendered as a hidden, spying spectator offering subjective observations of Lanthimos's and Kubrick's similar worlds, while distorted by idiosyncratic emotionless and banal dialogue where even murder becomes emotionless and antiseptic, couched in such a euphemism as "life functions terminated."

Lanthimos's cinematographer, Thimios Bakatakis, uses various dolly tracking shots along with drone shots to provide a camera gaze that follows the characters. Moreover, Lanthimos's use of ultra-wide-angle lenses (Panavision Ultra Speed & Zeiss Master Prime with focal lengths of 10 mm, 12 mm, and 17 mm) combined with a very slow zoom emulates Kubrick's style. In doing so, Lanthimos echoes Kubrick's use of these shots to instill anxiety, but where the former places his characters in areas well known to them (such as hospital corridors, etc.), the latter follows his characters through unknown, hostile, and disturbing terrains (e.g., as when Danny [Danny Lloyd] cycles around the Overlook Hotel in *The Shining* [Stanley Kubrick, 1980] or when he and Wendy [Shelley Duvall] explore the hedge maze).

In shots of long corridors, Lanthimos further resembles Kubrick's cinematic narratives by creating a distinct, invisible entity that silently observes people. These shots provide a spying camera gaze that mirrors "Kubrick's use of the unidentified narrator"[6] or rather an "impersonal narrator [who] is, in fact, a very personalized character" and "serves as an authorial device through which the film articulates many of its ideas."[7] In this way, both filmmakers create an off-screen omniscient narrator who serves as an authorial character and attempts to narrate the events, but who often passes sly, critical judgment upon the society depicted in these films to emphasize its corruptibility and masked culpability in which the bourgeois or aristocratic class appears to be moralistic but in truth is guilty of immoral and/or criminal behavior and actions. In the construction of his cinematic prologues and expositions, Lanthimos almost exactly replicates Kubrick frame by frame. *The Favourite* is divided into pseudoliterary supersegments with foretelling titles such as "This mud stinks," "I do fear confusion and accidents," and "What an outfit." These headings also suggest intertextual allusions and themes in *Paths of Glory* (Stanley Kubrick, 1957), *2001: A Space Odyssey* (Stanley Kubrick, 1968), and *Full Metal Jacket* (Stanley Kubrick, 1987) respectively. Lanthimos even chooses classical pieces by the same notable composers as Kubrick to dissociate, accentuate, or help narrate what is happening onscreen, including Beethoven, Schnittke, Strauss, and Shostakovich.

In classic Kubrickian fashion, Lanthimos's title sequence cuts are synchronized to the music. *The Lobster* begins with a black screen followed by a credits sequence with white title cards appearing onscreen. This cuts to a long shot and close-up of one side of a woman's face as she drives through rain amid dark colors and lighting with no dialogue. She stops the car and gets out as the camera cuts to a medium shot of three black donkeys idly grazing in a field with sullen looks just before she stands among them, takes out a gun, and shoots one dead. A white title card then appears onscreen in the Avenir font, which is near identical to Kubrick's trademark (and favorite) Futura as used across his oeuvre.[8] The camera then cuts to one side of David's (Colin Farrell) face as he sits on a couch next to a dog and has a conversation with a woman off-screen while crying because this canine is, in fact, his brother Bob, who has recently been transformed. A solemn Beethoven string quartet piece is the only sound heard aside from Short Sighted Woman (Rachel Weisz) who coldly and emotionlessly narrates the film's premise.

The Killing of a Sacred Deer opens in a similar fashion. A black screen with an identical credits sequence and white title cards accompany Franz Schubert's somber *Stabat Mater*. The camera then cuts to an extreme close-up of open-heart surgery, with the organ pumping furiously while being sewed up by a surgeon's white-gloved hand as the camera zooms out slowly to reveal the operating room. The film's title appears onscreen, again in Avenir. The scene follows without diegetic sound (aside from the classical piece), as Steven Murphy (Colin Farrell) removes his bloodstained plastic surgical gloves and attire.

The Favourite opens with a black screen and an identical credits sequence with white title cards, which cuts to a wide-angle shot within Queen Anne's eighteenth-century British aristocratic palace accompanied by the regal-sounding chords of a George Frideric Handel concerto. A slow tracking shot zooms in on the feeble, gout-stricken queen (Olivia Colman) as she is helped to remove her ceremonial robes along with her confidante, Lady Sarah (Weisz).[9] This exposition is reminiscent of *Barry Lyndon* (Stanley Kubrick, 1975), which, aside from opening with a black screen and an identical credits sequence with white title cards, is accompanied by the regal-sounding Sarabande sequence of Handel's *Keyboard suite in D minor*. A wide-angle shot establishes the eighteenth-century British regal-aristocratic hopeful (the father of protagonist Redmond Barry) who is killed in a duel as off-screen voice-over narration once again provides the context.

Lanthimos has used Kubrick's trademark reverse tracking shot zoom in many of his films. The reverse zoom and the unidentified narrator (as mentioned above) are among those techniques that have been interpreted as "representing familiar Kubrickian themes having to do with the loss of human freedom."[10] Similarly, in *The Killing of a Sacred Deer*, Lanthimos uses this characteristic camera movement within the long hospital corridor where Steven works. In *The Favourite*, a reverse tracking shot is used as Queen Anne is wheeled by Lady Sarah in her wheelchair through a long, dark palace corridor to emphasize her miserable condition and dependency on others. Other similar reverse tracking shots include when Anne and Sarah ride atop horses in a forest while discussing Abigail (Emma Stone) and their own estranged love for one another, thus mirroring the themes explored in *Barry Lyndon*. In sum, these visual techniques enhance the dark themes that both Lanthimos and Kubrick explore as outlined by Valerie Andrews in our introduction.[11]

Humanimalistic Domestication

As mentioned at the outset, the human/animal binary is a key notion shared by both directors. Kubrick and Lanthimos are concerned with the battle between the animalistic versus the rational sides of human beings, two characteristics that coexist simultaneously between what is considered civilization and barbarism. Their films question to what extent man is inherently born as "animal" or made into one: ideas that are informed by the Theseus story from Greek mythology, which represents the slaying of man's "lower animal" side in order to transcend the original, low-life state.[12] Thus, animals unleash havoc, terror, and chaos within human beings, a primary theme when Theseus kills the Minotaur. Lanthimos works on these themes by depicting worlds in which people and animals are either figuratively sacrificed, punished, or dependent on one another, or finally reduced to animal form literally when they cannot conform to societal norms. Both he and Kubrick convey that humans inherently possess animal instincts for sex, violence, and selfishness. Their ability to be tamed and domesticated is ultimately put to the test.

Kubrick and Lanthimos convey that, no matter where or when we are—whether the "real world," space, nature, or urban environments of the past, present, or future—we cannot escape from our animal instincts and violent, authoritative, forced power, and controlling behavior. In order to convey these messages more literally, both filmmakers often depict animals pitted against humans as a metaphorical amalgam or they show humans that mimic animals. These images exemplify what Barker refers to as "animalousness,"[13] a term that explains the relationality and relationship between human, animal, cinematic movement, and the world, thus depicting the "animalistic" side of *Homo sapiens*. Both Kubrick and Lanthimos often depict seemingly good-natured, ordinary characters who either become "violent animals" or their prey, all of which are attributed to fallible systems supportive of forced control.

Animalistic Experimentation: *The Lobster* and *A Clockwork Orange*

In *The Lobster*, Lanthimos creates a dystopian, fascistic, futuristic society world that tries to control the population through fear tactics and animalistic experiments that mirrors the world of *A Clockwork Orange* (Stanley Kubrick, 1971). In this society (mirroring the biblical injunction "It is not good for the Man to be alone"), being unattached is dangerous. In one scene, at the creepy mating hotel (mirroring the Overlook Hotel in *The Shining*), the staff instills fear in its guests by acting out scenarios theatrically to illustrate the detriments of being single and the benefits of coupling: a single woman walks down the street alone and is randomly raped by a stranger, echoing the multiple beatings and rapes of the first half of *A Clockwork Orange*. By contrast, when another woman walks down the street with her husband, the attacker is scared away.

Lanthimos takes "animalousness" even further as the fear of forced conversion starts to lead the "perfectly suited pairs" to transgress in new ways that are reflected in the transformations taking place before the active camera.[14] In this sense, the filmmaker's "wandering camera" or *camera gaze*[15] as a hidden, spying spectator offers subjective observations of "perfectly-mated" human couples whose actions become animalistic when they murder in cold blood devoid of emotion, or are literally transformed into beasts by force. At the mating hotel, guests have only forty-five days to find a "compatible" soulmate or else be turned into a beast and then ostracized to the woods, "a form of hell on earth."[16] If a guest fails to find love, they are literally and brutally transformed into an animal in the

Transformation Room (a name echoing Franz Kafka's *The Metamorphosis* [1915], an author much admired by Kubrick[17]).

While this remains off-screen (unlike the visceral and brutalizing Ludovico Treatment of *A Clockwork Orange*), "David and two other hotel guests share vivid details of the process as it is rumored to happen. The body is literally rendered animal, boiled down and reconstituted using only the necessary organs, while the unused parts (no need for kneecaps if one has chosen to be a fish, for example) are tossed out."[18] In many scenes, animals transformed from human form often "wander past nonchalantly in the back of shots—a flamingo, a camel, a peacock, a pony—suggesting their belonging to another world: these familiars of our world who inhabit another."[19] Hotel guests are then regularly expected to hunt and shoot down single "Loners" like the animals they have yet to become (just as Alex [Malcolm McDowell] in *A Clockwork Orange* runs over small animals with his car). The fascistic, Holocaust-like overtones here are clear. Thus, as Rubina Ramji points out,

> [t]his lack of variation becomes an underlying message through the movie; one cannot be different ... one cannot be pansexual. Compatibility is forced ... *The Lobster* portrays a world where life is rigid and ruthless. Both sides of this dystopian world are authoritarian—individual desires and needs have no place there. Love is irrelevant. In its own way, this film projects the fear that many of us have today of finding ourselves alone.[20]

The idea of forcibly conditioning humans to revert from their natural animalistic nature is also rendered stylistically. As Barker describes, "[i]n its use of slow motion, lateral camera movements, and the juxtaposition of multiple movements and rhythms, *The Lobster* also exhibits a "fantastic transversality at work" that troubles the notion of transformation from one to the other and reconfigures the relation between human and animal as a mutual entanglement."[21]

Lanthimos and Bakatakis incorporate Kubrick's classic slow zooms, while drawing us closer into a static scene or pulling us away at the same speed, consistently preparing us for horror that may or may not come. Kubrick employed similar shots and camera movements in *A Clockwork Orange* in order to accentuate Alex's animalistic and perverted violence. On the one hand, Alex mostly acts like a wild, dominant animal and leader of his pack that hunts and preys on victims. Yet, on the other, Alex is a "guinea pig" in a government-sponsored rehabilitation program called the Ludovico Treatment. A Pavlovian-response experiment, it is designed to "rehabilitate" him by removing his beastly and animalistic sexual and violent drives via an aversion therapy that includes viewing sex, horror, and atrocity films. After two weeks, he is left metaphorically lobotomized, neutered, and dehumanized, like a defanged and declawed animal, defenseless and emotionless just as David is progressively made at the mating hotel in *The Lobster*. After the Ludovico Treatment, implemented by the state to ensure that Alex will resist future urges, he expresses a "pain and sickness all over [him] like an animal," the exact fate that David has been threatened with should he give in to his sexual desires. His former Droogs, the gang members, Georgie and Dim, who are now police officers, take their revenge on Alex for the brutal treatment he inflicted on them as their leader. They handcuff and nearly drown him in an animal trough while cackling like hyenas.

When David meets the Heartless Woman (Angeliki Papoulia), he believes he has found his suitor. However, much like Alex, she is a violent sociopath,[22] and even murders David's brother, who has been transformed into a dog, in front of him. He stands idly by knowing that he must feign also being a "sociopath" in order to prove his compatibility with her and thus be deemed a legal "match." David fights back tears while watching his brother being murdered and, like Alex, "his psychic numbing is complete."[23]

Exacting revenge, David shoots the Heartless Woman with a tranquilizer dart and delivers her to the Transformation Room. Later, when he joins a group of rebels in the woods, he begins a courtship with Short Sighted Woman by "trapping rabbits—her favorite food—and presenting them to his inamorata as little love tokens,"[24] intertextually alluded to in *The Favourite*. Eventually, the renegade Loners launch an attack against the government-sponsored mating hotel, which "epitomizes the modern disciplinary institution, operating simultaneously as school, asylum, and hospital."[25] In doing so, they hope "to expose the lie at the heart of people's relationships"[26] as a fabrication of their fascist government's attempt to force "compatible" people to mate and therefore reveal that "love" in their society is instead based on a false foundation. Desperate to avoid transformation into a lobster by legally "mating" with Short Sighted Woman who has recently become blind, David contemplates stabbing himself in the eye with a knife. This draws striking parallels with the government-sponsored institution that administers the Ludovico Treatment in *A Clockwork Orange* by forcibly prying open Alex's eyelids, force-feeding him experimental drugs, and brainwashing him. In both films, the protagonists are conditioned to refrain from their innate desires. However, the experiment to forcibly turn Alex into a "good" person is eventually blamed by a sympathetic media for driving Alex to attempt suicide, and the heads of state immediately reverse the process so that "Alex can regress to his previous behavior."[27]

When David and the Loner rebels go to an urban mall, while glancing up in slow motion, he sees a framed photograph of horses racing on a track. A slight tracking movement reveals that the image is lenticular[28] as the horses' bodies appear to shift from one position to another with the camera's movement before cutting back to David. As a reference to famed motion photographer Eadweard Muybridge's experimentation with human and animal locomotion, and iconic of his 1877 study of a horse's gait, this shot suggests "an unsettling derealization of human and animal movement," thus "making it impossible to read David's glance simply as an uncanny moment of recognition, a glimpse of his own 'inner animal', ultimately staging 'an intimate encounter between human, animal, and cinema.' "[29]

David chooses to be transformed into a lobster because, according to him, they live long lives, have extended fertility, and are "blue-blooded like aristocrats." He also enjoyed watersports as a child. However, he is unaware that when a lobster sheds its shell, it is vulnerable to many predators on the ocean floor, which is symbolic of David's forced transformation (and Alex's conditioning) by the fascist dystopian government. Likewise, lobsters are blind like David is to his fascist government and, in order to be considered a legal match for the now blinded Short Sighted Woman, he must decide whether to literally take out his eyes with a steak knife in order to avoid being turned into a lobster before the film fades to black. However, "as [he] brings that knife to his eye, he hesitates and begins to awaken his *inner sight*"[30] of rebellion against the government and forest rebels. As Andrews points out, "[d]ealing with loss and loneliness, our anti-hero [David] faces a poignant and achingly familiar choice—to become as cold and unfeeling as the lobster or to accept the vulnerability and complexity that makes one fully human."[31]

Challenging the Nuclear Family: *The Killing of a Sacred Deer* and *The Shining*

Again, like with his previous film, the animal premise is foregrounded in the title of Lanthimos's *The Killing of a Sacred Deer*. It both draws upon and echoes Kubrick's *The Shining* in its fantastically-cursed and sacrificial characters, claustrophobic settings, and revenge-based, murderous themes. Furthermore, an individual is psychologically manipulated by an outside force that threatens to disrupt the nuclear family unit in order to enforce the ultimate sacrifice. Cardiologist Steven Murphy botches a heart surgery while under the influence of alcohol. The deceased patient's son, Martin (Barry Keoghan) seeks revenge by placing a curse on Steven's family. As Martin explains, each family member will die of an obscure disease unless Steven kills one of them as retribution. As the Murphy family becomes increasingly inflicted with paralysis, an inability to eat, and bleeding eyes, Steven must make a difficult choice in order to pay his "debt" to Martin and the "Gods" that have seemingly empowered him to curse the Murphy family unit. This scenario mirrors the Faustian pact Jack Torrance (Jack Nicholson) has made with the Overlook Hotel in *The Shining*, which demands that he "correct" his wife, Wendy, and son, Danny. Similarly, both couples are shown to have marital problems.

Both films are influenced by Greek mythology. Where Kubrick drew upon the myths of Oedipus and the Minotaur for his film, *The Killing of a Sacred Deer* is a retelling of Euripides's tragedy *Iphigenia in Aulis*,[32] in which the supernatural oracle demands that King Agamemnon sacrifice his daughter, Iphigenia, to appease the goddess Artemis so that Greek ships can set sail for the Trojan War. However, Iphigenia is saved at the last minute by Artemis, who sacrifices a deer in her place.

Lanthimos's film never provides an intelligible explanation as to how Martin has placed a mysterious curse on the Murphy family just as Kubrick refuses to explain the ethereal happenings in *The Shining*, privileging the psychological over the supernatural. Instead, this fantastical element forces Steven to make difficult moralistic choices about his family's survival in an attempt to resolve his own immoral behavior and animalistic actions. Like Jack, Steven is an alcoholic whose ambition to sustain a successful medical career, as well as prestige and honor, echoes the former's wishes to be a successful novelist. Although Jack loses his sanity, he fails to murder his young son, Danny, who outwits him in the hotel's maze. Steven, on the other hand, sacrifices his young son, Bob (Sunny Suljic, whose name is the same as David's brother-turned-canine sacrificed in *The Lobster*), in order to maintain his sanity and resolve himself of guilt in the hopes of appeasing Martin and the Gods that have empowered him to curse Steven's family.

As Jack descends into insanity, he becomes increasingly animalistic culminating in his transformation into a roaring beast, the Minotaur trapped in the maze, and the sacrificial ram demanded by the Overlook Hotel.[33] His growing writer's block, aggravated by the cabin fever, has him hurling a ball against the lobby wall where animal heads not only "signify the aggressive nature of the hotel's former guests,"[34] but also connect Jack to his increasing animalistic nature. In other scenes, Jack chases Wendy and Danny through the Overlook Hotel with "an inarticulate animal roar, signaling that he has finally degenerated into a savage beast."[35] When Steven learns that he must sacrifice a member of his family, he kidnaps, tortures, and almost murders the young Martin before succumbing to the dictate to kill one of his own children. The filmmakers pose an interesting question: is it natural or pathological—whether an animalistic or humanistic urge—for a parent to kill its own offspring?

The Shining, as Smith points out, addresses "Kubrick's thematic concern with the dark side of white American psychology and its connection to politics, sexuality, and family."[36] The upper-middle-class, lily-white, and pristine American neighborhood that Lanthimos depicts is highly immoral. Martin's mother (Alicia Silverstone) unabashedly attempts to seduce Steven right in front of her son. Moreover, Steven's wife, Anna, offers to masturbate Steven's colleague in exchange for clandestine information about her husband's botched surgery on Martin's father that he performed while under the influence. Desperate to break Martin's "curse," Steven, the highly revered heart surgeon, tortures and beats the young man before nearly murdering him, but then fearfully relents and chooses to sacrifice a member of his family instead. Much like Kubrick, Lanthimos depicts rampant culpability within American society—amid a seemingly picture-perfect, white suburbia and a large Midwestern city. And he does so while mirroring Kubrick's trademark Steadicam point-of-view tracking shots in many scenes that question and challenge ideals about the standard nuclear American family.

In addition, both films concern and depict a strong work ethic as a motivating factor in indoctrinating an ordinary man to murder his family. Steven is often seen at work with his colleagues just as Jack is often shown typing incessantly on his typewriter. These characters' strong work ethics and needs to be recognized as well-respected professionals in their respective fields are used as leverage to manipulate them to commit heinous crimes against their families, to swap the rational for the animalistic. Furthermore, the sanitary hospital where Steven works and the sterile Murphy home mirror the kitchen of the Overlook Hotel, the hospital in the final scene of *A Clockwork Orange*, and the futuristic room in the final section of *2001: A Space Odyssey*. This connection establishes false hope that the environments in Lanthimos's film are safe places with an ability to cure people—the hotel resembles a spa— when, in fact, they are places where people go to be killed or transformed into an animal.

Lanthimos updates *The Shining's* characters, too. Anna (Nicole Kidman, who is shown getting ready in front of a mirror with her hair pulled up in a ponytail, which mirrors her same depiction in *Eyes Wide Shut* [Stanley Kubrick, 1999]) contrasts with the more timid, faithful, and subservient Wendy as a successful, hardworking, and strong career woman who makes tough decisions equally with her husband. Wendy, on the other hand, is shown simply agreeing to accompany Jack for the entire winter in isolation at the ominous Overlook Hotel, and, as the film progresses, she is terrified of his violent, aggressive, and abusive behavior toward her and Danny. While Steven falls prey to his manipulator's curse and carries out the murderous deed that Jack failed to commit by sacrificing his son, he in essence "saves" the rest of his family from Martin's curse. Wendy and Danny, meanwhile, are only able to escape with their lives after Jack has failed to kill them and is frozen to death in the hedge maze.

In the final scene, the Murphy family eats at a local diner seemingly unrepentant and unafflicted after having just sacrificed their young son, Bob. The stereotypical American setting is emphasized by an emotionless glance between Martin and the Murphy daughter, Kim (Raffey Cassidy), which results in the latter pouring a gratuitous amount of tomato ketchup on her French fries, signifying the blood that has been spilled, as well as an intertextual reference to the torrents of blood emanating from the elevator in the Overlook Hotel. As Kim eats the standard American fare, she endeavors to hide a sly smile, as she and Martin exchange a few more portentous looks that, together with the motion, are suggestive of a raw, animalistic sexual energy between them. Lanthimos's portentous ending mirrors the final scene in *The Shining* in which a ballroom photograph of Jack suggests that he has been reincarnated and is now a part of the Overlook Hotel, which comes to symbolize recurring violent forces at the heart of the nation that will continue to haunt its caretakers and guests for time to come.

Eighteenth-Century Aristocratic Animalistic Competition: *Barry Lyndon* and *The Favourite*

Lanthimos's *The Favourite* mirrors Kubrick's *Barry Lyndon* in its satirizing of the animalistic competitiveness of eighteenth-century British aristocratic society (all blue-blooded like lobsters). Like Kubrick's eponymous protagonist, Abigail (Emma Stone) is a social climber desiring wealth and status; Molly Haskell describes her as a "cunning lady-in-waiting … whose glittering eyes see more than they let on."[37] Abigail (a more obviously Jewish name than Barry) also originates from the lower social stratum and attempts to rise in rank by using her charm and wits while "securing an aristocratic marriage to boot."[38] She, too, loses her father in a freak and accidental death: a horrendous gambler who gambled his daughter away at the age of 15, he was eventually killed for his countless unpaid debts. Similarly, just as Barry woos Lady Lyndon (Marisa Berenson), Abigail (sexually and otherwise) seduces the queen, thus stealing her away from the clutches of Lady Sarah before marrying Baron Samuel Masham (Joe Alwyn) to gain more social prominence among the aristocracy who are depicted mostly as outlandish, arrogant, hypocritical, desensitized, and cruel human beings.

Again, Lanthimos equates animals and humans. Queen Anne (Olivia Colman) has seventeen rabbits that symbolize the seventeen children she has lost owing to miscarriage, stillbirth, or premature newborn death (mirroring the loss of a child by Barry and Steven). The motherless queen is bitter and lonely, and she finds solace in her beloved pet rabbits whom she allows to roam freely in her chambers. Like Alex's pet boa constrictor, they are possibly the only thing she genuinely loves. When Abigail meets Anne initially, they bond over her pet rabbits as the queen discloses her secrets, and Abigail shows (feigned) empathy. However, as Abigail's disgust for the queen reaches its peak, she exhibits her distaste in the final scene by pressing her shoe onto one of her beloved rabbits while snickering, thus revealing her true feelings as she robs Anne of her royalty and humanity. This scene also works as an intertextual allusion to *The Lobster*'s "ghastly image of dead rabbits in a heap" when David courts Short Sighted Woman much as Abigail seduces Anne.[39]

In another scene, the queen's royal cabinet members cruelly and sacrificially raise ducks high in the air before forcing them to race for their own amusement while using a baton to edge them on. This scene mirrors *The Lobster*'s "duck–rabbit moments" in which David collects "gifts" for Short Sighted Woman in the woods, including dead rabbits and ducks, in his pathetic attempt to court the emotionless woman. The aristocracy also gorges on fancy delicacies, including feasting on rare and savory meats, such as deer (an intertextual allusion to Lanthimos's previous film). This scene is mostly shot in slow motion to accentuate their vileness. The *Favourite* ends with Anne ordering Abigail to rub her legs after witnessing her torture one of her rabbits. During the encounter, the queen grabs Abigail by her hair and holds her in place; as Abigail winces she resembles the helpless rabbit she was toying with only moments before. As the altercation progresses, shots of the two women are superimposed to suggest that they are one and the same vying for power at the expense of others as the film cuts to footage of Anne's seventeen rabbits with fade-ins and fade-outs.

In contrast, Barry cannot quell his animalistic urges and reacts against his enemy and stepson Lord Bullingdon (Leon Vitali) during a recital of a Bach concerto where he publicly beats the young lad before being ostracized from his aristocratic society, thus losing his social standing and fortune. Mario Falsetto writes of the sequence that "[t]he highly structured music perfectly reflects the ordered state of the aristocratic society. Moreover, a recital is the perfect event for Barry to stage in his quest for a peerage. It shows him to be cultured and the epitome of the 'civilized' moneyed class he so desperately wants to penetrate."[40] In a pivotal scene that follows, Kubrick utilizes a slow reverse zoom shot to accentuate Barry's severe loss as he sits lifelessly alone save for the only things he loves in life: his son, Brian, and their dog (recalled in David's insular relationship with his brother-turned-canine in *The Lobster*), all of them frozen and sullen while quietly fishing from a small rowboat as a swan waddles slowly by.

In *The Favourite*, Anne orders lobsters—a self-referential allusion to Lanthimos's earlier film, as well as a reference to the blue-blooded aristocracy in the film—to be sent to her bedroom to race for her own amusement before she intends to eat them. In a similar fashion, Sarah and Abigail's constant vying for power is captured brilliantly as they wittily threaten one another while discussing the hard sacrifices they have had to make in order to sustain their social positions as they leisurely skeet shoot pigeons for sport. These scenes are symbolic of an animalistic fight for survival and territory that occurs among the ranks in order to sustain titles and power.

Sarah is dragged through the forest while caught in her horse's stirrups. In a literal-metaphorical comparison, Barry's father dies because of an argument over horses, which is meant to be comical, while his young son, Brian, tragically falls off a horse that Barry buys for him and then dies. Horses, as a symbol of fate and bad luck, appear in other Kubrick films. A horse is shot in *The Killing* (1956) and, in a twist of fate, it is a horseshoe that causes the death of its assassin. In *Full Metal Jacket*, Private Cowboy (Arliss Howard), who is shot by the Vietnamese sniper, says that he hates Vietnam because "there's not one horse in the whole country."

Conclusion

This study explores how Lanthimos follows Graham Allen's discussion of intertextuality[41] by mirroring Kubrickian allusions and themes, in particular the human/animal binary, in his films. In this sense, Lanthimos cements his position as an auteur by creating a unique cinematic universe like Kubrick's, which, in turn, speaks volumes about our real world. Lanthimos's oeuvre raises interesting questions about morality and ethics by establishing emotionally distant characters that have little or no chance of escape. In this sense, Lanthimos builds upon Kubrick's cynicism about humanity as a victim of the absurdity and violence of the universe. Although humans may have evolved in some ways since the dawn of time, both filmmakers convey that at our core, we continue to kill and be killed like animals. It is inherent for *Homo sapiens* to compete, instill fear and obedience, and resort to either being sexual and/or violent predators or prey. In some cases, parents are willing to even murder their offspring, which may pose the ultimate threat to the once cherished but now dysfunctional family unit. These postmodern films feel eerily familiar to America's current political quandary regarding the representation of fear, power, and obedience. Specifically, Kubrick's and Lanthimos's films enable us to better understand human obedience through the notions of sex and animals and their symbolic links to violence and power. Aside from providing modern allusions to Greek mythology, Lanthimos provides many intertextual allusions to Kubrick and raises familiar Kubrickian themes using film aesthetics and atmospherically thematic visual cues. Moreover, both filmmakers provide a satirical criticism of and contempt for both American and British (aristocratic or bourgeois) societies by pushing the boundaries of moral gray zones with emotionless characters bound to their lot.

Notes

1 Molly Haskell, "*The Favourite*," *Film Comment*, 54, no. 6 (2018): 68–69, at p. 68.

2. Valerie Andrews, "Clawing Your Way to the Bottom," *Jung Journal*, 11, no. 1 (2017): 75–80, at p. 76.
3. Jennifer Barker, "A Horse Is a Horse, Of Course, Of Course: Animality, Transitivity, and the Double Take," *Somatechnics*, 8 (2018): 27–47, at p. 28.
4. Quoted in Xan Brooks, "Why Is Greece's Finest Young Director Making London His Home?" *The Guardian*, Nov 11, 2012, available at https://www.theguardian.com/film/2012/nov/11/greek-director-yorgos-lanthimos.
5. Kenneth Johnson, "The Point of View of the Wandering Camera," *Cinema Journal*, 32, no. 2 (1993): 49–56, at p. 49.
6. Jerold J. Abrams, "Introduction," in J. J. Abrams, ed., *The Philosophy of Stanley Kubrick* (Lexington: University Press of Kentucky, 2007), 1–8, at p. 5.
7. Mario Falsetto, *Stanley Kubrick: A Narrative and Stylistic Analysis* (Westport, CT, and London: Praeger, 2001), pp. 102, 146.
8. In the title sequences of his films, Lanthimos uses the Avenir font, a geometric sans-serif typeface designed in 1988 by Adrian Frutiger as a more "humanistic" version of traditional geometric typefaces like the Futura font utilized by Kubrick. See Cameron Chapman, "The Most Popular Fonts Used By Designers," *Web Designer Depot*, 2011, available at https://www.webdesignerdepot.com/2011/08/the-most-popular-fonts-used-by-designers/.
9. The reuse of an actor who previously appeared in a Lanthimos film is another Kubrickian tic as the director often cast actors in consecutive films. Farrell, Colman, and Weisz have all appeared in two of Lanthimos's films.
10. Chris P. Pliatska, "The Shape of Man: The Absurd and *Barry Lyndon*," in J. J. Abrams, ed., *The Philosophy of Stanley Kubrick* (Lexington: University Press of Kentucky, 2007), 183–200, at p. 185.
11. Andrews, "Clawing Your Way to the Bottom," 76.
12. Jill K. H. Geoffrion and Alain Pierre Louët, "CAERDROIA," *Journal of Mazes and Labyrinths*, 44 (2015): 8–27, at p. 20.
13. Barker, "A Horse Is a Horse," 32–36.
14. This echoes the couple in *Dogtooth* who use illusory linguistic signs and symbols to prevent their children from venturing into the outside world.
15. Johnson, "The Point of View of the Wandering Camera," 49.
16. Rubina Ramji, "*The Lobster*," *Journal of Religion and Film*, 20, no. 2 (2016): 1–3, at p. 1.
17. See Angelos Koutsourakis's chapter, "Kafkaesque Themes in *The Lobster*," in this volume.
18. Barker, "A Horse Is a Horse," 28.
19. Sarah Cooper, "Narcissus and *The Lobster*," *Studies in European Cinema*, 13, no. 2 (2016): 1–14, at p. 13.
20. Ramji, "*The Lobster*," 2–3.
21. Barker, "A Horse Is a Horse," 28.
22. Ramji, "*The Lobster*," 2.

23 Andrews, "Clawing Your Way to the Bottom," 77.
24 Ibid.
25 Yonca Talu, "Review: *The Lobster*," *Film Comment*, 52, no. 2 (2016), available at https://www.filmcomment.com/article/review-the-lobster-yorgos-lanthimos/.
26 Cooper, "Narcissus and *The Lobster*," 18.
27 Falsetto, *Stanley Kubrick: A Narrative and Stylistic Analysis*, 122.
28 According to Barker,

> a lenticular image is produced by having a lenticular lens placed above two or more still images (depicting the horses in successive positions on the track, here), then photographing these images in such a way that slices, interleaves, and prints them in an alternating pattern, which the movement of the final, interleaved/conjoined image or the eye itself translates into an image of movement.

See Barker, "A Horse Is a Horse," 47.
29 Ibid., 29–30.
30 Andrews, "Clawing Your Way to the Bottom," 78.
31 Ibid., 79.
32 Iro Filippaki, "Violence as Embodied Neoliberalism in the Neurothriller," *Lit: Literature Interpretation Theory*, 30, no. 2 (2019): 138–54, at p. 152.
33 See Nathan Abrams, *Stanley Kubrick: New York Jewish Intellectual* (Brunswick, NJ: Rutgers University Press, 2018).
34 Julian Rice, *Kubrick's Hope: Discovering Optimism from 2001 to Eyes Wide Shut* (Lanham, MD: Scarecrow Press, 2008), 251–52.
35 Gene D. Phillips and Rodney F. Hill, *The Encyclopedia of Stanley Kubrick* (New York: Facts on File, 2002), 209.
36 Greg Smith, "'Real Horrorshow': The Juxtaposition of Subtext, Satire, and Audience Implication in Stanley Kubrick's *The Shining*," *Literature/Film Quarterly*, 25, no. 4 (1997): 300–06, at p. 301.
37 Haskell, "*The Favourite*," 68–69.
38 Ibid., 69.
39 Barker, "A Horse Is a Horse," 28.
40 Falsetto, *Stanley Kubrick: A Narrative and Stylistic Analysis*, 61–62.
41 See Graham Allen, *Intertextuality* (London and New York: Routledge, 2000).

9

Consider the Absurd: Uneasy Proximity in *Dogtooth*, *The Lobster*, and *The Killing of a Sacred Deer*

Nepomuk Zettl

Some events seem unreal, out of touch with a rational concept of the world: people drowning in the Mediterranean, families forcefully separated at borders, police violence against people of color, child abuse in religious institutions on a massive scale, or a pandemic dictating "social distance." Indeed, there is a growing discrepancy between how the world should be and the actual experience of living in a present that can only be described as "absurd." The films of Yorgos Lanthimos combine tragedy with the banality of the everyday, depicting absurdist situations that are both otherworldly strange and yet strangely familiar. Instead of repressing the strange reality of the world at large, Lanthimos's films embrace the absurd, albeit at a distance.

This chapter investigates Lanthimos's cinema of the absurd with regard to three films that stem from a collaboration of the director with cowriter Efthymis Filippou and cinematographer Thimios Bakatakis: *Dogtooth*, *The Lobster*, and *The Killing of a Sacred Deer*. The first gives insight into the life of a family whose three children live in almost complete isolation from the world beyond their compound. Although they are of legal age, they follow the strict rule of not leaving the parental estate until they have lost their dogtooth, symbolic of their maturity—a treacherous rule, since they commonly last for most of an adult's life. Their daily routine consists of physical exercise and lessons expounding peculiar semantic forms: the word "sea," for example, translates to a "leather chair with wooden armrests like the one in the living room" and "road trip" is a "highly durable material used to make floors." The vocabulary is uncannily related to common language. Nonetheless, familiar signifiers are given a completely different meaning.[1] Every term that might inspire movement is supplanted.

In *The Lobster*, Lanthimos and Filippou create an even larger dystopic society, one that requires its members to live as couples. Single persons are therefore segregated and interned in an institute, where they are given forty-five days to build a lasting relationship. If they fail to form a relationship, they are then transformed into an animal of their choosing. In *The Lobster*, closeness requires submission to a discomforting social convention or risking physical harm. *The Lobster* marked Lanthimos's first film in the English language, starring international stars Rachel Weisz and Colin Farrell, bringing his work to a larger audience. Farrell returns in the main cast of Lanthimos's following film, *The Killing of a Sacred Deer*. In it, Farrell portrays a heart surgeon, Steven, whose family is haunted by an eerie young man wielding some kind of curse. Similar to in *Dogtooth*, the closeness of the family members in *The Killing of a Sacred Deer* is less defined by security; rather, the family consists of emotionally distanced individuals sharing a common destiny. Each one of these films juxtaposes the paradigms of proximity and distance in very specific ways. All three films open with a sequence of intense closeness. The reoccurring moments of discomfort in the films of Lanthimos become most evident in the opening shot of *The Killing of a Sacred Deer*. It is emblematic of the hypothesis to be explored in this chapter: the closer the protagonists get in Lanthimos's films, the wider the distance between the events on screen and the viewer becomes—on an emotional, cognitive, and/or semantic level.

After a short Overture (Franz Schubert's "Jesus Christus schwebt am Kreuze" (choir), *Stabat Mater in F minor, D 383, no. 1*), the viewer is faced with a most sensitive organ, the heart. In these first frames, we see it beating in close-up, filling the screen almost completely (see Figure 9.1a) before the shot retreats to expand the viewer's understanding of the space being presented. It also opens up to reveal medical devices—needle, thread, pliers, forceps—and finally the hands of surgeons appear (see Figure 9.1b). This initial sequence establishes a significant difference between proximity in relation to the viewing position, on one hand, and proximity in relation to the action on screen, on the other. Traditionally serving as a symbol for affection and thus remaining heavily guarded—after all, we hold dear what is close to our heart—the opening shot of *The Killing of a Sacred Deer* lays bare and makes grotesque what is commonly shielded and protected. Consequently, this opening creates a feeling of uneasiness, a feeling that

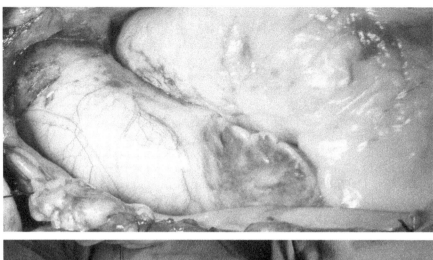

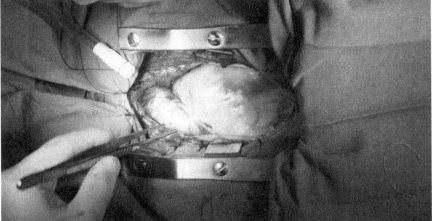

FIGURE 9.1a and b *Close-up of heart surgery opens* The Killing of a Sacred Deer.

is amplified by the faceless surgeon's operating hands that move freely (in and out of the frame) as the beating organ rests in place. The proximity presented on screen is marked by both threat and attention to detail—in short, the proximal relations are that of a hunter to its prey; Steven's hands may (or may not) be performing a life-saving operation. The proximity to the heart, in the depths of the patient's chest, lends a menacing, threatening atmosphere to the sequence. In a godlike dimension, the patient's fate lies in the surgeon's hands, a show of power that will be inverted for Steven later in the film. Accordingly, the position of the spectator is at this point highly ambivalent.

The opening sequence opaquely establishes the basic premise of *The Killing of a Sacred Deer*. Martin (Barry Keoghan), the son of a former patient, is convinced that Steven is responsible for the death of his father. In the course of the film, Martin approaches and gets closer to Steven's family. Shortly afterward, Steven's children fall ill and Martin instructs him that the only way to save his family would be to kill one of them in order to counterbalance the loss of Martin's father. In spite of the proclaimed principle of justice, the question of guilt remains ambiguous and unresolved throughout the film.

This premise in *The Killing of a Sacred Deer* is archetypically absurd, as is the obligation to live in a relationship or else be transformed into an animal in *The Lobster*, as is the autonomous microsociety in *Dogtooth* where maturity is determined by a tooth. Moreover, commentators have repeatedly characterized Lanthimos's films as "absurd." In most cases, this consignment stems from a diffuse feeling and serves as a buzzword to describe the director's style.[2] Stamos Metzidakis, for instance, regards Lanthimos's work as an example of "absurdist cinema"[3]:

> What I mean to do by using it [the adjective "absurdist"] here is to underscore the various ways this particular film presents a breakdown in typical human interaction, communication, and argumentation, and gives way to irrational or illogical speech and behavior, such as one finds in the plays of the Theater of the Absurd. Also, because the close examination and artistic exploitation of the irrational or illogical often recall the pioneering productions of Dada and especially Surrealism, it should come as no surprise to the reader that I will shortly have other occasions in this essay to refer to several Surrealist practices and their relation to Lanthimos's film.[4]

Although Metzidakis refers to the "theatre of the absurd" as a precursor to Lanthimos's style, he refrains from providing details of what is to be understood by such a cinema, associating it with surrealism and the practices of the so-called Greek Weird Wave[5] taking place in Greek cinema. I will begin by properly situating this cursory characterization and reframe the designation against the "absurdist" tradition as it was described by theater critic Martin Esslin.

Reexamining *The Theatre of the Absurd*

In his highly influential 1961 book *The Theatre of the Absurd*, Martin Esslin names Samuel Beckett, Arthur Adamov, Eugène Ionesco, and Jean Genet as primary representatives of what he calls the "theatre of the absurd." Esslin explains the "absurd" in reference to its etymological roots to describe something "out of harmony" from a dictionary definition that reads: "out of harmony with reason or propriety; incongruous, unreasonable, illogical."[6] For Esslin, the characteristics of the "theatre of the absurd" become most evident in Ionesco's *The Bald Soprano* (*La Cantatrice chauve*, 1950). Ionesco's play is largely uninterested in the psychology of its protagonists and lacks a structured narrative for the most part; for Esslin, it is "a theatre of the situation as against a theatre of events in sequence, and therefore it uses a language based on patterns of concrete images rather than arguments and discursive speech."[7] Esslin explains the function of absurdism in drama in the following terms: "The Theatre of the Absurd has renounced arguing about the absurdity of the human condition; it merely presents it in being— that is, in terms of concrete stage images. This is the difference between the approach of the philosopher and that of the poet; ... the difference between theory and experience."[8] The plays still rely heavily on language in the form of speech, but it no longer serves "as a means of communication and as a vehicle for the expression of valid statements, an instrument of thought."[9] Direct philosophical discourse, therefore, is almost nonexistent in the "theatre of the absurd," which provides the main difference to Albert Camus's concept of the "absurd." Camus imagined absurdity as an expression of religious uncertainty,[10] resulting from a rational individual's confrontation with the strangeness of the world in the wake of the Second World War. After the war, the "theatre of the absurd" emerged out of "the shattered religious and ideological certainties,"[11] primarily as a performative mode of expression. On the separation from the "existentialist theatre," Esslin writes,

> [t]he Theatre of the Absurd, on the other hand, tends toward a radical devaluation of language, toward a poetry that is to emerge from the concrete and objectified images of the stage itself. The element of language still plays an important part in this conception, but what happens on the stage transcends, and often contradicts, the words spoken by the characters.[12]

The nonsensical dialogue and the irrational action in the dramas of Ionesco and Beckett underline the formal nature of absurdist theater, confronting the audience with an/Other type of performance.[13] In this respect, the absurdist mode creates a kind of *Verfremdungseffekt* (the "alienation effect")[14] as typified by the early works of Bertolt Brecht.[15] As such, Esslin stresses that the absurdist mode was both shocking and incomprehensible to theater audiences of the 1950s and 1960s who were used to "the naturalistic and narrative conventions of the theatre."[16]

Similarly, Lanthimos's films are marked by an obfuscation (and therefore critique) of language, which does not radically reject its use per se, but casts traditional semantic relations into doubt. Dialogue in *Dogtooth*, *The Lobster*, and *The Killing of a Sacred Deer* is reduced to a minimum; when there is speech, characters speak pragmatically, in a reductive form that comes close to the absurd. Although the films do follow narrative lines, there are not necessarily causal connections between scenes, or between the protagonists' actions and their reactions. As drastic changes to the situations transpire—like the violent outbursts of the father in *Dogtooth* or Steven's kidnapping of Martin in *The Killing of a Sacred Deer*—they often occur suddenly, "out of harmony" with corresponding events in the films.

The alienating language of the films, which no longer solely serves as a means for communication, as well as the actions of apathetic protagonists, opens up space for absurdity as semantic playfulness in Lanthimos's films. Adopting a recognizable absurdist mode, Lanthimos's films recode familiar contexts to enable a different understanding. In my reading, Lanthimos's films create a relational play based on proximity and distance between the world as it is and the worlds they depict, providing a critical perspective on various aspects of the modern human condition. Accordingly, moments of close proximity in Lanthimos's films turn intimacy into something uneasy. In the remaining part of this chapter, I will observe three dimensions of proximity as they play out in the films by Lanthimos: the relationship between the protagonists and diegetic space, what I call corporeal proximity, and semantic closeness.

Absurd *mise-en-scène*: Dimensions of Space

For the most part, the protagonists in Lanthimos's films appear lost in space. The scenography is rarely introduced by clear establishing shots and there are often few or no causal connections between specific scenes. The diegetic spaces appear to be either enormous or claustrophobically small in relation to the bodies that occupy them. The *mise-en-scène* is generally asymmetrical, with the frame frequently filled with empty panes where shots feature wide-open spaces in the upper part of the image. Cinematographer Bakatakis's camera regularly faces the protagonists head-on in long shots while dialogues are often framed in a diagonal perspective and close-ups, in sequences that usually focus on just one person.

The relationship between the films' protagonists and their surroundings reflects their alienated status. In *Dogtooth*, only the patriarch is permitted to leave the insular estate. Society in *The Lobster* is organized in segregated sectors: the city is the domain of couples; the forest provides refuge for fugitive singles living in loose groups of so-called Loners; the hotel is an intermediary resort that encourages matchmaking, distinguishing areas for singles and couples. *The Killing of a Sacred Deer* features a multitude of different locations, each one in some way inhospitable. The protagonists pass through spaces with no apparent emotional connection to them; accordingly, both central settings, the hospital and the family's home, are equally impersonal. The proportional relations between protagonists and the spaces in which they are situated reveals much. In an early scene, the viewer finds Steven walking the hallways of his hospital workspace, followed by a camera at his back. The high angle of the continuous shot gives clear sight of what lies ahead as Steven passes seamlessly through sterile, straight-lined architecture matched to his body height (see Figure 9.2a). Later, however, after medical experts have failed to find an explanation for the mysterious paralysis of his children, Steven is engulfed by the spaces of the hospital's oversized rooms (see Figure 9.2b) in scenes shot at low angles. The visual effect of uncannily low ceilings is reminiscent of the narrow chambers in

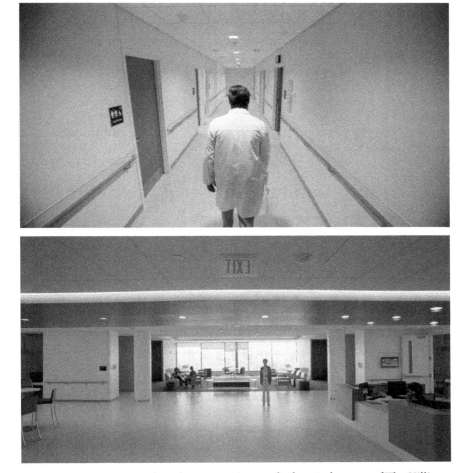

FIGURE 9.2a and b *Absurd* mise-en-scène *in the hospital spaces of* The Killing of a Sacred Deer.

Orson Welles's adaptation of Franz Kafka's *The Trial* (1962), where the protagonist is haunted by the persistent influence of an unknown power.[17] In *The Killing of a Sacred Deer*, the absence of clearly defined medical epistemology unhinges the stability of the hospital as a medical institution. Steven's powerlessness follows him elsewhere, into the home that impacts the familial dimensions of it; in all instances, Steven's loss of power is formally mirrored in the relation of his body to the surrounding spaces.

Another interesting case is the dimension of acoustic space in Lanthimos's films. *Dogtooth* for the most part forgoes the use of nondiegetic music and is therefore very different to the sound design of the other two films.[18] The music in *The Lobster* and *The Killing of a Sacred Deer* are shaped by distinctively dissonant passages,[19] as well as deep synthetic drones that feature in large portions of the films, which are not related to a diegetic source or a specific location—a passive acoustic *hors-champs*, as described by Michel Chion.[20] These soundscapes hold the audience in a complex relationship that increases feelings of uneasiness. Through such resonant procedures, the audience is affected by the acoustic signals even if they cannot find a corresponding cause for them on screen. The sound of the film—per se invisible—thus creates a new proximity, which immediately affects the viewing position; the failure to make sense of acoustic dimensions of the diegetic spaces amplifies the feeling of uneasiness, of being subjected to irrational, absurd influences.

Absurd Bodies: Corporeal Proximity

There are almost no depictions of emotional proximity or empathy in the films of Lanthimos. Emotional distance is supplanted by corporeal proximity in *The Lobster*, where relationships are established purely on the basis of corresponding characteristics—for example, the shared impairment of being short sighted. Moreover, the cinema of Lanthimos is characterized largely by a pragmatic economy of proximity in place of authentic affection. This is evident in *Alps*, where members of a group named Alps take up the roles of recently deceased people to aid the process of grief for their mourners. Elsewhere, sexual encounters in Lanthimos's films unfold as ritualistic role play. In *Dogtooth* and *The Lobster*, sex scenes are executed as mechanical processes that are devoid of passion. Sex in Lanthimos's films is not a taboo per se, but it is strictly regulated and employed economically. Furthermore, in *The Killing of a Sacred Deer*, the marital sex acquires an absurd, macabre element in a scene in which Steven's wife Anna (Nicole Kidman) presents herself lifelessly, mimicking a patient under general anesthetic.

Punishments that result from violations of rules outlined in Lanthimos's film worlds are equally harsh. Self-mutilating behavior is often enforced: in *The Lobster*, a resident of the hotel is urged to place one hand into a toaster for masturbating, while the son in *Dogtooth* has to hold mouthwash in his mouth for a painfully long period of time for throwing stones over the garden fence. Both punishments are absurdly arbitrary, follow minor misdemeanors and are therefore disproportional. In the final act of *The Killing of a Sacred Deer*, a powerless Steven takes Martin hostage, in order to forcibly make him end the suffering of his children. While Steven's violence harms Martin physically, his actions only serve to prove the strength of Martin's enigmatic power. Here, in the face of a phenomenon that goes beyond reason, the cardiologist—a man of science—reverts to violence. When Steven gets too close to his hostage, Martin bites him in the forearm "to show [him] an example." In response, Martin tears a piece of his own forearm with his teeth in order to disempower him and set up the nature of the eye-for-an-eye form of justice he seeks from Steven. "Do you understand?" Martin asks Steven, "my example, it's a metaphor. I mean, it's symbolic." Martin's uncertain categorical distinction between metaphor and symbol is interesting; the bite neither serves simply as a metaphor (it is too close to the substituted image and therefore tautological) nor as a pure symbol, but as a paradigm (in the sense of the Greek *parádeigma*) that explains Martin's philosophical position, his demand for a sacrificial offering in the form of the titular killing of a "sacred deer."

In Lanthimos's film worlds, irrational behavior is often employed to comment on the irrational conditions of the characters' existence, a theme that returns in his interest in human–animal relations. In her essay on *The Lobster*, Sarah Cooper draws on work by Jacques Derrida, who by "deconstructing [Emmanuel] Levinas and noting the problem in his philosophy more generally of prioritizing the human, suggests that the animal gaze, rather than sole contact through human language, offers one of the best ways of thinking about radical alterity."[21] Derrida develops this idea through the notion of shame, which he feels when facing his cat in the nude:

> Ashamed of what and before whom? Ashamed of being as naked as an animal *[bête]*. It is generally thought, although none of the philosophers I am about to examine actually mention it, that the property unique to animals and what in the final analysis distinguishes them from man, is their being naked without knowing it. Not being naked therefore, not having knowledge of their nudity, in short without consciousness of good and evil.[22]

For Derrida, that which is especially strange or distant provides a mirror image, by opposition, in which one's own identity may take shape.[23] He regards the difference expressed by "the inhuman or ahuman"[24] as the distinction that enables us to speak of the "human" in the first place. As mentioned earlier, the human–animal relation is a prominent feature in Lanthimos's films: in *Dogtooth* and *The Killing of a Sacred Deer*, the protagonists are directly equated to animals and in *The Lobster* they run the risk of becoming an animal if they fail to conform. The corporeal proximity of human to animal comes to bear critically on a philosophical project to determine what it is to be "human."

In his famous essay "Consider the Lobster," David Foster Wallace utilizes the format of a *Gourmet* magazine article to critique the violent preparation of lobster, which prompts a number of fundamental ethical issues for the author: "The lobster ... behaves very much as you or I would behave if we were plunged into boiling water (with the obvious exception of screaming)."[25] The proximity of the animal's behavior to plausible human behavior has an alienating effect on the reader. The human–animal relations may be superficially absurd, but they persist in the cinema of Lanthimos, as it does in the review by Wallace, to comment on the strange condition of being human. The protagonists in *Dogtooth*, *The Lobster*, and *The Killing of a Sacred Deer* are as naked animals, acting in a pragmatic if absurd manner that lays bare the mechanizations of human behavior.

Absurd Language: Semantic Distances

Although the dialogue in Lanthimos's films displays a tendency toward the absurd, language nevertheless plays a fundamentally important role. The commonplace functions and style of speech are replaced by systems of communication that are developed over the course of the films. Elder Daughter in *Dogtooth* experiences the world outside via video cassettes: *Rocky* and *Jaws* not only provide her with new vocabulary, but by watching them, she also learns new gestures, forms of action, and how to employ them. While her brother appears content with his mother's absolute definitions (e.g., "a zombie is a small yellow flower"), Elder Daughter takes up a "language game" (*Sprachpiel* in the sense of Ludwig Wittgenstein[26]) by testing the meaning of words and gestures practically by setting them in relation to each other. The videos reveal to her an alternative relationship with the world, which, up to this point, had been denied by the terms provided for her by her parents. However, Elder Daughter comes to realize that as long as she remains within the exclusive circle of her family, who do not participate in these games, she is caught up in an absurd environment that she must experience even if she is unable to fully interpret it.

In *The Lobster*, the Loners in the woods are not permitted to take a partner, therefore the central couple David (Colin Farrell) and Short Sighted Woman (Rachel Weisz) is forced to devise a new covert mode of communication. They develop a code with their bodies that enables them to convey secret messages to one another (see Figure 9.3a).

FIGURE 9.3a and b *Communication and sacrifice in* The Lobster.

The narrator explains:

> We developed a code so that we can communicate with each other, even in front of the others without them knowing what we are saying. When we turn our heads to the left, it means: "I love you more than anything in the world." And when we turn our heads to the right, it means: "Watch out, we're in danger!" We had to be very careful in the beginning not to mix up "I love you more than anything in the world" with "watch out, we're in danger!"

In the absurd world of *The Lobster* with opposing forms of totalitarianism in effect, the couple develops closeness (or proximity) through their own sign language, which is only perceivable at a distance. The couple is obliged to carve space in which they can safely communicate in the presence of others, their exclusive, illegal language system ironically forming the most genuine expression of intimacy in the film. In the middle of a forest, among the renegade singles, the couple uses gestures to stay in touch. The viewer is able to see an act of communication, but is unable to interpret the signs; as a consequence, even the audience is kept at a distance, as only a few of the encrypted exchanges are translated, in the voice-over transcribed above. After Short Sighted Woman is blinded for breaking the rules, the couple is forced to reintroduce their gestures as spoken language, verbally describing movements as they perform them, a process that further alienates the audience from the couple's intimacy.

Even after they have established genuine closeness, as well as a new language system, the couple cannot escape the absurdity of the world they live in. At the end of the film, having left the Loners in the woods, the couple chooses to rest at a roadside diner. It is the sort of place that Marc Augé might describe as a "non-place," a place that "cannot be defined as relational, or historical, or concerned with identity."[27] David leaves Short Sighted (now Blind) Woman at the table as he decides whether or not to take his own eyesight with a steak knife in the restroom (see Figure 9.3b). Absorbed in the relationship-based ideology of the society at large, David fears that he still must fulfill the social dogma of sharing a defining characteristic (short-sightedness, now blindness) in order to form a couple. They have escaped society, and yet they still adhere to its rules, the necessity of a mutual attribute to validate their union. This final scene crystallizes the absurdity of the human condition that is the target of much of Lanthimos's cinema. As in the theater of the absurd, which "is trying to present a *sense of being*,"[28] Lanthimos's films do not present specific moral resolutions; they do not provide closure, catharsis, or suggest some kind of rational way of understanding the irrational situations they present. Instead, by immersing his film worlds in the absurd, the irrational becomes a new normal through which to observe, in close proximity, the strangeness of human behavior.

Notes

1 Of course, these quotes are translations of the original version in Greek. For a critical perspective on the aspect of translation in film, with special reference to *Dogtooth*, see Dionysios Kapsaskis, "Translation as a Critical Tool in Film Analysis: Watching Yorgos Lanthimos's *Dogtooth* through a Translational Prism," *Translation Studies*, 10, no. 3 (2017): 247–62.

2 Discussion of Lanthimos's style has been ongoing: see Jonathan Romney, "Bad Education," *Sight and Sound*, 20, no. 5 (2010): 42–44, at p. 42: "*Dogtooth* ... presents its horrors in deceptively discreet terms, in an absurdist key"; Olga

Kourelou, "Dead Ringers," *Sight and Sound*, 22, no. 12 (2012): 52–53, at p. 52: "the *absurdity of human activity* and the unreliability of language are central concerns"; Trevor Johnston, "Animal Instincts," *Sight and Sound*, 25, no. 11 (2015): 28–30, at p. 29: "the Greek writer–director has been busily marking out his own cinematic territory, full of curious coteries, *absurd rules* and seemingly inevitable mischief ... There's a bracingly *absurd comic element* to all this, which might remind viewers of early Monty Python or even the skewed wit of 70s Luis Buñuel"; Carlos Aguilar, "Idiomatic Idiosyncrasy: Yorgos Lanthimos Talks *The Lobster*, Greek Cinema and Musical Subtlety," *MovieMaker*, May 12, 2016, available at https://www.moviemaker.com/news/idiomatic-idiosyncrasy-yorgos-lanthimos-the-lobster: "the films of Yorgos Lanthimos, in whatever language, confront those who brave them with *absurdist premises* that challenge what we consider 'normal' "; Jeremi Szaniawski, "*Nouvel Œdipe ou nouveau Sphinx? Yorgos Lanthimos, cinéaste européen*," *L'Avant-scène cinema*, 642, no. 4 (2017): 15: "une déconstruction, jusqu'à l'*absurde du symbolique traditionnel*." All emphases are mine.

3 Stamos Metzidakis, "No Bones to Pick with Lanthimos's Film *Dogtooth*," *Journal of Modern Greek Studies*, 32, no. 2 (2014): 367–92, at p. 367.

4 Ibid., 387.

5 Ibid., 368. Metzidakis adopts the definition of the "Greek Weird Wave" from Steve Rose, "*Attenberg, Dogtooth*, and the Weird Wave of Greek Cinema," *The Guardian*, Aug 26, 2011, available at www.theguardian.com/film/2011/aug/27/attenberg-dogtooth-greece-cinema.

6 Martin Esslin, *The Theatre of the Absurd* (New York: Vintage Books, 2001), 23; see also Wolfgang Fritz Haug, *Jean-Paul Sartre und die Konstruktion des Absurden* (Frankfurt: Suhrkamp, 1966), 15.

7 Esslin, *The Theatre of the Absurd*, 403.

8 Ibid., 25.

9 Ibid., 85.

10 See Uschi Quint-Wegemund, *Das Theater des Absurden auf der Bühne und im Spiegel der literaturwissenschaftlichen Kritik: eine Untersuchung zur Rezeption und Wirkung Becketts und Ionescos in der Bundesrepublik Deutschland* (Frankfurt: Rita G. Fischer, 1983), 19.

11 Liam Lacey, "Absurdism Is Back in Vogue at Cannes," *The Globe and Mail*, May 16, 2015, available at https://www.theglobeandmail.com/arts/film/absurdism-is-back-in-vogue-at-cannes/article24466258.

12 Esslin, *The Theatre of the Absurd*, 26.

13 See Leo Pollmann, *Geschichte der französischen Literatur der Gegenwart (1880–1980)* (Darmstadt: Wissenschaftliche Buchgesellschaft, 1984), 232–33.

14 Bertolt Brecht, "*Verfremdungseffekte in der chinesischen Schauspielkunst*" [1937], in W. Hecht et al., eds., *Bertolt Brecht Werke*, vol. 22, 2.I (Berlin and Weimar Frankfurt/M.: Aufbau Suhrkamp, 1993), 200: "Es handelt sich hier um Versuche, so zu spielen, daß der Zuschauer gehindert wurde, sich in die

Figuren des Stücks lediglich einzufühlen. Annahme oder Ablehnung ihrer Äußerungen oder Handlungen sollten im Bereich des Bewußtseins, anstatt wie bisher in dem des Unterbewußtseins des Zuschauers erfolgen." In 1964 John Willet translated *Verfremdungseffekt* as "alienation effect." Later the term was also translated as "distancing effect" and "estrangement effect," while some translators simply adhered to the abbreviated "V-effekt." See John Willett, "Alienation Effects in Chinese Acting," in John Willett, ed., *Brecht on Theatre. The Development of an Aesthetic* (New York: Hill & Wang, 1964), 91–99.

15 See Esslin, *The Theatre of the Absurd*, 403, at p. 411. See also, ibid., 412:

   The alienation effect in the Brechtian theatre is intended to activate the audience's critical, intellectual attitude. The Theatre of the Absurd speaks to a deeper level of the audience's mind. It activates psychological forces, releases and liberates hidden fears and repressed aggressions, and, above all, by confronting the audience with a picture of disintegration, it sets in motion an active process of integrative forces in the mind of each individual spectator.

   Esslin also claims that, against Brecht's intentions, the nuanced characters in his plays stimulate identification (ibid., 410).

16 Ibid., 327.

17 See the quotation from an article by Louis Chauvet at the opening of Welles's film: "*A partir d'une idée relativement simple, Kafka nous plonge dans un monde incohérent, absurde et surréel.*" Translation: "Starting with a relatively simple idea, Kafka plunges us into an incoherent, absurd and surreal world."

18 Nonetheless, *Dogtooth* also employs nondiegetic music, for example, when the French chanson from the parents' earphones accompanies images of the rest of the house.

19 In *The Killing of a Sacred Deer*, the moments of the highest intensity are highlighted by acoustic shock effects, as when Martin rips out a piece from his own arm with his teeth.

20 Michel Chion, *L'Audio-Vision. Son et image au cinéma* (Paris: Armand Colin, 2017 [1990]), 93.

21 Sarah Cooper, "Narcissus and *The Lobster*," *Studies in European Cinema*, 13, no. 2 (2016): 163–76, at p. 170.

22 Jacques Derrida, "The Animal That Therefore I Am (More to Follow)," trans. David Wills, *Critical Inquiry*, 28, no. 2 ([1997] 2002): 369–418, at p. 373.

23 Ibid., 418.3

24 Ibid., 381.

25 See David Foster Wallace, "Consider the Lobster," in D. F. Wallace, ed., *Consider the Lobster and Other Essays* (New York, Boston, MA, and London: Back Bay Books, [2004] 2007), 235–54, at p. 248. Like Derrida, Wallace mentions the capacity to verbally communicate only to problematize the difference between man and animal (ibid., 246): "The fact that even the most highly evolved nonhuman mammals can't use language to communicate with us about their subjective mental experience is only the first layer of

additional complication in trying to extend our reasoning about pain and morality to animals."

26 Ludwig Wittgenstein, *Philosophical Investigations*, trans. G. E. M. Anscombe (Oxford: Basil Blackwell, [1953] 1999), 11 (§ 23):

But how many kinds of sentence are there? Say assertion, question, and command?—There are *countless* kinds: countless different kinds of use of what we call "symbols," "words," "sentences." And this multiplicity is not something fixed, given once for all; but new types of language, new language-games, as we may say, come into existence, and others become obsolete and get forgotten ...

Here the term "language-*game*" is meant to bring into prominence the fact that the *speaking* of language is part of an activity, or of a form of life.

27 Marc Augé, *Non-Place. Introduction to an Anthropology of Supermodernity*, trans. John Howe (London and New York: Verso, 1997), 77–78.
28 Esslin, *The Theatre of the Absurd*, 403. Emphasis added.

10

Dog, Lobster, Deer, Rabbit: Yorgos Lanthimos's Animal Metaphors

Savina Petkova

Three twenty-something adult children are warned by their parents that if they misbehave, their mother will give birth to two babies and a dog. Equal parts humorous and discomforting, this peculiar threat typifies the uncanny fictional world of *Dogtooth*, Yorgos Lanthimos's second feature. The Greek-born director has made six feature films to date, all of which offer stylistic consistency with one another, depicting rigid social orders and systems of discipline. Lanthimos's corpus is characterized by political allegories and dystopian commentaries on heteronormativity, fittingly coupled with eruptive yet seemingly inconsequential violence. While humans and social criticism often take center stage, the peripheries of the films' narratives are almost always inhabited by animals; in Lanthimos's films, animals are *there* but they are not *themselves*. Therefore, the threat cited above can be seen as exemplary of how animals function both ironically and significantly within the diegesis: they are complex signifiers, both visually and rhetorically, that transfigure into metaphors for the human condition.

In this chapter, I will draw on the metaphorical properties of animals to explore the overlooked political aspects of Lanthimos's films. First, I will look at *Dogtooth*, which propelled Lanthimos to international fame. There, the animal metaphor presents a correspondence between child and dog that facilitates a meta-conversation about dog training and/as parenting. In

The Lobster, animals represent former human beings who have undergone a technical procedure of transformation. This metamorphosis, I argue, becomes a metaphor for the impossible separation between human and animal. The fact that no animal appears in *The Killing of a Sacred Deer* is a logical extension of the already existent hierarchy of humans over animals, which operate metaphorically as totems. To conclude, I turn to *The Favourite*, to explore the ethical charge of a negative metaphor, as in the case of Queen Anne's seventeen rabbits named after each of her deceased children.

Two films, *Kinetta* and *Alps*, are excluded from the present study since they do not include animals with a clear figurative function within their narratives. Rather, *Kinetta* and *Alps* are more straightforwardly concerned with a hermetic world of human bodies, identity, and role play, while always remaining within the realm of the Greek, marginal, and precarious human experiences that characterize Lanthimos's early films. In the four films to be discussed here, real animals appear before the camera, with the exception of "the sacred deer." In what follows, I contend that Lanthimos's "animal" films employ nonhuman creatures stretched out of shape into ironic extremes, as political metaphors designed to challenge social orders that imagine humans as exceptional.

What Metaphor Is (Not)

It is important to determine the difference between metaphor and substitution as both are relevant here. Common sense definitions usually equate metaphor to mean something similar to paraphrase or a comparison, but these terms remain vague and inherently reductive as definitions go. Metaphor, as it is understood here, is a composite rhetorical phenomenon used to form implicit, contextual relations between two things: it designates something (A) as something else (B), resulting in "a thing which acquires the quality of something not itself."[1] Furthermore, as Rachel Frazer observes, metaphors as new formations have a peculiar ability to not only generate new meaning, but also reconfigure our thinking about the base subject, while going as far as to offer a distinct political dimension.[2] The history of the animal metaphor as a comparative mode has to do with the proximity between humans and nonhuman animals, which dates back to the dawn of civilization. According to art critic John Berger, animals first entered our imagination not as a separate species, but as signifiers of human culture because they were already seen as a means of labor and sustenance. Berger goes on to state that the animal metaphor was originary because "the essential relation between man and animal was metaphoric."[3] Berger's assessment of the animal metaphor not only determines a conceptual proximity between human and nonhuman animals, but also identifies it as a violent, mutually defining dichotomy.

Humans and animals are almost intuitively configured together in literature and cinema, to the extent that one might find themselves tempted to suspect a case of substitution instead of metaphoric proximity when an animal symbolizes something of the human world. But metaphors are not mere substitutions, despite tendencies to read animal metaphors as a stand-in for a supposed animal nature in humans. Such hypotheses have been contested as presenting empty signifiers that perpetuate anthropocentric supremacy that others nonhuman animals, a fallacy explained by Giorgio Agamben as the "anthropological machine."[4] While Lanthimos does not dispense with human–animal hierarchies, his figurative use of animals is both ironic and exaggerated so as to perform an ethical function. Indeed, animals in Lanthimos's films are complex subjects that deserve close attention.

Another way of looking at animal metaphors is through the neologism *animetaphor* coined by Akira Mizuta Lippit, whose work has contributed to both film studies and critical animal studies. He conceptualizes animal metaphors in photography and cinema as "a limit of figurability, a limit of the very function of language."[5] He argues that even though metaphor as a figure of speech gestures toward new meaning in relation to its referent, utilizing an animal as a metaphoric device actively transforms language: "One finds a fantastic transversality at work between the animal and the metaphor—the animal is already a metaphor, the metaphor an animal. Together they transport to language, breathe into language, the vitality of another life, another expression: animal and metaphor, a metaphor made flesh, a living metaphor that is by definition not a metaphor, antimetaphor—'animetaphor.' "[6]

The ethical property of Lippit's *animetaphor* has to do with animals as both real creatures and fictional signifiers, where the animal forms a spectral presence upon an anthropocentric horizon. While Lanthimos's animal metaphors are, on the contrary, fleshed out, his ethical interests remain consistent with Lippit's. By unpacking what it means to be human within a contemporary social setting through the use of animal metaphors, Lanthimos adopts an ethically dubious mode (anthropocentrism) to place emphasis on the absurd logic that underpins a human–nonhuman hierarchy. This, in Lanthimos's films, becomes a viable way to address the violence of anthropocentrism from within.

But how can a rhetorical device possess an ethical quality? Within film studies, Lanthimos's animals have been critically addressed in various ways: as a "form of deviation as a governing principle";[7] as a core part of the films' symbolic order in Lacanian terms;[8] as commentary on the "humans they once were";[9] and as crucial to a European political aesthetic.[10] The intersections between humanistic and animal discourse to be found in each of these works makes apparent the complex state of human–animal relations both in Lanthimos's films and elsewhere. If a metaphorical alignment of these two concepts (human and animal) can restructure their respectively embedded meanings, it is clear that human–animal metaphors come to bear new understandings of what it means to be human. Indeed, the conflation of categories draws critical attention to certain behaviors, such as institutional discipline in *The Lobster* or the trauma of losing children in *The Favourite*, while also commenting on the suppression of other behaviors, such as language in *Dogtooth* or romantic bonds in *The Lobster*. Thus, it is clear that animal metaphors are complex sources of meaning in Lanthimos's films, functioning as tools for criticism and as objects to analyze.

"Your Mother Will Give Birth to a Dog": The Animal Metaphor in *Dogtooth*

In *Dogtooth*, words and meaning are dramatically restructured to enforce parental rule and to mark the sharp distinction between the center (the household) and the periphery (beyond the fence). The film presents an isolated family of five breaking apart, as one daughter attempts to overthrow her authoritarian father's (Christos Stergioglou) dominion. Throughout the film, a dog functions as a symbol for how the children are to be raised—trained according to the principle of obedience—even if the canine never enters the domestic space as a pet.

Here, it is the proximity of species that intimates toward a metaphoric realm. One visualization of how the children and the dog are equated comes halfway through the film's first act, when, tightly framed in a medium shot, Elder Daughter (Angeliki Papoulia) leans onto her father's white office door. Following an abrupt cut, the viewer is transported to a dog-training facility, far away from the home's strict bounds. The juxtaposition of Elder Daughter's silence as she eavesdrops with a dog's aggressive bark doubles the spatial rupture already signified by the cut. It is no coincidence that the dog, Rex, is also framed in a medium shot, which further highlights the human–nonhuman metaphor enabled by the film's narrative. A significant difference in the presentation of the two characters is that the dog, a Dobermann Pinscher, is paradoxically the only named character in the film (curiously fitting for such a dynamic is the fact that Rex is Latin for "king"). Likewise, the trainer's monologue positions parenting and training as analogous practices, with words connoting control ("to shape," "to teach," "to determine") referencing not only the dog, but also the Father's plans for his own children: "A dog is like clay. Our job here is to shape it. A dog can be dynamic, aggressive, a fighter, a coward, or affectionate. It requires work, patience, and attention from us. Every dog, your dog is waiting for us to teach it how to behave. Do you understand?" This instructive monologue serves as evidence of *Dogtooth*'s employment of metaphor, which makes permeable the boundary between child and canine. One will find that a simple substitution of the word dog with child fails to alter the meaning of the monologue; as a result, the human–animal dimension is both metaphoric and literal, given that the dog and the children are interchangeable. In *Dogtooth*, Lanthimos actualizes his metaphor in aural, visual, and rhetorical terms; in the end, it is through these formal devices that the film's ethical commentary on authoritarianism can be located.

Shortly after, the Father puts these training techniques into practice not on his dog, but on his children. Recognizing an opportunity, he covers himself with red paint and tears his clothes to imply the pretense of an attack by the most dangerous of animals beyond the fence: the house cat. After his strange performance an even more peculiar scene unfolds. As he towers above the other family members, who are all kneeling down, the patriarch barks twice before imitating a cat's meow. The whole sequence is brimming with both absurd humor and marked humorlessness, another contradictory tonal affect reflective of how animal metaphors function in Lanthimos's films. Such a staging introduces the growl of a dog as defensive behavior for the household. Beyond the overt farcicality of the scene, the father's forceful lesson in dog-like behavior is not an actual demand to become an animal, but an instruction to become a child with dog-like behavioral traits. The lesson intimates, albeit in a way that does not condone but scrutinizes the father's methods—the film itself, after all, is a metaphor for particular procedures of power—that in certain (oppressive) conditions, a child is just like "the dog [that is] waiting for us to teach it how to behave."

Following the Father's barking lesson, *Dogtooth* sets up another instance of intraspecies proximity to further advance the dog–child metaphor at work in the film. The children are threatened that, in the case that they misbehave, their Mother will give birth to two children and a dog: "If your behavior and your performances improve, I may not have to give birth. But if things don't change, I will have no other choice. But I won't hear a thing about the dog. He will be born as soon as possible." While the conditional aspects of the pregnancy only seem to add to the exchange's absurdity, the question of biological uncertainty goes completely unacknowledged. The Mother's supposed ability to birth a dog as well as a human child extends the film's metaphor to illustrate the power of ideologies that exert control over their subjects. As superficially comic as the threat might seem to be, the fact that the children do not contest the notion of a woman giving birth to a dog is telling of the extent of their imprisonment. Since everything including language is controlled by the parental unit, the children have been conditioned to accept and obey the logic laid out for them. Unlike the seemingly arbitrary nature of the connections established between nouns and their new meanings at the outset of the film—such as "sea" meaning "wooden armchair"—the film's human–animal approximation gains traction from the seeming dissonance that prompts interrogation of the human, the animal, and the complex parallels that emerge between those categories.

The mutual dependency between two objects, (A) and (B) for example, is crucial for structuring a metaphor, according to literary theorist Stanley Corngold. However, when a figurative comparison is made literal, as *Dogtooth* suggests in its approximation of child and/as dog, the substitution is never complete. Corngold writes, "[a]s we attempt to experience in (B) more and more qualities that can be accommodated by (A), we metamorphose (A); but we must stop before the metamorphosis is complete, if the metaphor is to be preserved, and (A) is to remain unlike (B)."[11] Importantly, a metaphor remains a metaphor when an irreducible element is left unchanged. Similarity or parallelism is traditionally thought to be the main feature of a metaphor but, as showcased in *Dogtooth*, it is the encroaching proximity between human and animal that sustains the metaphor without letting it collapse into itself. Eugenie Brinkema's formalist analysis of *Dogtooth* employs the allegory of "any" (any x can be y)[12] to explain how distance functions in the framing of the film's violence, yet the children–dog relationship operates on a different, though hardly less violent, kind of closeness. In my reading, the tentative proximity of species is facilitated, on one hand, by the film's aesthetics (the cut, accompanied by the aural transition of the bark), and on the other by cross-species mirroring through metaphor. In the end, the audience is invited to consider how the metaphoric currency of the film translates across to real-world referents.

Metamorphosis as Metaphor in *The Lobster*

The Lobster unfolds in a rule-governed heteronormative world of couples. David (Colin Farrell), newly single, is taken to a repurposed hotel where he is encouraged to form a romantic bond with a female resident in forty-five days. If any of the hotel guests fail to pair off during this time frame, they stand to be turned into an animal of their choosing. This, the film invites us to think, is the fate of several guests, although the transformation procedures take place off-screen and remain shrouded in mystery. The film invites various (bio)political interpretations, and while my reading borrows from this received framework, I will focus primarily on the metaphoric potential of animals that are said to have once been human. Here, the metamorphic element challenges established hierarchies that favor one species (the human) over another—which is referred to in animal studies as "speciesism"—since all of *The Lobster*'s animals are implied to be transformed human beings.[13] In keeping with Lanthimos's withholding style, the film does not offer a clear-cut position on the critical function of interspecies relations, yet its metaphor rests on the ambiguous border between human and animal.

The Lobster also radically interprets Agamben's "anthropological machine" by effectively negating it: indeed, the film presents an indeterminacy of species that collapses what both "human" and "animal" mean independently of each other and as corresponding categories. By erasing clear distinctions between the two categories, the film's logic defies a hierarchal construction of the human as superior to animal (and therefore of "the animal" as a devolved, prehuman state). Indeed, out-of-place animals including a peacock and camel occupy the Irish forest, their exotic presence both reconfiguring the biopolitical dynamics of the film while calling attention to the diegetic construction of interspecies boundaries. It is left ambiguous as to whether or not these animals have been human before. Ambivalence over the nature of the transformation procedure itself becomes a topic of conversation between characters. Later, a sequence conveys the final day of a young blonde girl before the action cuts rapidly to reveal a pony on a lead, the montage implying that that same girl has been turned into the animal. The transformation is only "visible" by cinematic elision; with the spectator's suspension of disbelief a prerequisite for the film's premise to function, the metamorphosis itself becomes a metaphor for our own cognitive power to configure the human as a particular type of subject.

The hotel positions metamorphosis as punishment for the crime of being single, though with the caveat that guests may choose the animal they wish to become. Upon his arrival at the hotel, the manager (Olivia Colman) congratulates David on his choice to become a lobster in the case that he fails to form a couple. She goes on: "Usually the first thing people think of is a dog and that's why the world is full of dogs. Very few choose to become unusual animals, which is why they are endangered."[14] David's choice to be a lobster (cold-blooded and hard-shelled) is notably estranged from the dogs (a nod to *Dogtooth*) that are popular among the other guests. David's decision to adopt the characteristics of such a singular animal echoes Jacques Derrida's appeal in *The Animal That Therefore I Am* to resist the flattening of the animal into a homogeneous category. The function of animals here, following Rosalind Galt, is to "make power visible";[15] as such, the metaphoric potential registers via differentiation, in their singularity as distinct animals as in the case of a lobster among dogs. The process of becoming an animal in *The Lobster* expresses individuality through a declared proximity to a specific animal, utilizing a metamorphic model that operates in a classically Ovidian fashion.[16] Indeed, classical links are maintained for Lanthimos's next feature, *The Killing of a Sacred Deer*, which makes reference to another mythical story while, unusually perhaps, omitting its focal animal referent. Whereas in *The Lobster* the metaphor is sustained via human-animal metamorphosis, in the latter film the fate of the characters is structured around the notable absence of the titular animal.

The Absent Animal as Metaphor: *The Killing of a Sacred Deer*

The Killing of a Sacred Deer sees a heart surgeon (Colin Farrell) establish a relationship with a deceased patient's teenage son, Martin (Barry Keoghan). However, the narrative takes a mysterious turn when, one by one, Steven's (Farrell) family fall victim to a mystical, lethal curse that requires a sacrificial act by the father to end it. No actual deer features in the film; beside the title, there is an off-hand reference to the Greek myth in relation to a school assignment. The referenced story is *Iphigenia in Aulis* by Euripides, an Ancient Greek tragedy in which Agamemnon, a hero of the Trojan War, is required to make a sacrifice to appease Artemis—goddess of the hunt— and bring honor to his troops. When Agamemnon is forced to sacrifice his daughter—Iphigenia—she voluntarily steps upon the sacrificial altar, but the goddess replaces the girl's body with a hind, thus sparing her life.[17] While Lanthimos's film is loose as adaptations go, it nevertheless has a mythopoetic quality that stretches the tale to extreme lengths.

While the film does not feature a deer per se, the Greek tragedy equally has no human sacrifice; the murder that occurs in *The Killing of a Sacred Deer*, as Steven takes the life of his son, is itself a metaphorical stand-in for the sacrificial animal that is missing from the source text. Such interchangeability—one is present where the other is absent—embodies an important rhetorical feature of the human–animal metaphor, even if the filicide demanded by Martin's curse reverses more familiar adoptions of the human–animal trope that involve animal death. With a human death, the film's narrative exposes how metaphorical substitutions between humans and animals are inherently anthropocentric. Following *Dogtooth* and *The Lobster*, by undoing the metaphors, Lanthimos's adoption of animals enacts a form of social criticism about allegorical language, anthropocentric logic, and the human condition without merely evoking the reductive notion that humans and animals share common tendencies. In *The Killing of a Sacred Deer*, Lanthimos explores what happens to a familial structure if there is no scapegoat (in the biblical sense) to save humans from themselves. Nevertheless, the deer performs extratextual functions, to scrutinize rhetorical devices and demonstrate what is gained and lost when human–animal hierarchies are transposed onto human–animal metaphors.[18] The absent deer reinstates the violence of the original metaphor, thus revealing how human–animal metaphors often evade human culpability behind a wall of language and rhetoric.

The Killing of a Sacred Deer disentangles human–animal ethics to remain focused on human actions and their consequences. Undoubtedly, the film's causal chain of events—the violation of the Hippocratic oath, the mysterious curse that follows, as well as the sacrificial killing—entirely pertains to a realm of human ethics often negated when it comes to classical allegories.

The minimal presence of the animal is confined to the film's title, yet that structuring element is enough in itself to engineer readings that relate to the human–animal dichotomy that is implied by it. More than that, though, the film draws attention to a normative absence of real animals in human–animal metaphors if they are only accounted for by a rhetorical function (see also *The Lobster*'s essentially missing lobster).

Metaphor as Negation in *The Favourite*

Lanthimos's next film, *The Favourite*, is arguably the least animal-oriented film of the four under discussion here, but nevertheless makes candid use of seventeen rabbits to present an unorthodox form of human–animal metaphor. *The Favourite* is a queer period drama that focuses on various political dynamics, and the plays of power and lust they engender, in the court of Queen Anne (Olivia Colman) as both Lady Sarah Marlborough (Rachel Weisz) and her distant, out-of-grace relative Abigail Hill (Emma Stone) fight for her favor. Animals also feature in minor but significant roles. One early sequence includes a race (though ironically conveyed in slow motion) of domesticated ducks where Horatio, Lord Marlborough's champion, is crowned "the fastest in England," a sarcastically deployed token of manhood proffered to the ever-emasculated court members. On a different occasion, Anne sends for a supply of lobsters to race before eating. While *The Lobster*'s protagonist takes pride in describing the film's eponymous animal as "blue-blooded and royal," *The Favourite* presents both crustacea and wildfowl as a source of amusement illustrative of aristocratic excess: indeed, food-value is supplanted by entertainment-value in service of Anne's caprice. However, among all the animals, the most glaringly significant are the seventeen rabbits that reside in Anne's bedchamber.

Anne's rabbits are domesticated to the point of fetishism. Moreover, the film presents them as an unequivocal metaphor for Anne's deceased children. Keeping in mind the high rate of reproduction in rabbits (females remain fertile for their entire lives), the rabbit metaphor negates the primary, colloquial procreative frame of reference (i.e., "to fuck like rabbits"). The use of a negative metaphor—one that indicates a lack rather than a presence—proves that metaphors can be antieconomical and generate both new meaning as well as further questions. Not discounting Lanthimos's tendency toward satire, it is productive to explore the film's rabbit metaphor as precisely that: a rhetorical move that gives and takes.

As previously discussed, metaphor conventionally relies on an overlap of meaning. Here, it is built on an abrogation: fertility *vis-à-vis* childlessness. As a visualization of her trauma, the presence of actual rabbits is traded against Anne's deteriorating state of mind; the deceased (or absent) children are signified by abundantly present animals, an antithetical approach to the notably absent animal referent in *The Killing of a Sacred Deer*. In his previous film, Lanthimos's animal metaphor is purely rhetorical, but here it interweaves with the image of actual animals, *à la Dogtooth*. For Anne, the animals are individual beings, not merely a mass of rabbits; she accentuates the singularity of each animal, naming the rabbits after her children and celebrating each rabbit's birthday to mark the date of a child's passing. After climbing the ladder of Anne's good graces, Abigail recognizes the value of the rabbits as a measure of devotion to the queen. As such, the rabbits are a substantial mark of social capital and its acquisition—in this way, they become instruments of power over the ruling body, with the absurdity of that dynamic being another crucial part of their visual and thematic function in the film.

In the film's closing sequence, Anne observes an inebriated Abigail stepping on one of her rabbits, taking perverse pleasure as she smothers it. Having already secured her a place in court, the rabbit is thus stripped of its power-acquisition potential regarding Abigail's relation to Anne, though her actions here reveal that her devotion to the queen was ultimately only self-serving and therefore false. For Abigail, the rabbit is now just a rabbit and a source of play, while for Anne the metaphor remains strong to the point that it might not even be metaphorical (they are, in a way, her babies). As a rhetorical device, the rabbit beneath Abigail's foot is helpless, just as Anne's children were, as Anne now is, and as Abigail could be now that her true nature has been found out. The actual and metaphorical position of the rabbit extends further, for it cannot know its own end;[19] its proximity to death serving to punctuate the metaphor by bringing its parts ever closer: the dying rabbit with the deceased child, as well as Anne and Abigail's figuration in the new metaphorical diagram offered by the scene.

Animal death in a film is an extreme example of the limits of human–animal metaphors, since animals do not act or react in the same way as humans. Furthermore, any distance established between an animal character and the real animal disappears as acts of violence can only be conferred as real against the animal; it is the animal and not merely its image that is being threatened with violence or death. Lippit insists that animal peril is never purely figurative, and that animals achieve agency in their death cry.[20] In *The Favourite*, the animal is spared, but its proximity to death remains at the center of this final scene, even more so since rabbits do not make a sound when distressed; they express discomfort by either thumping or jumping. The absence of a death cry extends the rabbit's metaphorical qualities even further. The smothering sequence unfolds over just a few seconds, and yet the potency of the threat toward a real rabbit makes it all the more distressing, simultaneously providing a metaphor that is both meticulously constructed and deconstructed in its coming together. The threatened animal is both real and not, which in turn provides a meta-commentary on what is at stake when animals feature as metaphors at the expense of their also being flesh and blood animals. *The Favourite*, by negating the metaphor's origins, once again illustrates the complex relationality of animal metaphors in Lanthimos's films.

Metaphor and Conclusion

Lanthimos's films do not offer simple remedies to complex ethical–political issues regarding human–animal dynamics. Nevertheless, I argue that they do provide an entry point for exploring animal metaphors as a recurring, albeit knotty, trope in cinema. Even though the director himself does not specifically advocate for animal rights and ethics, his genuinely critical approach to humanism and human subjectivity, social norms, and anthropocentrism positions him as one of the more vocal diagnosticians of human–animal issues. Therefore, his animal films should be studied as such and scrutinized for their employment of and commentary on human–animal taxonomies, as well as the anthropocentric ethics at work (including the way we talk about animals), which seek to question distinctions between human and animal. Instead of employing direct philosophical referents, the films "act out" the trope in question, revealing new political orders by stretching humans and animals from their meeting points to metaphorical extremes and back again.

Animal metaphors in Lanthimos's films point to the ethical challenges of a mutually defining bond. His films make use of the two-way relationship between the metaphoric constituents and investigate the violence held in such bonds, especially where they fail to fully overlap. I argue that it is precisely this indeterminacy of species that mobilizes Lanthimos's ethical and political commentary. From the gray areas that Lanthimos creates, one can identify a pressing desire to interrogate how oppressive forces create, maintain, and wield their power. In Lanthimos's films, one might recognize "the capacity for metaphor [to] distinguish [the human] from the animal,"[21] as well as a deeper mission to understand the rhetorical dimensions that have taken root in animal comparisons. In the four films discussed here, animal metaphors can take many forms—substitution (*Dogtooth*), transformation (*The Lobster*), sacrifice (*The Killing of a Sacred Deer*), or proxy for trauma (*The Favourite*)—and it is in the films' oscillation between categories of difference, between presence and absence, that Lanthimos reveals how humans and animals can be equally other.

Notes

1 Stanley Corngold, "Kafka's '*Die Verwandlung*': Metamorphosis of the Metaphor," *Mosaic: A Journal for the Interdisciplinary Study of Literature*, 3, no. 4 (1970): 91–106, at p. 97.

2   Rachel Elizabeth Fraser, "The Ethics of Metaphor," *Ethics*, 128 (2018): 728–55, at p. 731.
3   John Berger, *About Looking* (New York: Vintage Books, 1980), 7.
4   See Giorgio Agamben, *The Open: Man and Animal*, trans. Kevin Attell (Stanford, CA: Stanford University Press, 2004).
5   Akira Mizuta Lippit, *Electric Animal: Toward a Rhetoric of Wildlife* (Minneapolis: University of Minnesota Press, 2000), 163.
6   Ibid., 165.
7   Eugenie Brinkema, "e.g., *Dogtooth*," *World Picture*, 7 (2012): 1–26, at p. 7.
8   Ben Tyrer, "'This Tongue Is Not My Own': *Dogtooth*, Phobia and the Paternal Metaphor," in T. Kazakopoulou and M. Fotiou, eds., *Contemporary Greek Film Cultures from 1990 to the Present* (Oxford: Peter Lang, 2017), 101–29, at p. 112.
9   Sarah Cooper, "Narcissus and *The Lobster*," *Studies in European Cinema*, 13, no. 2 (2016): 163–76, at p. 160.
10 Rosalind Galt, "The Animal Logic of Contemporary Greek Cinema," *Framework*, 58, nos. 1–2 (2017): 7–29, at pp. 9–10.
11 Corngold, "Kafka's *Die Verwandlung*,'" 98.
12 See Brinkema, "e.g. *Dogtooth*," 2. Her analysis centers on substitutional logic, the principle of control and allegorical disjunction.
13 See Cooper, "Narcissus and *The Lobster*," 169. Cooper remarks that "it is difficult to look at any of the animals in the film without wondering whether they too were once human."
14 Whether or not such a narrative arc conceals vegan or ecoactivist messages, and how this dialogue relates to questions of speciesism, remain interesting points of inquiry but are beyond the scope of this chapter.
15 Galt, "The Animal Logic," 21.
16 Richard Buxton writes of the significance of "the expression of the human being's previous moral character within the new form" as characteristic of Ovid's *Metamorphoses*. See Richard Buxton, *Forms of Astonishment: Greek Myths of Metamorphosis* (Oxford: Oxford University Press, 2009), 6. Also see the work of Marina Warner, who connects Ovidian metamorphoses with the Pythagorean doctrine of metempsychosis, that is, the transmigration of souls. See Marina Warner, *Fantastic Metamorphoses, Other Worlds: Ways of Telling the Self* (Oxford: Oxford University Press, 2002).
17 A messenger then enters and recounts how, as the blow was struck, a deer appeared in the maiden's place. It is generally agreed that the last 100 lines containing the messenger's speech are interpolated and were added as late as the seventh-century CE. See Naomi A. Weiss, "The Antiphonal Ending of Euripides's *Iphigenia in Aulis*," *Classical Philology*, 109 (2014): 119–29.
18 This specific function of the animal signifier echoes the work of Dominick LaCapra, who criticized Agamben's approach to the human–animal

relationship as an abstract topos. See Dominick LaCapra, *Human, Animal, Violence* (Ithaca, NY: Cornell University Press, 2009), 166.

19 Akira Mizuta Lippit, "The Death of an Animal," *Film Quarterly*, 56, no. 1 (2002): 9–22, at p. 11.
20 Ibid., 13.
21 Kelly Oliver, *Animal Lessons: How They Teach Us to Be Human* (New York: Columbia University Press, 2009), 67.

PART IV

Genre and Variation

11

Art-House Thriller: Auteur Meets Genre in *The Killing of a Sacred Deer*

Geoff King

Two notable sequences early in *The Killing of a Sacred Deer* feature camera movement tracking the progress of the main protagonist along pristine and brightly lit hospital corridors. The first, in which he is accompanied by a colleague, creates an impression of expressive art-cinema stylization, resulting partly from the extended length of the shot, the camera smoothly retreating ahead of the two figures. A wide-angle lens produces a somewhat hypnotic effect. The deep perspective appears forced and exaggerated, strong vanishing point lines being established at each of the four corners of the corridor, echoed by ceiling tiles and lines on the walls, the camera seeming to move faster than the characters. The impression is striking and a little disorienting, although in a manner that remains implicit and nonspecific, a style that fits with the strategies of certain varieties of art cinema, including the early films of Yorgos Lanthimos. The second combines such an effect with a dimension that also seems rooted in genre. The camera this time follows the cardiothoracic surgeon Steven Murphy (Colin Farrell) from behind and is positioned at a higher angle that increases the level of stylization and adds a sense of threat in the way it looms above him; a dimension reinforced through the addition of high-pitched strings on the soundtrack. Such an impression seems confirmed when the sequence leads to an unplanned meeting with the character who will prove to be his nemesis, the youthful

Martin (Barry Keoghan), although none of the underlying reasons are at this point apparent to the viewer.

The impressions created by these corridor shots are symptomatic of two dimensions of the film examined in this chapter: its mixture of material of the kind associated with both art cinema and the more generic, the latter in this case involving aspects of the psychological revenge thriller. The generic is often positioned as opposite to notions of the artistic, in film and in discourses relating to cultural production more broadly. This is an opposition that can be traced to the origins of institutionalized distinctions between notions of art and craft that date back especially to the eighteenth century in the Western tradition, a process explored by Larry Shiner[1] that I have examined previously in relation to the forms of cultural value accorded to art cinema.[2] In the face of the increasing commercialization of many forms of cultural production, a number of overlapping distinctions became sedimented into the process of marking off notions of "higher" that were accorded a more lofty status. These include the distinction between the artist and the artisan and frameworks directly relevant to the denigration of the generic such as "creative imagination" versus "reproductive imagination" and "originality" versus "imitation of models."[3] *The Killing of a Sacred Deer* is viewed here, however, as an example of a tendency for the two dimensions to be combined in certain ways in work that exists at the relatively more commercial end of the art-house spectrum.

The combination of aspects of art cinema and genre is nothing new, elements of the latter having been employed by many previous examples, including the use of crime formats in canonical examples such as early Jean-Luc Godard and François Truffaut. The art-house field has never been purely "artistic" in character—austere and intellectual or harshly social-realist, for example. It has often overlapped with the market for more generic and/or exploitation-oriented material, as I have also argued elsewhere.[4] Qualities associated with art cinema can be mixed with elements of genre in variable degrees, from the substantial maintenance of genre convention to its wholesale deconstruction. The mobilization of recognizable genre components is likely, however, all other things being equal, to give any individual example relatively larger commercial traction. The main focus of this chapter is on how the combination of art cinema and genre in *The Killing of a Sacred Deer* is manifested at the textual level, in dimensions such as narrative, audiovisual style, characterization and resulting moral ambiguity. It also situates the balance of textual qualities in the industrial–institutional context of its production and circulation, as an example of the work of an already-noted international art-house "auteur" figure seeking, as with his previous film, *The Lobster*, to move into a relatively more commercial arena, key components of which also include the use of the English language and the employment of central star performers, Farrell and Nicole Kidman. The position of Lanthimos here is viewed as a manifestation of a broader mobility available to global filmmakers, although in this instance one that occupies a geographical and industrial space between those of his low-budget Greek origins and a move toward the Hollywood mainstream.

Narrative Withholding, Style, Music

A key marker of the art-film status of *The Killing of a Sacred Deer* is its approach to narrative, although this can also be seen as partially rooted in the genre location. The early stages are characterized by a notable withholding of narrative information. The scenario, once revealed, is clearly within the scope of the revenge thriller, a reasonably distinct and established subgenre. Steven is required by Martin to choose one member of his family to kill to make amends for what Martin takes to be the former's responsibility for the death of his father during surgery. Martin has an unexplained power to inflict suffering, initially on Steven's young son Bob (Sunny Suljic): a paralysis of the legs and an inability to eat, later to be followed by bleeding from the eyes and a subsequently rapid death. Bob's condition is followed by the same affliction on his teenage sister Kim (Raffey Cassidy) and a similar one is promised for Steven's wife, Anna (Kidman). This is a distinctly larger-than-life, outlandish fictional scenario, the title indicating an element parallel with the Greek mythic story of Iphigenia. In the version told in Euripides's *Iphigenia in Aulis* (*c*. 405 BCE), Agamemnon is required to sacrifice his daughter to the goddess Artemis to enable a becalmed fleet to be allowed to sail to participate in the battle against Troy; other variants indicate that Agamemnon has offended Artemis by accidentally killing a sacred deer. Such unlikely and melodramatic material is atypical of the more "heavyweight" forms of art cinema, although perhaps less so if understood as reference to sources with the cultural cachet possessed by classical mythology. Art cinema is often associated with the opposite of the melodramatic, a term frequently used pejoratively, even if the two can also overlap in some ways.[5] The treatment of this material in *The Killing of a Sacred Deer* remains consistent with established art-cinema norms, however, both generally and in relation to the earlier films of Lanthimos and his principal collaborator, co-screenwriter Efthymis Filippou.

The revelation of the plot scenario outlined above does not come until the fiftieth minute, nearly half way through the film. Before this, the viewer witnesses a number of encounters between Steven and Martin, without any indication of the nature of their relationship, although with intimations that something sinister is involved. First, they meet in a diner. Nothing of substance is discussed, leaving the viewer uninformed about the relationship between the two. At the end of the sequence, head-and-shoulders-scale shots of each character are accompanied by quiet, high-pitched and needling strings on the soundtrack, which remain a heightened indicator of tone and consequent generic location throughout the film. A cut to an exterior—a very wide-angle shot of the two leaning on the bonnet of Steven's car, parked close to a river—is marked by the addition of a menacingly low and undeveloped base rumble. The camera glides past the pair, the two figures diminutive in the shot, the movement and aural accompaniment creating an impression of sinister threat of some unspecified variety. Another notable feature of all the scenes so far is the combination of such perspectives with overtly banal dialogue, a source of marked incongruity.

Martin next features a couple of scenes later, turning up without prior warning at the hospital, the more generically unsettling quality of which is underlined by the repeated use of the needling strings. Martin apologizes, saying he did not want to put Steven in an awkward position. Why this might be the case is again left unexplained, the continued use of the same elements on the soundtrack maintaining a more marked but still unspecific sense that something is awry. A similar accompaniment features in their next meeting, a walk along the waterside that ends with Steven inviting Martin to his home to meet his family. A slight extra frisson is added to the strings, quietly wavering, as we cut to a gliding camera observing his arrival at the door, implying the presence of some kind of threat, although unspecified. During the visit, Martin is polite and well received by Steven's family, but there is an odd flatness in his manner of speaking. The sinister music is left behind but the visuals at times maintain a sense of something being off kilter. An odd perspective is employed in Kim's bedroom, for example, where the three young people have gathered, in which the camera moves slowly inward during a shot that frames only the lower halves of Kim and Martin, followed by a cut to a relatively high wide-angle view of the room.

All of this material is bristling with unease, awkwardness and discomfort of a kind that characterizes the Greek films through which Lanthimos and Filippou gained their international reputation, most notably *Dogtooth*, a dimension I examine elsewhere.[6] This includes a unsettling bedroom sequence between Steven and Anna, a game they term "general anesthetic" that involves the latter sprawling motionless on the bed for the former's sexual pleasure. Sources of such awkwardness feature in many varieties of art cinema more generally, the qualities of which often challenge more mainstream-conventional forms of cinematic comfort.[7] The lack of any spelling out of the underlying scenario is another quality familiar from the earlier work of the filmmakers. In another approach that can be taken as characteristic of certain forms of art cinema more widely, which often put greater than usual demands on the audience, the viewer is left to deduce what exactly is going on in the treatment of the sequestered children in *Dogtooth* or the enactment of the roles of the recently deceased in *Alps*. *The Killing of a Sacred Deer* is broadly similar in this respect, although the marked connotations of the music, in particular, make a significant difference to the overall impression. Viewers are left to wonder what the basis might be of the relationship between Steven and Martin. Martin, as performed by Keoghan, has an innocent and vulnerable appearance, with blandly child-like features that might also imply some kind of unstated plain-faced threat in this context, potential film-generic resonances here ranging from the likes of *Village of the Damned* (Wolf Rilla, 1960) to *Funny Games* (Michael Haneke, 1997). Steven's offer of money to buy food in the diner suggests the youth might come from a more disadvantaged background, a point confirmed by Martin during his visit to the home of the cardiologist.

The first explanation we are given for Steven's relationship with Martin comes when he introduces Martin to a colleague as a school-friend of his daughter. He subsequently tells Anna that Martin was a patient of his some years previously, the latter's father having died instantly after a car crash. The fact that Martin's father was treated in a hospital—and so did not die instantly from anything—is intimated twice: once in a phone call from Martin to Steven and again during a dinner visit made by Steven to Martin's home, during which he escapes from an embarrassing pass from the latter's mother (Alicia Silverstone). Martin's invitation to dinner is given its own dark undertones, not just in the presence of quietly sinister notes on the soundtrack but also his insistence that it happen the following night. A sound bridge has his words overlap a sequence taking place the next day, in which Steven drives out of the hospital parking garage, during which the troubling tones recur. An overtly thriller- or even horror-generic moment occurs, in which a blurry figure passes close to the camera, after which we catch what seems to be a fleeting glimpse of Martin. A cut to an exterior of Martin's home is accompanied by Steven asking if he came to the hospital that day, which the former denies (the implication being that this is untrue and thus something openly dishonest is now involved). That it was Martin's father rather than Martin who was a former patient, who died on the operating table, is spelled out by Martin after he turns up at Steven's office at the hospital—following another high-angle, unnervingly scored corridor sequence—claiming to be suffering from heart pains.

Following the awkward failure of what appears to have been Martin's attempt to set Steven up with his mother, a call from Martin interrupts a lunch at the Murphy residence. By this stage, Martin is gaining what appears to be the status of a stalker of some kind, the implications of which are increased when, shortly afterward, he turns out to have driven Kim home from her school choir practice on a borrowed motorcycle—a more clearly invasive move at the vulnerable level of family, all the more so for not being shown—after which he lurks outside. The following morning is when the first of the physical symptoms strike Bob, although no logical basis yet seems to exist for any connection to be made between the two sets of events. It is the day after this that Martin reveals his apparent responsibility for Bob's condition and the fact that Steven must choose one of his family to kill "to balance things out" if they are not all to succumb. The clear implication is that Steven was responsible for the death of Martin's father, although this is not discussed. Later dialogue between Steven and Anna, and then the latter and the anesthesiologist Matthew (Bill Camp), informs us that Steven had been drinking before an operation involving the father, although the latter contests responsibility.

Narrative withholding of the kind that characterizes most of the first half of the film can be interpreted as a product of both art-cinema and generic conventions. The former is a mark of continuity with the earlier films of Lanthimos (although not his first non-Greek production, *The Lobster*, the bizarre scenario of which is spelled out much earlier) and established art-cinema traditions (whether those associated with certain forms of downplayed realism or more obscure modernist or minimalist tendencies). Such reticence, or more active concealing, is also a convention of certain kinds of thriller or horror narratives, however. Generic conventions allow films of this kind to be narratively uncommunicative or sometimes outrightly misleading, but in a manner that might broadly be expected or accepted as within the norm.[8] That *The Killing of a Sacred Deer* leans toward generic as much as art-cinematic motivation for its approach is implied most clearly by the connotations of the music. The overall valence of the scenes outlined above would be very different were the music to be removed and the viewer left without the overtly interpretive steer it provides, as tends to be the case in the earlier films of Lanthimos and much of the art-cinema landscape within which they can be located. The sinister tones create an impression of discomfort and dislocation, along with some of the visual qualities, but of a very particular kind. This is an overt signaling of grounds for discomfort, even where their exact basis remains unclear. It implies something as-yet-unknown that will be revealed, as opposed to the ultimately perhaps more discomforting absence of encouragement of interpretive or emotional response found in works such as *Dogtooth*.

Mixing Arthouse and the Generic

In the second half, *The Killing of a Sacred Deer* moves in a more clearly channeled direction. The revelation of the central plot dilemma establishes an explicit generic scenario. We move away from any notion of a broadly unsettling portrayal of relatively ordinary existence into an explicitly heightened and abnormal narrative of threat, crisis, and required response. That is, this involves a move into the kind of special, separate fictional world associated with many film genres, the conventions of which encourage the viewer to accept and engage with situations that might not otherwise be likely to be deemed plausible (the irrational or "evil" of horror, the alien worlds of science fiction, the bursting into song of the non-backstage musical, etc.). The film seems here unambiguously to gain the status of a thriller. There is a threat to life to be faced, a raising of the stakes beyond the material of the everyday, and a clearly identified antagonist. Subgenerically, this might be situated further as a *psychological* thriller, in that the abiding modality is one that primarily involves personal–psychological control and response rather than outward sources of action, plotting or violence. As Martin Rubin suggests, in general, "the thriller works primarily to evoke such feelings as suspense, fright, mystery, exhilaration, excitement, speed, movement."[9] He adds, "it emphasizes visceral, gut-level feelings rather than more sensitive, cerebral, or emotional heavy feelings, such as tragedy, pathos, pity, love, nostalgia."[10] The psychological thriller, as Rubin suggests, focuses more on "the psychological motivations and emotional relationships of characters affected by a crime."[11] As a feature that mixes elements of this genre and those associated with art cinema, and that leans toward the psychological, *The Killing of a Sacred Deer* is lower in its offering of more mainstream-conventional entertainment qualities such as excitement, speed and movement and is more emotionally heavy in tone. It offers a potential exhilaration of its own, however, in some of the striking use of wide-angle visuals, particularly combined with the unsettling music, and in what might be seen as the audacity of some of its treatment of family relationships and its climax, to which I return below.

The Killing of a Sacred Deer also has resonances of the horror genre, again located chiefly as an interior or psychological variety. Music or sound design again features prominently in the establishment of such resonances, one implicit source of connection between the events before and after the first collapse of Bob. The reason for Bob's condition is, at first, unclear, although given horror-like audio resonances. The initial revelation that he cannot move his legs is accompanied by a low percussive rattle-rumbling that marks an incursion of heightened material. Early scenes at the hospital feature louder and more intrusively dissonant and dark sounds, an unresolved, discordant and sometimes darkly brassy rattling-grating commotion. Bob seems to recover and is on the way out of the building when he collapses again at the foot of an escalator, to similar accompaniment, in a high overhead shot the fatalistic connotations of which—implying some force from above—seem to presage what is to come. The audio effects used here and elsewhere are somewhat oppressive in nature, offering elements of the "constrictive immersion" associated by Julian Hanich with the bodily impact of certain kinds of horror or thriller sequences.[12] For Hanich, a central dynamic of such material is created by shifts between such tightening/compression and relieving moments of extrication out of the film world. This, he suggests, is the basis of the pleasure that can be taken from cinematic experiences of fear. In the escalator sequence of *The Killing of a Sacred Deer*, however, the two seem simultaneously to be combined: the oppressive sound occurs at a moment of distanced withdrawal from proximity to character. A general favoring of distancing of this kind is a marker of the more art-cinema qualities of the film, an issue addressed in more detail below. While the source of Martin's power is never made clear, it seems almost to be manifested within the disturbing field of the sound design, from earlier intimations to its full-blown exercise from this point onward. Similar sources of aural dislocation feature in scenes in which Bob undergoes a range of medical tests, including a horror-type organ note at one point during a scan.

Having eventually moved into a more defined and generically coded scenario, *The Killing of a Sacred Deer* retains central qualities that can be associated with the realm of art cinema. If genre elements offer a source of greater commercial traction, the balance between the generic and that which is more characteristic of art cinema leaves plenty of space for variation, as I have argued elsewhere.[13] Genre components might relatively conventionalize the art-cinematic, but the latter can also render genre territory more challenging and less clear-cut, in some cases blurring the lines between the two. This is the case in *The Killing of a Sacred Deer*, I suggest, at levels including additional aspects of narrative structure and in dimensions such as central characterization and resulting moral ambiguity.

The major "revelation" moment offered by Martin is itself unconventionally deployed. If much of the narrative withholds rather than reveals, this is a moment of strikingly rushed exposition. Having turned up unbidden and complaining about being stood up the day before, Martin insists that Steven join him in the hospital cafeteria. In response to the latter's complaint that he does not have much time, Martin reacts literally, blurting out his ultimatum in an extremely rapid and condensed manner. The effect is incongruous: material of great moment—within the diegesis and to the viewer—is rattled off flatly and without what would seem to be the appropriate level of emotional expression. The impact of what Martin claims also seems underplayed, with little explicit discussion of this between Steven and Anna or much direct evidence until close to the end of the film of Steven's response other than what might be taken to be a state of disbelief or denial. When a visit to Bob's hospital room after the encounter confirms that he is unable to eat, Steven tries to force food into his mouth. As further tests are carried out and Anna declares her opinion that it is a psychosomatic disorder, Steven tries to make Bob walk. In an attempt to get his son to admit if it is all pretense, he offers a deeply inappropriate and uncomfortable revelation of a secret of his own, relating to his first masturbation and an incident in which he masturbated his sleeping father. Even after Kim has also fallen victim to the first two stages of incapacity, Steven seems to remain in denial, either just outwardly or to himself, and fails to admit any culpability for the death of Martin's father. That Martin really has the power he claims over the family seems confirmed when he speaks by phone to Kim from outside the hospital and tells her to get up and go to the window, which she is then able to do. What the basis of any such influence might be is left entirely unaddressed, however, a prominent and substantial narrative lacuna the viewer is left to deal with without explanation—an area in which a more conventional generic fiction might be expected to offer some kind of rationale. All the viewer is left with on this count is, for those sufficiently informed, an entirely external and abstract application of part of a Greek tragic model that is given no specific purchase on the events of the film.

Once well established in its genre dimensions, *The Killing of a Sacred Deer* continues to challenge more mainstream-conventional approaches in its treatment of character. Steven and Anna are not conventionally sympathetic figures with whom viewers are encouraged to feel emotional allegiance, despite the highly emotive nature of the dilemma they face. Both are presented as somewhat cold and flat, given to the expression of stilted and often unconvincing banalities, another feature the film has in common with the earlier work of Lanthimos. *The Killing of a Sacred Deer* offers alignment with Steven, in the first sense in which the term is used by Murray Smith to examine what he terms the "structure of sympathy" offered by films.[14] That is, alignment in the form of a "spatio-temporal attachment" to character: a general sense of proximity to the character, who offers the primary source of focalization for the diegetic events. This is not accompanied by a strong sense of "subjective access" to character, however, the approach found generally toward the main protagonists of more mainstream-conventionally articulated features.

The recurrent use of wider than usual angles and long shots is one way the film tends to remain distant from its characters, including Steven. Wide-angle lenses, in some cases as short as 10 mm or 12 mm,[15] create an impression of characters being oppressed by their surroundings. Distortion of this kind does not create an impression of access to subjectivity, as can be the case with many expressive audio-visual effects employed in works of art or independent cinema, but of something closer to their subjection to exterior forces in a manner more likely to be associated with certain forms of horror. When closer shots are used, these are also at times relatively disjunctive. When not viewed in distancing wide-angle perspectives, characters are often shot from a sideways-on position, looking toward the edge of the frame more than outward to a position closer to that of the viewer, an approach the cumulative effect of which seems to block a more conventional sense of access to their emotions. Framing that locates characters toward the lateral margins of the frame has a constricting effect, creating a general impression of tension that might at times have a particular character orientation. In the early part of the film, Martin is particularly subjected to such treatment, sometimes along with Steven. In the first waterside encounter between the pair, for example, one low-angle, shallow-focus shot has the latter to the left of the center of the frame, facing left, with the former's shoulder visible at the edge of the screen, seemingly hemmed in. Martin hugs Steven, in response to the gift of a watch, his face now moving to the left extremity. A reverse angle keeps both similarly squeezed into the margins. A cut follows to a low wide-angle long shot of the pair, perched on the bonnet of Martin's car in front of the waterside background and positioned toward the bottom of the frame and slightly off-center to the right. As the camera moves in closer, the effect is to push them again toward the right-hand edge of the screen.

A similar sense of constriction is created in the scene at the hospital during which Martin shows Steven the new strap he has obtained for the watch. A cut is made to a head-and-shoulders-scale shot in which Steven's head is located in between the middle and right-hand side of the screen and Martin is only partially visible at the right-hand edge. A sense of off-center confinement is also created in the second waterside scene, in which wide-angle long shots, trailing the pair from behind, are combined with closer framing from low and slightly canted angles as well as some moments of marginal positioning. At times, the impression might be that Martin poses an intrusive threat from the margins, at the formal as well as at the plot level. This seems particularly the case when he arrives at the Murphy household and a shot from outside is followed by a lateral perspective after Anna opens the door to him: at first, Martin remains off-screen to the right, passing flowers across the threshold while still out of vision. After being invited in by Anna, he stands for a moment at the edge of the screen before walking across the hallway, now kept centered along with Anna as the camera pans to follow them. This might be taken as formally underlining what is intimated to be an almost vampiric intrusion into the family sanctum. It is notable that early individual shots of Kim and Bob present them centered in the frame, as if to imply a state of more balanced everyday normality, although across the film as a whole, Martin is far from the only character to be presented either positioned or looking flatly toward the margins of the image. The general stylistic approach is another dimension in which the film is broadly in keeping with the style of Lanthimos's early work, such as *Dogtooth*, which includes some shots that frame figures without including their heads. Distance of the kind that often results, combined with some more conventional treatment, gives the film something of the "cerebral" quality that Rubin suggests is not usually associated with the thriller.

Following from but also going beyond this, *The Killing of a Sacred Deer* also withholds any great encouragement of what Smith terms "allegiance" with any of the characters: a sense of moral approval of their behavior and siding with them in evaluative terms. This is a striking feature in a work that involves stark moral–emotional issues and another key marker of less-mainstream film status. Is Steven to blame for what happens? Does he in any way *deserve* the kind of justice meted out by Martin? It might be hard to say that he is or does, but neither does the film seem to offer exculpation. Instead, it tends to occupy an awkward space in between. The exact facts surrounding responsibility for the death of Martin's father are left unclear. Steven admits to having had a couple of drinks before the operation, but whether or not that was a causal factor is left open. Instead, we are left with little more than the banalities offered by the surgeon and the anesthesiologist, each of whom ritually says it is always the other who is to blame for any deaths in the operating theater. Even if Steven were to blame, we might not consider this to merit the brutal eye-for-an-eye punishment required by Martin.

Steven is not presented in an overwhelmingly positive or negative light but no concerted working-through of the moral rights and wrongs is offered. The film is here unlike some examples of art cinema characterized by an attempt to offer an explicit articulation of what can be a nonjudgmental plurality of different perspectives, as, for example, in *A Separation* (*Jodaeiye Nader az Simin*, Asghar Farhadi, 2011). The coldly distant treatment of Steven does not give him the status of a more typically commercial film version of a sympathetic flawed "everyman" with whom the viewer is encouraged to have a high level of personal empathy, caught up in some such situation beyond his control. Anna is presented in much the same way, if anything more coldly detached, certainly not as a source of warmth or family nourishment. The film could be read as an indictment of a cold, shallow, upper-middle-class professional existence of the kind often found in works of art cinema set in such a milieu (e.g., the films of Haneke), but nothing of this kind is made explicit. This is another dimension in which the film is reminiscent of earlier Lanthimos films such as *Dogtooth*, containing plenty of potential for the application of such sociopolitical readings while remaining elusively nonspecific in itself.

A similar quality of the morally ambiguous and disquieting, again characteristic of art cinema and notions of higher art more generally, is found in the responses of Bob, Kim and Anna in the later stages of the film. It becomes apparent, without any initial statement or discussion, that they are each competing not to be chosen by Steven to be given the role of sacrificial victim. At this point it is clear the children are aware of the scenario, although it is characteristic of the film that no moment of revelation to them is dramatized. After Kim intimates in one exchange with Bob that it is he who will die, not because she or his parents do not love him, Bob replies to the effect that his parents have bought him a piano, to which allusion was made earlier in the film. Their mother told him it would arrive the following month, he adds: "They didn't tell you so you wouldn't be scared." The implication is that he expects to be the one still to be around at that time. Kim responds by asking if she can have his MP3 player when he is dead.

Such cold competition for life between siblings is a highly unconventional and disturbing representation of family relations, a clear marker of art or independent status. The same goes for subsequent sequences in which each sets about trying to win over Steven. Bob drags himself along the floor into the kitchen to cut his hair—an earlier bone of contention with his father— and offers to water the plants, a chore he has previously evaded. Having earlier declared his desire to be an ophthalmologist when he grows up, a marker of allegiance to his mother's profession, he now says he has changed his mind and would prefer to do what his father does. Such blatant sucking up to a parent in order to have a greater chance to be allowed to live is, again, deeply against more conventional representations of even the more troubled of fictional families. Kim later abases herself in a broadly similar manner, after first seeking to escape with Martin. She offers to be the one to atone for her father's sins, telling him he gave her life and has the right to take it away. This appears not to be a heartfelt declaration but another cynical ploy for sympathy. Anna, meanwhile, having gained no response from the offer of another bout of "general anesthetic," suggests coldly that "the most logical thing, no matter how harsh it sounds" is to kill one of the children because they can always have another, or if not, they can try IVF. She is, effectively, competing for her own life against one of her own children, a clear transgression of a more sacrificial maternal stereotype. Steven, for his part, resorts to a visit to the children's school principal to ask which of them is best, a question that the latter unsurprisingly declines to answer. A nod to the mythic reference of the title is offered here in the principal's reference to an excellent paper written by Kim about Iphigenia, which might lead the suitably informed viewer to suppose that her apparent offer to be the sacrificial victim might be lifted from a similar *volte face* enacted by Euripides's version of the character.

The ending of the film is one that spares Steven the difficulty of making a choice but is extremely harsh in conventional cinematic-cultural terms. Presumably unable to decide, or to live with such a burden, he arranges his wife and children in the living room: seated, bound, gagged and hooded. Armed with a rifle, he covers his own eyes, spins himself around and shoots in a random direction, the weapon aimed at approximately body height. After two misses, he eventually hits Bob, presumably fatally, in the chest. A cut is made to a scene in the diner where Steven met Martin earlier in the film. Martin enters, passing the other three. A number of looks are exchanged before the film ends with a shot of Martin and a cut to the main title. Life appears to have carried on for the survivors. The viewer might wonder how the death of Bob would have been explained but, such detail aside, the end is one that can be classified as "tough" and uncompromising, a quality that fits with the expectations of the art house as well as those of harsher versions of psychological horror or thriller. There is no last-minute rescue of the kind found in *Iphigenia in Aulis*, in which, just at the moment of sacrifice, the title character is magically replaced by a deer, which is accepted as an alternative. Neither does there appear to be any price to be paid by the instigator, Martin, or any outward sense of the kind of emotional agonizing undergone by Agamemnon in Euripides's play; none of the kinds of mediations, consolations or relief that might be expected in more comfortable treatments of such territory.

Between Hollywood and the Local

The combination of art-house and genre qualities found in *The Killing of a Sacred Deer* at the textual level can be understood in the context of a particular phase of the career of the filmmaker/s. Creators of small-scale independent art-house-type features are often faced with difficult choices once having established an initial presence and recognition within the field. One option is to continue making films of a broadly similar kind to those upon which their careers have been launched. This means relying usually on a mixture of limited sources of funding, often difficult to acquire even for those with an established reputation, and being restricted to an international festival and art-house arena, particularly for films made in languages that have only local reach and that, as a result, require subtitling or dubbing in order to be consumed beyond their country or region of production. Many examples of this can be found, ranging from figures such as Jean-Luc Godard, in the latter category, to Hal Hartley in the English-language American indie sector. Lanthimos is an example of a filmmaker who has sought access to larger resources—and, concomitantly, broader audiences—by moving to a different location and mode of production, from *The Lobster* onward. Key ingredients of the recipe involved, as in *The Killing of a Sacred Deer*, are a move to London as a base, production in the English language and the recruitment of substantial star names as lead performers, notably Colin Farrell in both *The Lobster* and *The Killing of a Sacred Deer*, with the latter also featuring the marquee name of Kidman. In keeping with these moves toward a larger scale commercial arena is the use of generic components such as romance in the former and the elements of thriller and horror examined above in the latter. The particular relocation achieved by Lanthimos represents a middle position, in industrial terms, away from the limitations imposed by Greece-based and Greek-language independent production but not all the way into the fully mainstream arena of Hollywood. *The Killing of a Sacred Deer* occupies a middle space, at this level, that maps quite closely onto the territory represented by the mix of art-cinema and generic elements at the textual level.

Lanthimos has, as of the time of writing, actively resisted any call from Hollywood, the primary gravitational force of attraction for many filmmakers who move from smaller industries in their countries of origin in search of increased resources and/or rewards. After achieving an Oscar nomination for *Dogtooth*, the film that marked his international breakthrough in the art-house sector, he was taken around Hollywood by his agent and offered a number of existing projects that he declined because, unsurprisingly, there was no guarantee that he would have any of the control to which he was accustomed.[16] As Melis Behlil suggests, the Hollywood studios have a long history of recruiting directing talent from smaller cinemas overseas, a tendency that has, if anything, increased in the intensely globalized neoliberal film economy of recent decades.[17] As Behlil puts it, citing two dimensions that would apply to Lanthimos, the most common path to Hollywood "seems to be to achieve box-office success or a significant reputation in one's own country or region or on the global festival circuit, possibly leading to an Oscar nomination, something that often translates into a contract with a major studio."[18] Hollywood is generally keen to recruit new talent to maintain the quality of its output. For filmmakers from elsewhere, work in Hollywood offers new opportunities, including greater remuneration, higher production budgets and access to better equipment, along with bigger marketing budgets and distribution networks, resulting in an ability to reach larger audiences. In return, as Behlil suggests, "the directors are expected to play the game by the rules and make films that make a profit."[19] The latter is almost always likely to involve a surrender of any total control over their work (a luxury enjoyed by few even among established studio directors), including an emphasis on projects of more mainstream credentials than any of the work of Lanthimos to date. It is for this reason that he declined any such move (although *The Killing of a Sacred Deer* was his first film to be shot in the United States, in Cincinnati).

Lanthimos has been frank, however, about some of the commercial benefits of his move away from Greece. Working in English from *The Lobster* onward was a clear statement of intention to access filmmaking on a larger scale than the very low-budget, "available means" (which also often means virtually "unpaid") model found in his early career. It was this in particular that enabled him to employ internationally recognized performers such as Farrell and Kidman, along with Rachel Weisz in both *The Lobster* and *The Favourite*. A clear marker of the status of the developing international auteur career—however much this might need to be qualified by his long-term collaboration with Filippou and others, including director of photography Thimios Bakatakis and editor Yorgos Mavropsaridis—was the fact that it was the stars who approached Lanthimos, rather than vice versa, at least as far as Weisz and Kidman were concerned, the latter having also been considered at one point for *The Lobster*.[20] The director also apparently insisted that the stars worked on his own terms, including a requirement to have seen his films and to accept that he will not give them any background information on the story or their characters beyond what is in the screenplay.[21]

Lanthimos acknowledged that the central focus on a love relationship in *The Lobster* provided a theme that was "accessible" and made the film "financially appealing," at least on the basis of a "multi-part European coproduction model,"[22] with funding from Ireland, the UK, Greece, France and the Netherlands, including a number of state agencies.[23] *The Killing of a Sacred Deer* is listed as an Ireland, UK, Greece production. Principal funding came from the UK-based Film4, the Irish Film Board and New Sparta Film,[24] the film having been developed by Film4 with the Ireland- and

London-based Element Pictures. It also received support from the European Union's MEDIA program: a development grant of €58,000 and €179,000 in support of its distribution.[25] The budget of *The Lobster* has been estimated at €4 million, no figure being available for the latter. Both films were given selective releases in the US market by the relatively youthful independent distributor, A24, the slate of which has mixed international features with exploitation-genre elements of the kind found in *The Killing of a Sacred Deer* (e.g., *Climax* [Gaspar Noé, 2018], and *Midsommar* [Ari Aster, 2019]) with lower-key American indies such as *The Florida Project* (Sean Baker, 2017) and *Lady Bird* (Greta Gerwig, 2017). These are models not so different from those followed by many non-English-language art-house productions, however, and modest in scope. The combination of genre and art-film status of *The Killing of a Sacred Deer* was also reflected in its festival career, a key component in the life cycle of art and independent films. It followed a standard prestige-art-film model in having its premiere at Cannes and also showing at high-profile events such as Toronto and London, but it was also screened at Fantastic Fest and Beyond Fest, each of which is specifically identified as a genre-oriented showcase.[26]

What this industrial location amounts to is the availability of considerably more resources than were employed in the Greek films of Lanthimos, but still a relatively marginal position when compared with that of Hollywood or other larger-budget mainstream-oriented cinemas. Such a position was actively chosen by Lanthimos, who said at the time of the release of *The Killing of a Sacred Deer*: "For the moment, I'd rather make smaller films that I can control than just going and making a much bigger film and not being able to maintain my vision."[27] He has expressed some reservations about even this degree of move from origins he characterizes as working with a group of close friends. He had "craved professionalism," he says in another interview, but was "a bit frustrated with it" when it was achieved because he missed the degree of flexibility he had when just working with intimates.[28] His struggle, he says, has been to try to regain some such flexibility after moving into what he describes as "a much more composed structure."[29]

The case of Lanthimos in general, and *The Killing of a Sacred Deer* in particular, can be seen as an example of one of the many positions that exist for filmmakers, in between smaller production in their countries of origin and any move to the larger-scale arena of Hollywood.[30] His next film, *The Favourite*, offers a mix of qualities that might be viewed as bearing the marks of the auteur (including the use of pronouncedly even wider-angle, sometimes fish-eye lenses) and the more conventional production category of the British-based royal-period-heritage film. In this case, some more degree of movement can be identified from the origins of the filmmaker, *The Favourite* not being scripted by Lanthimos or Filippou and moving a stage closer to Hollywood in having a larger budget, estimated at $15 million, and being distributed by the specialty division of one of the studios, Fox

Searchlight Pictures. This remained some distance from Lanthimos having the status of a more mainstream director-for-hire, a situation from which he had previously distanced himself,[31] but further illustrates the variety of positions that can be taken up within the wider landscape of international film culture and industry.

Notes

1. See Larry Shiner, *The Invention of Art: A Cultural History* (Chicago: University of Chicago Press, 2001).
2. See Geoff King, *Positioning Art Cinema: Film and Cultural Value* (London: I.B. Tauris, 2019).
3. Shiner, *The Invention of Art*, 155.
4. King, *Positioning Art Cinema*.
5. Ibid., 97–98, 180, 216–35.
6. See Geoff King, *The Cinema of Discomfort: Disquieting, Awkward and Uncomfortable Experiences in Contemporary Art and Indie Film* (New York: Bloomsbury, 2021).
7. Ibid.
8. For an analysis of "puzzle" or "twist" narratives in contexts ranging from the art and indie film sectors to Hollywood, see Warren Buckland, ed., *Puzzle Films: Complex Storytelling in Contemporary Cinema* (Chichester: Wiley-Blackwell, 2009) and *Hollywood Puzzle Films* (New York: Routledge, 2014).
9. Martin Rubin, *Thrillers* (Cambridge: Cambridge University Press, 1999), 5.
10. Ibid.
11. Ibid., 203.
12. Julian Hanich, *Cinematic Emotion in Horror Films and Thrillers: The Aesthetic Paradox of Pleasurable Fear* (New York: Routledge, 2010), 24.
13. King, *Positioning Art Cinema*, 212–54.
14. See Murray Smith, *Engaging Characters: Fiction, Emotion, and the Cinema* (Oxford: Clarendon Press, 1995).
15. See Kodak, "Yorgos Lanthimos, Director of *The Killing of a Sacred Deer*, Says He Doesn't Want to Shoot Digitally Again," *Kodak*, Jan 24, 2018, available at https://www.kodak.com/za/en/motion/blog/blog_post/?contentid=4295005986.
16. See Eric Kohn, "How Yorgos Lanthimos Got Nicole Kidman to Go Disturbing Places with *The Killing of a Sacred Deer*," *Indiewire*, Nov 10, 2017, available at https://www.indiewire.com/2017/11/yorgos-lanthimos-interview-the-killing-of-a-sacred-deer-nicole-kidman-1201896185/.
17. See Melis Behlil, *Hollywood Is Everywhere: Global Directors in the Blockbuster Era* (Amsterdam: Amsterdam University Press, 2016).

18 Ibid., 24.
19 Ibid., 20.
20 See Danny Leigh, "Interview: Yorgos Lanthimos, Director of *The Lobster*," *Financial Times*, Oct 13, 2015, available at https://www.ft.com/content/f5f489ca-719f-11e5-9b9e-690fdae72044.
21 Kohn, "How Yorgos Lanthimos Got Nicole Kidman to Go Disturbing Places."
22 Amir Ganjavie, "Futureworlds: Talking with Yorgos Lanthimos about *The Lobster*," *Bright Lights Film Journal*, May 19, 2016, available at https://brightlightsfilm.com/talking-yorgos-lanthimos-lobster/.
23 Leigh, "Interview: Yorgos Lanthimos, Director of *The Lobster*."
24 Element Distribution, "*The Killing of a Sacred Deer* Production Notes," *Element Distribution*, 2017, available at http://elementdistribution.ie/wp-content/uploads/THE-KILLING-OF-A-SACRED-DEER-Production-Notes-FINAL.pdf.
25 European Commission, "EU-Funded Movie Awarded Prestigious Palme d'Or at Cannes Film Festival," June 1, 2017, available at https://ec.europa.eu/unitedkingdom/news/eu-funded-movie-awarded-prestigious-palme-dor-cannes-film-festival_en.
26 Mark Olsen, "Not Even Nicole Kidman and Colin Farrell Can Answer the Mysteries of *The Killing of a Sacred Deer*," *Los Angeles Times*, Oct 20, 2017, available at https://www.latimes.com/entertainment/movies/la-et-mn-the-killing-of-a-sacred-deer-answers-20171020-story.html.
27 Quoted in Kohn, "How Yorgos Lanthimos Got Nicole Kidman to Go Disturbing Places."
28 Quoted in Sarah Bradbury, "*The Killing of a Sacred Deer*: An Interview with Director Yorgos Lanthimos," *The Upcoming*, Nov 1, 2017, available at https://www.theupcoming.co.uk/2017/11/01/the-killing-of-a-sacred-deer-an-interview-with-director-yorgos-lanthimos/.
29 Ibid.
30 For useful analysis of a variety of positions within this spectrum taken up by the Mexican-born directors Guillermo del Toro, Alejandro González Iñárritu, and Alfonso Cuarón, see Deborah Shaw, *The Three Amigos: The Transnational Filmmaking of Guillermo del Toro, Alejandro González Iñárritu and Alfonso Cuarón* (Manchester: Manchester University Press, 2013); for more case studies relating specifically to moves to Hollywood, see Behlil, *Hollywood Is Everywhere*.
31 Kohn, "How Yorgos Lanthimos Got Nicole Kidman to Go Disturbing Places."

12

Myth and Mythopoeia in the Films of Yorgos Lanthimos

James J. Clauss

Film scholars agree: the films of Yorgos Lanthimos are weird.[1] After seeing *The Killing of a Sacred Deer*, my initial response was negative. I had a similar reaction to Pier Paolo Pasolini's *Oedipus Rex* (*Edipo Re*, 1967) and *Medea* (1969) upon the first viewings. It was only after seeing those films numerous times that I came to grasp the depth of their meaning and the formal intelligence of the artist behind them.[2] So, with Pasolini in mind, not only did I revisit *The Killing of a Scared Deer* several times, but other Lanthimos films as well, including *Kinetta*, *Dogtooth*, *Alps*, *The Lobster*, and *The Favourite*. I have now come to see how *The Killing of a Sacred Deer* reflects his broader cinematic and, dare I say, mythopoeic representation of human behaviors. As a classicist, I tend to view films through an ancient lens.[3] In this case, Lanthimos specifically invites us to approach *The Killing of a Sacred Deer* as an adaptation of the myth of Iphigenia, daughter of Agamemnon, since it is alluded to in the title and specifically mentioned near the end of the film. As it happens, I suggest that a central theme of *The Killing of a Sacred Deer*—found in the ancient myth involving Iphigenia in general and central to Euripides's *Iphigenia in Aulis* (405 BCE) in particular, the model for the film—provides insight into understanding all of Lanthimos's films. Since coming to this understanding by studying *The Killing of a Sacred Deer*, I will begin my analysis of his oeuvre with this film and thereafter proceed chronologically. I start, however, with a diachronic look at the ancient myth, as it accounts for the central crisis in the film and the way in which the characters respond. As we shall see, the heart of *The Killing of a Sacred Deer* transcends the Greek myth and the specific tragedy Lanthimos updates in the film by more directly engaging an underlying universal anxiety: guilt.

The earliest reference to the daughters of Agamemnon occurs at *Iliad* 9.144–45, when their father offers any of three to an irate Achilles as part of his attempt to bring him back into the Trojan War.[4] Homer names Agamemnon's daughters Chrysothemis, Laodike, and Iphianassa, with the last of which being alternatively named Iphigenia elsewhere.[5] The poet of the post-Homeric *Cypria*, however, named four daughters, including both Iphigenia and Iphianassa.[6] The same epic introduces the story that Agamemnon angered the goddess Artemis because he killed a deer and boasted that he was a better hunter than she. For this reason, the prophet Calchas stated that Agamemnon must sacrifice his daughter, identified as Iphigenia, to appease the goddess's anger. Marriage with Achilles was offered as a way to bring the girl to Aulis, where the fleet was stuck due to foul weather. In this account, however, Iphigenia was not sacrificed, but taken to the land of the Tauri, with a deer substituted in her place, and made immortal.[7] In the fragmentary *Catalogue of Women* ascribed to Hesiod, the princess was called Iphimede and a phantom of the girl was sacrificed, while she likewise was made immortal and called "Artemis of the Wayside," equated with the goddess Hecate.[8]

In the first half of the fifth century BCE, Iphigenia's lot changed. Both Pindar and Aeschylus report that the young girl died in the sacrifice.[9] Neither, however, mentions the killing of a deer or a boast by Agamemnon. These return in Sophocles's *Electra* (c. 410 BCE), in which Agamemnon kills a deer in a sanctuary of Artemis and utters his boast.[10] Since a deer was imagined as the theriomorphic manifestation of the goddess and as this deer resided within her precinct, it was indeed a sacred deer, as alluded to in the title of Lanthimos's film.[11] Artemis required the sacrifice and the king had no choice but to offer it, different from Aeschylus's play as well as Euripides's *Iphigenia in Aulis*, in each of which he had the option to choose. The motivation for Artemis's anger differs in Euripides's *Iphigenia among the Taurians* (c. 413 BCE). In this version, Agamemnon promises to sacrifice the most beautiful thing born that year which turns out to be his daughter. The winds kicked up, preventing the fleet from sailing to Troy because he failed to fulfill his vow.[12] In both of the Euripidean plays, Iphigenia is replaced by a deer. As we know from other sources, including Aeschylus's *Agamemnon*, the sacrifice of Iphigenia, actual or intended, prompted Agamemnon's wife, Clytemnestra, to have an affair with his estranged cousin, Aegisthus, during the king's absence in the Trojan War; upon his return from Troy, they killed him, together with Cassandra, a princess of Troy whom Agamemnon brought home as his concubine.

Iphigenia's sacrifice is not unique in ancient literature. The Greek myth parallels the story of Abraham and Isaac in *Genesis* 22.1–19, where a father is ordered by Yahweh to sacrifice his child, here a son. In this instance, however, the father has not offended the deity but is being tested. Passing the test by taking Isaac to Mount Moriah to sacrifice him, Abraham is instructed by an angel to sacrifice a ram instead, comparable to the case of Iphigenia.[13] In both stories the father must agree to sacrifice his own child or face divine wrath. It is possible that behind both stories lies the eventual rejection of human in favor of animal sacrifice.[14] In sum, in the background of *The Killing of a Sacred Deer* lies not only a well-known Greek myth that has evolved over time, but also a universal tale of parental anxiety surrounding the guilt of losing a child, represented in all cases by the need to sacrifice a child (often firstborn) to appease a divine (or supernatural) power.[15]

Before turning to the film, I would like to look briefly at Euripides's *Iphigenia in Aulis*, since two features of its plot are especially relevant to *The Killing of a Sacred Deer*.[16] The play, performed posthumously, engages the themes of power and control.[17] Prevented from sailing because of the weather, Agamemnon is informed by the prophet Calchas—without explanation—that if they sail to Troy he will have to sacrifice his daughter to the goddess Artemis.[18] In order to make this happen, as in the *Cypria*, he tricks his wife, Clytemnestra, into sending Iphigenia to Aulis under the pretext of marriage with Achilles, an action that precedes the play. In the opening scene, Agamemnon attempts to prevent his daughter from coming by sending a second letter, but is foiled by his brother, Menelaus, who intercepts it. In the course of their argument, we learn why Agamemnon was willing to kill his own daughter in the first place: according to Menelaus, he wants the glory of leading the greatest expedition ever assembled.[19] Agamemnon in turn accuses Menelaus of wanting the war only to retrieve his trophy wife, Helen.[20] We also learn that only Calchas and Odysseus are aware of the required sacrifice.[21] As such, in Agamemnon's mind the latter pair has complete control over the situation: both because of their knowledge of the prophecy and in particular because of Odysseus's ability to manipulate the army. In fact, to make sure that the sacrifice will take place, Odysseus informs the soldiers of the prophecy and leads them to seize Iphigenia, thus sealing her fate.[22] Ironically, the general who controls the vast armada has no control of his fate.

Second, when Iphigenia arrives with her mother and infant brother, Orestes, she has no idea of the plan. Achilles and Clytemnestra are later informed of her impending death by the servant instructed to deliver the second letter.[23] At this point, Clytemnestra pleads with Achilles to help and suggests that Iphigenia plead for his help as well.[24] Achilles advises Clytemnestra to plead with her husband not to go through with the slaughter.[25] Iphigenia in turn pleads with her father to spare her life.[26] Not only does Agamemnon not acquiesce, but he also masks his vaulting ambition by stating that the war is necessary to stop the abduction of Greek women by barbarians and to keep Hellas free, the same false rationale proclaimed by Menelaus earlier in the play.²⁷ When Achilles promises to fight to save her life, suddenly Iphigenia, with growing affection for the hero, accepts her death in service of Greece.²⁸ Iphigenia willingly sacrifices her life, believing that she is serving her country, for which she will achieve immortal fame, but, according to the surviving ending, a deer is substituted and she is received among the gods.²⁹ Two prominent features of this ancient tragedy play out conspicuously in Lanthimos's film: first, a father, his wife, and children find themselves under the control of a human (Martin in place of Calchas and Odysseus) who wields inescapable power and requires a human sacrifice; second, the potential victims are forced to plead, unsuccessfully, for their lives.

As in Lanthimos's other films, *The Killing of a Sacred Deer* begins *in medias res*. The first shot of the film is of a throbbing human heart accompanied then by a bloody glove, suggesting without context that we are witnessing open-heart surgery.³⁰ We soon learn that the central character, Steven Murphy (Colin Farrell), is a heart surgeon.³¹ Later we discover that he lost a patient during an operation, the father of Martin (Barry Keoghan), whose close relationship with Steven is mystifying, even to Martin's wife, Anna (Nicole Kidman). We wonder: why is Steven buying lunch for, offering money to, and then giving an expensive watch to this boy, and then inviting him into his home to meet his family? To make matters even more puzzling, Steven's relationship with his own children, Kim (Raffey Cassidy) and Bob (Sunny Suljic), is far less loving.³²

It is not surprising, given Lanthimos's other films, that sexual activity is employed as a prominent characterizing device, though in a considerably more muted fashion than in *Dogtooth* and *Alps*. Steven's relationship with Anna comes across as strained, and their sexual ritual, in which Steven masturbates while Anna lies at the foot of the bed, as if anesthetized, suggests that intimacy between them is strange and perfunctory.³³ Steven and Anna later attend a banquet at which Steven is acknowledged for his outstanding practice in cardiology. We learn from a conversation between his anesthesiologist and Anna that Steven has not had a drink in three years, a fact that invites us to imagine alcoholism as a contributing factor to the complex nature of his various relationships, not to mention the death of Martin's father. Nonetheless, this scene establishes Steven as a decorated and highly respected surgeon and, as such, the modern-day equivalent of Agamemnon who, like his ancient analogue, will soon be under the control of a supernatural force.³⁴

Steven and Martin meet again, near the bridge where the former gives the latter the watch, and they have a conversation about friends. Martin's father had encouraged him to have many, but none are ever mentioned. Martin comes to Steven's house, where he has dinner and spends time in Kim's room. There, Martin oddly speaks about subaxillary hair, a topic that later plays out when Steven is asked to show him his armpits. It would appear that Martin is aching for a father with whom he can have conversations about puberty. During the same evening, Kim and Martin take a walk and Kim sings for her guest, leading us to suspect a potential love connection that recalls Iphigenia's budding affection for Achilles in Euripides's play. Martin refuses to stay the night because he does not like to leave his mother alone. At the end of the evening, Anna learns that Martin's father was a patient some time ago. The mystery continues.

Steven goes to Martin's house for dinner where he meets his mother (Alicia Silverstone). They eventually watch Martin's favorite film, *Groundhog Day* (Harold Ramis, 1993), during which Martin hugs Steven and goes to bed, allowing his mother to be alone with Steven. The set-up is an apparent attempt to resurrect a father for Martin.[35] Martin's mother makes a not-so-subtle move on the doctor, admiring his hands, kissing them, and recalling the times when she came to the hospital to visit her husband. She even suggestively states that she will not let him leave until he tastes her tart.[36] The longing for a father-son relationship with Steven continues in a subsequent scene. Martin, worried about his heart, visits Steven at the hospital, noting that his father should have survived the surgery and that he sleeps with his mother because of her anxiety.[37] After Steven shows Martin his armpits, the young boy invites him to come to his house again, adding that his mother will be upset if he doesn't because she is attracted to him, stating that they are perfect for each other. Steven refuses, responding that he is married and loves his wife and children. This, as we will see, is the moment when the story takes a turn toward the supernatural as Martin resorts to seeking his revenge against Steven.[38]

Several days later, Bob is unable to get out of bed and is taken to the hospital. Tests detect no abnormalities, but as he tries to leave, he collapses. An MRI scan also reveals no evidence of illness. Martin visits Bob in the hospital where, in the cafeteria, he finally has an opportunity to speak with Steven alone. Having complained that he is spending less time with him, Martin declares that Steven must now kill a member of his family, just as he killed his father, to regain balance. If he does not, his family members will each succumb to paralysis, loss of appetite, followed by bleeding from the eyes, and then death shortly afterward. Martin makes it plain that if he does not kill one of them, all including Steven will eventually die. Steven now faces Agamemnon's dilemma and Martin is in complete control.[39]

In the scenes that follow, the viewer observes the unfolding of Martin's revenge. Kim and Martin are in her room and she lies partially unclothed on the bed, emulating her mother's ritual before sex. However, Martin is focused on Steven, stating that he feels sorry for him. Soon afterward, Bob is no longer interested in eating. In his frustration, Steven tries to coerce Bob into revealing what lies behind his condition by telling him a secret of when he once masturbated his sleeping father. At choir practice, Kim collapses and ends up in the hospital, in the same room as Bob, where she too has no interest in eating.[40] As all of this is happening, Anna wonders again about Martin and why her husband did not mention their relationship. Her curiosity leads her to visit Martin at his home. He informs her that Steven killed his father and falsely declares that he has shown interest in his mother. Why, she asks, must she and the children pay the price for the actions of her husband? Anna's inquiry over why the burden falls on them echoes a similar question that lies at the heart of many Greek tragedies and is a central question in *Iphigenia in Aulis*: why must Iphigenia die in support of a war to bring home another man's wife?[41]

Anna continues in her quest to understand and speaks with his colleagues, asking if Steven had been drinking when he operated on Martin's father. He replies that two drinks before an operation were not unusual back then, implying that Steven may have been impaired at the time. As payment for his information, Anna performs manual sex on him in a car. As mentioned above, Clytemnestra similarly cheated on Agamemnon while he was in Troy and, once again, the ancient story reveals itself slowly but methodically in Lanthimos's film.

Though still in the grip of Martin's power, the children return home from the hospital. In a vain attempt to gain the upper hand, Steven imprisons Martin in their basement, beating him from time to time as he tries with force to get him to release his family.[42] All now know of their fate, as is the case in *Iphigenia in Aulis* when Clytemnestra confronts Agamemnon together with Iphigenia and Orestes.[43] As in the Euripidean play, Steven's family begins to plead for their lives in different ways. Bob cuts his hair and promises to become a cardiologist like Steven, hoping that for this devotion his father will spare his life. Meanwhile, Anna cleans Martin's wounds and kisses his feet. Later, accepting the inevitable loss of one of her children, she proposes to have sex with Steven in order to conceive another child, a self-serving suggestion that makes a case for Steven saving her. At night, Kim drags herself down to the basement, pleading with Martin to let her walk again so that they can run away together. Nothing succeeds. The next day, Anna reveals that she released Martin, admitting failure, just as Bob starts to bleed from his eyes.

Like Agamemnon, Steven must now kill a member of his family to satisfy a power beyond his control. In an attempt to determine on the basis of intelligence which of his children he should save, Steven visits their school, inquiring about their successes. It is here we learn that Kim had written an essay about *Iphigenia*, directly referencing the ancient text from which Lanthimos is drawing influence. Instead of choosing either of his children or his wife, Steven ultimately opts for chance. He secures them all in chairs arrayed in a circle, covers their heads with pillowcases, and covers his own face as well. With a rifle in hand, he turns in circles and fires several times, missing at first, but eventually killing Bob. From a writing perspective where nothing is left to chance, the choice to have Bob die is interesting: having offered to become a cardiologist like his father, Steven effectively kills himself, figuratively speaking, making Martin's revenge all the more complete.

In the final scene of the film, Steven, Anna, and Kim are at the diner where Steven used to meet Martin. Martin enters and looks at them. In silence the survivors exit the diner, and the film ends, leaving Martin by himself. The scene recalls another meeting place between Martin and Steven, the bridge. It was there that we learned that Martin's father encouraged him to have many friends. While Martin has achieved balance and justice, he finds himself alone, abandoned by the only people we see him with apart from his mother. While Steven, Anna, and Kim leave the restaurant, able to move on in their lives, although embittered, Martin, because of and in spite of his power, fails to regain a father as he desired and has equally lost a friend in Steven and a potential lover in Kim. In what could be called an emerging Lanthimosian tradition, what transpires here is the message that there are no winners when abuse of power is the source of one's control.

As I suggested above, stories of child sacrifices might well have arisen from feelings of guilt that accompany the loss of a child, a loss that is subsequently attributed to a divinity wherein the notion that "this is what God wanted" morphs into a divine command in its mythic form. Martin's power comes across as absolutely irresistible and as such unreal, comparable to that of the god upon whom this particular myth is based. Given Steven's battle with alcoholism and the primordial guilt that emerges when people are responsible for the unintended death of another person, I wonder if the story we observe can be understood, even apart from what Lanthimos intended, as something that is playing out in Steven's mind. In *The Matrix* (The Wachowskis, 1999), a young boy famously announces to Neo that "there is no spoon." Could it be that Martin is an incarnation of Steven's guilt as it takes complete control of his life? A guilt so consuming that he conjures up a divine power to demand the ultimate retribution: self-annihilation? As Rodney Farnsworth once stated: "archetypes deconstruct authorial intentions and reconstruct atavism";[44] choosing to take on an ancient myth can bring along with it the most unexpected outcomes and invite a range of readings, whether directly intended or not.

Kinetta tells the story of three unnamed individuals: Hotel Maid (Evangelia Randou), Photo-store Clerk (Aris Servetalis), and Plainclothes Officer (Costas Xikominos), who has a passion for German cars and Russian women. The unlikely trio practice for and film murder scenes that take place near a seaside resort. In fact, these disconnected scenes mirror the discontinuous narrative that comprises *Kinetta*.[45] While the ultimate significance of the film remains obscure, the theme of control resides at its center. Plainclothes Officer, who writes the scripts, is the primary power figure both in the scenes enacted and with the Russian prostitutes he sees. He represents the authority driving the scripts filmed by Photo-store Clerk and the violence directed at Hotel Maid playing the role of the female victims. *Kinetta* bears the hallmarks of Lanthimos's weird style and ends inconclusively. Yet, when viewed from the perspective of his subsequent films, it presages the director's ongoing interest in power, systems of control, and violence that frequently adopt mythical dimensions. To this end, Plainclothes Officer resembles Calchas and Odysseus in *Iphigenia in Aulis*, for whom control is an exercise with no purpose beyond its exertion.

Dogtooth raises the theme of control to a degree that perhaps only Lanthimos could imagine.[46] With the exception of the dog Rex, as in *Kinetta*, the main characters do not have names, but the narrative is much more cohesive and arguably more disturbing. Father (Christos Stergioglou) and Mother (Michele Valley) keep their young-adult children—Elder Daughter (Angeliki Papoulia), Son (Hristos Passalis), and Younger Daughter (Mary Tsoni)—imprisoned in their suburban compound, although we never learn why.[47] So profound is the parental control that the children are taught the wrong meanings of words ("sea" is a "leather armchair with wooden arms," "motorway" is a "strong wind," the word that Elder Daughter uses for vagina is "keyboard"). One evening, the father plays a song supposedly sung by their grandfather, but it is in fact Frank Sinatra singing "Fly Me to the Moon," which he completely mistranslates.[48] Another aspect of their total captivity lies in the fact that the children are told that they will only leave the compound when they lose their "dogtooth," which of course will never happen on its own. As the film progresses, the systems of control exhibited by the father in particular acquire ever more insidious dimensions: in order to satisfy the expected libido of Son, Father brings home an employee of his factory, Christina (Anna Kalaitzidou), to satisfy his needs. When it turns out that she has traded VCRs for cunnilingus offered by Elder Daughter, both Elder Daughter and Christina are struck on the head by Father and the parents, lacking a suitable partner from outside, send in Elder Daughter to have sex with her brother.[49] After being forced to have sex with her brother, Elder Daughter smashes out her "dogtooth" with a dumbbell and climbs into the trunk of Father's car, from which we never see her leave. We are left to imagine that the only recourse within this familial autocracy is death or life-long submission. Similar to *The Killing of a Sacred Deer*, the parents lose a child as a result of extreme control, here their own.

Sadistic control again features in *Alps*, which tells the story of a foursome—Nurse (Angeliki Papoulia), Stretcher-bearer (Aris Servetalis), Coach (Johnny Vekris), and Gymnast (Ariane Labed)—with a strange business proposition: to pretend to be the deceased relatives of surviving loved ones.[50] The collective adopt the name "Alps" because no one will know what it means, and mountains are imposing and cannot be replaced.[51] The leader (Stretcher-bearer) takes on the name Mont Blanc, as it is the largest mountain; Nurse becomes Monte Rosa; Coach calls himself Matterhorn because it reminds him of his father, a choice that brings with it an Oedipal element. At the beginning of the film, Gymnast longs to do routines to pop music, but Coach not only does not allow it, but also tells her he will bash her head and mouth if she insists (echoing the father's punishment of Elder Daughter in *Dogtooth*); even when he reprimands her work, Gymnast calls him the best coach, repeated at the end when she finally performs her routine to pop. Her tortured facial expression, evocative of abject surrender, marks the end of the film. Monte Rosa's father (Stavros Psyllakis) similarly strives for control, insisting that she wear a jacket and let him know where she is. Since their occupation involves finding out about the preferences of dead people in order to impersonate them, at one point Monte Rosa, losing her grip on reality, asks her father about her deceased mother's interests and then reaches toward his groin (more Oedipal posturing that simultaneously evokes *Dogtooth*), only to be slapped.[52] Impersonating other people in such intimate ways eventually takes its toll on Monte Rosa who appears to believe she is the deceased daughter of one of her clients, a tennis player (Maria Kyrozi). She is ultimately released from the "Alps" with a smash to the head by Mont Blanc. Like *Kinetta*, *Alps* offers up cinematic staccato, and its insistence on control through violence follows naturally on from *Dogtooth*. *Alps* also posits an existential question, as it represents its protagonists, especially Monte Rosa, blurring the boundaries of their own identities: "Who Am I?" also being one of Oedipus's burning questions in versions of that myth.

The Lobster tells the story of a bizarre society in which it is illegal for individuals to remain single. Once a person no longer has a spouse, he or she is required to register at a hotel that provides counseling and opportunities to remarry. A successful couple (like Limping Man [Ben Whishaw] and Nosebleed Woman [Jessica Barden]) will spend time on a yacht; if one does not find a spouse within forty-five days, they are turned into the animal of their choice. When David (Colin Farrell), whose wife leaves him in the film's opening scenes, arrives with his dog (and former brother) Bob, he informs Hotel Manager (Olivia Colman) of his choice to become a lobster should he fail (hence the title). Outside of the hotel in the woods there exists a group of loners, led by Loner Leader (Léa Seydoux). Both she and Hotel Manager have complete control over their respective domains. Within the hotel, in order to make residents open to finding a partner, masturbation is forbidden and punished by having one's hand put into a toaster. Later, after David has escaped to the forest, he admits to masturbating to Loner Leader without retribution, because in the forest it is physical intimacy with others that is brutally punished. Both societies are thus inverted images of each other. Loner Leader leads an attack on the hotel where they tie up Hotel Manager and force her partner (Garry Mountaine) to shoot her. There are no bullets in the gun, so the attack appears intended to prove the hollowness of the relationship offered as a model match to the residents. While living among the Loners, David falls in love with Short Sighted Woman (Rachel Weisz) and their intimacy is eventually discovered. Loner Leader has Short Sighted

Woman blinded, after which she and David escape to the city, but not before he drugs, binds, and places Loner Leader in a shallow depression where she will be torn apart by dogs (recalling Actaeon in Greek mythology). The last scene finds David contemplating blinding himself with a steak knife (recalling, not for the first time in Lanthimos's films, Oedipus).[53] Once again, *The Lobster* presents a narrative in which certain individuals exert absolute control within their particular sphere of power. David and Short Sighted Woman escape, but at a horrific cost, precisely as we observe at the conclusion of *The Killing of a Sacred Deer*, which follows *The Lobster* in Lanthimos's feature filmography.

Lanthimos's most recent film, *The Favourite*, also explores the theme of control; this time, however, set within a historical context, with named characters similar to *The Killing of a Sacred Deer*, but not in a contrived dystopian setting that features in his other films. The story takes place during the reign of Queen Anne (Olivia Colman) in the early 1700s, at which point England was at war with France. As the queen is weak and temperamental, she requires the assistance of her close friend and sexual partner, Lady Sarah (Rachel Weisz). Her status as friend and advisor, however, is soon challenged by the arrival of her cousin, Abigail (Emma Stone), who, sold by her father to a German who once controlled her, now finds herself under the control of yet others. In time, when the queen becomes ill, Abigail goes to the forest to pick medicinal herbs; these cure the queen and prompt Sarah and Abigail to become friends. At one point, however, Abigail observes Sarah having sex with the queen—a decisive moment. Not long afterward, Sarah finds Abigail in bed with the queen and fires her.[54] The queen, in tenuous control, wants to keep both women in her service, enjoying their attention and sexual favors. In time Abigail drugs Sarah's tea and the latter ends up outside of a brothel, after passing out and being dragged unconscious by her horse.[55] With Sarah gone, Abigail manages to become a Lady and takes on the role of her chief advisor, operating in direct opposition to the position Sarah took with regard to the war.[56] When Sarah returns, she is rebuffed by the queen and moves out of the palace. She contemplates a letter of apology, but Abigail counters any move on her part by stating that Sarah has been stealing from the queen and burns her letter when it arrives. Sarah is then banished from the country, and Abigail appears to have gained complete control. In the final scene, however, as she is about to crush one of the queen's pet rabbits, she lets it go when Anne orders her to tend to her, a command she timidly obeys, recalling the Gymnast at the end of *Alps*. *The Favourite* offers a less tragic conclusion than the other films but remains thematically concerned with unnatural power dynamics and the prevailing theme of control.

The Killing of a Sacred Deer, based on a Euripidean play that features control apparently for its own sake, reflects a constant theme in Lanthimos's films in which central characters submit to the dominance of empowered individuals. The director's last two films have evolved from their predecessors by being based on a specific myth and a specific historical personage, respectively; also, the main characters have names. What sets *The Killing of a Sacred Deer* apart from all is that the person in control is not an abusive older male—*pater familias* (father of the household)—or a passive-aggressive queen, but a traumatized teen, aching for the father he lost and possessing a power well beyond the other controlling figures in Lanthimos's films. This well suits the ancient myth, as Martin is based on a Greek divinity who was represented as eternally adolescent, a virgin as Martin remains within the film. As noted above, Artemis's totemic animal was the deer, so when Agamemnon kills the sacred deer, he in turn kills an avatar of the goddess. Martin's revenge effectively replicates the ancient model: by killing Bob, who offered to become a cardiologist, Steven kills a younger replica of himself. Lanthimos has done more than update an ancient myth in a modern setting; he saw what lies at the heart of the story and recast it according to his own thematic preoccupations and personal mode of storytelling. The choice to revisit the myth of Iphigenia, a story that has appeared in various forms across cultures, should now seem natural in the context of Lanthimos's cinematic corpus to date. The universal tale of a parent sacrificing a child in obedience to a divine power clearly spoke to the director's vision of how absolute control brutalizes those under its command and sometimes even those in its possession. Euripides's *Iphigenia in Aulis*, therefore, offered an apt narrative scaffolding for a modern retelling that engages Lanthimos's cinematic vision. Moreover, the lack of names in the early films, which comes across as odd at first, actually succeeds in further universalizing the films' tragic emplotments. The early films evince not only a weird but also breathtaking mythopoeia, in which the *dramatis personae* are represented as types: mean-spirited people in control and powerless people under control. In the ongoing exploration of this theme, it seems reasonable, perhaps even predictable, that Lanthimos would eventually move from the universal toward the particular, a development that happens to parallel the shift in antiquity from generic folktales (e.g., heroes killing ogres) to myths and legends anchored in time and place (such as Odysseus killing Polyphemus on Sicily after the Trojan War). It will be fascinating to see where Lanthimos's mythopoeic interests lead him from here.

Notes

1 See Steve Rose, "*Attenberg, Dogtooth* and the Weird Wave of Greek Cinema," *The Guardian*, Aug 27, 2011, available at https://www.theguardian.com/film/2011/aug/27/attenberg-dogtooth-greece-cinema, and Geli Mademli, "From the Crisis of Cinema to the Cinema of Crisis: A 'Weird' Label for Contemporary Greek Cinema," *Frames Cinema Journal*, 2013, available at

https://framescinemajournal.com/article/from-the-crisis-of-cinema-to-the-cinema-of-crisis-a-weird-label-for-contemporary-greek-cinema/.

2. See James J. Clauss, "When Nature Becomes Natural: Spiritual Catastrophe in Pasolini's *Medea*," *Phasis*, 10, no. 2 (2007): 147–52; for an overview of Pasolini's films on Greek myth in general, see Massimo Fusillo, *Greece According to Pasolini: Myth and Cinema* (Rome: Carocci, 2007).

3. For a reading of John Ford's *The Searchers* from such a perspective, see James J. Clauss, "Descent into Hell: Mythic Paradigms in John Ford's *The Searchers*," *Journal of Popular Film and Television*, 27 (1999): 2–17.

4. Timothy Gantz provides an outstanding resource for reconstructing early Greek mythological narratives. See Timothy Gantz, *Early Greek Myth* (Baltimore, MD: John Hopkins University Press, 1993).

5. If this is the case, then the sacrifice of Iphigenia must postdate the *Iliad*, as she is still alive during the Trojan War.

6. Martin L. West, *Greek Epic Fragments* (Cambridge, MA, and London: Loeb Classical Library, 2003), 99.

7. Ibid., 75.

8. Glenn W. Most, *Hesiod. The Shield, Catalogue of Women and Other Fragments* (Cambridge, MA, and London: Loeb Classical Library, 2007), fr. 19–20.

9. See Pindar, *P* (474 or 454 BCE), fr. 11.17–25, and Aeschylus, *Agamemnon* (458 BCE), lines 228–49.

10. See Sophocles, *Electra*, lines 563–76.

11. The killing of a sacred deer is featured at the beginning of Michael Cacoyannis's film *Iphigenia* (1977), which I suspect may also have influenced Lanthimos's title, among other things.

12. Euripides, *Iphigenia among the Taurians*, lines 15–25. On this play in general, see Jennifer Clarke Kosak, "Iphigenia in Tauris," in L. K. McClure, ed., *A Companion to Euripides* (Chichester: Wiley Blackwell, 2017), 214–27.

13. For a comparison of the myths and a more detailed discussion of the Greek tale, see Jan Bremmer, "Sacrificing a Child in Ancient Greece: The Case of Iphigenia," in E. Noort and E. Tigchelaar, eds., *The Sacrifice of Isaac* (Leiden: Brill, 2001), 21–43.

14. See John Skinner, *A Critical and Exegetical Commentary on Genesis* (New York: Scribner, 1910), 332; Michael D. Coogan and Cynthia R. Chapman, *The Old Testament* (Oxford: Oxford University Press, 2018), 74. Euripides's *Ion* offers another parallel: a mother (unknowingly) intends to kill her own son who is replaced by a dove.

15. The sacrifice of children, required for various reasons, can be found among many cultures worldwide. See Stith Thompson, *Motif-Index of Folk-Literature: A Classification of Narrative Elements in Folktales, Ballads, Myths, Fables, Mediaeval Romances, Exempla, Fabliaux, Jest-Books, and Local Legends* (Bloomington: Indiana University Press, 1989), S260.

16. David Kovacs offers both the Greek text and an English translation with basic but important commentary. See David Kovacs, *Euripides: Bacchae*,

Iphigenia at Aulis, Rhesus (Cambridge, MA: Harvard University Press, 2002). Andy Hinds and Martine Cuypers include two translations: one literal and one intended for stage production. See Andy Hinds and Martine Cuypers, eds., *Euripides' Iphigenia in Aulis* (New York and London: Bloomsbury, 2017).

17 Evidence suggests that the play, left unfinished, was completed by his son or nephew, also named Euripides, and put on in 405 BCE. See Kovacs, *Euripides: Bacchae, Iphigenia at Aulis, Rhesus*, 157–58.

18 Euripides, *Iphigenia in Aulis*, lines 358–60.

19 Ibid., lines 334–75.

20 Ibid., lines 378–401.

21 Ibid., lines 506–27.

22 Ibid., lines 1345–69.

23 Ibid., lines 855–94.

24 Ibid., lines 900–16, 992–94.

25 Ibid., lines 1015–16.

26 Ibid., lines 1211–52.

27 Ibid., lines 1259–75, 366–75. As noted by Isabelle Torrence, there is considerable irony in Agamemnon's claiming this as his rationale, since, according to Clytemnestra he had killed both her first husband and their child (lines 1148–56). See Isabelle Torrence, "Iphigenia at Aulis," in L. K. McClure, ed., *A Companion to Euripides* (Chichester: Wiley Blackwell, 2017), 284–97, at p. 294.

28 On the theme of patriotism in the play, see Justina Gregory, *Cheiron's Way: Youthful Education in Homer and Tragedy* (Oxford: Oxford University Press, 2019), 224–25.

29 Euripides, *Iphigenia in Aulis*, lines 1368–1401, 1608, 1614, 1622. Another ancient source suggests that in the original ending of the play, the goddess Artemis herself appeared and announced the substitution of a deer. See Kovacs, *Euripides: Bacchae, Iphigenia at Aulis, Rhesus*, 343.

30 The classical music in the background, Franz Schubert's *Stabat Mater in F Minor* (1816), refers to another human sacrifice demanded by a divinity, that of Jesus. Its contrast with the eerie background music heard elsewhere, suggestive of a horror film, elegantly reflects this odd combination of ancient myth and modern horror narrative.

31 The beginning parallels that of *The Lobster* in that it is only after you learn that humans are being turned into animals that the opening scene makes any sense: a woman kills a donkey, who must have been her former husband or another loved one.

32 The older Kim and younger Bob, intentionally or not, parallel the older Iphigenia and younger Orestes in Euripides's play.

33 A parallel, intended or unintended, to Clytemnestra's insistence of having been a dutiful wife to Agamemnon (lines 1148–65).

34 I wonder if the decision to have Farrell wear a beard is a nod to Agamemnon as represented in Cacoyannis's *Iphigenia*, or perhaps to the iconography of ancient kings in general?

35 *Groundhog Day* describes the transformation of a cynical person whose deaths and resurrections prepare him for marriage, so its selection seems purposeful.

36 With *Alps* and *Dogtooth* in mind, cunnilingus seems to be insinuated.

37 This is given as a reason for not staying overnight at Steven's house, as mentioned above. On the ubiquity of Oedipus in cinema, see Martin Winkler, "Oedipus in the Cinema," *Arethusa*, 41 (2008): 67–94, and, more broadly, Kenneth Glazer, *Searching for Oedipus: How I Found Meaning in an Ancient Masterpiece* (Lanham, MD: Hamilton Books, 2018). This theme plays out elsewhere in Lanthimos's films, as will be noted below.

38 This recalls Euripides's *Medea*. Medea wanted to take revenge for Jason's abandonment by killing his new bride, her father, and Jason himself. But the unexpected arrival of Aegeus, who longed for a son, changed Medea's plans, diverting them to the killing of her own children. Martin may have discovered in Steven's confession of love the best approach for avenging the loss of his father.

39 In *Iphigenia in Aulis*, Agamemnon observes that if he does not kill Iphigenia, the soldiers will attack Mycenae and kill him, Menelaus, his daughter, and everyone in his city as well (lines 528–37, repeated at 1267–68).

40 As a further indication that Martin possesses total power over the family, he calls Kim and tells her to go to the window, which she can do. When he disappears, she collapses.

41 Euripides, *Iphigenia in Aulis*, lines 396–99, 1166–70, 1192–1208, 1236–40.

42 This compares to the case of Menelaus who threatened to have Calchas killed before he could inform the troops of his prophecy and thus avoid the sacrifice (ibid., lines 512–20).

43 Ibid., lines 1115–21.

44 Rodney Farnsworth, *The Infernal Return: The Recurrence of the Primordial in Films of the Reaction Years, 1977–1983* (Westport, CN: Praeger, 2002), 111.

45 While Kinetta is a beach resort west of Athens, the choice of the location, whose name suggests cinema, seems to underscore the metacinematic nature of the film. What Angelos Koutsourakis says about *Dogtooth*—that it instantiates a "paratactic style"—is especially evident here. See Angelos Koursourakis, "Cinema of the Body: The Politics of Performativity in Lars von Trier's *Dogville* (2003) and Yorgos Lanthimos's *Dogtooth* (2008)," *Cinema: Journal of Philosophy and the Moving Image*, 3 (2012): 84–108, at pp. 84–85.

46 While Mademli, for instance, sees the film as "a parable for the political and economic cul-de-sac of the Greek state of affairs," I will avoid a political reading of this and the other films. My focus will remain literary. See Mademli, "From the Crisis of Cinema to the Cinema of Crisis."

47 This is similar to *Iphigenia in Aulis*, where we never learn why Agamemnon must sacrifice Iphigenia.

48 Dionysios Kapsakis addresses the fascinating issue of mistranslation and its representation in the subtitles; regarding this Sinatra song, he states: "The lack of reference between language and reality is transposed to the level of the nonequivalence between source and target languages. Translation here is a form of taming of reality, a defence mechanism against the fear but also the seduction of the foreign, symbolized in the local context by Frank Sinatra." See Dionysios Kapsakis, "Translation as a Critical Tool in Film Analysis: Watching Yorgos Lanthimos' *Dogtooth* through a Translational Prism," *Translation Studies*, 10 (2017): 247–62, at p. 255. He goes on to tease out the political implications of Lanthimos's strategy, but as mentioned in n. 46, I limit my discussion here to the film narratives themselves.

49 In addition to the overt incest in this scene, sanctioned by the parents, Younger Daughter offers to lick her father for his harpoon.

50 As Afroditi Nikolaidou aptly notes, *Alps* and *Dogtooth* both feature games and reenactments. See Afroditi Nikolaidou, "The Performative Aesthetics of the Greek New Wave," *FilmIcon: Journal of Greek Film Studies*, 2 (2014): 20–44, at p. 30.

51 The use of ambiguous names to conceal identity parallels the parents' duplicitous definitions in *Dogtooth*. See Mademli, "From the Crisis of Cinema to the Cinema of Crisis."

52 Cunnilingus also occurs when Monte Rosa pretends to be the dead wife of Lamp Shop Owner (Efthymis Filippou).

53 Sarah Cooper offers an interesting interpretation of *The Lobster*, but her focus on Narcissus ignores the larger engagement with Ovid's *Metamorphoses*, as we observe in the background a number of different animals, including a horse, peacock, and camel, which we are led to believe are transformed human beings also. See Sarah Cooper, "Narcissus and *The Lobster*," *Studies in European Cinema*, 13, no. 2 (2016): 163–76.

54 As a result, Abigail strikes her own face with a book, an action that recalls both Lame Man in *The Lobster*, who causes nose bleeds to be with Nosebleed Woman, and Elder Daughter in *Dogtooth*, who knocks out her dogtooth.

55 The venue would seem to reflect the meretricious behavior of both Sarah and Abigail.

56 The queen sanctions Abigail's marriage with Masham (Joe Alwyn), now that she is a Lady. On their wedding night, the bride is so fixated on her situation that she consummates their vows by manually stimulating the groom, recalling the scene with Anna and Steven's colleague in *The Killing of a Sacred Deer*.

13

Rethinking the Heritage Film: Gothic Critique in *The Favourite*

Alex Lykidis

The British heritage genre has been accused of being passive, uncritical, and pretentious entertainment, "[f]ormally unchallenging, while nevertheless replete with visual strategies that signify 'art.'"[1] Critics have argued that heritage films occupy a middlebrow middle ground, "neither genuine art nor genuinely popular," designed primarily to confirm the cultural knowledge of their privileged viewers.[2] Foreign-born directors have tended to produce more critical perspectives on British history and society, avoiding the fetishization of upper-class lifestyles and nostalgic investment in national unity usually attributed to the genre.[3] Belen Vidal contends that since the mid-1990s, heritage films have become "a fully-fledged international genre" with "changing notions of realism, authenticity and ideological purpose in order to address diverse audiences."[4] There has been a recent upsurge in "anti-national" heritage films that "move away from the consensual national narratives" of the past and "towards the reconfiguration of the myths of national identity."[5]

Contemporary themes and transnational styles have supplanted earlier investments in period authenticity, historical accuracy, and national identity in what has come to be known as post-heritage cinema. First theorized by Claire Monk in reference to films such as *Orlando* (Sally Potter, 1992), *The Piano* (Jane Campion, 1993), and *Carrington* (Christopher Hampton, 1995), the post-heritage label is used to describe films that provide more self-conscious and critical portrayals of the past and often focus on queer sexuality and gender fluidity. It is associated with performative, reflexive, or ironic portrayals of identity and with the anachronisms, hybridity, and referentiality of postmodernism. The languid, immersive, and reassuring style of heritage cinema is replaced in post-heritage films by more challenging, destabilizing, and heterodox modes of address.[6] A film commonly associated with post-heritage aesthetics is *Elizabeth* (Shekhar Kapur, 1998), which, instead of the quaint pastoralism and tasteful pictorialism of the heritage genre, uses " 'violent juxtapositions' between 'beauty and violence' " to create "stylistic clashes [that] reflect the tension and conflict that characterise the film's events."[7]

Films about early modern monarchs like *Elizabeth* are usually more critical of the monarchy because they focus on the abuses of power endemic to autocratic rule, whereas many films about twentieth-century monarchs like *The Queen* (Stephen Frears, 2006) and *The King's Speech* (Tom Hooper, 2010) humanize the British royal family by focusing on the tension between its ceremonial public role and its domestic struggles. Andrew Higson notes that "as the monarchy loses any real political power, it retreats into … the domestic space of the family." This "de-politicisation and domestication of the monarchy" emphasizes "monarchical benevolence" and duty, which Mandy Merck argues has transformed "the meaning of the Crown … from physical force to visual splendor to model family."[8] Heritage films that present a nostalgic vision of British national identity tend to be set in the Regency or late Victorian periods, whereas those, like *Elizabeth*, focusing on early modern monarchs portray an unstable nation still in the process of formation.[9] And yet, even post-heritage films like *Elizabeth* can legitimate the British monarchy by associating it with innovative styles and contemporary genres.[10] According to Higson, all monarchy films, by "exploiting a fascination with the British royal families, and almost regardless of whether they represent the royals in a sympathetic manner … play a role in maintaining the monarchy as a contemporary cultural presence."[11]

While the validation of the monarchy seems inescapable, *The Favourite* has all the characteristics associated with more critical cinematic representations of British royals: it is helmed by a foreign director, it focuses on the absolutism of an early modern monarch, and it features post-heritage stylistic elements: genre hybridity, historical anachronisms, queerness, performativity, and a confrontational style. Yorgos Lanthimos's approach to the film's acting, script, music, and production design sought to distance *The Favourite* from the specificities of its historical subject matter and the conventions of the heritage genre. He held rehearsals to focus the cast's attention on their physicality so that their performances would make the film "feel like its own world" and not "like another period piece [in which] people speak and walk in a certain way."[12] He asked the film's original screenwriter, Deborah Davis, to rewrite the script with less emphasis on the intricate political details of Queen Anne's reign and brought in Tony McNamara to make the language and tone of the dialogue more irreverent, acerbic, and contemporary.[13] Similarly, the make-up, costumes, and music in the film are an amalgam of period-appropriate and anachronistic material.[14] In these ways, Lanthimos sought to make "a film that feels relevant to us today, so you could imagine this happening anywhere in the world or anytime or place."[15]

Kara McKechnie has shown that in monarchy films "the filmic depiction of the monarch [has] always depended on the contemporary situation."[16] Scholars have usually connected cinematic depictions of the monarchy to public perceptions of the British royal family at the time of a film's release, but in this chapter the portrayal of Queen Anne's court in *The Favourite* will be related to the social and political dynamics of neoliberalism that have provided an important ideological context for Lanthimos's work throughout his career.[17] The democratic deficits of contemporary political institutions are portrayed in Lanthimos's films through the antisociality and miscommunicativeness of character interactions that reflect the empty proceduralism and unaccountable authority of neoliberal governance. The preponderance of misguided, incongruous, imitative, or overly referential expressions in *Dogtooth* and *Alps* conveys the impoverishment of our collective political imagination in a time of policy convergence, technocratic decision making, and declining electoral participation that have reduced the democratic process to a largely ceremonial exercise.[18] Even though *The Favourite* seems to bear little relation to Lanthimos's Greek-language cinema because he didn't write the screenplay and its subject is British political history, the film shows Lanthimos's continued thematic preoccupation with the dysfunctional relationships that result from authoritarian social arrangements.

This chapter will consider the deviations from heritage characteristics in *The Favourite* in relation to the gothic tradition. The film does not feature the vampires, demons, and ghosts that we associate with gothic texts, yet its withering portrayal of Queen Anne's court presents monarchical rule as monstrous and artificial. The social and political criticism embedded in Lanthimos's unconventional style accords with the gothic emphasis on "the impositions of an unjust and unjustifiable society," while the pervasiveness of cruel and antisocial behavior in the film is consistent with the gothic's "deep pessimism about the human condition."[19] The links between its gothic elements and neoliberalism situate *The Favourite* within what Linnie Blake and Agnieszka Soltysik Monnet describe as neoliberal gothic: texts that incorporate gothic elements "to interrogate the ways in which neoliberal economics has impacted the modern world, has pervaded our very consciousness and, in so doing, has refashioned the very subjectivities we inhabit."[20] Focusing on the political rather than the economic aspects of neoliberalism, Lanthimos uses gothic tropes like denaturalization and grotesquerie to defamiliarize the film's social and political context, providing us with a timely critique of undemocratic systems of government.

Denaturalization as Structural Analysis

The Favourite is a story about the real-life personal and political intrigue in the court of Queen Anne (1702–1714), played by Olivia Colman. It chronicles the rivalry between Sarah Churchill (Rachel Weisz), the duchess of Marlborough and the queen's powerful advisor and lover, and her cousin Abigail Hill (Emma Stone), who arrives at the palace penniless due to her father's mismanagement of the family fortune. Sarah is married to John Churchill (Mark Gatiss), the duke of Marlborough, who is a government minister and the leader of the Allied army waging war against France. Abigail navigates the conflict between pro-war (the Marlboroughs, Sidney Godolphin [James Smith], and the Whigs) and antiwar (Robert Harley [Nicholas Hoult], Samuel Masham [Joe Alwyn], and the Tories) forces as she gains the queen's favor, in part by sleeping with her. Sarah is drugged and nearly killed by Abigail and later exiled from the court, while Abigail manages to rehabilitate her social standing by becoming keeper of the privy purse and marrying Samuel Masham. Queen Anne is a tragicomic figure at the center of the narrative: ailing, grieving for her dead children, desperate for affection, disinterested in her duties, and manipulated by all sides. The plot of *The Favourite* is certainly interesting, despite or perhaps because of its historical inaccuracies, and yet the film systematically directs our attention elsewhere.

In the first scene, after the initial credit sequence, the camera is situated in one corner of Anne's bedroom and is pointed diagonally at the other corner, maximizing the perceived scale of the room and suggesting that narrative space rather than narrative action is the subject of the shot. The colorful decorations on the walls and ceiling draw our attention more than the muted tones of Sarah and Anne's black-and-white costumes. When we return to the credits, all we hear is the jangle of keys and a door being unlocked, making the built environment again more prominent than the characters. The shift of our focus in *The Favourite* from narrative actions to the film's setting is consistent with the pictorialism of the heritage genre, which often features "camera movement [that] is dictated less by a desire to follow the movement of characters than by a desire to offer the spectator a more aesthetic angle on the period setting and the objects that fill it."[21] In heritage films, "shots, angles, camera movements frequently exceed narrative motivation" and are "divorced from character point of view" in order "to display ostentatiously the seductive *mise-en-scène* of the films."[22]

In *The Favourite* the emphasis on set design defamiliarizes the social context in which the narrative occurs rather than seducing us into accepting it. Whereas the "display of loosely period-appropriate objects, decor, architecture and man-made landscapes" leads to "the fetishisation of material culture in the quality heritage film," the setting in *The Favourite* is presented as alienating and unwelcoming.[23] Lanthimos emphasizes the inhuman scale of the palace through uncentered long shots that create considerable amounts of negative space in the frame, diagonal compositions, low angles, and narratively excessive shots of characters walking in the hallways of the palace. Each of the film's three protagonists has a scene in which she walks for a long time along a corridor after something emotionally distressing has occurred—Anne after she screams at a music teacher and his pupils, Sarah after she discovers Abigail in Anne's bed, and Abigail after Sarah regains Anne's favor—so that the enormity of the palace is made to amplify their misery. Fish-eye lenses are used occasionally to distort the edges of the frame, making it appear as if the walls of the palace are caving in on its inhabitants. At certain moments the camera slowly tracks forward or back while facing a wall, door, ceiling, or floor. The movement is not fast enough to suggest dynamic action or momentum and the absence of characters in the frame evacuates any sense of purpose from these changes of perspective. The resulting effect is one in which our surroundings seem to shift around us, creating a disorientation that undermines our comfort with the film's setting.

The denaturalization of narrative space in *The Favourite* counters the heritage genre's fetishization of upper-class lifestyles. The exclusion of the working class in British heritage films, whose narratives frequently revolve around "monarchs, nobility, or aristocrats," produces a "nostalgic, upper-class version of Englishness."[24] The fascination in these films with private property and the culture of "those with inherited or accumulated wealth and cultural capital" leads to "private interest becom[ing] naturalised as public interest."[25] By contrast, in *The Favourite*, the unnaturalness of social and political relationships in Queen Anne's palace is emphasized from the outset. In the first scene, Sarah and Anne do not face the camera or each other, a long framing distance prevents us from seeing their faces, backlighting obscures Anne's face completely, a low framing angle directs our eye to the ornate ceiling rather than the characters, and there is awkward spacing between the characters so that Sarah occupies a nebulous middle ground between being close enough to comfortably speak with Anne and far enough away to afford her privacy as she changes. The loud orchestral music we hear during this early part of the scene suggests that ceremonial protocol overwhelms any potential for authentic social interaction. We are disoriented by a cut that violates the 180-degree rule and the ensuing shot-reverse shot sequence of a conversation between Sarah and Anne isolates each of them in the frame. In every shot of this sequence the camera inches forward eerily and Anne's depiction through a lower angle than Sarah creates graphic discontinuities. Throughout the rest of the film, fish-eye lenses, extreme low angles, backlighting, elliptical editing (that skips dialogue), and a lack of two-shots are used to defamiliarize conversations and convey how socialization is strained by the artificiality of monarchical social relations.

The denaturalization of the *mise-en-scène* in *The Favourite* is akin to "the historically embedded techniques of estrangement that gothic has employed with such regularity" and to the gothic trope of "spectralization," which involves "a mental turning of every perceived object into a ghost-like figure that is distanced from what it signifies."[26] The angular distortions that are generated by Lanthimos's diagonal compositions, unmotivated camera movements, and use of a fish-eye lens are commensurate with gothic "disruptions of scale and perspective."[27] The film's emphasis on the oppressiveness of the palace's never-ending passageways and cavernous chambers aligns with "the prevalence of claustrophobia ... the foreclosure of escape from institution or destitution, the grotesque exaggeration of character and location" in gothic texts.[28] The cumulative effect of these techniques is to make Anne's court resonate with the malevolent energies unleashed by the extreme concentration of power of monarchical regimes. The palace comes to resemble the Gothic castle or mansion marked by "disorientation or danger," a place "beyond reason" where power is formed in the "conjunction of family line, social status and physical property."[29]

Denaturalization is an apposite representational strategy in the current political climate because of the ideological mechanisms used to legitimate neoliberal rule. The naturalization of the neoliberal order kicked into high gear after the collapse of Eastern European Communism in 1989, spawning "end of history" narratives that conceived of capitalism as the only viable way to organize society. At the policy level, this has produced TINA (there is no alternative) rhetoric that presents the neoliberal agenda, including harsh and ineffective austerity measures, as the only possible response to a wide variety of socioeconomic problems.[30] The construction of neoliberalism as an incontrovertible system of governance relies on the naturalization of the market and uses "an appearance of scientificity and incontestability" to disguise the class antagonism of its proposals, portraying them "as a sociological fact and not as a political, partisan gesture."[31] When an ideological program is naturalized in this way, "it is not open to political contestation and it is shielded from democratic discussion."[32] The denaturalization of narrative space in Lanthimos's films encourages us to question the seemingly incontestable social and political structures that shape our lives.

In the subsequent scene of *The Favourite*, Sarah is blindfolded as Anne shows her a model of the palace that she has decided to build for her. We are initially unaware of why Sarah is blindfolded and being led down a dark corridor; elliptical editing and a lack of dialogue are used to reduce narrative coherence and keep us on edge. The third shot of the scene is a rapid forward track through the empty room that is their destination, turning right to show Sarah and Anne entering. As soon as the women appear, the shot ends, which again gives the impression that the camera is more interested in narrative space rather than the characters. This sequence is similar to many dialogue-free interludes in the film in which all we hear is nondiegetic music or diegetic environmental sounds. By shifting our attention from narrative to *mise-en-scène*, these moments emphasize how social and political arrangements influence character behavior. The focus on the built environment in *The Favourite* encourages us to adopt a structural understanding of power. But Lanthimos does not just redirect our focus from narrative to *mise-en-scène*, he also aligns these two stylistic elements in order to produce an uncompromising critique of undemocratic societies then and now.

Theater of the Grotesque

Whatever social or historical criticism is contained in a heritage film's narrative is often blunted by the visual sumptuousness of its *mise-en-scène*. According to Andrew Higson, "[e]ven those films that develop an ironic narrative of the past end up celebrating and legitimating the spectacle of one class and one cultural tradition and identity at the expense of others through the ... obsession with the visual splendours of period detail. *Mise-en-scène* and drama thus work against each other in their construction of the national past."[33]

In reference to the Merchant Ivory productions *Howards End* (1992) and *The Remains of the Day* (1993), Pamela Church Gibson concurs with Higson's assessment of the genre, noting that the "palpable pleasure in parading the visual splendour of the past undermines the social criticism of Forster's novel ... and visual excess ... [neuters] the irony of Ishiguro's novel."[34] By contrast, the *mise-en-scène* in *The Favourite* contributes to the criticism of monarchical absolutism and concentration of power articulated in the film's narrative. What connects these two elements is the grotesquerie that Lanthimos uses to portray the characters and their social context in the film.

This is most evident in two narratively excessive scenes of aristocratic amusement, one involving a duck race and the other an orange pelting. In the first scene, members of the royal court (including Marlborough and Godolphin) watch and gamble on a duck race in one of the rooms of the palace. The absurdity of this social activity is emphasized by the use of various techniques that denaturalize image and sound, including extreme low angles, slow motion, orchestral music that drowns out most diegetic sounds, and audio distortion of faint screams, grunts, and quacks. The incomprehensibility of the assembled scene is emphasized in several shots of aristocrats cheering on ducks that remain off-screen, a framing style that portrays character behavior as artificial or unwarranted by keeping the object of their attention out of view. There is an incongruity between the earnest vociferousness of the crowd's cheers and the comic waddling of the ducks in the race. The absence of cues to explain the scene's significance or connect it to the rest of the narrative emphasizes the gratuitousness of this courtly entertainment. Narrative excess is complemented by the vulgarity of the *mise-en-scène*, with close-ups of grimacing, open-mouthed, or wildly gesticulating aristocrats next to extravagant displays of meat and fruit on tabletops. In the latter scene, a group is shown in another room of the palace pelting a naked man with blood oranges. Here, too, there is an expressionistic departure from the conventions of realism through slow motion and an orchestral score that drowns out diegetic sounds, while the arbitrariness of the depicted activity is again emphasized by the absence of cues that would explain its narrative relevance. This later scene is crosscut with Sarah's horse riding accident (which is caused by Abigail), using Sarah's brush with death to underscore the frivolousness of the nobility's eccentric amusements and to place their seemingly harmless aggression on a continuum with more malicious and consequential acts of violence in the narrative.

These two scenes feature many elements of gothic grotesquerie. The absurd behavior on display corresponds with what Michael Hollington, drawing on the work of Thomas Wright, asserts is grotesque art's "irreverent readiness to turn into burlesque the most sacred and popular [customs]."[35] The visual correlation of pompous aristocrats with waddling ducks follows in the gothic tradition of "comic animism" that relies on satirical "comparisons of human and animal appearance and behaviour."[36] Intercutting the orange pelting activity with Sarah's horse riding accident creates a tonal hybridity characteristic of gothic grotesquerie, which Hollington describes as an "amalgam of contradictory spectacles," a "mingling of laughter and tears."[37] The use of jarring close-ups and the disconnection of these scenes from the rest of the narrative produce "grotesque incongruities in scale or context," while the grimaces and garish make-up of the assembled aristocrats accord with the gothic emphasis on ugliness: "replete with a range of negative features: not beautiful, they display no harmony or proportion. Ill-formed, obscure, ugly, gloomy ... gothic texts register revulsion, abhorrence ... disgust."[38]

The portrayal of monarchical rule in *The Favourite* focuses on the psychological regression, irrational decision making, and susceptibility to manipulation of unelected leaders. Anne frequently acts like a petulant child, such as when she shouts at the teenage footman outside her room for looking at her, then orders him to look at her and then chastises him for doing so. Anne's indecisiveness as a leader is shown when she collapses on the floor of parliament after she has been placed in a difficult position by Harley who praises her for not raising the landowners' tax right before she is set to announce that it will be raised. Anne is repeatedly outmaneuvered by Sarah, who tells Anne that the war with France is not over and must continue, and she unthinkingly parrots the rhetoric that Sarah has drilled into her. At one point she tells Harley in reference to the war with France: "We must fight for what we fight for." Anne's emotional anguish, self-destructive behavior, and abject loneliness make her a pathetic figure who elicits our sympathy. We see Anne gorging on cake and then vomiting, playing solitaire in her empty bedroom, threatening to jump out of the window, crying after being thrown to the floor by Sarah and whimpering "you do not care." Anne's naiveté, the tragic loss of her children, her physical discomfort due to gout and her disinterest in her official duties make her a relatable character. But any sympathy we might feel for Anne is undercut by her mood swings that reveal her to be sullen, selfish, and spiteful. An example of Anne's abrupt transitions from victimized lament to vengeful malevolence occurs in a conversation between the queen and Abigail that takes place when Sarah has gone missing after her riding accident: Anne says, "I'm tired. It hurts. Everything hurts. Everyone leaves me and dies. Finally her. If she's not dead, I will cut her throat. She may be doing this to hurt me."

The depiction of Anne as an immature, capricious, and vindictive monarch in *The Favourite* coincides with the gothic interest in the intersections of madness, social status, and political power. Fred Botting states that "[g]othic texts are, overtly but ambiguously, not rational, depicting disturbances of sanity and security, from ... displays of uncontrolled passion, violent emotion or flights of fancy to portrayals of perversion and obsession."[39] Anne is one in a long line of "exorbitant tyrants" in the gothic repertoire, which has always concerned itself with "tyranny and its effects" and "the horrific and seemingly limitless powers of the despot."[40] The queen's eccentric personality and erratic behavior in *The Favourite* create a gothic "pageant of folly, a theater of lurid exploitation, placing disturbed, vulnerable, and unsettling figures on display."[41]

Lanthimos has said that Anne's character in *The Favourite* shows how "[p]ersonal relationships, mood, chance, or anything like that can actually affect people's decisions, and when they're in a position of power, their capriciousness can affect the fate of a nation. And that's quite scary to think about, and quite relevant."[42] Anne's contemporary relevance is heightened by the authoritarianism of neoliberal governance. The earliest implementation of neoliberalism in Pinochet's Chile and other South American countries in the 1970s relied on military dictatorships to usher in unpopular policies such as privatization, regressive taxation, and deregulation. More recently, emergency conditions established in the wake of military conflict or economic collapse, such as the Iraq War and the 2008 financial crisis, have been used to impose neoliberal programs on populations that might, under different circumstances, have rejected them.[43] William Davies describes this as an assertion of the "'ultimate' (extra-juridical, undemocratic) authority of executive decision."[44] More generally, the spread of neoliberalism has relied on a "constitutional authoritarianism" in which policies are codified without popular consent through international treaties, constitutional amendments, technocratic rule making, entry criteria for transnational institutions, common currency agreements, and debt repayment schemes.[45]

In the past few years, right-wing demagogues like Donald Trump, Jair Bolsonaro, and Viktor Orbán have gained power by taking advantage of popular discontent with the neoliberal order. The corruption, jingoism, factionalism, and authoritarian inclinations of these leaders have only amplified the democratic deficits of the neoliberal era.[46]

The focus on petty tyrants obsessed with rules in Lanthimos's Greek-language films captures the technocratic coldness of "constitutional authoritarianism," whereas Queen Anne's evidence-free, personality-driven decision making in *The Favourite* conveys the leadership style of right-wing populists. The rationality of political debates is undermined by Anne's unpredictable whims, such as when she gets annoyed at Sarah at a ball and decides to reverse her earlier decision to raise taxes on landowners, and by the patrimonialism of the royal court: the queen and her main advisor are sleeping together and the queen's advisor is married to a government minister. The tangled web of personal and political relationships in the film reflects the conflation of private and public affairs in monarchical systems of rule. At one point, Anne proclaims: "It's my state. I'm the business of state." The meeting that the bedridden queen conducts with her ministers provides an apt visualization of this breakdown in the divisions between personal and political space, private and public authority. Godolphin, Marlborough, Sarah, and a few others are assembled around Anne's bed, while the map of France they are discussing is placed on her prostrate body, creating a contoured effect like in raised relief maps. Anne's eyes are closed as Marlborough pokes the map and, by extension, her torso with his cane. The ailing queen's body is here symbolically coincident with the nation's military ambitions, superimposing the body politic onto the body natural, but her mind is elsewhere. Anne's first words are, "Which country is that again?" An example of the conflation of private desires and public decisions occurs later in the film when Anne justifies hiring Abigail as her maid of the bedchamber by telling Sarah: "I like it when she puts her tongue inside me."

The commingling of private and public realms in *The Favourite* is in line with the representation of early modern monarchs in heritage cinema. Films about late modern monarchs such as Victoria or Elizabeth II emphasize the "tension between domesticity, romance and family life on the one hand and the obligations of public appearances and ceremonial occasions on the other."[47] However, in films about early modern monarchs, such as Henry VIII or Elizabeth I, the private realm "is constructed almost entirely in terms of romantic and/or sexual liaisons, which themselves spill over into the public sphere."[48] Heritage cinema humanizes contemporary royals as relatively powerless yet well-meaning individuals overwhelmed by their public duties and domestic commitments, whereas early modern monarchs are associated with "selfish irresponsibility rather than familial responsibility" and by "an irresponsible, absolutist wielding of power."[49] By erasing private/public divisions and focusing on early modern absolutism, *The Favourite* provides a more critical perspective on the monarchy.[50]

In some ways, early modern monarchs like Anne are more relevant to an understanding of power in the neoliberal era than contemporary monarchs. This is because the divisions between public and private domains are increasingly being transgressed by the ubiquity of neoliberalism as a system of thought. Under neoliberalism, the personal sphere is not a haven from the ruling order because it is suffused with the ethos of competitive individualism. Wendy Brown describes neoliberalism as "a normative order of reason developed over three decades into a widely and deeply disseminated governing rationality [which] transmogrifies every human domain and endeavor, along with humans themselves."[51] The consequences of neoliberal policies, such as insecure employment, social isolation, indebtedness, and the lack of a safety net, incentivize us to discipline our bodies, our time, our labor, and our personal relationships in order to eke out a precarious existence. This process of self-discipline involves applying the values of entrepreneurialism and financialization—promotion, assessment, investment, and the pursuit of competitive advantage—to all aspects of our lives in an attempt to maximize our social capital and economic productivity.[52] In Lanthimos's films, the antisociality that results from authoritarian social structures manifests itself in every facet of character experience, including family interactions, sexual relations, leisure activities, and everyday speech.

Aesthetics of Antisociality

The ball scene, in which Sarah and Masham dance exuberantly in front of Anne until she gets upset and demands to be taken to her room, is reminiscent of the dancing in other Lanthimos films such as *Dogtooth* and *Alps*. The common thread is the excessive, competitive, and performative nature of the dancing and the emotional disconnection between the dancers and their audience. Sarah and Masham's ebullient movements display a lack of sensitivity to the ailing queen's inability to participate in the ball. Their obliviousness to Anne's disposition is characteristic of the function of nonverbal expression in Lanthimos's films: it is an eruption of energy, motivated by a genuine desire to communicate, that is often misread, ignored, or rejected. The perfect synchronicity of Sarah and Masham's dance moves, despite their anachronistic eccentricity, shows how in Lanthimos's films, the highly referential and imitative qualities of language and gesture limit the ability of characters to express themselves in an authentic way.[53] Even the way characters walk in *The Favourite* conveys the disconnectedness of social relations in the royal court. Throughout the film, characters walk away from each other without explanation, follow each other at a distance, or rush to keep up, and, in general, tend not to face each other or to explain their movements to others. The most self-conscious example of this pattern occurs when Abigail follows Masham at some distance; he notices and slows down, and as he turns around Abigail does too, so that when they begin to walk again he is now following her. Masham exclaims, "Are you following me?" to which Abigail responds, "You seem to be following me, sir, as I am in front of you."

Antisociality is presented in *The Favourite* as a series of shocks for characters and audiences alike. There are sudden (uncued) cuts to new narrative locations and events, violence directed at characters from off-screen (cold water being thrown on Abigail, for instance), surprising off-screen sound (Sarah's voice startling Abigail before Sarah starts to hurl books at her), abrupt shifts in tone, sudden stops and starts of nondiegetic music, and scenes starting or ending with screams (Abigail's when her hand is burned with lye; Anne's when she is bedridden with painful gout). In *The Favourite*, apparently innocent or charitable actions often turn out to be self-serving or ignoble. Early in the film, Abigail is in a carriage on her way to the palace. She smiles pleasantly at someone off-screen, but a cut reveals a man on the other side of the cabin leering at her and then putting his hand down his pants. The final shot of the sequence is a fast-moving tracking shot from behind the carriage following its rapid movement toward the palace. This type of camera movement occurs several times in the film, aligning us behind the forward momentum of a character whose intentions we find out later are less admirable than we may have at first assumed. In this instance, Abigail's seeming innocence and vulnerability disguises her ruthless pursuit of social advancement. Later we see Abigail pushed out of the carriage face-first into excrement. Here, as elsewhere in the film, the impression of forward progress or noble purpose is revealed to be illusory.

Characters in *The Favourite*, like in Lanthimos's other films, inflict a litany of cruelties upon each other. Many of these unkind acts are part of the political machinations in the royal court, but we also see a maid trick Abigail by taking her to Sarah before she has a chance to clean up and not warning her to wear gloves when she washes the floor with lye. The film suggests that the only ethical response to an inhumane social order is brutal honesty. Despite her manipulation of the queen, Sarah appears to be the most forthright character in the narrative. We get a good sense of this in one of the final scenes when Sarah is drafting a reconciliatory letter to Anne. Her first attempts at an opening line are "You cunt" and "I dreamt I stabbed you in the eye." In an earlier moment, Anne tells Sarah, "I wish you could love me as [Abigail] does," to which Sarah responds, "You wish me to lie to you? Oh, you look like an angel fell from heaven your majesty. No, sometimes you look like a badger. And you can rely on me to tell you ... I will not lie. That is love." Sarah's harsh truths are certainly preferable to a pretense of civility that would mask the structural violence of the women's social context. Such a conceit is employed by the villains in Lanthimos's films: the father (Christos

Stergioglou) in *Dogtooth*, Mont Blanc (Aris Servetalis) in *Alps*, the hotel manager (Olivia Colman) in *The Lobster*, and Abigail in *The Favourite*.

The myriad cruelties in Lanthimos's narratives allow us to better understand the entrenched antisociality of our times. By transferring enormous amounts of wealth and power from labor to capital, neoliberal measures have led to higher levels of inequality and insecurity. Attacks on the welfare state and labor unions and the proliferation of contingent employment and indebtedness are eroding social bonds: "the most basic circuits of social life—alliances, obligations, and solidarities—have been hotwired to disseminate corrosively antisocial energies."[54] In order to justify these deleterious policies, the poor and the indebted are moralistically blamed for their economic plight: "In capitalism … solvency serves as the measure of the 'morality' of man."[55] The shocks of Lanthimos's editing and narrational style capture the bewildering effects of neoliberal forms of exploitation that are harder to discern due to the abstractions of financialized capitalism.[56]

The Hollowness of the System

The Favourite initially makes us believe that it is a film about a sensitive and innocent young woman who enters a royal court beset by cruelty and deceit and tries to humanize it. In one scene, Abigail spends an afternoon with Anne, talking with her and feeding cake to her pet rabbits. She finds out that Anne has lost seventeen children through miscarriage, stillbirth, or illness. Abigail seems genuinely touched by Anne's personal tragedy and authentically fond of the seventeen rabbits that Anne has assembled around her to represent each of her lost offspring. This provides a strong contrast to Sarah who seems totally uninterested in the rabbits: in the film's first scene, Anne says, "Sarah, you must say hello to the little ones," to which Sarah responds, "No. It is macabre … No, I love you but that I will not do." In a later scene, when Anne mentions Hildebrand, one of the rabbits, Sarah responds: "Is that a rabbit?" At the end of the film we see Abigail intentionally step on one of the rabbits, which makes us realize that her earlier displays of affection for these animals was probably a pretense designed to curry favor with the queen. We are encouraged to develop a more skeptical perspective on the relationship between Abigail and Anne even earlier in the narrative. When the two women dance together in Anne's bedroom, we hear non-simultaneous sounds of the pigeon shooting that will take place in the subsequent scene. Cooing, shots fired, and shouts of "throw" provide a dark undertone to the women's dancing, linking it to the competition between Sarah and Abigail for influence in the royal court, which is about to enter a more violent phase. This eruption of violence is hinted at by the splatter of blood that strikes Sarah after Abigail shoots a pigeon at close range in the scene that follows.

At several times in the film, a closely framed shot of Abigail is shown as other characters have a conversation off-screen. Their dialogue in these instances gives us premonitions about Abigail's ruthless ambition, her apolitical and purely selfish motivations, her willingness to destroy Sarah, and the misery she will bring upon herself: "there is always a price to pay [and] I'm prepared to pay it; this is [a] disgusting distortion of the system; he is a useful ally but a dangerous enemy; we'll make a killer of you yet." The "distortion of the system" that Abigail represents can be understood if we compare her to Sarah, whose machinations are all associated with specific political positions that she is trying to advance. By contrast, Abigail's scheming consists of cold calculation and naked ambition; it is a politics devoid of normative values, without a concern for the greater good. This is made clear during a conversation between Abigail and Harley. Harley says, "Have you counseled her for our side? ... The country's future hangs in the balance ... You do not care? I thought you were on our side," to which Abigail responds, "I'm on my side. Always. Sometimes it's a happy coincidence for you. Like now. You'll get a chance to save the country." Later in the film, Sarah hints at the fact that Abigail and Sarah have different motivations (one purely personal, the other political): Sarah says, "Oh my god, you actually think you have won ... We're playing very different games."

Abigail's purely personal aspirations in *The Favourite* reflect the absence of normative considerations of the common good in neoliberal discourse. As Wendy Brown notes, "technical in orientation, [neoliberal] governance buries contestable norms and structural striations (such as class), as well as the norms and exclusions circulated by its procedures and decisions."[57] The removal of substantive, value-based concerns from political discussions is based in part on economism, which is "the targeted use of economics ... to replace normative, critical evaluation with economic, technical evaluation."[58] The narrowing of politics to purely technical questions allows neoliberal politicians to present their decisions as neutral and scientific and to label any political opposition to their policies as biased and irrational. As William Davies asserts, neoliberals "seek to replace moral rules ... with scientific rules ... by ignoring the irredeemably normative constitutions of socio-economic life."[59] Under such circumstances, the "field of politics" is reduced to a competition between elites whose only motivation is power itself: "their objective is merely to dislodge others in order to occupy their place."[60]

The Favourite implicates us by gradually revealing that the most cynical and self-centered character in the narrative is the person with whom we have been initially encouraged to identify. Our alignment with Abigail is a function of her extensive screen time, her portrayal through close-ups more than any other character, her arrival in the royal court at the start of the narrative (coinciding with our "arrival"), the sharing of her backstory, her initial characterization through admirable qualities (sensitivity, resourcefulness), and the intimate depiction of her quotidian routine (sleeping, washing herself). It is only once her true character is revealed that we might begin to disidentify with her, and, by extension, with the unbridled self-interest that she embodies. When Abigail becomes a dominant figure in the royal court, her corrosive influence is rendered visible on Anne's body, on her partially paralyzed face and limbs, ashen complexion, and slurred speech, and reflected in the queen's lethargic public appearances with unkempt hair, an unmade face, and informal attire. Abigail's narrative function in *The Favourite* is that of the parasitical guest who erodes the social fabric and moral character of the institution that she enters. Parasitical guests are common in gothic texts, as Joanne Watkiss explains:

> The Gothic has always been concerned with the invited, parasitical guest. Contrary to the reassuring position of the uninvited, the threat to the home, institution, and individual has always been invited; the threat is permitted entry to the space of the home before its influences can be felt. Therefore, the Gothic highlights the villainous capabilities of those who have been wrongly trusted, suggesting an inaccuracy of judgment ... the persistent Gothic threat is that of the hostile guest: the invited visitor who usurps the space she/he enters.[61]

The gothic trope of the "parasitical guest" is an apt metaphor for the neoliberal order, which has insinuated itself into every facet of our lives, corrupting even our most private thoughts and relationships. Our initial alignment with Abigail makes her an "invited visitor," someone we allow in, accept, and support. By encouraging us to identify with Abigail at first, Lanthimos implicates us in the ruthless antipolitics that she comes to represent. Disidentification, denaturalization, and grotesquerie are used in *The Favourite* to alienate us from the undemocratic social context of its narrative, helping us to recognize that neoliberalism is a "hostile guest" destroying us from within.

Notes

1. Charlotte Brundson quoted in Belen Vidal, *Heritage Film: Nation, Genre and Representation* (New York: Columbia University Press, 2012), 24.
2. Ibid., 26–27. In recent years, feminist scholars have countered earlier dismissals of the genre as uncritical or unserious, in part by focusing on its activation of the female gaze and the gender politics of its often overlooked costume design (ibid., 100–03).
3. Andrew Higson notes that many of the heritage films that are "interrogative and critical, exploring the underside of the nostalgic vision ... are made not by upper middle-class English film-makers, but by directors and producers

raised in other cultures. Inevitably, many such film-makers approach their subject-matter from a less than reverential position, from that of an outsider rather than the insider." See Andrew Higson, *English Heritage, English Cinema: Costume Drama since 1980* (Oxford: Oxford University Press, 2003), 28–29.

4   Vidal, *Heritage Film*, 74. Claire Monk argues that heritage films have always had international characteristics: financed through international coproductions, with an international cast and crew and an aesthetic sensibility designed to appeal to international audiences. See Claire Monk, "The British Heritage-Film Debate Revisited," in C. Monk and A. Sargeant, eds., *British Historical Cinema: The History, Heritage and Costume Film* (London: Routledge, 2002), 176–98, at pp. 176–77, 186.

5   Vidal, *Heritage Film*, 68.

6   Ibid., 100–01.

7   Kara McKechnie, "Taking Liberties with the Monarch: The Royal Bio-pic in the 1990s," in C. Monk and A. Sargeant, eds., *British Historical Cinema: The History, Heritage and Costume Film* (London: Routledge, 2002), 217–36, at p. 229; see also Pamela Church Gibson, "From Dancing Queen to Plaster Virgin: Elizabeth and the End of English Heritage?" *Journal of Popular British Cinema*, 5 (2002): 133–41, at p. 137.

8   Andrew Higson, "From Political Power to the Power of the Image: Contemporary 'British' Cinema and the Nation's Monarchs," in M. Merck, ed., *The British Monarchy on Screen* (Manchester: Manchester University Press, 2016), 339–62, at p. 357; Mandy Merck, "Introduction," in Mandy Merck, ed., *The British Monarchy on Screen* (Manchester: Manchester University Press, 2016), 1–19, at p. 15.

9   Higson, *English Heritage, English Cinema*, 26.

10 Vidal, *Heritage Film*, 19.

11 Higson, "From Political Power to the Power of the Image," 348.

12 Yorgos Lanthimos quoted in Eric Kohn, "*The Favourite* Director Yorgos Lanthimos Reveals the Method to His Madness," *IndieWire*, Nov 21, 2018, available at https://www.indiewire.com/2018/11/yorgos-lanthimos-interview-the-favourite-greece-1202022576/.

13 Emily Zemler, "*The Favourite* Is One of the Year's Most Original Screenplays; Here's How It Came About," *Los Angeles Times*, Nov 23, 2018, available at https://www.latimes.com/entertainment/movies/la-et-mn-the-favourite-screenplay-deborah-davis-tony-mcnamara-20181123-story.html.

14 Alissa Wilkinson, "*The Favourite* Director Yorgos Lanthimos on Why His Films Aren't as Mean as People Say," *Vox*, Nov 21, 2018, available at https://www.vox.com/2018/11/21/18069744/yorgos-lanthimos-interview-favourite-lobster-history-costumes-dancing; see also Emily Poenisch, "Yorgos Lanthimos Explodes the Period Drama with *The Favourite*," *Esquire*, Nov 16, 2018, available at https://www.esquire.com/entertainment/movies/a23695276/yorgos-lanthimos-the-favorite-interview/.

15 Yorgos Lanthimos quoted in Kohn, "*The Favourite* Director Yorgos Lanthimos Reveals the Method to His Madness."
16 McKechnie, "Taking Liberties with the Monarch," 220.
17 Ibid., 220–21; Merck, "Introduction," 15; Vidal, *Heritage Film*, 18–19.
18 Peter Mair, *Ruling the Void: The Hollowing of Western Democracy* (London: Verso, 2014), 22–55.
19 David Punter and Glennis Byron, *The Gothic* (Malden, MA: Wiley, 2004), 16; Martin Parker, "Organisational Gothic," *Culture and Organization*, 11, no. 3 (2005): 153–66, at p. 155.
20 Linnie Blake and Agnieszka Soltysik Monnet, "Introduction: Neoliberal Gothic," in L. Blake and A. Soltysik Monnet, eds., *Neoliberal Gothic: International Gothic in the Neoliberal Age* (Manchester: Manchester University Press, 2017), 1–18, at p. 3.
21 Andrew Higson, "Re-Presenting the National Past: Nostalgia and Pastiche in the Heritage Film," in L. D. Friedman, ed., *Fires Were Started: British Cinema and Thatcherism* (London: Wallflower Press, 2006), 99–109, at p. 99.
22 Ibid. See also Higson, *English Heritage, English Cinema*, 38–39.
23 Higson, "From Political Power to the Power of the Image," 348.
24 Higson, *English Heritage, English Cinema*, 26; Vidal, *Heritage Film*, 14.
25 Higson, *English Heritage, English Cinema*, 27; Higson, "Re-Presenting the National Past," 96.
26 Parker, "Organisational Gothic," 165; Jerrod E. Hogle, "The Gothic Ghost of the Counterfeit and the Progress of Abjection," in D. Punter, ed., *A New Companion to* The Gothic (Malden, MA: Wiley, 2015), 496–509, at p. 497.
27 Punter and Byron, *The Gothic*, 50.
28 David Punter, "Introduction: The Ghost of a History," in D. Punter, ed., *A New Companion to* The Gothic (Malden, MA: Wiley, 2015), 1–10, at pp. 1–2.
29 Fred Botting, *Gothic* (London: Routledge, 2014), 4.
30 Bart Cammaerts, "Neoliberalism and the Post-Hegemonic War of Position: The Dialectic between Invisibility and Visibilities," *European Journal of Communication*, 30, no. 5 (2015): 522–38, at p. 528.
31 Chantal Mouffe, *On the Political* (London: Routledge, 2005), 54–55; see also Philip Mirowski, "Postface: Defining Neoliberalism," in D. Plehwe and P. Mirowski, eds., *The Road from Mont Pelerin: The Making of the Neoliberal Thought Collective* (Cambridge, MA: Harvard University Press, 2015), 417–55, at pp. 435–36.
32 Mouffe, *On the Political*, 56; see also Wendy Brown, *Undoing the Demos: Neoliberalism's Stealth Revolution* (Brooklyn, NY: Zone Books, 2015), 127–31.
33 Higson, "Re-Presenting the National Past," 100.

34 Pamela Church Gibson, "Fewer Weddings and More Funerals: Changes in the Heritage Film," in R. Murphy, ed., *British Cinema of the 90s* (London: British Film Institute, 2000), 115–24, at p. 116.

35 Michael Hollington, *Dickens and the Grotesque* (London: Routledge, 2015), 4.

36 Ibid., 8.

37 Ibid., 10. See also p. 24.

38 Ibid., 10; Botting, *Gothic*, 2.

39 Botting, *Gothic*, 2.

40 Scott Brewster, "Seeing Things: Gothic and the Madness of Interpretation," in D. Punter, ed., *A New Companion to* The Gothic (Malden, MA: Wiley, 2015), 481–95, at p. 483; Punter and Byron, *The Gothic*, 14.

41 Ibid., 483.

42 Poenisch, "Yorgos Lanthimos Explodes the Period Drama with *The Favourite*."

43 Thomas Biebricher, "Neoliberalism and Democracy," *Constellations an International Journal of Critical and Democratic Theory*, 22, no. 2 (2015): 255–66, at p. 255.

44 William Davies, *The Limits of Neoliberalism: Authority, Sovereignty and the Logic of Competition* (London: Sage, 2016), 27.

45 Alison J. Ayers and Alfredo Saad-Filho, "Democracy against Neoliberalism: Paradoxes, Limitations, Transcendence," *Critical Sociology*, 41, nos. 4–5 (2015): 597–618, at p. 606.

46 Donatella della Porta, "Progressive and Regressive Politics in Late Neoliberalism," in H. Geiselberger, ed., *The Great Regression* (Malden, MA: Wiley, 2017), 26–39, at pp. 34–37; Nancy Fraser, "Progressive Neoliberalism versus Reactionary Populism: A Hobson's Choice," in H. Geiselberger, ed., *The Great Regression* (Malden, MA: Wiley, 2017), 40–48, at pp. 44–47.

47 Higson, "From Political Power to the Power of the Image," 351; see also pp. 354, 357; Gibson, "From Dancing Queen to Plaster Virgin," 134–37; Merck, "Introduction," 4–5.

48 Higson, "From Political Power to the Power of the Image," 351.

49 Ibid.

50 Regardless of time period, all monarchs in heritage films are portrayed as "spectacular creatures who command awe" and participate in "a theatre of ceremonial spectacle, a projection of public splendour, grandeur and majesty" that cements their "status as national figurehead[s]" (ibid., 354). In *The Favourite*, the aura associated with royal office is undermined, though not entirely eliminated, through an emphasis on Anne's infirmity, ignorance of state affairs, and public tantrums.

51 Brown, *Undoing the Demos*, 9–10.

52 Wendy Brown states that "[a]s human capital, the subject is at once in charge of itself, responsible for itself, yet an instrumentalizable and potentially dispensable element of the whole" (ibid., 38).

53 Alex Lykidis, "Crisis of Sovereignty in Recent Greek Cinema," *Journal of Greek Media and Culture*, 1, no. 1 (2015): 9–27, at pp. 15–20.
54 Richard Dienst, *The Bonds of Debt* (London: Verso, 2011), 3.
55 Maurizio Lazzarato, *The Making of the Indebted Man: An Essay on the Neoliberal Condition* (Cambridge: Semiotexte/Smart Art, 2012), 58.
56 As Susanne Soederberg states, "[t]he relationships between capitalists and workers, for instance, are converted, through the credit system, into relations between debtor and creditor. The latter relations are mediated by formalised abstractions (e.g., interest rates, late fees) as opposed to direct forms of domination between employer and employee." See Susanne Soederberg, *Debtfare States and the Poverty Industry: Money, Discipline and the Surplus Population* (London: Routledge, 2014), 34; see also Miranda Joseph, *Debt to Society: Accounting for Life under Capitalism* (Minneapolis, MN: University of Minnesota Press, 2014), 20–21.
57 Brown, *Undoing the Demos*, 131.
58 Davies, *The Limits of Neoliberalism*, 22.
59 Ibid., 14.
60 Mouffe, *On the Political*, 21.
61 Joanne Watkiss, "Welcome the Coming, Speed the Parting Guest: Hospitality and the Gothic," in D. Punter, ed., *A New Companion to* The Gothic (Malden, MA: Wiley, 2015), 523–34, at p. 523.

PART V

Gender, Sex, and Sexuality

14

Young Women's Deadly Rebellions in the Early Films of Yorgos Lanthimos

Tonia Kazakopoulou

A chambermaid, a nurse, and a daughter each walk into a film, with some hope …

This may sound like the start of a bad joke, but it rather sets the scene for the consistent representational approach to young women that feature in Yorgos Lanthimos's early films,[1] where hopeful rebellious acts in search of agency and self-determination invariably lead them to annihilation. In this chapter, I argue that representations of women in Lanthimos's films remain problematic, despite these characters' centrality in the director's work, and despite a general acknowledgment of his work's progressive credentials. Moreover, the way women are inserted—and kept—within certain systems of representation in the films, and the way that such representations of women are in turn often bypassed in criticism about the films, can have very serious (and not at all funny) real-life consequences in how women are perceived, treated, and (de)valued. Representations—across all artistic and linguistic fields—make a claim about their subject, and it is often through representations that we get to know and question social realities. All the more reason to pay close attention to these characters, their functions, and the ways they are filmed.[2]

Systems of Representation in Film and Film Criticism

One of my wider research interests concerns the politics of representation in film, and women's representation in particular.[3] Although Lanthimos does not necessarily share my pre-occupations when he makes his films, it is noticeable that female characters occupy a central position in his oeuvre. This is significant and its consistency suggests this choice is a conscious, rather than a coincidental, practice. Despite this tendency, there has been little writing about women in the scholarship that has been produced about Lanthimos in the last few years, and mostly since the success of *Dogtooth*. There is, however, considerable writing on the ways stringent neoliberal, or capitalist, systems of governance, all of them patriarchal, are critiqued as a menacing force against the family and/or the individual in Greek films produced in the last couple of decades more generally, and in Lanthimos's films more specifically.[4] Alex Lykidis,[5] as a case in point, argues that systems of control in Lanthimos's oeuvre can be seen as allegorical of wider neoliberal and technocratic regimes that deprive individuals from the sovereignty of their selves. Meanwhile, others have focused on the formal accomplishments of Lanthimos's films, commenting on linguistic tropes and/or modes of performance.[6]

International and Greek film critics (although the latter less favorably so) have been quick to focus their commentary on the "weird" Greek families, the strangeness of form and content, and the context of the financial crisis in Greece that serves as a thematic backdrop and analytical index for a number of Greek art-house films produced in the first couple of decades of the twenty-first century, including Lanthimos's Greek-language features.[7] Indeed, some theorists and critics already referenced in this chapter consider Lanthimos and his work paradigmatic of the so-called Greek Weird Wave or Greek New Wave, which is a less contested term for grouping these films.

I agree with most such analyses of Lanthimos's work—and of contemporary, mostly art-house, Greek cinema more generally—though I believe that what has not been pointed out enough is how gendered, and severely misogynist, these systems of representation are, even as they purport to examine the failures of patriarchal structures, though they often go unnamed as such. Through close textual analysis, this chapter seeks to address this gap in the current thinking about Lanthimos's films, and discusses how the young women in his films are systematically driven/written to their deaths, literally and/or symbolically. Within masculinist systems of governance and control, women, I argue, are additionally subjugated, and therefore their acts of resistance in the films acquire further political significance; at the same time, it is these very acts that unfailingly lead the women to self-annihilation. In the current context of increased gendered violence and feminicide in Greece,[8] as elsewhere, there is a consistent and often violent push-back against gains made by various feminist movements for women's self-determination and sovereignty over their own bodies. Therefore, it is important to turn our gaze, again, toward the ways that women have been, and continue to be, conceptualized in cultural productions, and particularly in those texts that are perceived as progressive in terms of their form, content, and politics.[9] It is important that biases that find their way into objects of cultural significance are checked, and that those that garner higher critical acclaim are also scrutinized and accordingly critiqued, if a change in imaging and imagining is to be effected.

Moreover, while many have celebrated the idea that binary, heteronormative conceptions of gender and sexuality have been put to rest, the discourse generated by the current—at the time of writing—Greek government, and always by the church that is newly empowered by conservative politics in the country, persistently refers back to older conceptions.[10] Although Lanthimos does not seem to assign particular importance to the sexuality or sexual orientation of his characters—indeed, sex is often a function, a product for sale, something one engages with in the same deadpan fashion as any other action—by and large the representations he engages in are heteronormative and hierarchical, as this chapter will show. To this end, textual analysis, my main methodological tool, is continuously significant within the field of film studies as a means of contesting complacent images and imaginings in cultural productions, and for examining responses to challenges and changes in sociopolitical contexts.

Each section in this chapter discusses a film in the order of its release: *Kinetta*, *Dogtooth*, and *Alps*. This is not to evidence any particular chronological progression, but rather to demonstrate the consistency of a pattern. My analysis focuses on the act of rebellion by the young female protagonist in each film—on the level of plot—and I also discuss the formal systems that help frame these acts as rebellious. Focusing, then, on Lanthimos's Greek-language features, and following Joanne Clarke Dillman's[11] study into the circulation of images of dead women in our visual landscapes from the turn of the millennium onward, I question the films' politics of representation and argue that they repeat misogynistic and damaging notions about women in the very instant that they appear to be granting them agency. Bringing to the fore such paradoxical articulations of young women's rebellions in Lanthimos's films, I seek to upset the cultural complacency surrounding representations of gendered violence in otherwise progressive works. This complacency, I might add, manifests itself in the art *and* in its critical reception, where questions relating to representations of women are dealt with superficially, deemed irrelevant or outdated, or are outright ignored.

The Haunting Specter in *Kinetta*

Lanthimos's first art-house film in Greece, *Kinetta*, follows a trio—two men, a police officer (Costas Xikominos) and a photographer (Aris Servetalis), and one woman, a hotel chambermaid (Evangelia Randou)—who reenact and film or photograph local murder scenes. The motivation for this "pastime," for lack of a better word, is unknown, though the film registers the police officer's delight in narrating the crimes, invariably committed against women. The characters are not given names.

The opening sequence sees a deadly car accident on a desolate motorway. A man watches from across the street and approaches the scene. A woman is dead inside the badly damaged, overturned car. He does not help; instead, he takes the cassette that is still playing in the car's sound system and walks away. The song, sung by Greek singer Tzeni Vanou, becomes a haunting soundtrack in key moments throughout the rest of the film and constitutes one of the formal systems that persistently returns to the image of a dead woman, who is additionally fragmented by the agitated camera and close-up framing; only body parts are seen, not a whole woman. After this prelude, the next scene takes us to a cemetery where the man stands in front of a grave (whose occupant remains unknown), listening to the cassette he found in the car. As set out by these formal markers, one might immediately construe that *Kinetta* is a film about (a) woman's death.

In hindsight, and because this opening sequence is not being recorded by the photographer, nor narrated by the police officer, one might assume that this first death of a woman on our screen is not a reenactment. Rather, it acts as a template and a key for some of the film's recurring audiovisual systems of representation. Visually, the camera is jittery, very mobile and unstable, establishing a haunting presence for the viewer; moreover, the framing is frequently executed in close-ups, which offers only fragments of visual information and not a whole picture. Aurally, intimate scenes of death and love are overpowered by the haunting musical accompaniment of the opening sequence and/or stretches of silence. In both cases, the haunting "presence," evident in Lanthimos's style, is coded female from the outset.

The concept of haunting is indeed an interesting one and can be productive in the context of this analysis, up to a point. Avery Gordon uses the term to describe "those singular yet repetitive instances when ... the over-and-done-with comes alive, when what's been in your blind spot comes into view," concluding that "haunting raises spectres."[12] She continues:

> These spectres or ghosts appear when the trouble they represent and symptomize is no longer being contained or repressed or blocked from view ... Haunting and the appearance of spectres or ghosts is one way we are notified that what's been concealed is very much alive and present,

interfering precisely with those always incomplete forms of containment and repression ceaselessly directed toward us. Haunting … always registers the harm inflicted or the loss sustained by a social violence done in the past or in the present.[13]

Misogyny and sexism are perennial violences in both reality and representation. At first glance, Lanthimos's representational systems suggest a critique against patriarchal forms of oppression and violence against women. In representation, too, there is a critically present camera—both inside and outside the film world—that implies an awareness of and an active commentary on the politics of representation. To use Gordon's terminology, spectral women make their "presence" felt, here and elsewhere in Lanthimos's oeuvre, raising into view forms of repression ceaselessly directed toward them; yet, this kind of presence presupposes actual death, and the haunting presence is of immaterial significance when real lives are at stake.

As aforementioned, the police officer sets up reenacted murders, giving instructions via voice recording. Michel Chion[14] has spoken of sound in film as voco- and verbocentric, where the presence of a human voice (and words) capture and focus our attention above all other sounds. As such, these voices structure our vision and understanding; or, to put it another way, the human voice prevails in the hierarchy of perception.[15] What is important to note is that Chion argues for a noncompetitive codependence of image and sound in film; what we see and what we hear make sense together and not independently of one another. In *Kinetta*'s audio-vision, to appropriate Chion's term, there is a male, authoritative figure whose voice dictates the narrative. The film goes to some lengths to establish this character's control over the way each story is told. If one were to suspect that his dry, monotone narration is restricted to his pastime of crime reconstruction, then it is soon revealed that the same occurs when he exploits migrant women who require documents from the police. He narrates the actions that the women must enact—not just the removal of clothes and waving of their hair, but also sex—in a clear demonstration of abusive power. Quite visibly, and aurally, the character does not accommodate stereotypical notions of virile masculinity, nor those of a potent patriarch; indeed, it is easy to dismiss him as a pathetic little man with funny fixations on cars and go-carting; a police clerk with pretentions of solving crimes. Yet, despite this vision of aspirational patriarchy, the film—and all the subsequent ones I discuss in this chapter—does very little to disrupt his authority.

The dominance of the police officer's (recorded) voice is supported by the photographer's gaze through his camera. Lanthimos observes this process of representation and quite often maintains a critical distance, pulling back to a long or extreme long shot, especially during the crime reenactment scenes. However, the director also affords the spectator a privileged insight into his character when he looks without his camera. He often looks at the chambermaid, mostly when she is unaware, which establishes a hierarchical power structure in the act of gazing. One can indulge in thinking that this character is perhaps more attentive, less imposing, even tender and shy; a representation akin to that of the "new man" who surfaced in mainstream Western cinemas sometime in the early 1990s.[16] He asks after the maid's welfare, brings food to her room but hesitates to knock on her door, and even carries her to the hospital after she gets hurt during a reenactment. Nevertheless, he also participates in the production of her characters by arranging costumes, reiterating instructions, and, of course, filming or photographing her. In perhaps the most intimate scene in the film, the two sit in his van and listen to music, the same cassette he lifted from the car crash during the opening sequence. The ghost of the dead woman is evoked at the expense of the living character. Despite the poignancy of this scene, it remains consistent with the formal systems of the film. When confronted with an actual deadly accident, the photographer walks away; and when he is later confronted once again with the reality of death, as opposed to the reenacted facsimiles of it in which he participates, after the maid's suicide attempt, his impulse is to reach for his camera. Lanthimos appears to be commenting on power structures that determine how and what we see, but one might equally ask, is the director being critical enough of representation and its politics?

During the reenactments we see the chambermaid get hurt repeatedly: she gets bruised, her leg gets a gash, and her arm is sprained. The police officer recklessly—or perhaps sadistically—puts her in harm's way. Toward the end of the film, however, the chambermaid rebels against this structure by rehearsing her own death by strangulation. This unprompted *pre*-enactment of her death places her attempted suicide within the system of representation established by the film. Perhaps this is also in a way a *re*enactment: she is already dead, a specter that haunts the film with no agency of her own. When she does try to commit suicide, it is by swallowing pills—not something pre-rehearsed, even if it has been prefigured. One cannot celebrate her act of rebellion without first considering that the film presents this as the only way out for this young woman in the world she inhabits. But death is hardly to be celebrated. It may be the case that patriarchy, or any other system, loses its control over a woman, her body, her subjectivity, in death, but the sticky point for me is that so does the woman, for the simple reason that she is now dead. Any acquisition of agency in her taking control is undermined and undone by her annihilation. I also want to question the presentation of agency here. On the level of plot, perhaps the woman's suicide may be read as a forceful political act: a means for her resistance and finally liberation.[17] However, any cause for celebration is short-lived and bitter to taste if one considers how this moment of rebellion is filmed. On the level of form, the film returns to the system it established in the opening scene of the car crash. Short glimpses of body parts—therefore not a whole woman—in close, tight shots, instead of the wider long shots that capture in fullness the murder reenactments. On the level of plot, the photographer "saves" the young woman, but not before photographing her dying body; he resuscitates her and soon after we see her return to her regular duties before the film concludes.

Two things are problematic in the way this is formally treated by Lanthimos. First, by having one of the men, albeit the more sympathetic one, photograph this scene, any implied agency is undermined, and the suicide is resignified as yet another reenactment, with the outcome being determined by men both textually (in the photographer) and extra-textually (in Lanthimos himself). Second, the "life" that this woman must continue living has also been resignified as a symbolic death that, effectively, kills her, even if it constitutes some form of middle ground between life and death. The jittery handheld camerawork and the obscure framing in close shots renders her a spectral figure, emulating the same spectral impression of the first dead woman that opened the film. There is no way out of this system it seems, in reality and in representation, and once the annihilation, literal and symbolic, has been established beyond doubt, the camera steadies for the closing shot of her walking back toward the hotel. Women's death and its representation are observed by Lanthimos from the outset, but are not adequately resolved, which is itself a violence toward those represented in this formula. It is critiqued, to some extent, but not dismantled—at least not representationally. I do not imply intentionality in this by the director or his films; rather, a complacency in operating with and within existing systems of representation.

The Living Dead in *Dogtooth*

Dogtooth focuses on a self-contained family living in a house at the edge of a city. The only person allowed to leave the house is the father. The mother and the three adult, but infantilized, children (two daughters and a son) remain enclosed. When the outside world finds its way into the house, one of the children, Elder Daughter, stages an exodus.

Dogtooth is populated by multiple female characters. Following *Kinetta*, the central family are not named. Instead, they are defined by their relation to one another, pointing to a self-contained system of existence and representation: the female family members are Mother (Michele Valley), Elder Daughter (Angeliki Papoulia), and Younger Daughter (Mary Tsoni). The only named character is significantly a woman, Christina (Anna Kalaitzidou), an outsider brought into the house by Father (Christos Stergioglou) to satisfy Son's (Christos Passalis) sexual needs. Many possibilities arise from the close-knit community of women in *Dogtooth*, even within the hermetically closed system of the film (as argued by Ben Tyrer, for example, from a psychoanalytical perspective[18]); to put it simply, the very idea of a *community* of women holds a promise to break the regime that the patriarch (and, indeed, Lanthimos) has put in place. Alas, while Lanthimos places the women on the screen and in close proximity to one another—their centrality in the film's visual strategies is evident—they act without agency and when they communicate, they do so in a language that is not their own. Their exchanges take place in a compromised field of communication that has been determined by the director and cowriters Lanthimos and Efthymis Filippou. In order to pursue this line of inquiry, I will focus on two women characters, whose seeming rebellions against the established structure are most plainly realized: Christina, who is granted access to the family's otherwise impenetrable environment; and Elder Daughter, who exists within the confines of the house, but wishes to escape to the world beyond it.

In an early sequence in the film, Christina approaches Elder Daughter for a conversation after a sexual encounter with Son. The young women are alone and unsupervised, and the scene is filmed in intimate close and mid-shots. The discussions are childish and allude to an exchange system of objects that is already in place between the two sisters that Christina has become privy to and will later exploit. However, the camerawork also registers an unspoken desire for companionship in the women. The hopeful fissure in the visual economy of the film gets quickly contained in the next sequence, when Christina is firmly entered into the representational regime of the father, who videos the family with her, and directs that she smiles more. Lanthimos offers hope of a crack in the dominant patriarchal system, only to pull it away quite pointedly and transform it into a representation of control orchestrated by a man and his camera. Formally, a long shot of the father standing and looking down through his camera on the young, seated women leaves no doubt of the hierarchy at play; it is a double system of representation—with the father's camera matched by the director's—that not only fails to imagine women outside established hierarchical systems, but also quickly refutes their agency when any prospect of it arises. If such a nihilistic approach is intentional, it is not any less problematic. This is a punishing visual regime that results in violence that is carried through to the film's end.

Christina's rebellion comes in her attempt to appropriate the existing system of exchange and reward to her advantage. She brings in objects from the outside world, which she barters for sexual favors from Elder Daughter. While these are undertaken for Christina's benefit, they also open an imaginative possibility for Elder Daughter, who attempts to reproduce them with Younger Sister. And because all these encounters operate outside of heteronormativity, the father cannot countenance that something inappropriate might be taking place, leaving the women to briefly take advantage of this blind spot in his patriarchal order. Following *Kinetta*, on the level of plot, glimpses of female desire find a way through a tight system, but formally, women's desire belongs to a representational regime that is controlled by men. The video technology that Father used to record Christina is part of the same technology that brings about her undoing: having found out she has supplied Elder Daughter with video tapes, the father visits Christina in her house and violently beats her with the VCR, a former source of currency for her. Elder Daughter is similarly punished for her part in the exchange as Father hits her in the head with a video tape strapped to his hand. The community and desires of women are violently undone, both narratively and formally.

I do not object to the representations of raw violence perpetrated by the patriarch against the vulnerable. In this respect, the film does not shy away from representing the realities of gender-based domestic violence and abuse that disproportionately affect women. Dimitris Eleftheriotis[19] writes convincingly about the need for introspective criticism and the examination of the deeply problematic and specifically Greek ways in which the family (dys)functions, and calls for literal, rather than allegorical analyses of films like *Dogtooth*.[20] Indeed, one could argue that *Dogtooth* is Lanthimos's film that most clearly allows a recognizable reality to infiltrate its systems of representation. On an extratextual level, viewers can identify the film's engagement with real violence that women are subjected to daily, but within the text, Lanthimos constrains the opportunities for the women to imagine and to act, and, crucially, constrains any opportunity for women to *be* imagined outside of the system of violence he presents.

A key component in the construction of this locked system, both narratively and in terms of *mise-en-scène*, is the father's car. It is a significant location in the film that is coded as masculine, here as well as in broader cultural (and filmic) terms. It is the place where the father constructs their "reality." There, in close-up shots he removes labels from water bottles in the car boot before taking them into the house or prepares his costume for the staged death of a potentially imaginary second son supposedly existing precariously on the other side of the villa's fence. In this sense, the car is already compromised as a means of escape and is another part of the iconography of containment and annihilation that the film generates.

At this point, Elder Daughter has taken on the name Bruce, which she will have heard in one of the video tapes brought into the house by Christina. The name Bruce, therefore, forms part of Christina's legacy, whereby she has gifted Elder Daughter the opportunity to imagine a world beyond her family home, though that world is also unforgiving to women, as Christina's fate testifies to. While Bruce, in name and deed, appears to rebel from the family's oppressive system, she cannot escape its reach: having already mutilated herself, it is there, in the car, and correspondingly in the film's patriarchal system of representation, that she is entombed.

As I have written elsewhere[21]—and following *Thelma and Louise* (Ridley Scott, 1991)—the choice of death over subjugation to patriarchy has been celebrated in some feminist writing. I remain unconvinced, for some of the reasons I have already mentioned above in my discussion of *Kinetta*. I am also skeptical that Bruce's ending up in the boot of the car creates a fate that is akin to Schrödinger's cat: that unless and until the boot opens, she is both dead and alive.[22] Due to the way Lanthimos systematizes and codes life and death in his films, Elder Daughter is bound to fail. To reach any other conclusion, one must ignore the car as a visual motif of containment and a locus of production for the film's stringent representational regime. Moreover, the only person who has access to the car is the father; it requires no leap of the imagination to expect that he will open the boot at some point. If, at that point, Bruce is alive, then her "life" has already been coded as worse than death within the violent reality of the family home; if she miraculously escapes, then Christina is the only point of contact she has to a world she has been systemically coded not to understand. Additionally, Christina has already functioned as a powerful referent to woman's precarious existence in the world. And if, finally, she is dead, then her annihilation is absolute, and death cannot be taken as a victory. In this way, I find Lanthimos's films less open-ended than some critics have suggested, for the director has already put in place a system that ensures she will not get out. I must emphasize, I am not looking for happy endings, but rather arguing for less complacent representational practices than those that consistently conceptualize women as entombed and decidedly dead, even as they are living.

The Hollow Shell in *Alps*

Alps is, at the time of writing, the last Greek-language feature to be directed by Lanthimos. In the film, two men and two younger women form a group that provides consolation services to bereaved relatives by impersonating their dead loved ones. The group name themselves Alps and each participant acquires the name of a mountain in that range; the characters, like in the previous films, are known by their profession or function.

As an entrepreneurial group, the Alps offers a type of grief management for a fee; I would argue that *Alps* is the film among Lanthimos's that can most explicitly be seen to critique a neoliberal, globalized, capitalist system and to comment on the Greek financial crisis. All characters also hold other jobs, all of which offer limited reward in a capitalist value system. A paramedic (Aris Servetalis) leads the group, working with a nurse (Angeliki Papoulia), a gymnast (Ariane Labed), and her coach (Johnny Vekris). At the level of plot, such contextual considerations can help unlock a particular set of readings that others have already discussed.[23] Beyond established analytical frameworks conveying interest in the film's commentary on contemporary economic systems, it is worth considering the additionally precarious position of women as expendable entities. As Dillman puts it, "the economic and social effects of globalization are reinforced through a variety of discourses, one of the most prominent of which implicitly situates women as exploitable, replaceable, and disposable."[24]

Women's participation in any given system is invariably predicated on following the rules, rather than setting them, and as recent developments across the globe have demonstrated, financial, and resultant sociopolitical and cultural, crises invariably become opportunities for a push back on women's gains for equality and self-determination. This narrative plays out rather explicitly in *Alps* as the nurse tries to participate in the economic system as a decision-maker rather than a laborer: she secures a client for herself without the knowledge of the male group leader. When she is found out, she is punished in an excessively violent way by the leader; she is also expelled from the group and dropped by her clients, too, who decide upon a younger model for their dead daughter. By the end, the film shows the nurse as a broken and abandoned character lacking direction or purpose: a dispossessed entity[25] and a disposable body. Such analysis of the film's commentary on biopolitical power can be productive far beyond the few lines I have dedicated here—indeed, Dimitris Papanikolaou has written most eloquently and convincingly about Greek cinema of the twenty-first century and biopolitics[26]—yet this is not a direction I will follow further at this time.

Instead, I want to draw attention to the audiovisual economy of the film and once again unpick the systems of representation in relation to the female characters. I particularly want to focus on the nurse character, though it is important to note that her narrative and representational trajectory operates in relation to the gymnast, which I will also briefly touch upon. Primarily, I argue that in *Alps* Lanthimos offers a critical and self-reflective commentary on the mechanics of film representation and performance.

Alps conveys a hierarchical system that privileges the male; a trope that is consistent with the director's work even where he focuses on women. More than simply an entrepreneur, the paramedic, as leader of the Alps, is presented as director of the whole operation. In an early scene, he names the group and writes its characters: the group, he determines, will be called Alps, and each member must adopt the name of a corresponding mountain. He is henceforth to be referred to as Mont Blanc, the tallest of all the Alps. The scene is shot in medium close-ups that bring each character in and out of focus, centering on each in turn while pushing the others to the edge of the frame. It is difficult not to notice the technique on display and to not be aware of a doubled directorial presence both in and out of the film world. Lanthimos makes his presence felt, directing the audience's perspective in a way that reinforces Mont Blanc's authority within the group. The soundtrack further determines the male authority that punctuates the scene, which is layered consistently across the changing images. Any interjection by other characters only serves to confirm his authorial dominion. Thus, the film form presents an audiovisual system by which to understand the film's characters, and especially its women.

Soon after, Mont Blanc is in his office, where he prepares scripts and plans casting and costuming for the group's next performance. As in his previous features, Lanthimos establishes a male director as a figure of control, a man in charge of mediating systems of power and representation. In *Alps*, Mont Blanc's directorial persona establishes his authority as the ultimate decision-maker: he has the "vision" redolent of filmmaking auteurs, as well as an overarching control over the structure and shape of the group's performances. Following *Kinetta* and *Dogtooth*, the characters speak monotonically; here, however, the style of delivery acquires further significance as a system that explores and comments on the nature of performing. Whether they play a role or not, the characters speak the same way, and as the film progresses, it becomes increasingly difficult to identify when and how the characters are performing;[27] this later becomes especially poignant for Monte Rosa, the nurse. Despite this blurring, however, the roles remain clear: there is a strict hierarchy that operates within the group, whereby Mont Blanc serves only as its leader and relies heavily on the women's labor.

Monte Rosa attempts to subvert the hierarchical system, which constitutes the film's primary act of women's rebellion. She seizes an opportunity to secure a client for herself in a transaction wherein she controls the rules of the performance and takes the payment. Monte Rosa's attempt to take over the system is noteworthy because it signifies not only a refusal to continue to be directed and authored by Mont Blanc, but because she also briefly assumes an entrepreneurial role for herself with which she is able to determine (or author) her own role(s). The rebellion here is arguably more consequential than in Lanthimos's earlier films; unlike Bruce's attempt to escape in the car boot that determines her death inevitable, the nurse seeks to control the means of production, to take the driver's seat in the system of patriarchal–capitalist production in which she is enmeshed. I contend, however, that this is still achieved within a fixed audiovisual system of representation.

There are two moments when the strong authorial presence recedes to offer the viewer a glimmer of a shift within the prevailing structure. First, when Monte Rosa takes over, her interaction with the grieving parents is filmed in a medium-long shot, with all the characters in view: we see her talking, and she performs a display of empathy in a way that engages her potential clients. She has a different way of doing business, after all. Consistent with practices identified earlier, however, this hopeful respite is simultaneously refuted by the film, which maintains a monotonal vocal style to counter the images of compassion. The second instance occurs as Monte Rosa stops the gymnast's attempted suicide. On the level of plot, they act and interact independently of the men who control them. On the level of form, however, the audiovisual system established during the Alps naming sequence is still intact: Monte Rosa is out of focus at the edge of the frame, even when speaking, while the camera focuses on the gymnast as she listens and occasionally responds. Thus, Monte Rosa's attempt to establish a different set of interactions and solidarity is undermined by a representational regime that continues to subjugate her. The narrative might be saying something, but the form (established by a male auteur, Lanthimos) says otherwise.

In keeping with Lanthimos's tendencies, these quests for emancipation will not end well for the women. When Mont Blanc discovers Monte Rosa's insubordination, he beats her on the head with a club. At this point, the perspective changes as both characters are brought into focus. In this formal maneuver, Lanthimos reestablishes Mont Blanc's power: Monte Rosa has reentered Mont Blanc's field of vision and now sits at the edge of the frame looking up at him as he holds the club. Monte Rosa is then expelled from the group; this is the beginning of her symbolic death. Having been expelled, Monte Rosa finds herself increasingly immersed in her last role as reality and performance start to merge for her. The more she is immersed, the more the camera distances itself from her, formally emphasizing the process of the character's dismantling. At the end of the film, Monte Rosa stands outside her last clients' home with her identity and agency stripped from her: she is a hollow shell, the living dead.

Without fail, the operational systems of representation in Lanthimos's films prove entirely detrimental for the female characters. Not only do his films observe women's vulnerable state, but they also reinforce it to the point of obliteration. Lykidis points out that "the pessimistic ending of *Alps* reflects the common perception in peripheral societies that agency is fundamentally compromised by external influences, a recurring theme in modern Greek culture."[28] The problem is that in speaking about "societies," Lykidis elides the very real power imbalances that exist within the social systems identified. And while Lanthimos's film certainly shows these gendered power differentials, it does nothing to destabilize them.

A chambermaid, a daughter, and a nurse enter a chapter…

The critical framework that constructs women's death as resistance is unsatisfactory for me, and I remain deeply suspicious of any attempt to celebrate women's death, both in representation and in real life. I am compelled to believe that cultural representations are crucial to how we—women and humans more generally—may differently and diversely envision our future. My analysis in this chapter centers on the women in Lanthimos's films who tend to be routinely sidelined in the wider criticism of the director's work. I have shown that women's lives in Lanthimos's films, at least the ones I have looked at here, are rendered systematically disposable, both narratively and formally; or, as Dillman writes, "the woman is put under erasure as a condition of her visibility in the text."[29] It is important to note, in conclusion, that I do not consider Lanthimos to be a misogynistic filmmaker; in fact, I study his work precisely because I find he provides astute observations of the misogynist cultures that emanate from existing patriarchal structures that systemically and systematically treat women as expendable entities. What I argue is that more attention should be paid to how Lanthimos goes about making these observations, not only from the privileged position of white masculinity, but also by using representational tropes that confer women to inevitable annihilation. In other words, rather than getting carried away with the progressiveness of his films, we must recognize Lanthimos's system of representation as a closed circle that complacently indulges in images of death for its women.

Notes

I would like to offer my thanks to Dimitris Papanikolaou for a constructive and encouraging discussion during the early presentations of this chapter. Thanks are also owed to Pedro de Senna, who has always been a challenging and trusted discussant of ideas explored in my work. Last, but not least, I owe gratitude to Eddie Falvey for his gracious humanity while I was writing this chapter under very difficult circumstances and for his careful editing of my work.

1. This chapter focuses on Lanthimos's Greek-speaking films: *Kinetta*, *Dogtooth*, and *Alps*. Although my argument may be extended to his English-speaking features, that would be the basis of a much larger study than this space permits.

2. An earlier and shorter version of this chapter was published as a blog post hosted by *Rethinking Modern Greek Studies in the 21st Century: A Cultural Analysis Network*. See Tonia Kazakopoulou, "Young Women's Deadly Rebellions: Cultural Complacency in the Films of Yorgos Lanthimos," *The Oxford Research Centre in the Humanities*, 2020, available at https://www.torch.ox.ac.uk/article/young-womens-deadly-rebellions-cultural-complacency-in-the-films-of-yorgos-lanthimos.

3. See, for example, my articles: Tonia Kazakopoulou, "Schemes of Comedy in *The Cow's Orgasm*," *Journal of the Hellenic Diaspora*, 37, no. 1 and 2 (2011): 61–74; "The Mother Accomplice: Questions of Representation in *Dogtooth* and *Miss Violence*," *Journal of Greek Media and Culture*, 2, no. 2 (2016): 187–200; "In Crisis: Greek Cultural Heritage, Masculinity and a Female Pig," *FilmIcon: Journal of Greek Film Studies*, 5 (2018), available at https://filmiconjournal.com/journal/article/page/76/2018/5/2.

4. See, for example, Mark Fisher, "*Dogtooth*: The Family Syndrome," *Film Quarterly*, 64, no. 4 (2011): 22–27; Ipek A. Celik, "Family as Internal Border in *Dogtooth*," in R. Merivirta, K. Ahonen, H. Mulari, and R. Mähkä, eds., *Frontiers of Screen History: Imagining European Borders in*

Cinema, 1945–2010 (Bristol and Chicago, IL: Intellect, 2011), 217–33; Stamos Metzidakis, "No Bones to Pick with Lanthimos's Film *Dogtooth*," *Journal of Modern Greek Studies*, 32, no. 4 (2014): 367–92; Tatjana Aleksić, "Sex, Violence, Dogs and the Impossibility of Escape: Why Contemporary Greek Film Is so Focused on Family," *Journal of Greek Media and Culture*, 2, no. 2 (2016): 155–71; Dimitris Papanikolaou, *Κατι Τρεχει με την Οικογενεια: Εθνος, Ποθος και Συγγενεια την Εποχη της Κρισης/There Is Something about the Family: Nation, Desire and Kinship at a Time of Crisis* (Athens: Patakis, 2018).

5 Alex Lykidis, "Crisis of Sovereignty in Recent Greek Cinema," *Journal of Greek Media and Culture*, 1, no. 1 (2015): 9–27.

6 See, for example, Angelos Koutsourakis, "Cinema of the Body: The Politics of Performativity in Lars von Trier's *Dogville* and Yorgos Lanthimos' *Dogtooth*," *Cinema: Journal of Philosophy and the Moving Image*, 3 (2012): 84–108; Chrysa Ariadni Kousela and Ioannis Mazarakis, "Η παρωδιακή χρήση της γλώσσας στις ταινίες του Γιώργου Λάνθιμου/The Parodic Use of Language in the Films of Yorgos Lanthimos" [my translation], *Filmicon: Journal of Greek Film Studies*, 4 (2017): 257–80; Dionysios Kapsaskis, "Translation as a Critical Tool in Film Analysis: Watching Yorgos Lanthimos's *Dogtooth* through a Translational Prism," *Translation Studies*, 10, no. 3 (2017): 247–62; Carlo Comanducci, "Empty Gestures: Mimesis and Subjection in the Cinema of Yorgos Lanthimos," in A. Hedberg Olenina and I. Schulzki, eds., *Mise en geste: Studies of Gesture in Cinema and Art*, Special Issue of *Apparatus: Film, Media and Digital Cultures in Central and Eastern Europe*, 5, 2017, available at http://www.apparatusjournal.net/index.php/apparatus/article/view/56/128.

7 See, for example, Peter Bradshaw, "*Dogtooth*: Review," *The Guardian*, Apr 22, 2010, available at https://www.theguardian.com/film/2010/apr/22/dogtooth-review; Philip French, "*Dogtooth*," *The Observer*, Apr 25, 2010, available at https://www.theguardian.com/film/2010/apr/25/dogtooth-film-review; Steve Rose, "*Attenberg, Dogtooth* and the Weird Wave of Greek Cinema," *The Guardian*, Aug 27, 2011, available at https://www.theguardian.com/film/2011/aug/27/attenberg-dogtooth-greece-cinema; Yiannis Zoumboulakis, "Οι ταινίες της εβδομάδας: Τρέχα—γύρευε στις «Άλπεις»/Films of the Week: 'Whatever' in *Alps*" [my translation], *To Vima*, Oct 26, 2011, available at https://www.tovima.gr/2011/10/26/culture/oi-tainies-tis-ebdomadas-trexa-gyreye-stis-alpeis/; Achilleas Ntellis, "Η ανολοκλήρωτη τριλογία της παλαιάς Ελλάδας (Κινέττα, Κυνόδοντας, Άλπεις)/The Incomplete Trilogy of Old Greece: *Kinetta, Dogtooth, Alps*" [my translation], *Frear Online*, June 3, 2013, available at https://frear.gr/?p=652.

8 See, for example, John Smith, "Greece Records 13,700 Cases of Domestic Violence," *The Greek Reporter*, Jan 28, 2018, available at https://greece.greekreporter.com/2018/01/28/greece-records-13700-cases-of-domestic-violence/; TaNeaTeam, "Γυναικοκτονίες: Οι γυναίκες στην Ελλάδα που δολοφονήθηκαν από συζύγους, συντρόφους και συγγενείς/ Feminicides: The Women in Greece that Were Murdered by Their Husbands, Partners and Relatives" [my translation], *Ta Nea*, June 19, 2021, available at https://www.tanea.gr/2021/06/19/people/

gynaikoktonies-oi-gynaikes-stin-ellada-pou-dolofonithikan-apo-syzygous-syn trofous-kai-syggeneis/; Myrto Lialiouti, "Από τη «Στέλλα» στον «Ζορμπά» και από τον Παπαχρόνη στην υπόθεση Φραντζή/From *Stella* to *Zorba the Greek* and from Papachronis to the Frantzis Case" [my translation], *Ta Nea*, June 28, 2021, available at https://www.tanea.gr/2021/06/28/greece/astynomika/apo-ti-stella-ston-zormpa-kai-apo-ton-papaxroni-stin-ypothesi-frantzi-2/; Lialiouti draws explicit links between representation of feminicide in Greek film and the lived experience of women in Greece.

9   Outside of Greece, I would encourage a closer look at the works of David Lynch and Lars von Trier, for example, for the use of persistent misogynist tropes in their films that warrant further scrutiny.

10 Globally, the picture is not much different, but any exploration of a wider context is beyond the scope of this chapter. However, and despite this chapter's focus on Greece and Lanthimos's Greek-language features, it is important to note that the director's work has resonated with audiences worldwide, so I would encourage more research on the female characters.

11 Joanne Clarke Dillman, *Women and Death in Film, Television, and News* (New York and Basingstoke: Palgrave Macmillan, 2014).

12 Avery F. Gordon and Janice Radway, *Ghostly Matters: Haunting and the Sociological Imagination* (Minneapolis, MN: University of Minnesota Press, 2008), xvi.

13 Ibid.

14 Michel Chion, *The Voice in Cinema*, trans. Claudia Gorbman (New York: Columbia University Press, 1999); Michel Chion, *Audio-Vision: Sound on Screen* (New York: Columbia University Press, 2019).

15 I have written about this in relation to *Dogtooth*; an argument that is still applicable to this chapter, but not one that is necessary to reproduce here. See Tonia Kazakopoulou, "The Mother Accomplice," 187–200.

16 See Yvonne Tasker, *Spectacular Bodies: Gender, Genre and the Action Cinema* (London: Routledge, 1993); Rosalind Gill, "Power and the Production of Subjects: A Genealogy of the New Man and the New Lad," *Sociological Review*, 51, no. 1 (May 2003): 34–56; Tim Edwards, *Cultures of Masculinity* (London: Routledge, 2005); Tamar Jeffers McDonald, *Romantic Comedy: Boy Meets Girl Meets Genre* (London and New York: Columbia University Press, 2007).

17 See Judith Butler and Athena Athanasiou, *Dispossession: The Performative in the Political* (Cambridge: Polity Press, 2013); Judith Butler, Zeynep Gambetti, and Leticia Sabsay, *Vulnerability in Resistance* (Durham, NC: Duke University Press, 2016).

18 Ben Tyrer, "This Tongue Is Not My Own: *Dogtooth*, Phobia and the Paternal Metaphor," in T. Kazakopoulou and M. Fotiou, eds., *Contemporary Greek Film Cultures from 1990 to the Present* (Oxford: Peter Lang, 2017), 101–30.

19 Dimitris Eleftheriotis, "Introspective Cosmopolitanism: The Family in the Greek Weird Wave," *Journal of Greek Media and Culture*, 6, no. 1 (2020): 3–27.

20 Although this is not a line of argument I will follow in this chapter, it is important to point out the very literal hold that patriarchal structures have on many aspects of Greek life and its dominance in representation.
21 Kazakopoulou, "The Mother Accomplice."
22 See Tyrer, "This Tongue Is Not My Own."
23 See, in particular, Lykidis, "Crisis of Sovereignty."
24 Dillman, *Women and Death*, 15.
25 Butler and Athanasiou offer an influential discussion on the political significance of dispossessed subjects and communities and conceptualize dispossession as a form of resistance to individualist neoliberal forms of oppression. See Butler and Athanasiou, *Dispossession*.
26 Dimitris Papanikolaou, *Greek Weird Wave: A Cinema of Biopolitics* (Edinburgh: Edinburgh University Press, 2021).
27 The field of Performance Studies has examined this continuum between life and performance extensively. Richard Schechner's seminal work *Performance Theory* (London and New York: Routledge, 1988) sets the foundation for such analyses.
28 Lykidis, "Crisis of Sovereignty," 17.
29 Dillman, *Women and Death*, 25.

15

The "Weird" Sex Scenes of Yorgos Lanthimos

Alice Haylett Bryan

The directors of the so-called Greek Weird Wave have always been located on the edge of European cinematic extremism. One obvious reason for this is the wave's position in cinematic history, coming into being around the release and international reception of *Dogtooth* in 2009, five years after the publication of James Quandt's notorious *Artforum* essay "Flesh and Blood: Sex and Violence in Recent French Cinema."[1] Therefore, the majority of the work of directors such as Yorgos Lanthimos, Alexandros Avranas, Athina Rachel Tsangari, and the others that make up the wave was released after the height of European extremism. Although the latter continues in various forms, by 2009, the world had seen quite a lot of sex and violence. Accordingly, scholarly texts on European extremism position Greek directors on the periphery—a footnote here, a passing reference there—rarely dedicating a whole study or chapter to films from the country. In Tanya Horeck and Tina Kendall's edited collection on the subject, the only Greek director referenced is Lanthimos, and he is only mentioned twice in passing.[2] Likewise, in Nikolaj Lübecker's *The Feel-Bad Film*, Lanthimos receives a small reference in a note, whilst in *Extreme Cinema: The Transgressive Rhetoric of Today's Art Film Culture*, Mattias Frey goes as far as referring to the "significant number" of extreme productions in the Greek Weird Wave, but again this is only a passing comment that circumvents specifics.[3] These are just a few examples that demonstrate the small, intermittent, and fluid borders between certain films of the Greek

Weird Wave and European extreme cinema. Another reason why the Greek Weird Wave is often adjacent to European extremism is that although many of its films deal with difficult topics (sexual abuse, willing or enforced incest, prostitution, but also positive representation of queer identities and sexual freedom), their imagery is not always quite extreme enough to push them over the boundary of what is widely accepted in European art cinema. Or when extreme imagery is utilized, it may only be once or twice in a film rather than a sustained onslaught of sex and violence. Instead, the films and filmmakers that could be classified under the banner of the Greek Weird Wave move in and out of extremity, at times intersecting with it and at other times not.

Out of all the directors of the Greek Weird Wave, Lanthimos is the one most referenced in relation to European extremism, and also the one who has received the most mainstream international recognition and acclaim, with films such as *The Lobster* and *The Favourite* positioning him as a well-known figure in the global film market. Having moved away from his Greek production roots, his films are now English-language productions financed via a broad range of national and private funding bodies and, unlike many directors who are positioned within the category of extremism, they win awards not only at festivals such as Cannes and Venice, but also at mainstream events like the Oscars. Therefore, it could be argued that Lanthimos's position at the intersection of varying filmic tropes and categories—Greek weirdness, extremism, art cinema—has allowed him to successfully conquer the international market, creating films that are weird enough to be interesting, but not too weird, brutal enough to shock, but not too shocking, and with a strong individual style that invites audiences in, rather than only appealing to those with an exclusive taste for the art house. And it is in his depiction of sex where one can most clearly see this navigation between these—at times opposing—forces. This chapter will argue that Lanthimos's depiction of sex and sexual activity is where his works most closely align with extreme cinema through a combination of formal (and, as I will argue, sexual) realism and emotional disconnection. This chapter will propose that sex in these works is not about connection, but rather the characters use sex as part of a transaction, a way of achieving a specific personal goal, or a means of obtaining pleasure for the self. Therefore, the sex act in Lanthimos's films is at once "real" and jarring (or extreme) in both its depiction and for what it reveals about the characters' motivations, and as such operates as the pivotal example of how the director straddles the mainstream and art cinema, ordinary and weird, the acceptable and the extreme.

The Greek Weird Wave and European extremism are both slippery and problematic categorizations. As documented by scholars such as Maria Chalkou and Lydia Papadimitriou, the Greek Weird Wave arose at a point in Greek history where the country—and its filmmakers—were conscious of their relationship with Europe.[4] Furthermore, the wave consisted of a rush of young talent aspiring to push back against the stagnant Greek film industry that prioritized popular local comedies for funding and failed to deliver promised financial support to emerging filmmakers. Instead, these young directors adopted a creative and collaborative approach to filmmaking, favoring narratives that engaged with Greece's social–cultural and political debates in imaginative, and often "weird," ways. Eleni Varmazi argues that the films of these directors share many formal approaches and narrative characteristics. She writes: "A certain loss of logical succession, a spastic physicality, spasmodic sexuality, sporadic and broken relationships, as well as the merging of different genres, are common elements characterizing contemporary Greek cinema, which nevertheless also contains an impressive diversity of cinematic references."[5] In 2009, the same year that Lanthimos released *Dogtooth*, he was part of a group of young directors who set up FOG—Filmmakers of Greece—to protest against the government's lack of support for Greek film culture. Later joined by over 250 film professionals, FOG challenged existing methods of funding for Greek film including the Greek State Film Awards, claiming that rigging and favoritism were rife, stifling the growth of new talent. Their protests were successful, and a new era was born in Greek cinema, one that looked outward to Europe (and the European art-cinema circuit) instead of prioritizing local return. This combination of a history of independence and then an influx of fresh support resulted in a creative boom for Greek film. However, many have challenged the idea that this new wave was particularly "weird," or indeed, a unified "wave." Lanthimos himself has rejected the idea of any cohesion among Greek directors arguing that "there's no movement, no common filmic language. Just different films here and there that are happening. And people are noticing them because of the country's exposure internationally."[6]

This variation in style and content across the films of these Greek directors could be why the wave's position in relation to European extremism is fluid and intermittent. Whereas a film such as *Miss Violence* (Alexandros Avranas, 2013), with its opening sequence of a young girl choosing to commit suicide on her eleventh birthday rather than enter into an incestuous relationship with her father, could easily be presented as an example of European extremism, a film such as *Attenberg* (Athina Rachel Tsangari, 2010) hovers just on the other side of the border in the domain of European art cinema. But, as with the so-called Greek Weird Wave, the categorization of European extremism is equally impossible to define. As Frey explains, it is difficult to demarcate the boundaries of extreme cinema as it crosses over into horror, pornography, exploitation, and art cinema. Frey proposes that instead of using an "in or out" definition, extremity should be considered as a spectrum: "Speaking roughly and simply, extreme cinema is an international production trend of graphically sexual or violent "quality" films that often stoke critical or popular controversy ... these productions depend on (offending) culturally inscribed boundaries between art and exploitation."[7] Furthermore, the extreme is first subjective and second a threshold. What is extreme for one person may be quite tame and acceptable for another. Therefore, it is a cultural and ideological question—a decision about what kinds of sex and violence are normative and/or part of mainstream cinema and what kinds are unacceptable or difficult. This threshold is constantly shifting according to political and other cultural factors, personal preferences, and changes in time and space.

Subsequently, rather than trying to define extremism in cinema using any form of specific generic classifications—or as Frey argues, an "in or out" system—what can be seen to link the films of Catherine Breillat, Gaspar Noé, Michael Haneke, and Lukas Moodysson to name but a few, is the manner in which these films utilize experimental formal styles to depict sex and violence in a way that directly—and therefore actively—engages the spectator. This engagement has been theorized in a number of different ways. For example, Horeck and Kendall define European extreme cinema as containing "graphic and confrontational images of sex and violence ... designed deliberately to shock or provoke the spectator" arguing that such works are not intended to wash over a passive spectator but seek to constantly jar and provoke the audience.[8] Martine Beugnet takes a more phenomenological approach, proposing that the transgressive nature of these films is found in the way that they encourage their audiences to experience a physical affect that is intense and at times overwhelming.[9] In contrast to Beugnet's sensorial audience response, Catherine Wheatley argues that the films of Haneke—one of the few other "extreme" directors more widely accepted by mainstream audiences—encourage an "ethical reflexivity," inciting the audience to distance themselves from the film and question what they are seeing on-screen and how it relates to them.[10] What is consistent across all these approaches is that it is this affective audience confrontation, and the potential for deeper—often philosophical—enquiry, that separates European extremism from other extreme cinemas, such as the more generic labeling of Asian extreme cinema, or the independent hardcore horror of the United States. Subsequently, European extremism is better treated as a style of filmmaking rather than a movement or genre. It embraces transgression in both form and content, with directors utilizing experimental and distinctive formal techniques to elicit active, and often embodied, responses in the spectator. As Tim Palmer writes, "[t]hese narratives of the flesh ... are rendered via a radical, innovative use of film style, an ingeniously crafted barrage of visual and aural techniques ... Besides the undeniably inflammatory subject area, it is this startlingly experimental stylistic treatment that makes these films so affecting in conception and execution."[11] Subsequently, European extremism is not just about the depiction of sex and violence—for these are abundant in the horror genre or pornography—but about the way that sex and violence are depicted and their "use" to create affect in the spectator, that demarcates this style of filmmaking.

There is a distinct lack of romance involved in the sex scenes of European extreme cinema. Rare is the depiction of loving sex between a couple. More common is sex between strangers, rape, or fleeting relationships focused on sexual pleasure and experimentation rather than human connection. For example, *Irréversible* (Gaspar Noé, 2002) does feature a loving relationship between Alex and Marcus, but the majority of the film is dominated by Marcus's quest for vengeance against Alex's rapist, and her rape is the film's most affecting moment, depicted in a nine-minute-long stationary single take. Likewise, in *Romance* (Catherine Breillat, 1999), Marie is in a sexless relationship with her self-absorbed boyfriend, causing her to seek sexual pleasure elsewhere. These include episodes of bondage with her employer and being willing to let a man perform cunnilingus on her, which then turns into a brutal rape. In the few films where sex is between adults in a relationship, things are often far from romantic. In *Twentynine Palms* (Bruno Dumont, 2003), David and Katia are in a relationship, but their sex is rough and needy, often following an argument. The film follows them as they drive through the American desert searching for a location for a magazine shoot. They argue and fuck from one location to the next until the film's final few minutes, where they are attacked by a group of men on the road and David is violently raped. Returning to their motel, David cuts off his hair and then stabs Katia to death. Such a brutal ending removes any sense of tenderness or intimacy between the couple from the viewer's mind. Another example of adults in a consenting relationship, but this time where the sex is more tender and about the other's pleasure as much as self-gratification, is *9 Songs* (Michael Winterbottom, 2004). Labeled the most sexually explicit mainstream British film ever, *9 Songs* follows the relationship of Matt and Lisa over the course of a year via nine concerts and features graphic and unsimulated sexual acts (including unsimulated penetration).[12] Here, the extreme nature of the sex act lies not in its brutality or questions of consent, but in its actual depiction as the actors perform real sex acts in front of the camera. However, as Asbjørn Grønstad argues, Winterbottom's "deadpan" formal style when filming these explicit scenes and his unwillingness to depict his characters in a range of sexual positions as is common in pornography reinforces on which side of the divide this film falls. Unlike a lot of pornographic material, *9 Songs* depicts real sex; not just unsimulated sex, but the sex that people actually have.[13]

I propose that this is the context where the films of Lanthimos most clearly align with European extremism. If, for the most part, the Greek Weird Wave could be called extreme adjacent—that is, operating alongside and occasionally overlapping with the extreme—with Lanthimos's films, it is in the depiction of sex and its use (in a narrative context or in creating affect in the spectator) where this overlapping most commonly occurs. As with European extremism, sex in Lanthimos's films is rarely about love or mutual pleasure. Instead, the director utilizes distinct formal and performative styles—combined with narrative events—to depict sex as having three specific outcomes: as a transaction, as a means for personal gain, or as a self-focused search for pleasure. By paying attention to the sexual exploits of his characters, it is possible to more fully explain why the director is often included within texts on European extremism; to go further than the previous brief references and passing comments or footnotes. Furthermore, Lanthimos's films provide an opportunity to see what happens when a director with a willingness to embrace extremity via the depiction of sex enters the mainstream.

Lanthimos's second feature-length film *Dogtooth* is the Greek film most referenced in relation to European extremism. Released in the same year as the Greek financial crisis (pushing the country—and to some extent the film—into the international spotlight), *Dogtooth* is the story of a dominating patriarch (Christos Stergioglou) and his wife (Michele Valley) who have kept their children locked away into adulthood. The parents keep their grown-up children inside the grounds of their house, pretending that the outside world is a dangerous land only traversable by car and inhabited by deadly felines. Throughout the film Lanthimos utilizes a distinctive formal style that would become a signature in his later work. He favors stationary cameras and long shots, creating a distancing affect in the audience by drawing attention to the construction of the image. Characters enter and depart the frame, negative space at times dominates the shot, and awkward arrangements of bodies and objects create blockages in the audience's line of sight. This awkwardness extends to the actors' performance styles. In an approach to acting that is now synonymous with the director, the cast performs its roles with an almost monotone expression, delivering lines in a stilted manner as though reading from a list, with little variation in their vocal tonality. This blank awkwardness is startlingly present in the film's sex scenes. In order to satisfy the libidinal urges of his son (Christos Passalis), the father organizes a woman named Christina (Anna Kalaitzidou) from his workplace to have sex with him in return for money. When the two first have sex, the entire scene is filmed using just two static camera positions: first a long shot that initially cuts the top off the actors' heads before centrally framing them as she masturbates him on the bed; and then a close-up that is positioned off to the side, taking in more of the blank wall than the couple's faces. Subsequently, Lanthimos's camera is as awkward as his actors' performance styles. Bodies are one moment center-screen, and in the next, completely obscured, facial expressions hard to read or blocked out entirely due to the framing or the position of objects in the room. The lighting is harsh, and the couple's behavior is devoid of affection and desire. Son seems to approach sex as another form of exercise, purely an addendum to the chest curls he is doing as Christina enters the room. Later in the film the woman attempts to get Son to perform oral sex on her, but he refuses and they have sex doggy style instead. Christina then goes and visits Elder Daughter (Angeliki Papoulia), offering to exchange a coveted headband in return for oral sex. Due to her closeted upbringing, Elder Daughter has no idea that licking Christina's genitals is a sexual act and is more than willing to carry it out as payment in the transaction. Christina is therefore taking advantage of her naïveté in order to gain sexual satisfaction, the mirroring of her own prostitution accentuated through the repetition of bodily posture as Elder Daughter is now the one on all fours performing cunnilingus.

Christina and Elder Daughter's exchanges continue during subsequent visits, before they are eventually caught out by the father. After beating and dismissing Christina, the parents decide to let Son choose which of his sisters he would like to have sex with. Selecting the elder, they have sex, again captured via a succession of static camera shots. As Son and Elder Daughter sit side by side on the bed, he instructs her how to make him erect with her hand before the camera cuts to a similar straight-on shot as before, initially cutting off the siblings' heads and framing only their torsos before they lie down center-screen. Lanthimos then cuts to another medium close-up, this time of Son's back with Elder Daughter's face hidden behind his body. The shot lasts for a drawn-out thirty-five seconds, with the lack of visual change drawing the viewer's attention to the sounds of the scene. Devoid of nondiegetic music, the soundtrack is filled with the creaks of the bed, Elder Daughter's small yelps of pain, and Son's sexual grunting. The use of diegetic sound enhances the realism of the scene, hammering home not only the corruption of this parentally arranged incest, but also the shock and pain that the sex act must be causing Elder Daughter. The camera cuts once more, this time to a shot of her head leant painfully over the bedframe, a grimace on her face as her brother's hand clasps around her breast (see Figure 15.1). His reflection is visible in a mirror behind them,

FIGURE 15.1 *Incestuous sex in* Dogtooth.

but this fades into the background as attention cannot be anywhere other than the expressions of pain on Elder Daughter's face. For a film that is at times incredibly funny—encouraging its audience to laugh at the lies of the parents and the behavior of their children—this scene is hauntingly cold.

Although the penetration in *Dogtooth* is simulated, the actors do engage in real acts of sexual foreplay as Elder Daughter masturbates her brother as Christina did. This inclusion of unsimulated sexual acts, along with an image from a pornographic movie that the parents watch together, suggests that *Dogtooth* is not only Lanthimos's most explicit film, but also explains why this film is often referenced in texts on European extremism. But this connection is down to more than just genitals onscreen. It is the way that the characters think about sex in combination with its detached and emotionless depiction by Lanthimos that renders this film so odd and unsettling for the audience, and therefore incites an "extreme" affect. Rather than be about love, emotional connection, or even just mutual pleasure, sex in *Dogtooth* is almost a mundane obligation. As Mark Fisher writes, there is a "dutifulness" about it, not only on behalf of Christina, who is being paid for the act, but also with the son and even the parents.[14] The audience does not see the parents educating Son about sex but it can be imagined that there has been little talk of emotional connection with one's partner (for there is no suggestion of leaving the house to find a wife or a husband). For Son, sex is purely for male libidinal release. Even when the parents are shown having sex there is very little romance involved. They watch hardcore pornography in a detached state or have foreplay-less missionary sex whilst listening to music played through headphones, transforming something that could be shared (music/sex) into something insular. It is this combination of graphic sex with a lack of emotion that makes such scenes so unnerving and difficult to watch, which subsequently creates an "extreme" affect.

But there is one other factor to take into consideration. As with many other examples of European extremism, the sex that is presented in *Dogtooth* is almost disturbingly realistic in its banality. By rejecting the overtly sensuous and romanticized sex of mainstream cinema that favors soft lighting and instant orgasms, and replacing it with awkward thrusting and perfunctory intercourse, Lanthimos presents sexual situations that are in a way more familiar, or real, than those of Hollywood. This is not arguing that sex in real life is boring, but rare is the person who lost their virginity in a manner that did not include some awkward fumbling, or the long-term loving couple who have not shared a quicky that felt more like a race to the finish line than a real emotional connection. The sex scenes in *Dogtooth* are too close for comfort, filmed using an aesthetic and sexual realism that snaps the audience out of their identification with the filmic image. They are at once familiar and shocking, relatable through their realism, and abhorrent in their context.

Subsequently, *Dogtooth* presents sex as distinct from emotional attachment and the exchanging of pleasure. Instead, sex in this world—and indeed across much of the director's work as a whole—has three main motivations: as something that is used as part of a transaction (Christina, the sisters trading licking for objects), for personal gain (the parents keeping the son under their control), or for self-focused pleasure (the son, and to some extent the parents). These sexual acts are presented in a manner that continues the director's wider project of distanciation, and indeed may even represent its peak. However, there is one exception to Lanthimos's portrayal of relationships as devoid of real care and devotion, and that is in *The Lobster*. In this strange tale of compulsory relationships, David (Colin Farrell) attends a hotel where single people have a limited amount of time to find a partner or they are turned into an animal of their choice. Relationships are based on small similar characteristics between partners, such as having a nice smile or susceptibility for nosebleeds. This necessity, combined with the need to save one's life by finding a mate, results in many of the relationships that come out of the arrangement feeling fake, and David himself enters into such a coupling with a particularly cruel woman (Angeliki Papoulia) by pretending to be as heartless as she is. He ends the relationship after she kills his brother—who is now a dog after having failed to find a mate at the hotel. Yet, David does find love. He leaves the hotel confines and joins the Loners, a group of escaped hotel occupants who live in the woods and are hunted by current guests to gain extra days to find a mate. The Loners have banned any form of relationship or romance, with both being punishable by mutilation. David falls in love with Short Sighted Woman (Rachel Weisz) and their relationship progresses in secret as the gang attempts to sabotage the work of the hotel. The leader of the Loners suspects the relationship between David and the woman and arranges for her to be blinded. At the end of the film the two lovers escape, and David prepares to blind himself so that they can be the same.

There is something wonderfully strange about the sexual contact displayed in the world of *The Lobster*. In the confines of the hotel, masturbation is banned, yet all guests are sexually stimulated by the maid to just before the point of orgasm as part of their mandatory routine. This stimulation is carried out in a rather odd way, with the maid rubbing her behind over David's crotch as though it were a medical procedure. Rather than being extreme in its emotional detachment, the scene is more amusing in its oddity. However, it is immediately followed by a shocking act of punishment as one of David's fellow guests has his hand publicly burned in a toaster during breakfast when the hotel manager accuses him of masturbating. This reprimand works to reinforce the unspoken rule that sexual release can only be granted to those who are part of a couple. During his time with the Loners, David and Short Sighted Woman go on trips into the city with the group's leader. In order to pass in this world of compulsory relationships they are instructed to behave as a couple, giving them the opportunity to openly express their desire for each other and have the physical contact that

FIGURE 15.2 *Genuine affection in* The Lobster.

is banned by the group. However, they get a little carried away with their performance, passionately kissing and groping each other when visiting the home of the leader's parents. In comparison to Lanthimos's other films, this is a rare moment of real passion and mutual care, yet it is rendered comical and absurd due to the inappropriateness of their embrace in front of the older couple (see Figure 15.2).

Despite this absurdity, there is also something quite normal about David and Short Sighted Woman's public display of affection. Their embrace is slightly awkward, their bodies turned in to one another as they sit side by side on a chair. Hands fumble about in laps, her hair is frizzy, his glasses steamed up. If one were to ignore the setting and the man sitting next to them, their affection would appear quite lifelike; a sexual realism that is neither pretty nor perfect, but natural. Therefore, this sequence provides an interesting contribution to the study of sexual behavior in Lanthimos's films as it is a rare example of a mutually enjoyable and loving embrace of equals, where no transaction is taking place and each participant responds to and gives the other pleasure. The additional element that distinguishes it from many of the director's other films is that both characters involved in the liaison are to a certain degree likable and "good." Although spectatorial identification may be a push too far due to Colin Farrell and Rachel Weisz's stilted performance style—this is a film by Lanthimos after all—at least here the audience have a couple whom they want to succeed in life and love.

This denial of audience identification with his characters is one of the constant traits of Lanthimos's corpus. The men and women who populate his narratives range from the pleasantly awkward to the outright corrupt, performed by actors in a manner that encourages distance through a stilted delivery of lines and jerky bodily movements. This awkwardness is taken to extremes during the director's depiction of sexual acts, which in line with European extremism are either formally jarring or feature a corruptive element. The latter is certainly true of the sex lives of married couple Steven (Colin Farrell) and Anna (Nicole Kidman) in *The Killing of a Sacred Deer*. Steven, a surgeon, has befriended teenager Martin (Barry Keoghan) and invites him home to meet his wife, Anna, who is also a doctor, and their two children, Kim and Bob (Raffey Cassidy and Sunny Suljic). It transpires that Martin's father was a patient of Steven's who died on the operating table. When Bob becomes mysteriously paralyzed, Martin issues the following ultimatum: the surgeon must kill a member of his own family in order to balance the books or, instead, they will all die from the mystery illness. Martin appears torn between wanting Steven as a father substitute and taking revenge on him for the death of his "real" dad. Yet this confusion can only be guessed at by the audience due to Keoghan's hauntingly emotionless performance. Mirroring the lack of narrative clarity (e.g., Martin's ability to induce and then relieve the illness goes unexplained), the characters too are often blank and emotionless. This heightens the force of emotional or violent outbursts when they do occur, such as when Steven kidnaps Martin and beats him as he is tied to a chair, or when the boy rips out a chunk of his own flesh as a "metaphorical" example of a death for a death.

As with *Dogtooth*, there is little mutual pleasure or love in the sexual acts depicted in *The Killing of a Sacred Deer*. Anna, in particular, is willing to use sex to get what she wants. In order to understand what happened with Martin's father's death, she provides sexual gratification to one of Steven's colleagues in exchange for information, jerking him off in his car. In a scene that recalls the "real" but shocking sex of siblings discussed above, Lanthimos's formal approach to capturing this event is jarring in its mundanity. Throughout the act the camera remains focused on Anna's face, drawing attention to her blank and business-like expression. The film's audience is denied any sign of emotion from Anna or nondiegetic music, making the sticky pumping sounds of her hand moving back and forth across the man's penis disturbingly and realistically pronounced; it is almost *too* intimate. Although this is a simulated sex act and no genitals are displayed, as with many examples of European extremism, it is the extent of the formal realism of its depiction that shocks the audience. However, when it comes to Anna and Steven's sex life, it is the nature of Steven's desire and Anna's complicity in it that is worryingly corrupt. Early in the film the couple are shown about to have sex. Anna lies spread out across the bed, pretending to be an anesthetized patient. Lanthimos does not seek to criticize individual sexual kinks, but rather he is using sex to fill in the gaps in character motivation that remain due to his particular approach to actor performance and lack of narrative expansion. The depiction of a doctor being turned on by imagining having sex with an unconscious patient is deeply disturbing and speaks to Steven's own feelings of almost God-like

FIGURE 15.3 *Marital sex in* The Killing of a Sacred Deer.

power, a delusion that is fully unleashed during the film's climax. But his penchant for anesthetized women also represents an emotional disconnect in his marital sex life. Anna seemingly remains motionless throughout, potentially gaining pleasure but in a completely passive manner, mirroring the emotional blankness that is seen when she exchanges sex for information (see Figure 15.3).

Speaking of the French films that initiated the trend to categorize European extremism as an amorphous whole, Palmer argues that such works are a *cinéma du corps*, a cinema of the body that seeks to provoke and discomfort its audiences. He proposes that this form of filmmaking features "dispassionate physical encounters involving filmed sex that is sometimes unsimulated; physical desire embodied by the performances of actors or non-professionals as harshly insular; intimacy itself is depicted as fundamentally aggressive, devoid of romance, lacking a nurturing instinct or empathy of any kind; and social relationships that disintegrate in the face of such violent compulsions."[15] Such a description could easily be applied to *The Killing of a Sacred Deer*, and indeed many of Lanthimos's films. Not only is Steven and Anna's relationship profoundly insular, but their relationship and their relationships with their children crumble instantly at the hands of Martin. It is clear early on in the film that each parent openly favors the child of their opposite sex, with both Martin and Anna being physically rough with or assaulting Bob and Kim, respectively. Yet even more shocking is how neither parent offers their own life up to save their child, and Anna even coldly states that "logically" Steven should kill one of the children as they can always have another. As partners and as parents, Steven and Anna are devoid of sentimentality and love, with the only emotion clearly displayed being anger. Beyond the reference to unsimulated sex, Palmer could otherwise be writing specifically about Lanthimos's film. In the face of death, the characters all think of themselves first and foremost, and even Kim's willingness to be sacrificed feels like a performance put on to come across as the devoted "good" child and to play up to Steven's illusions of being the all-powerful Father. Furthermore, not only is the sex in the film devoid of romance, but there is also something "fundamentally aggressive" about Steven's fantasy of having sex with someone who is unconscious, due to the lack of consent. He is effectively fantasizing about raping his patients via his consenting sex life with his wife, implicating her in his guilt through her willingness to take part.

The Killing of a Sacred Deer is therefore a film that could easily be labeled as an example of European extremism. It features sexual acts that either have shocking undercurrents or are jarringly mundane in both procedure and presentation. Such acts are carried out by emotionless people with a susceptibility for violence. As with *Dogtooth* and *The Lobster*, the film did well on the art festival circuit (which as Frey argues is the prime exhibition ground for European extremism), nominated for the *Palme d'Or* at Cannes and winning the award for Best Screenplay.[16] However, it was with his next film that Lanthimos was able to make the move into the mainstream. *The Favourite* won the Grand Jury prize at Venice Film Festival, signaling its "art cinema" credentials, but it also went on to receive nine Academy Award nominations, including Best Picture and Best Director, and won in the category of Best Actress for Olivia Colman's performance. Lanthimos was suddenly a household name. But to be mainstream problematizes his status as a director of extreme films; one cannot be simultaneously in the center (mainstream) and on the periphery (extreme). Directors such as Haneke and Lars von Trier have had their films exhibited in large cinema chains but while remaining entrenched in the stylistic and narrative confines of art cinema and therefore never quite possessing the widespread mass appeal that is enjoyed by *The Favourite*. *The Favourite*, on the other hand, attracted audiences from across the board, and made $95.9 million at the global box office (compared to *Amour*'s [Michael Haneke, 2012] $29.9 million and *Nymphomaniac*'s [Lars von Trier, 2013] $18.5 million). The film therefore presents an interesting case study to see if and how this move to the mainstream impacted the content of Lanthimos's work and his formal style. When it comes to his approach to sex, it appears that it did result in small changes. In *The Favourite* there are no visible genitals, although at one point we do see the bottom of a middle-aged male thrusting away whilst having sex with a prostitute. Most sexual acts that occur are off-screen, removed from view by careful framing and attention to the actors' faces. Also, in contrast to Anna's hand job in the car, Lanthimos moves away from the sticky aural reality of that scene to instead focus more on the intentions and preoccupations of the servicing party. For in this film sex equals power.

Lanthimos opens *The Favourite* with a scene that straightaway removes any sense of romance or tenderness from sexual desire. A young woman called Abigail (Emma Stone) travels to visit her cousin Sarah Churchill, the Duchess of Marlborough (Rachel Weisz). As she rides along in a packed carriage, a solider openly masturbates in front of her, before pinching her behind as she makes her exit, causing her to fall face-first into the mud. An instant statement that this is no prim and proper period drama, Lanthimos presents us with a situation where consensual and nonconsensual public sexual acts are considered normal—everyone else in the carriage ignores the man's furious pumping—yet at the same time there is a connection established between sex and filth, with Abigail falling into the stinking mud, which a maid later informs her probably contains human excrement. As the film continues, Lanthimos presents sex as having two clear goals: as a means of personal satisfaction (but not necessarily the satisfaction of one's partner) or for personal gain whether as part of a transaction or a manipulation. For example, Abigail's wedding night is far from one of marital bliss. She frets openly about the whereabouts of Sarah, whom she has just poisoned, and only joins her husband in the marital bed when he complains angrily that he is "as hard as a rock." As Abigail instructs her spouse to lie still, the film cuts to a close-up of her deep in thought as she reaches behind herself and starts to jerk him off. Her face is stern with worry over what Sarah might do in retribution and her body posture is awkward and uncomfortable, sitting upright and apart from her husband and rejecting his attempts to make further contact. There is a complete detachment between the sexual act she is carrying out and the thoughts that preoccupy her. The hand job she is giving to her husband is just that, a job that must be done to placate him so that she can get on with more pressing concerns. Their relationship is, after all, purely a means for her to protect herself, and therefore sex between them is a necessary task to complete as part of the transaction: his pleasure for her security. Lanthimos's combination of a close-up of Abigail's preoccupied expression with careful staging that positions her groaning husband out of focus in the background, formally cements the disconnection between sex and romance (see Figure 15.4).

Joanna Di Mattia argues that *The Favourite* is about power and its acquisition through sex, predominantly with Queen Anne (Olivia Colman), but also with the various men who exist in the background. Di Mattia writes: "Both Sarah and Abigail play games with each other, with Anne and with the men around them—not for fun, but because surviving as a woman in eighteenth-century England demands it."[17] As such, Di Mattia locates the body as a source of power in the film, in particular in Anne's overweight and (sadly) barren form. Those who can give sexual gratification to Anne receive access to her power, money, and the safety she can provide, so therefore again any sexual relationship with her is devoid of mutual satisfaction and instead replaced with an undercurrent of the companion's

FIGURE 15.4 *Abigail's wedding night in* The Favourite.

own personal gain. Although Sarah appears to have fond feelings for her "friend" the monarch, she is still willing to manipulate Anne by using sex to get what she wants, casting a shadow of doubt over the sincerity of their relationship. Furthermore, if sex is about power in the film, then it is also crucially depicted as an activity not belonging to more traditional cultural accompaniments to sex, such as romance and family. Although Sarah and Abigail are both married, their partners are pushed to the background, and historical accuracy is completely snubbed as Anne's husband—Prince George of Denmark—does not feature at all beyond a phantom presence suggested by the seventeen rabbits she keeps as reminders of her dead children. By removing the husbands, and indeed the children, from the lives of Anne and Sarah, sex becomes only about the pleasure and power achieved in its exchange, rather than any traditional ideas or ideals relating to love and familial relationships.

It would be quite difficult, indeed problematic, to classify *The Favourite* as part of European extremism. The basic narrative arc—two women manipulating a third with sex to gain power—does open itself up to extremity with its focus on sex outside of the bounds of equal loving relationships, but it is not hugely challenging. And the images of sexual acts are neither particularly graphic, nor unsimulated. However, if extremity is defined as a style that creates degrees of affect in the audience, encouraging a distanced and active spectatorship, Lanthimos certainly continues this approach. It could be proposed that across his corpus that this, Lanthimos's most mainstream and arguably unweird film, contains his most provocative formal style. *The Favourite*'s continual use of wide and fish-eye lenses, camera pivots, and low-level framing results in an uncanny affect that both pulls the viewer sensorially close to the world of the film (and the film as a medium) and pushes us away again. This push–pull spectatorial phenomenon is one often found within many films that are classified as European extremism, films that invite a sensorial and embodied reception, yet also ethically and intellectually push the audience away with their brutal imagery and provocative narratives. The use of a fish-eye lens in particular in *The Favourite* draws the viewer into the chaos of its diegetic world, and indeed its absurdity, enhancing the feeling of enclosure and isolation as the characters traipse from one area of the palace to another, trapped as though in a fishbowl. The curved interiors conveyed by the fish-eye lens come to embody the circularity of the events that unfold within the palace: the rotation of power back and forth between Sarah and Abigail, the Tories and the Whigs, and the decision whether to end the war or let it continue on its bloody course indefinitely. At the same time, the distortion of the image and the slight queasiness it creates in the viewer, combined with the raw and dirty representation of eighteenth-century life above and below stairs, creates a disconcerting and difficult spectatorial experience. Rather than be swept into a solid identification with the characters and a fantasy of period charm, the viewer is sensorially assaulted by the chaos, noise, and grime that lurks behind the pristine dresses and polished floors.

In her influential book *Cinema and Sensation: French Film and the Art of Transgression*, Beugnet explores the reemergence of a focus on the sensorial that occurred in French filmmaking at the turn of the century. In a work that is often cited in relation to European extremism—as the New French Extremity can be considered its founding body of work—Beugnet argues that a number of French films of this period present a direct call to be experienced by *all* the senses, "stressing, in particular, cinema's tactile quality."[18] Discussing films commonly listed as examples of European extremism such as *Sombre* (Philippe Grandrieux, 1999), *Twentynine Palms* (Bruno Dumont, 2003), *Dans ma peau* (Marina de Van, 2002), and *Romance* (Catherine Breillat, 1999), Beugnet writes that "[t]here is an inherently transgressive element to this kind of filmmaking ... to open oneself to sensory awareness and let oneself be physically affected by an artwork or a spectacle is to relinquish the will to gain full mastery over it, choosing intensity and chaos over rational detachment."[19] Beugnet argues that in the conventional relationship between the observer and the observed there is a detachment between the two: the observer stands apart from what they observe. Yet with the French cinema that she studies, and arguably in European extremism more generally, this gap is closed, and "the effect of looking and listening takes on a mimetic quality indicative of an involvement with the object of the gaze that preempts or supersedes this state of detached self-awareness."[20] This is not the suture of continuity editing, but a more embodied and emotional connection between viewer and film. I propose that although *The Favourite* does not directly call to the senses in the same manner as Beugnet's corpus, Lanthimos utilizes the film's cinematography to play with its audience, resulting in the aforementioned push–pull connection between emotional (and identificatory) absorption and dazed detachment. As such, the chaos of the eighteenth-century court is replicated in the spectatorial experience; we are spun, coerced, and constrained just like those within the walls of the palace. Returning to the scene of Abigail's wedding night it is possible to see such a formal manipulation of the audience. Devoid of any of the normal editing choices associated with sex such as identificatory shot-reverse shot patterns, close-ups of skin-on-skin contact, or even a focus on the sex act itself, the scene starts with an exchange between Abigail and her husband, each shot individually and positioned in the center of the screen, enhancing the sense of disconnection between them. As he demands that she join him in the marital bed the camera breaks the 180° line and pans round as Abigail crosses from one side of the room to the other. Due to the wide angle of the lens, it is as though the whole room is pivoting around the camera, an effect that Lanthimos developed when shooting *The Killing of a Sacred Deer*. The effect is jarring and inelegant, much like their impending sexual encounter, drawing attention to the camera itself whilst simultaneously translating the sexual awkwardness and mundanity into an aesthetic style that eschews romance and the delicate gesture. In the next shot, the camera slowly zooms in toward Abigail's face as she frets about Sarah's intentions, inviting the audience to focus not on her action but her interiority. The sex act that she is engaged in is little more than necessary labor to maintain her position, so unemotional on her part that it is almost comical. It remains firmly off-screen, with his pleasure ignored and obfuscated by the film's central point of focus.

Consequently, the formal manner through which Lanthimos depicts sexual encounters in *The Favourite* can be seen as a continuation of his approach to the subject in earlier works such as *Dogtooth*. Sex in the director's films remains a point of rupture in audience identification, through a combination of a formal style and character motivation that subverts the norms of cinematic sexual depiction. Although this later work does not feature "extreme" imagery such as the on-screen genitals and sexual acts that preceded it, or even the lifelike soundtrack of a film such as *The Killing of a Sacred Deer*, it still uses sex to play with audience's expectations and present a degree of sexual realism. Indeed, the use of sex in this way floods out across the narrative of *The Favourite*; it is all about sex beyond the confines of love and mutual pleasure. The same is true with the perfunctory sexual interactions of *Dogtooth*, the compulsory relationships of *The Lobster*, and the god-like fantasies of Steven in *The Killing of a Sacred Deer*. If there is one constant across the many worlds created by Lanthimos it is that sex equals power.

In conclusion, the sex scenes in Lanthimos's films are pivotal when analyzing his distinct approach to filmmaking. This should be of no surprise for he is a director known for the awkwardness of his characters; sexual acts naturally provide prime opportunities for clumsy and impersonal movements, personalities jarringly devoid of expression, and relationships that subvert traditional romantic—or even social—expectations. Viewing Lanthimos's work through the prism of extremity offers a productive approach for understanding such sexual encounters and how they can be seen as representative of his wider project, and indeed, his appeal. Lanthimos's sex scenes perfectly represent how the director's films result in a push–pull spectatorial experience; one that draws the audience in through a formal experimentation that adds an affectual layer to narrative events, but simultaneously pushes them back again with awkward performance styles, the breaking of expectations, and visual weirdness. Therefore, although Lanthimos has arguably entered the mainstream, he has managed to do so in a way that formally still keeps one foot in the extreme. Or rather, he continues to straddle multiple forms at once: ordinary and weird, acceptable and extreme, mainstream and art cinema.

Notes

1. James Quandt, "Flesh and Blood: Sex and Violence in Recent French Cinema," *Artforum International*, 42, no. 6 (2004): 126–32.
2. Tanya Horeck and Tina Kendall, eds., *The New Extremism in Cinema: From France to Europe* (Edinburgh: Edinburgh University Press, 2011).
3. Nickolaj Lübecker, *The Feel-Bad Film* (Edinburgh: Edinburgh University Press, 2015); Mattias Frey, *Extreme Cinema: The Transgressive Rhetoric of Today's Art Film Culture* (London: Rutgers University Press, 2016), 157.
4. Maria Chalkou, "A New Cinema of 'Emancipation': Tendencies of Independence in Greek Cinema of the 2000s," *Interactions: Studies in Communication and Culture*, 3, no. 2 (2012): 243–61; Lydia Papadimitriou, "Locating Contemporary Greek Film Cultures: Past, Present, Future and the Crisis," *FilmIcon: Journal of Greek Film Studies*, 2 (2014): 1–19.
5. Eleni Varmazi, "The Weirdness of Contemporary Greek Cinema," *Film International*, 17, no. 1 (2019): 42–43.
6. Joshua Chaplinsky, "Yorgos Lanthimos Is Not the Leader of the Greek New Wave: An Interview with the Director of *Alps* and *Dogtooth*," *Screen Anarchy*, July 2012, available at https://screenanarchy.com/2012/07/yorgos-lanthimos-is-not-a-prude-an-interview-with-the-director-of-alps-and-dogtooth.html.
7. Frey, *Extreme Cinema*, 7.
8. Horeck and Kendall, *The New Extremism*, 1.

9 Martine Beugnet, *Cinema and Sensation: French Film and the Art of Transgression* (Edinburgh: Edinburgh University Press, 2007), 3.
10 Catherine Wheatley, *Michael Haneke's Cinema: The Ethic of the Image* (Oxford: Berghahn Books, 2009).
11 Tim Palmer, *Brutal Intimacy* (Middleton, CT: Wesleyan University Press, 2011), 59.
12 Andrew Anthony, "Caught in the Act," *The Guardian*, Feb 2005, available at https://www.theguardian.com/film/2005/feb/20/features.magazine.
13 Asbjørn Grønstad, *Screening the Unwatchable: Spaces of Negation in Post-Millennial Art Cinema* (Houndmills, Basingstoke: Palgrave Macmillan, 2012), 68.
14 Mark Fisher, "*Dogtooth*: The Family Syndrome," *Film Quarterly*, 64, no. 4 (2011): 22–27, at p. 22.
15 Palmer, *Brutal Intimacy*, 57–58.
16 Frey, *Extreme Cinema*, 46–68.
17 Joanna di Mattia, "Bedroom Games: Sex and Power in *The Favourite*," *Screen Education*, 95 (2019): 8–15, at p. 10.
18 Beugnet, *Cinema and Sensation*, 2.
19 Ibid., 5. Crucially Beugnet goes at length to distance her corpus from the categorization "extreme" as she finds it too limiting and prioritizes sensationalism over sensation.
20 Ibid., 5.

16

The Queer Posthumanism of *The Lobster*

Marios Psaras

> [T]he as yet unnamable which is proclaiming itself and which can do so, as is necessary whenever a birth is in the offing, only under the species of the non-species, in the formless, mute, infant and terrifying form of monstrosity.[1]
>
> JACQUES DERRIDA

Yorgos Lanthimos's *The Lobster* opens with an extended shot of a woman driving her car down a country road amidst torrential rain. Finally she pulls over and exits the car, walking toward a pair of unsuspecting horses, before unexpectedly pulling out a pistol and shooting one of them three times. Shot entirely from inside the car, the windshield wipers intermittently clear the obscuring rain for the viewer, framing and reframing the human and the animal/nonhuman onscreen, and which signals the beginning of a story that focuses on the space between species and the stories and discourses that have historically occupied that space. All the while, the animal's blood spills onto the wet ground.

Drawing on a range of cinematic traditions, Lanthimos's first English-language feature invites discussions as old as our species and ever topical, as the current period of racist panic, xenophobia, exclusion, seclusion, self-isolation, and insularity, amidst a turbulent global, post-pandemic, sociopolitical climate, explicates. "The only way to reach the human may be to overreach it, to exceed the boundaries that fundamentally delimit and define the human," argues Diana Fuss.[2] In this chapter, I discuss the way Lanthimos's film departs from both historical and contemporary representations of the posthuman, constructing a queer posthumanist film form, through which he explores precisely such boundaries, ultimately exercising a caustic critique of the heteropatriarchal premises of humanism.

The film's premise is simple: in a highly regulated societal setting, those who end up single are expelled to a hotel where they are given forty-five days to find their perfect match, or else they will be converted into an animal of their choice. The narrative follows David's (Colin Farrell) stay at the hotel and his subsequent escape to the woods, where he joins the Loners and falls in love with Short Sighted Woman (Rachel Weisz), with whom he decides to escape to the city to live as a couple. The story is narrated by Short Sighted Woman, but her narration, which appears in infrequent voiceover, is less a revelation of narratively significant information and more a comic commentary on the action taking place.

At first glance, *The Lobster* might give the impression of a love story, a fairy tale featuring A-list Hollywood stars, albeit a weird one. There is nothing sentimental, metaphorical, or dreamy in the deadpan dystopian universe that Lanthimos creates; the narrative meanderings rather spiral out of control to invent new generic possibilities beyond realism, defying—as one would expect from the *enfant terrible* of contemporary Greek cinema—verisimilitude and engendering affective responses that oscillate between the weird, almost indulgent, feeling of the uncanny and the terror that underpins the film's overarching existential premise. For *The Lobster* is essentially a dark and deeply weird love story; one that, I argue, reconfigures both "love" and "story" through the distorting lens of a queer critique of the humanist foundations of the biopolitical and its representational means. It is, as such, a posthumanist study of the body: an aesthetic enquiry into the discursive, epistemological, if not ontological, histories of the human body with its volatile temporalities placed under the spotlight. It is a film that is, ultimately, meant to remind us of precariousness and vulnerability as our primary existential condition and interdependence as our primary ethical concern.

Posthumanism, for Francesca Ferrando, responds to an "urgency for the integral redefinition of the notion of the human following the onto-epistemological as well as scientific and bio-technological developments of the twentieth and twenty-first centuries."[3] According to Andy Miah, "*technological change* has become a core component of contemporary imaginations about posthumanity"; however, the posthuman project is more generally concerned with such concepts as "becoming, alterity, transgression of boundaries and the position of humanity."[4] In this way, though the term appears prominently in debates about the ethical ramifications of biotechnology and medical enhancements, its analytical power extends to broader—and, for the purposes of this chapter, more useful—philosophical preoccupations that take to task the massive project of the critique of humanism, its history, ethics, and politics.

Differentially allocated to categories of (human) bodies across time and space, the "human" is broadly acknowledged as the subject of the Enlightenment and of traditional liberal humanism. As Tony Davies explains, this "human" is understood as "always singular, always in the present ... [it] inhabits not a time or a place but a condition, timeless and unlocalized."[5] In this chapter, I draw specifically on the kind of critical posthumanism that aims at deconstructing the universal, liberal humanist subject, rejecting Enlightenment's universal claims and exposing its processes of mutation, variation, and becoming. Most significantly, I find particularly useful critical works that investigate the representational history of the categories of the human and the nonhuman, while attempting to (re-)establish or (re-)conceptualize them.

Popular culture offers an abundance of posthuman representations, dating back to ancient art and literature. Perhaps one of the most popular tropes to appear in historical posthuman representation is the posthuman hybrid. Hybridity is conceptualized in the form of a cross or crossing between human and animal and is ubiquitous in both verbal and literary traditions linked with mythology and religious narratives. Anthropomorphism is also predominant in such representations, as is the representation of the hybrid beast as violent and threatening to human survival. Hybridity, anthropomorphism, and crossing infuse not only the ancient Greek canon (mythology, Greek drama, literature) but also the Christian parables and folk songs of the Byzantine and medieval periods.

Myra Seaman observes that representations of human-animal hybridity in the Middle Ages have religious origins, rooted in the medieval conception of the relationship between human beings and the divine, which dictated that whatever physical boundaries may be crossed in these stories, the constancy of an "essential human nature," centered on reason and courtesy, remained.[6] After all, as she notes, "hybridity is essential to Christ's participation in the human," though no hierarchy within Christ's hybrid identity was ever accepted by the Church; instead, Christ was constructed as a single, unified, humano-divine being, which valorized "individual embodied identity," and was indispensable for "bodily resurrection."[7]

Such a consideration of the integrity of the individual self in relation to a particular body is challenged by contemporary popular culture's fascination with the posthuman, which foregrounds processes of mind-uploading, body-hopping, genetic manipulation, reproductive technologies, virtual reality, medical enhancement, eugenics, and more. In such representations, which speak directly to the project of transhumanism,[8] the body is presented as limiting and constraining individual freedom, while human consciousness— its ethical superiority and vitality for the preservation of the anthropocene— remains the centrifugal force of all narratives.[9] As Seaman observes, such a "physical counterpart (and successor) to the universal human ... reveals certain cultural anxieties about embodiment—perhaps most especially when that embodiment is rejected or overcome in the attempt to release a supposedly 'pure' cognition."[10] Nevertheless, "altering the body through mechanical and biomedical improvements necessarily challenges our sense of identity, 'integrally bound' as it is to 'physicality' ... As expectations of body change, expectations of selfhood change as well," she warns.[11]

Unlike the above technoscientific fantasies, which have often offered imaginative versions of the apocalyptic posthuman (including the likes of *The Terminator* [James Cameron, 1984] and *RoboCop* [Paul Verhoeven, 1987]), Seaman identifies a particular strand of contemporary posthuman representations that rather favor a

> hybrid posthuman who retains a very familiar "natural self" and is an extension of rather than "successor" to the human being ... The resilient characteristic affiliated by these texts with the human—typically presented in terms of "human nature"—is not the quality most esteemed by liberal humanism or the scientific posthuman, the "universal instrument" of Cartesian reason; rather, it is an embodied affectivity [that makes them still] vulnerable to manipulation, suffering, and possible extinction [while allowing] them to overcome those who threaten to extinguish and replace the human.[12]

Narratives such as *Dark City* (Alex Proyas, 1998), the 2000s reboot of the TV series *Battlestar Galactica* (2004–2009) and *Never Let Me Go* (Mark Romanek, 2010) expose "techno-science's insufficient ability to *feel*" and reveal a psychological disposition in human nature, which, though it makes people vulnerable, nonetheless adds value in their lives; this disposition is something opaque, uncanny, that "cannot be seen as a moving part, nor mechanized."[13] Featuring vulnerable characters who make irrational yet principled choices, based on their own moral judgments, such narratives reject science's certainty of its own objectivity and reason, used invariably to justify all kinds of atrocities, rather retaining "a nostalgia for the weaknesses that result from particular *embodied* affectivities."[14]

Arguably, *The Lobster* investigates the liminal space between the human and the nonhuman without offering alternative or inventive depictions of the human or the posthuman, but it does so by attacking the very discursive means—linguistic, social, representational—of producing these categories, as well as the norms, styles, and language that accompanies them. In this, it follows N. Katherine Hayle's seminal proposal that the posthuman "does not really mean the end of humanity. It signals instead the end of a certain conception of the human, a conception that may have applied, at best, to that fraction of humanity who had the wealth, power, and leisure to conceptualize themselves as autonomous beings exercising their will through individual agency and choice."[15]

Indeed, Lanthimos's "sci-fi" scenario does not seek to unveil a hidden affective or mental interiority (or superiority, for that matter) that defines humanness, nor does it corroborate a departure from the human body to release pure cognition. It instead, dramatizes a perseverance to protect and secure the integrity of the human body as a definitive vessel of the self, both viewed as indispensable qualities for humanness in its dystopian universe. But a socially based humanness, the film reminds us, prescribes that the embodied self is aligned with the particular ideological framework of a given social structure, one that is clearly defined in gendered and sexual terms. The human body in Lanthimos is, thus, fully present and center-stage with a focus on the way it aligns with or deviates from the imagined universe's social norms. The film brims with instances of aligned or deviant embodiment, respectively affixing to or opposing the set ideology, producing and reproducing the threshold between the human and the animal, or better yet the human and the nonhuman.

Life at the hotel includes participation in a series of performative tasks and presentations, through which the guests are made to appreciate the value of the couple form. In one scene, two waiters and a maid reenact instances from everyday life, which juxtapose the difficulties of life as a single with the perks of being in a couple: a single 70-year-old man suddenly chokes to death at dinner, and a single young woman is presented as prey to violence and rape. Conversely, when the two are escorted, the risks are eliminated. Short and sketch-like, the performances stand out for their exaggerated yet deadpan corporeality: the old man's mechanical choking and the younger bodies' robotic movements in the rape reenactment verge on the grotesque, overriding the horrific connotations of rape and death behind the travesty of an autocratic social structure.

A characteristic element of Lanthimos's cinema, grotesque performativity also imbues the daily tasks that the guests themselves are asked to perform. Attending glamorous dance balls appears to be such a daily routine, as an indispensable avenue through which the singles get to meet their potential perfect match. Astonishingly, perfect matching in *The Lobster*'s universe is translated into the sharing of the same "defining characteristic," which is also highlighted as corporeal: a limp, a lisp, short-sightedness, heartlessness. All dressed the same—men in black suits and women in floral cocktail dresses—the guests seem to eagerly attend the balls, presenting themselves to the secluded microcosm of the hotel and their future suitors where they dance to the accompaniment of the hotel manager and her partner's singing. If successful, new couples are awarded a double bedroom and two weeks on a yacht, and are absurdly assigned a child if there appears to be trouble in paradise. In a self-reflexive nod to cinematic illusionism, at the end of one such ball scene, loud horns suddenly sound and the curtains open wide, flooding the ballroom with daylight while the guests start running in panic to change quickly for the hunting task that follows.

Hunting in *The Lobster*'s universe is specifically targeted at the Loners. The Loners are the singles who have escaped the hotel to the nearby woods, where an alternative—yet equally regulated—social structure exists, which opposes the couple form and, generally, prohibits any form of erotic attachment and sexual contact. *The Lobster*'s "hunting games" are first introduced in a striking scene of abounding authorial presence, as Lanthimos's filmic brushstrokes resemble a Van Gogh painting. Wearing raincoats and carrying tranquilizer guns, the hunters jump off the vans and run into the woods in search of Loners. Played in extreme slow motion and over the eerie accompaniment of a Greek song (*"Apo Mesa Pethamenos,"* which translates to "Dead Inside"), the hunting scene becomes a study in morbid caricature. As they jump or climb over bushes, fallen tree trunks, and branches, shooting, punching, and pulling the Loners' unconscious bodies, the hunters' movements and face gestures are accentuated, distorted, and ridiculed; the content falls flat due to the absurdly extreme stylization of the form and the characters' violent acts are annulled of narrative significance and ethical controversy.

The question of ethics is, clearly, very much embedded in posthumanist discourse; however, what is more exciting when it comes to film is not so much the different approaches to the posthuman condition proposed at the level of content, but the ethical premise—or promise—suggested at the level of form. In an effort to shed light on this ethical dimension and reveal how Lanthimos's film operates on a radically different level from previous posthuman narratives, I would like to consider the ethical repercussions of Gilles Deleuze's famous distinction between the movement-image and the time-image, as outlined in *Cinema 2: The Time-Image*.[16] According to Deleuze, traditional narration is understood as always referring to a *system of judgment*. As Deleuze claims, classical narrative cinema insists on "organic" narration, which claims to be true by preserving "the legal connections in space and the chronological relations in time,"[17] thus offering an indirect representation of time, as a consequence of action, dependent on movement, and inferred from space.[18] Drawing on Deleuze, Janet Harbord argues that normative cinema's spatiotemporal structure "implicitly stages a higher moral authority, a transcendental legislation" with "the revelatory acts of narrative, bent on exposing error and reasserting a moral order."[19] This "notion of a greater or absolute truth," nonetheless, collapses in postwar cinema and cinema cultures at the margins, which privilege repetition or the accumulation of acts with "no 'greater' meaning," without performing "a revelation or exposure of 'truth' that suggests an appeal to justice."[20] It is interesting how techno-transhuman fantasies speak directly to the first category with their appeal to the reestablishment of unambiguous moral orders (think, for example, of *The Terminator* or *RoboCop*), while the hybrid posthuman narratives, identified by Seaman, offer more complicated spatiotemporal structures with denouements that oscillate between the hopeful and the dystopian, thus blurring the notion of a greater truth or meaning and bringing them closer to the signifying operations of the postwar time images.

True to form, Lanthimos creates an (un-)ethical universe distinct from both of the above categories: a universe that refuses to signify, with ambivalence and indeterminacy infusing not only the film's ending but also its entire construction of time and space, thus being consistent with his earlier Greek-language films that helped initiate the so-called Greek Weird Wave. As I argue elsewhere, the films that form this particular strand of contemporary independent Greek cinema offer neither a reestablishment of a moral order nor a definite resolution, their denouements rather encompassing a relentless negation of meaningful closure and, at the same time, an ethically laden opening of meaning to the indefinite and the irreducible.[21] Calling for a metonymic move from the weird to the queer in my understanding of these films' narrative operations, I draw on Lee Edelman's radical queer "refusal of meaning,"[22] and Teresa de Lauretis's delineation of queer textuality as one that disrupts referentiality and works against narrativity, understood here as the generic pressure of all narrative toward closure and the fulfilment of meaning.[23]

Interestingly, *The Lobster* can be read as a queer text not only at the level of form, as a film that undermines verisimilitude and canonical representation's meaning-making practices, but also on the basis of its subversive thematics. De Lauretis adds another "not sufficient but necessary specification" for queer textuality, which is that of carrying the inscription of sexuality as something more than sex, "an unmanageable excess of affect ... an undomesticated, unsymbolizable force, not bound to objects and beyond the purview of the ego, a figure of sexuality as, precisely, drive."[24] *The Lobster* takes such a consideration of sexuality as its point of departure, as the—otherwise different—ethical structures that govern the hotel and the woods both aim at precisely containing, controlling, and regulating sexual relations, each in their own ways. And, despite there being little if any sex shown on screen, sex looms everywhere as the structurally absent image that navigates not only the film's narrative, but also its polemic queer posthumanist rhetoric, through alienating and deconstructing devices that expose its historical links to violence, abuse, and, yes, power.

Indeed, the only sex scene in the film, between David and the Heartless Woman (Angeliki Papoulia), is utterly deglamorized and uncomfortable both stylistically, by a complete absence of romantic lighting, set, and soundtrack, and narratively, as David holds tightly any form of feelings to prove he is equally heartless and, thus, a perfect match for her. Lying on her back completely inexpressive and dispassionate, while David is penetrating her, the Heartless Woman uses sex not for pleasure but to confirm his lack of emotions. Desire is, literally, out of the window, rather hiding in the woods, where sex and affection are, nonetheless, absolutely forbidden, persecuted, and punished by means of extreme corporeal violence, including mutilation (the "red kiss" and "red intercourse"). However, this does not stop David from falling in love with Short Sighted Woman, pursuing affection whenever they are given the opportunity. In a hilarious scene taking place in the city during a visit to the Loner Leader's (Léa Seydoux) parents, David and Short Sighted Woman release their mutual attraction by passionately making out on the sofa in front of everyone, while the parents play the theme tune of *Forbidden Games* (René Clément, 1952) on the guitar. As their passion escalates, an annoyed Loner Leader stands up and separates them, reprimanding them for their misbehavior. In the scene's final shot, David and Short Sighted Woman sit on the sofa embarrassed, casting guilty glances off-screen and tapping their legs to the beat of the music.

The absurdity of the above scenes produces the kind of comedy that results from surreal excess as an relentless satire designed to confound the discursive (realist, white, heterosexist) premises of humanist knowledge. Humanism's pervasive and repressive moralization of sex and sexuality, which invariably seeks authority in "nature," is unveiled as nothing but a pure social construct. Much as it happens in Lanthimos's previous films, sex is deployed as a mechanism for the production and reproduction of highly regimented social structures and associated power relations. Though here, as some of the scenes above testify, sex is also emphasized as uncontainable excess, which risks the structure's implosion and which those in power acknowledge and strive to anticipate and contain. In this way, the film offers a "radical critique of the religious and social conventions that [have] ideologically constrained, systematically essentialized, and ultimately threatened to de-sensualize the erotic practices of" humans, but also a reconsideration of human sexuality as "neither purely 'animalistic' nor fully 'human.' "[25] Sexuality rather assumes a taxonomic and existential function, producing human nature or naturalizing the "human" construct, allocating precarious bodies the status and privileges of a specific(ally) sexualized humanness. And, as such, it ultimately occupies that perpetually negotiated and liminal space between animal and the human, as do language, reason, and affect.[26]

The power of *The Lobster*'s posthumanist discourse is precisely located in the film's thematic and formal dramatization of humanism's perpetual deferral of this liminal space, which constitutes the boundary between the human and the animal. At the level of its thematic preoccupations and narrative construction, the audience witnesses the characters' absurd meandering across spaces of varied levels of (human) access, privilege, and benefits, all equally highly regulated, surveilled, and haunting. Where the city appears as the locus of human residence and activity, the woods as the animals' or nonhumans' natural habitat, and the hotel as the threshold between human "rehabilitation" and animal crossing, the three main spaces though clearly delineated are, nonetheless, greatly interchangeable and penetrable.

At the level of form, the human/animal divide is both underlined and obscured by the representational power and narrative function ascribed to the animal onscreen, while also being invariably compromised by the satirical quality of the otherwise overwhelming horror embedded in the film's premise, that is, the threat of the irrecoverable loss of the human body. For it is not only that the film places the animal at the center of its queer critique of the hetero/homo-normative, binary forms of gender and sexuality, and the insistence on the couple form as the only permissible form of social and familial organization. As Rosalind Galt notices, "the film at once depends on and problematizes dominant attitudes to animals (shooting the cute pony, turning people into dogs), creating a viewer who is often uncomfortable and uncertain how to feel."[27] In addition, Galt suggests, "animality encodes the film's disciplinary discourse" as is evident in the violent power relations that govern the realms of both the hotel and the woods.[28]

In effect, the ultimate punishment of corporeal conversion into an actual animal that carries the heavy weight of safeguarding the human–animal border in Lanthimos's surreal universe draws on a long history of corporeal signification associated with the human versus the animal. Derrida calls this phenomenon the narrative war against animals, referring to the "Judeo-Christian-Islamic tradition of a war against the animal, of a sacrificial war as old as Genesis."[29] Jonathan Burt observes that killing defines the relative status of living beings; "killing [is] the ground of difference."[30] As he explains, it is difficult "to avoid the presence of death, killing, and sacrifice at all levels of inquiry into animal representation. Within this arena of morbidity, the animal symbol or image is understood not so much as a sign of absence, or non-presence, but as a symptom of a deeper and more permanent loss."[31] Indeed, while human bodies in the film are incarcerated, violated, or shot unconscious, it is only after they have turned into animals that they are killed, more often than not, viciously and unremorsefully. Burt continues, "[t]he idea of sacrifice is integral to the inflated logic at work here. Understood as essential to the structure of subjectivity, culture, and law, sacrifice is taken as defining the 'us' and the 'them,' it provides the criteria for the 'noncriminal putting to death' and the identity of those beings that it is acceptable to subject to total control."[32]

Unconvinced about David's truly heartless nature, Heartless Woman wakes him up to announce that she has killed Bob, his brother, who had previously been converted into a dog: "I killed your brother. I left him to die very slowly. He may not be dead yet even as we speak. I was kicking him for ages." David strives to hide his devastation behind exasperated brief responses, as Heartless Woman, framed in a medium low-angle shot, blinding light behind her creating a sharp contrast with her shadowed deadpan face, mimics the dog's whine and continues: "It must have been from the pain. You didn't hear anything?" Devastated yet inexpressive, David goes to the bathroom to find Bob's body covered in blood. A turning point in the narrative, David forces Heartless Woman to the transformation room with the help of the maid before escaping into the woods.

The scene begs the question: what if this metaphor of deep emotional attachment to animals channeled through the precondition of a previous human-to-human relationship points toward a potential rethinking of the way we relate to animals, to rethinking the biblically sanctified, supposedly transcendental domination over and mastering of the animal kingdom? What if such a reconfiguration of animal–human relationships could take the form of an interdependency between different life forms that Burt proposes under the term "livingness."[33] In Burt's words, "I define livingness as the mode of active coexistence whereby an individual's ability to live (or die) depends on the nature of its interaction with others. This coexistence does not require any form of identity between different species as such, but it does require an understanding that organisms in livingness are unavoidably co-constitutive."[34]

The film's proposal of a radical reframing of human–animal relations is literalized through an impressive formal device, which Galt calls "shared enframement"—a term she borrows from Jennifer Fay.[35] As Galt observes, "if animal bodies often signify in cinema primarily as markers of indexicality, *The Lobster* quickly decouples them from any straightforward realism" by filling the *mise-en-scène* of the woods with exotic animals (a peacock, a camel, a flamingo), whose conspicuous onscreen presence distracts attention from otherwise narratively significant scenes.[36] Galt argues that this kind of "shared enframement ... mak[es] visible the human power of life and death over animals (through a metaphoric use of humans *as* animals) *and* deploy[s] that power relation to speak about political violence in Europe," as these "animetaphors," as she calls them, refer both "to animality itself and to those subjects who have been forcefully excluded from full humanity in Europe."[37] Galt continues, "*The Lobster*'s non-human animals create gestures in a Brechtian sense, their bodily movements interrupting the smooth unfolding of narrative and arresting the function of dominant ideologies,"[38] punctuating the violated and excluded (human) bodies, which nonetheless remain present and visible in the fringes of society (as well as the frame).

In discussing the on-screen coexistence of animals and humans, Burt acknowledges an "unresolved ambiguity" that stems from the irreducible difference between the two categories of beings. As he explains,

> [t]his refers back to the asymmetry in becoming-animal and the idea that one could not become "an animal" as such, a logical consequence of valorizing becoming over all else; in other words, where becoming-animal

is only ever virtual and never actual, animal becoming is of a totally different order. The asymmetry can cut both ways: on the one hand, it may indicate a more utopian situation of the coexistence of ever emerging difference; or on the other, it may highlight a more problematic inequality in becoming.[39]

This is an interesting thesis to apply to a film that literalizes the becoming-animal process through its dystopian spatiotemporal structure. Lanthimos actualizes the possibility of becoming-animal, creating powerful animetaphors that comment on traditional significations of animality and concomitant narratives of sacrifice and killing, but which also corroborate the film's queer posthumanist discourse on the vices and violence of both historical and contemporary differential allocations of humanness.

This brings to mind Achille Mbembe's notion of "necropolitics," which pertains to a "global modality of power that subjects populations to conditions that ascribe them the status of the living dead."[40] As such, necropolitics control whose lives matter and should be protected, and who can be disposed of—in other words, it determines who can be deprived of the conditions for life and being "human."[41] Associated with this line of thought is the question of recognition, which Judith Butler and Athena Athanasiou define as "an apparatus that discursively produces subjects as human (or inhuman, subhuman, less than human) by normative and disciplinary terms such as those of gender, sexuality, race, and class."[42] As Butler points out, "the differential distribution of norms of recognition directly implies the differential allocation of precarity."[43] Put differently, for those who count as human or as subjects of rights under the hegemonic norms "precarity can be minimized through inclusion within a scheme of recognition" that automatically renders their lives valuable.[44] At the same time, those same norms would produce criminalizing and pathologizing regimes; schemes that, based on legal violence, reserve the right to kill or to let die, thus attesting to what Butler frames as the existential condition of our irreversible "vulnerability to injury and loss."[45] For, we are only ever partially interpolated within the established schemes of recognition, our status as subjects of rights being perennially provisional. Accordingly, in *The Lobster*, after Limping Man (Ben Whishaw) tricks Nosebleed Woman (Jessica Barden) into thinking they share the same defining characteristic of frequent nosebleeds, the pair is announced and applauded by the hotel community as a new successful match, transferred to a double room and then to a yacht, before they are finally assigned a child. However, their delicate relationship is bound to hang on the balance of Limping Man's secret, which David eventually discloses on the night of the Loners' attack.

David's own storyline is also filled with agonizing attempts at securing a match, which should get him re-recognized as human. And though he eventually achieves that outside the grounds of the hotel, the film's denouement highlights his anxiety to validate his match with Short Sighted Woman within the scheme of recognition prescribed by the hegemonic norms of the city. In the (anti-)climactic final scene of David facing off against the mirror ready to inflict violence upon himself, Butler and Athanasiou's notion of "dispossession" meets a most fitting aesthetic application. As Athanasiou argues, dispossession "signifies an inaugural submission of the subject-to-be to norms of intelligibility," thus resonating with "the psychic foreclosures that determine which 'passionate attachments' are possible and plausible for 'one' to become a subject."[46] Butler suggests that dispossession is what effectively establishes the self as social, while also revealing it as interdependent, "driven by passions it cannot fully consciously ground or know" and "dependent on environments and others who sustain and even motivate the life of the self itself."[47] Failing the hotel's test and struggling with the Loners' equally oppressive regime, David and Short Sighted Woman decide to escape, yet back into the city where the fragile statuses of their relationship and humanness (both unrecognized per the city's norms) relegate them to perennially precarious subjects, vulnerable less-than-humans; yet unable to live or even envision a life outside the contours of society. The dilemma facing David in the final scene—namely, to lose his sight or not so as to match with his now-blinded love object—reveals the self's inherent interdependency, which, as Butler warns, is what precisely "establishes our vulnerability to social forms of deprivation."[48]

For Butler and Athanasiou, the way out is conceived of as an "insurrection at the level of ontology," namely, "the constant questioning of conditions in which the human is determined by normative and normalizing regimes of intelligibility in terms of gender, sexuality, race, nationality, class."[49] The "barbarian, the monster and the animal," as well as the "stranger, the *sans papiers* ['without papers'], the unemployed, the queer," generally those forms of life historically excluded from the realm of the normative human might emerge as radicalized forces of resistance that aim at exposing or challenging the regulative fictions that produce them as unintelligible.[50] As Athanasiou contends, to radically reframe the fantasy of the self-sufficient human is to think through "amalgamation and reassemblages of the animate and the inanimate, human and non-human, animal and human animal, life and death," as well as to form "communities with other forms of life, in social realms of co-implicated and differently embodied bodies."[51] Whereas the narrative refuses to offer a vision of this potentiality—Lanthimos, indeed, never resorts to unambiguous endings, let alone happy ones—the film's form does not shy away from throwing in traces of radical posthumanism in the fleeting frames of animal imagery, which, precisely because they are neither narratively significant nor mere background fodder, disturb the canonical representational lexicon of humanism as well as its realist underpinnings through what I would suggest to name antirealist satire.

According to Robert C. Elliot, satire as an artistic form holds human vices, follies, abuses, or shortcomings up to censure by means of ridicule, derision, burlesque, irony, parody, caricature, or other methods, with an intent to inspire social reform.[52] The form traces a thread that goes back millennia to ancient Greek drama and, more specifically, to the satyr play. Though originally performed for comic relief addressed toward a less educated audience unaccustomed to the more serious genre of the tragedy, the satyr play evolved into a politically significant dramatic form, often capitalizing on light humor to exercise social and political critique among Athenian audiences.[53] Most importantly, situated in the threshold between tragedy and comedy, the satyr play deploys theatrical devices of estrangement and distanciation, conveyed by the interactions and the interlocutions between satyrs and heroes in the context of a playful metafiction, where actions, situations, and relationships between characters have no value in themselves.[54] Interestingly, the animal and posthuman elements are, indeed, ubiquitous in the satyr play, as the irreverent and transgressive satyrs are animal–human hybrid male spirits, associated with the Greek mythological figure of Dionysus who signifies fertility and excessive sexuality. Through the centuries, the main tenets of the satyr play have impregnated a range of dramatic and literary forms, primarily the instrumental function of its transgressive motifs in the service of social and political critique.

Julian Murphet describes satire as the most political genre of modernity, claiming it as "humanism's constant inhumanist companion and undoing."[55] He explains:

> its function has long been to ... expose [man's] violent hypocrisies and excremental obscenity, "his" utter inability to live up to his own mythic self-image. [...] Humanism is a smokescreen of sentimental affection for the universal in "man," draped over the pornographic spectacle of his rape of the universe. Satire, conversely, is viscerally disgusted by the universal in "man"; it loves only the particular, the irreducible quality or truth.[56]

Deploying such tactics as displacement, exaggeration, black humor, mordant satiric bite—in effect, the acerbic style of Nietzsche, Brecht, Duchamp, Eliot, Marx—satire capitalizes on the abounding contradiction between word and deed in compelling figural, narrative, and allegorical forms, in order to expose the abounding contradiction between "the ideological currency of humanism and the inhumanity of the industrializing marketplace."[57] Exposing the inhumanist dimensions of humanism, satire augments antagonism, provokes it, and takes it to a political limit; ridicule and grotesque representation serve a direct confrontation between oppositional groups. In Murphet's own words,

> [h]umanism is the constant ideological apology, among dominant classes, for an ever-spreading world system bent on ... the structural treatment of the vast majority of human beings not as members of the set "humanity," but precisely as exceptions to it: beasts, things, integers, manipulable code. In such a situation, the rhetoric-political solution is surely not more and more "humanism," which invariably decodes as biopolitical cynicism and the regulation of populations—a disgusting accommodation with what degrades human beings. Rather, what is required is the political instinct for drawing battlelines between the various groups and classes whose competing interests are dissembled as "the human condition."[58]

In *The Lobster*, the filmic terrain emerges precisely as such a battlefield, characterized by layered processes of separation and division. The film refrains from realism's canonical Manichaeism, indeed, from creating distinct narrative and characterological spheres of good and evil. Lanthimos does not insist on the perceived humanness (or humanity) of the excluded group that is relegated to the status of the animal. His film rather emerges as a battlefield between singularities, who—often formed in temporary alliances—either passionately pursue or passionately repudiate the "human condition," at any point highlighting the precarious status of "humanness" and the blurred discursive lines between human and inhuman. The film, indeed, refuses to resolve this argument. Its satirical antirealism insists on antagonism and militancy and not on resolution. As Murphet contends, ironic style is

> issued on behalf of a "post-subject," a non-person, whose function as stylist is less to shore up belief in the fiction of a durable subjectivity than it is to enlist an army for the ensuing melee ... [S]tyles are fashioned with no reason to exist other than to show that there is no humanity, no Man, no subject, only temporary alliances of misfits, objects, and techniques, united by the nonconformities of a *sui generis* style.[59]

A unique match of style and content, *The Lobster* is an inexhaustible antithesis between characters and landscapes, word and deed, image and sound, a stylistic killing machine, severing realism, humanism, and the concomitant pleasures and comforts of cinematic spectatorship; a queer, weird, antihumanist text punctuating the contradictions of heteropatriarchal humanist discourse. A genuine model of posthumanist antirealist satire, *The Lobster* is "that hijacking, the willful exposure of a 'parallax view' at the heart of a heartless world through a merciless ridiculing of every discourse that apologizes for it."[60]

As Derrida reminds us, the ahuman is the "excluded, foreclosed, disavowed, tamed, and sacrificed foundation of what it founds, namely, the symbolic order, the human order, law and justice."[61] One can only wonder, are we forever trapped within these arbitrary, historically and politically contingent, and more often than not violent, schemes of recognition that would announce us humans, subjects of rights, less precarious and with valuable lives? Is this our only way out of the formless, mute, infant, and terrifying form of monstrosity? "What's worse? To die of cold and hunger in the woods, to become an animal that would be killed or eaten by some bigger animal, or have a nosebleed from time to time?" Limping Man asks David when confronted about his fake nosebleeds. "To become an animal that would be killed or eaten by some bigger animal," replies David.

Lanthimos's posthumanist project is precisely one that departs from Enlightenment, Modernism, or even Postmodernism's fixations on an ontological delineation of the category of the human, which seeks to locate its difference from either the animal (following Michel de Montaigne and René Descartes)[62] or machine and automata (following Francis Fukuyama).[63] *The Lobster* is neither a science-fiction blockbuster, entertaining contemporary anxieties over biotechnological evolution, nor a dystopian drama that seeks to unearth a superior and exclusively human ability for transcendental thought: the likes of morality, conscience, or religion. Losing the status of the human in the parallel universe that Lanthimos creates is as easy as failing to find Mr. or Mrs. Right within forty-five days. And yet, as I have emphatically argued in this chapter, the film's seemingly naïve premise offers the opportunity for a satirical yet vicious queer reframing of the ethical and political underpinnings of humanism. For, the delineation of Otherness (or nonhumanness, for that matter) is effectively the delineation of the boundaries of our moral concern: which bodies fall within these boundaries and which ones are left out, left to be killed or eaten by a bigger animal?

Notes

1 Jacques Derrida, "Structure, Sign, and Play in the Discourse of the Human Sciences," in K. M. Newton, ed., *Twentieth-Century Literary Theory* (London: Palgrave Macmillan, 1997), 115–20, at p. 119.
2 Diana Fuss, *Human, All Too Human* (London and New York: Routledge), 4.
3 Francesca Ferrando, "Posthumanism, Transhumanism, Antihumanism, Metahumanism, and New Materialisms: Differences and Relations," *Existenz*, 8, no. 2 (2013): 26–32, at p. 26.
4 Andy Miah, "Posthumanism: A Critical History," in B. Gordijn and R. Chadwick, eds., *Medical Enhancements and Posthumanity* (New York: Routledge, 2007), 1–28, at p. 2, emphasis in the original.
5 Tony Davies, *Humanism* (New York: Routledge, 1996), 32.

6   Myra J. Seaman, "Becoming More (than) Human: Affective Posthumanisms, Past and Future," *Journal of Narrative Theory*, 37, no. 2 (2007): 246–75, at p. 254.
7   Ibid., 254–55.
8   According to the Transhumanist Declaration, written by an international group of authors in 1998, "humanity's potential is still mostly unrealized." In this sense, transhumanism is a project that expresses an optimism for entering an era of an ultra-human version assisted by technology (Ferrando, "Posthumanism, Transhumanism, Antihumanism," 27), having much in common with liberal humanism in its "unalloyed faith in the primacy of the Enlightenment subject—rational, autonomous, self-determining"; see Elaine L. Graham, *Representations of the Post/Human: Monsters, Aliens and Others in Popular Culture* (New Brunswick, NJ: Rutgers University Press, 2002), 159.
9   Seaman, "Becoming More (than) Human," 248.
10 Ibid., 247.
11 Ibid., 249.
12 Ibid., 259–60.
13 Ibid., 264, emphasis in the original.
14 Ibid., 267, emphasis in the original.
15 N. Katherine Hayle, *How We Became Posthuman: Virtual Bodies in Cybernetics, Literature and Informatics* (Chicago: University of Chicago Press, 1999), 286.
16 Gilles Deleuze, *Cinema 2: The Time-Image*, trans. Hugh Tomlinson and Robert Caleta (London: Continuum, 2009 [1985]).
17 Ibid., 133.
18 Ibid., 128.
19 Janet Harbord, *Evolution of Film: Rethinking Film Studies* (Cambridge: Polity Press, 2007), 157–58.
20 Ibid., 158.
21 Marios Psaras, *The Queer Greek Weird Wave: Ethics, Politics and the Crisis of Meaning* (London: Palgrave Macmillan, 2016).
22 Lee Edelman, *No Future: Queer Theory and the Death Drive* (Durham, NC, and London: Duke University Press, 2004), 120.
23 Teresa de Lauretis, "Queer Texts, Bad Habits, and the Issue of a Future," *GLQ: A Journal of Lesbian and Gay Studies*, 17 (2011): 243–63, at p. 244.
24 Ibid., 245.
25 Michael O'Driscoll, "Entoporn, Remy de Gourmont, and the Limits of Posthuman Sexuality," *Modernism/Modernity*, 20, no. 4 (2014): 627–43, at p. 628.
26 Ibid., 631–32.

27 Rosalind Galt, "The Animal Logic of Contemporary Greek Cinema," *Framework: Journal of Cinema and Media*, 58, no. 1 & 2 (2017): 7–29, at pp. 22–23.
28 Ibid., 24.
29 Jacques Derrida, *L' animal que Donc Je Suis* (Paris: Galilée, 2006), 140.
30 Jonathan Burt, "Morbidity and Vitalism: Derrida, Bergson, Deleuze, and Animal Film Imagery," *Configurations*, 14, no. 1 & 2 (2006): 157–79, at p. 157.
31 Ibid.
32 Ibid., 159.
33 Ibid., 169.
34 Ibid.
35 Galt, "The Animal Logic of Contemporary Greek Cinema," 25.
36 Ibid., 23.
37 Ibid., 26. Emphases in the original.
38 Ibid.
39 Burt, "Morbidity and Vitalism," 175–76.
40 Achille Mbembe quoted and discussed in Judith Butler and Athena Athanasiou, *Dispossession: The Performative in the Political* (Cambridge: Polity Press, 2013), 20.
41 Ibid.
42 Ibid., 90.
43 Ibid., 89.
44 Ibid.
45 Ibid., 20.
46 Ibid., 1.
47 Ibid., 4.
48 Ibid., 5.
49 Ibid., 119.
50 Ibid., 34–37.
51 Ibid., 37.
52 Robert C. Elliot, "Satire," *Encyclopedia Britannica*, 2019, available at http://www.britannica.com/art/satire.
53 See Massimo Di Marco, "What Is the Function of the Satyr Play?" *Polis: Journal for Ancient Greek Political Thought*, 34 (2017): 432–48.
54 Ibid.
55 Julian Murphet, "A Modest Proposal for the Inhuman," *Modernism/Modernity*, 23, no. 3 (2016): 651–70, at p. 662.
56 Ibid.

57 Ibid., 659.
58 Ibid., 665.
59 Ibid., 667.
60 Ibid., 666.
61 See Jacques Derrida, "And Say the Animal Responded?" in C. Wolfe, ed., *Zoontologies: The Question of the Animal* (Minneapolis, MN: University of Minnesota Press, 2003), 121–45, at p. 134.
62 Michel de Montaigne, "Man is No Better Than the Animals," trans. Donald M. Frame, in "An Apology for Raymond Sebond," in *The Complete Works: Essays, Travel Journal, Letters* (London: Everyman's Library, 2003 [1580–92]), 401–35. Also see Peter Harrison, "Descartes on Animals," *Philosophical Quarterly*, 42, no. 167 (1992): 219–27.
63 Francis Fukuyama, *Our Posthuman Future: Consequences of the Biotechnology Revolution* (London: Profile Books, 2002).

Yorgos Lanthimos's Primary Feature Filmography

2005	*Kinetta*
	95 min
	Director: Yorgos Lanthimos
	Producer: Athina Rachel Tsangari
	Screenplay: Yorgos Kakanakis, Yorgos Lanthimos
	Cinematographer: Thimios Bakatakis
	Editor: Yorgos Mavropsaridis
	Actors (main): Evangelia Randou, Aris Servetalis, Coastas Xikominos, Youlika Skafida, Hector Kaloudis
	Country: Greece
	Language: Greek
	Budget (approx.): N/A
	Box office (approx.): N/A
	Awards and nominations (main): Thessaloniki Film Festival (*Nominated*: Golden Alexander)
2009	*Dogtooth (Kynodontas)*
	97 min
	Director: Yorgos Lanthimos

	Producers: Iraklis Mavroidis, Athina Rachel Tsangari, Yorgos Tsourianis
	Screenplay: Efthymis Filippou, Yorgos Lanthimo
	Cinematographer: Thimios Bakatakis
	Editor: Yorgos Mavropsaridis
	Actors (main): Christos Stergioglou, Michelle Valley, Angeliki Papoulia, Mary Tsoni, Christos Passalis, Anna Kalaitzidou
	Country: Greece
	Language: Greek
	Budget (approx.): $323,000
	Box office (approx.): $1.37 million
	Awards and nominations (main): Academy Awards, USA (*Nominated*: Best Foreign Language Film); Cannes Film Festival (*Won*: *Prix de la Jeunesse, Prix Un Certain Regard*); Hellenic Film Academy Awards (*Won*: Best Film, Best Director, Best Screenplay, Best Supporting Actor, Best Editing; *Nominated*: Best Actor, Best Actress, Best Effects, Best Make-Up)
2011	*Alps (Alpeis)*
	93 min
	Director: Yorgos Lanthimos
	Producers: Yorgos Lanthimos, Athina Rachel Tsangari
	Screenplay: Efthymis Filippou, Yorgos Lanthimos
	Cinematographer: Christos Voudouris
	Editor: Yorgos Mavropsaridis
	Actors (main): Angeliki Papoulia, Ariane Labed, Aris Servetalis, Johnny Vekris, Efthymis Filippou, Stavros Psyllakis, Eftychia Stefanidou, Sotiris Papastamatiou, Maria Kyrozi, Tina Papanikolaou, Konstadina Papoulia, Nikos Galgadis
	Country: Greece
	Language: Greek
	Budget (approx.): N/A

	Box office (approx.): $243,000
	Awards and nominations (main): Hellenic Film Academy Awards (*Won*: Best Make-Up; Best Screenplay); Venice Film Festival (*Won*: Best Screenplay; *Nominated*: Golden Lion)
2015	*The Lobster*
	118 min
	Director: Yorgos Lanthimos
	Producers: Ceci Dempsey, Ed Guiney, Yorgos Lanthimos, Lee Magiday
	Screenplay: Efthymis Filippou, Yorgos Lanthimos
	Cinematographer: Thimios Bakatakis
	Editor: Yorgos Mavropsaridis
	Actors (main): Colin Farrell, Rachel Weisz, Jessica Barden, Olivia Colman, Ashley Jensen, Ariane Labed, Angeliki Papoulia, John C. Reilly, Léa Seydoux, Michael Smiley, Ben Whishaw
	Country: Ireland, United Kingdom, Greece, France, Netherlands
	Languages: English, French
	Budget (approx.): $4.5 million
	Box office (approx.): $18 million
	Awards and nominations (main): Academy Awards, USA (*Nominated*: Best Original Screenplay); BAFTA Awards (*Nominated*: Best British Film); Cannes Film Festival (*Won*: Jury Prize, Palm Dog, Queer Palm; *Nominated*: *Palme d'Or*); Hellenic Film Academy Awards (*Won*: Best Foreign Film)
2017	*The Killing of a Sacred Deer*
	121 min
	Director: Yorgos Lanthimos
	Producers: Ed Guiney, Yorgos Lanthimos
	Screenplay: Efthymis Filippou, Yorgos Lanthimos
	Cinematographer: Thimios Bakatakis
	Editor: Yorgos Mavropsaridis

		Actors (main): Colin Farrell, Nicole Kidman, Barry Keoghan, Raffey Cassidy, Sunny Suljic, Alicia Silverstone, Bill Camp
		Country: Ireland, United Kingdom
		Language: English
		Budget (approx.): N/A
		Box office (approx.): $6.12 million
		Awards and nominations (main): Cannes Film Festival (*Won*: Best Screenplay; *Nominated*: *Palme d'Or*)
2018	*The Favourite*	
		119 min
		Director: Yorgos Lanthimos
		Producers: Ceci Dempsey, Ed Guiney, Yorgos Lanthimos, Lee Magiday
		Screenplay: Deborah Davis, Tony McNamara
		Cinematographer: Robbie Ryan
		Editor: Yorgos Mavropsaridis
		Actors (main): Olivia Colman, Rachel Weisz, Emma Stone, Nicholas Hoult, Joe Alwyn, James Smith, Mark Gatiss, Jenny Rainsford, Jack Veal
		Country: Ireland, United Kingdom, United States
		Language: English
		Budget (approx.): $15 million
		Box office (approx.): $95.87 million
		Awards and nominations (main): Academy Awards, USA (*Won*: Best Actress; *Nominated*: Best Picture, Best Director, Best Supporting Actress [twice], Best Cinematography, Best Editing, Best Original Screenplay, Best Production Design, Best Costume Design); BAFTA Awards (*Won*: Best British Film, Best Actress, Best Supporting Actress, Best Screenplay, Best Make-Up, Best Costume, Best Production Design; *Nominated*: Best Film, Best Director, Best Supporting Actress, Best Editing, Best Cinematography); Venice Film Festival (*Won*: Grand Jury Prize, Best Actress; *Nominated*: Golden Lion, Queer Lion)

CONTRIBUTORS

Nathan Abrams is Professor in Film at Bangor University in Wales. He is the author of, most recently, *Stanley Kubrick: New York Intellectual* (2018), *Eyes Wide Shut: Stanley Kubrick and the Making of His Final Film* (with Robert P. Kolker, 2019), and *The Bloomsbury Companion to Stanley Kubrick* (with I. Q. Hunter, 2021).

James J. Clauss is Professor of Classics at the University of Washington, USA. Most of his work pertains to Classical antiquity, especially Hellenistic Greek and Roman literature, although he has a special interest in film as classical reception and has published scholarship on *The Searchers* (John Ford, 1956), *Medea* (Pier Paolo Pasolini, 1969), and *Clash of the Titans* (Desmond Davis, 1981).

Eddie Falvey is Lecturer in the School of Arts and Media at Plymouth College of Art, UK. He holds a PhD from the University of Exeter and is the author of a number of chapters and books, which include *Re-Animator* (2021) and *The Archive and the City: Visualizing New York on Early Film* (2022), and is the coeditor of *New Blood: Critical Approaches to Contemporary Horror* (with Joe Hickinbottom and Jonathan Wroot, 2020) and *ReFocus: The Films of Nicolas Winding Refn* (with Thomas Joseph Watson and Kate Moffat, 2022).

Asbjørn Grønstad is Professor of Visual Culture at the University of Bergen, Norway. He has published twelve books and over sixty scholarly articles. His most recent monographs are *Rethinking Art and Visual Culture: The Poetics of Opacity* (2020) and *Ways of Seeing in the Neoliberal State* (2021).

Alice Haylett Bryan is a visiting Research Fellow in Film Studies at King's College London, UK. Her publications include "'I Only Like Seeing Myself in Small Bits': Catherine Breillat's Reflections of the Female Body" (2016) in *Cine-Excess* and "Inhospitable Landscapes: Contemporary French Horror Cinema, Immigration and Identity" (2021) in *French Screen Studies*.

Vrasidas Karalis is Sir Nicholas Laurantus Professor of Modern Greek at the University of Sydney, Australia. He is the author of *A History of Greek Cinema* (2012), *Realism in Greek Cinema: From the Post-War Period to the Present* (2017), and most recently, *The Cinematic Language of Theo Angelopoulos* (2021).

Ina Karkani is a PhD researcher at the Freie Universität Berlin, Germany. She works as a film curator for the International Film Festival Berlin (Berlinale, Section Generation). Her most recent publications include "Bergman's Women, Female Gender Representation in *Summer with Monika*, *Persona*, and *Scenes from A Marriage*" (2019) in *Film International*, "Aesthetics of Recession: Urban Space and Identity in *Attenberg and Beautiful Youth*" (2016) in the *Journal of Greek Media and Culture*, and "Framing the Weird Body in Contemporary European Cinema" (2015) in *The Funambulist Papers*.

Tonia Kazakopoulou is Lecturer in Film and Television at the University of Reading, UK. She is the coeditor of *Contemporary Greek Film Cultures: From 1990 to the Present* (with Mikela Fotiou, 2017) and is currently working on a forthcoming monograph on the topic of dejection in Greek film.

Geoff King is Professor of Film Studies at the Brunel University London, UK. His recent publications include *Indiewood, USA: Where Hollywood Meets Independent Cinema* (2009), *Indie 2.0: Change and Continuity in Contemporary American Indie Film* (2014), *Quality Hollywood: Markers of Distinction in Contemporary Studio Film* (2016), *Positioning Art Cinema: Film and Cultural Value* (2019), and *The Cinema of Discomfort: Disquieting, Awkward and Uncomfortable Experiences in Contemporary Art and Indie Film* (2022).

Angelos Koutsourakis is Associate Professor in Film and Cultural Studies at the University of Leeds, UK. He is the author of *Politics as Form in Lars von Trier* (2013) and *Rethinking Brechtian Film Theory and Cinema* (2018), and the coeditor of two books, *The Cinema of Theo Angelopoulos* (with Mark Steven, 2015) and *Cinema of Crisis: Film and Contemporary Europe* (with Thomas Austin, 2020).

Michael Lipiner is currently a PhD candidate in Film Studies at Bangor University in Wales. His most recent publication is "The Grotesque Social Outcast in the Films of Tim Burton" in *Tim Burton's Bodies: Gothic, Animated, Creaturely and Corporeal* (S. Hockenhull and F. Pheasant-Kelly, eds., 2021).

Alex Lykidis is Associate Professor of Film Studies at Montclair State University, USA. He is the author of *Art Cinema and Neoliberalism* (2021). His previous work on Greek cinema has been published in the *Journal of Greek Media and Culture*, the *Journal of Modern Greek Studies*, and the edited collection *Cinema of Crisis: Film and Contemporary Europe* (T. Austin and A. Koutsourakis, eds., 2020).

Afroditi Nikolaidou is Assistant Professor in the Department of Communication and Media Studies at the National and Kapodistrian University of Athens. She has coedited several volumes on Greek cinema and culture including *Athens: World Film Location* (with Irini Sifaki and Anna Poupou, 2014), *Apo ton proimo ston sihrono elliniko kinimatografo/From the Early to Contemporary Greek Cinema: Methodology, Theory, History* (with Maria Paradeisi, 2017), and *I hameni leoforos tou ellinikou cinema* (with Anna Poupou, 2019). She is a co-curator of *Motherland, I See You*, a year-long public screening, film preservation and publication project on Greek cinema, organized by the Hellenic Film Academy.

Savina Petkova is currently completing her LAHP-funded PhD at King's College London, UK, on the topic of animal metaphors and metamorphoses in contemporary European cinema. Savina is also a film critic across the European festival circuit and a regular contributor to *MUBI Notebook*.

Marios Psaras is Cultural Counselor at the Cyprus High Commission in the UK and Visiting Research Fellow at King's College London, UK. He received his PhD from Queen Mary University of London, UK, and has lectured at universities across the UK and Europe. He has published journal articles, book chapters, and reviews on contemporary Greek and European queer cinema, including *The Queer Greek Weird Wave: Ethics, Politics and the Crisis of Meaning* (2016). He is a member of the Hellenic Film Academy, an independent filmmaker, film festival programmer, jury member, and producer.

Nepomuk Zettl is an author and independent researcher. He received his doctorate in Film from the University of Zurich, Switzerland, and works at the Goethe-Institut as a consultant in the Department of Film and Media which supports European film festivals around the globe. His book *Enclosed Spaces: The Box as Cinematic Motif* (2020) investigates the epistemological, narrative, and aesthetic potential of spatial enclosures.

INDEX

absurdity 3, 12, 13, 38, 40–5, 48, 55, 57, 60, 81, 88, 89, 103, 108–12, 129, 133–47, 151, 153, 158, 205, 206, 248, 254, 264–6
aesthetics 2, 5, 19, 21, 24, 26–7, 36, 42, 47, 49, 56, 58, 68, 70, 93, 97, 103, 115, 118–20, 151, 202, 214, 246, 255, 260, 270
Alps 8, 12, 20, 29, 44, 45, 55–65, 140, 150, 168, 183, 186, 190–2, 196, 197, 201, 209, 211, 223, 230–3, 234
Andersson, Roy 4, 40, 41, 43
Angelopoulos, Theo 4, 37–40, 43–4, 46–7, 48
animality 12, 13, 57–8, 67–79, 103–16, 117–31, 134, 136, 141–2, 149–61, 191, 193, 206, 211, 247, 259–76
art film 1–11, 19, 46, 96, 99, 165–81, 222, 240–2, 251
auteurism *see* authorship
authoritarianism 8, 12, 55, 77, 86, 88, 89, 94, 103, 118, 121–4, 152–3, 189, 201, 207–9, 225, 264, 266
authorship 2, 7, 10, 12, 19–23, 29–30, 37, 43, 68, 103–16, 117–31, 165–81, 232, 233, 264

Bakatakis, Thimios 25, 28, 74, 118, 122, 133, 138, 178
Bergman, Ingmar 7, 62, 85
Bresson, Robert 4, 56

Cinema of Cruelty 84–6

Dogtooth 1, 3, 4, 6–8, 20, 25, 27, 28, 29, 35, 38, 43, 45, 48, 49, 55, 56–8, 60, 62, 71, 77, 81, 81–99, 133–47, 149–61, 168, 170, 174, 175, 177, 183, 186, 190–1, 201, 209, 211, 221–3, 227–30, 232, 239, 241, 244–7, 249, 251, 255

extreme film 3–4, 56, 81–2, 96–7, 98, 239–44, 246, 251, 255–6, 266

Farrell, Colin 2, 9, 48, 51, 59, 69, 90, 93, 106, 114, 119, 130, 134, 142, 154, 156, 165, 166, 177–8, 186, 191, 196, 247–9, 260
Favourite, The 2, 3, 9–11, 13, 44, 46, 48, 60, 117, 119–20, 123, 127–9, 150, 152, 157–9, 178, 179, 183, 192, 199–217, 240, 251–5
Filippou, Efthymis 2, 39, 133, 134, 167, 168, 178, 179, 197, 228

Greek cinema 1–3, 4–9, 12, 14, 19–33, 35–51, 57–8, 71, 136, 222–3, 239–44, 265
Greek New Wave *see* Greek Weird Wave
Greek Weird Wave 1–3, 7, 9, 12, 22, 27, 29, 38, 49, 57, 136, 222, 239–43, 265

Haneke, Michael 3, 56, 82–5, 96, 169, 175, 242, 251

Iphigenia in Aulis 3, 125, 156–7, 167, 176, 183–97

Kafka, Franz 13, 103–16, 122, 140, 146

Killing of a Sacred Deer, The 2, 3, 9, 13, 28, 44, 48, 49, 55, 82, 85, 86, 92–7, 99, 117, 119–20, 124–7, 133–47, 150, 155–9, 165–81, 183–6, 190, 192–3, 197, 249–51, 255

Kinetta 6–9, 11–12, 35–51, 150, 183, 189–91, 196, 223, 224–7, 228, 230, 232, 234

Kubrick, Stanley 4, 13, 49, 117–31

Lobster, The 1, 3, 9–10, 12, 13, 14, 27, 28, 36, 48, 55–65, 67–79, 81, 86, 88, 89–92, 96, 103–16, 117, 119, 121–4, 125, 127, 128, 133–47, 150, 152, 154–5, 156, 157, 159, 166, 170, 177–9, 183, 191–2, 195, 197, 211, 240, 247, 251, 255, 259–76

music videos 1, 5, 21, 23, 24–6, 28

My Best Friend (O kalyteros mou filos) 6, 20, 25, 40

mythic elements 2, 3, 12, 13, 39, 41, 46, 49, 94, 120, 125, 129, 155–6, 160, 167, 176, 183–97, 199, 261, 271

national cinema 4–11, 42, 199–202
  see also Greek cinema

neoliberalism 13, 61, 89, 103–16, 178, 201, 204, 207–13, 222, 230, 237

Nimic 11

politics 2, 8, 10, 13, 20, 22–3, 37, 41–4, 48, 55–65, 70, 76, 89–90, 103–16, 125, 129, 149–61, 197, 199–217, 222–6, 231, 241–2, 259–76

Poor Things 11

postmodernism 3, 4, 11, 21–6, 49, 129, 200, 273

power 4, 10, 12, 13, 22, 45, 55–6, 58, 59, 85, 86, 89, 93, 94, 113, 118, 121, 128–9, 135, 140–1, 153, 155, 157–9, 185–6, 189, 190–3, 200, 202–5, 207–12, 225–6, 231–3, 249–55, 262, 265–9

Rouvas, Sakis 5, 23–5, 40

sex 6, 10, 14, 24–6, 47, 56–8, 61–2, 69, 87–9, 91, 94, 118, 121–3, 129, 140, 168, 186–8, 190, 192, 208, 221–37, 239–57, 259–76

state (commentary on) 5, 7–8, 12, 77, 88–9, 103–16, 122–3, 128, 196, 211–3, 216

state funding 8–9, 20, 22, 29, 41, 178, 241

style 1–11, 20, 23, 25–6, 28–9, 37, 40, 42, 44, 48, 56, 61, 68, 71, 74–7, 81–5, 89–90, 93, 96, 99, 108, 117–8, 136, 142, 144, 154, 165–7, 174, 190, 199–201, 203, 211, 224, 240–5, 248, 251, 253, 255, 262, 271–2

transnationality 1, 2, 3, 4–11, 19–20, 29, 36, 38, 199, 207

Tsangari, Athina Rachel 2, 3, 6, 7, 22, 29, 37, 38, 42, 71, 239, 241

Uranisco Disco 20, 25, 40

video dance 5, 21, 23, 26–30

violence 2, 6, 12, 13, 57, 74, 81–6, 88, 92, 95–7, 98, 118, 121–4, 129, 133, 141, 149, 151, 154, 156, 158, 159, 171, 189–91, 200, 206, 210, 211, 223, 225, 227–30, 239–42, 251, 263, 265–70

weirdness (as style) 1–3, 7, 11–14, 27, 29, 38–9, 42, 49, 57, 71, 81–3, 87, 94, 96, 136, 183, 190, 193, 222, 239–41, 256, 260, 265, 272

Weisz, Rachel 2, 9, 10, 92, 107, 114, 119, 120, 130, 134, 142, 157, 178, 191, 192, 202, 247, 248, 252, 260

CPSIA information can be obtained
at www.ICGtesting.com
Printed in the USA
LVHW080213120922
728136LV00003B/49